A BOTANICAL MATERIA MEDICA • VOLUME 3 • JONATHAN STOKES

Publisher's Note

The book descriptions we ask booksellers to display prominently warn that this is an historic book with numerous typos or missing text; it is not indexed or illustrated.

The book was created using optical character recognition software. The software is 99 percent accurate if the book is in good condition. However, we do understand that even one percent can be an annoying number of typos! And sometimes all or part of a page may be missing from our copy of the book. Or the paper may be so discolored from age that it is difficult to read. We apologize and gratefully acknowledge Google's assistance.

After we re-typeset and design a book, the page numbers change so the old index and table of contents no longer work. Therefore, we often remove them; otherwise, please ignore them.

Our books sell so few copies that you would have to pay hundreds of dollars to cover the cost of our proof reading and fixing the typos, missing text and index. Instead we let most customers download a free copy of the original typo-free scanned book. Simply enter the barcode number from the back cover of the paperback in the Free Book form at www.RareBooksClub.com. You may also qualify for a free trial membership in our book club to download up to four books for free. Simply enter the barcode number from the back cover onto the membership form on our home page. The book club entitles you to select from more than a million books at no additional charge. Simply enter the title or subject onto the search form to find the books.

If you have any questions, could you please be so kind as to consult our Frequently Asked Questions page at www.RareBooksClub.com/faqs.cfm? You are also welcome to contact us there.

General Books LLC™, Memphis, USA, 2012.

A BOTANICAL MATERIA MEDICA, cOnsISTInG OF TIIE GENERIC AND SPECIFIC CHARACTERS OP THE PLANTS USED In MEDICINE AND DIET, WITH SYNONYMS, AND REFERENCES TO MEDICAL AUTHORS, BY JONATHAN STOKES M. D. IN FOUR VOLUMES. VOL. III. LONDON,

PrInTED FOr J. JoHnSon AnD Co. ST. PAULS cHUrcHYArD.

Class U DODECANDRIA.
Order 1. MONOGYNIA. 1. *Flowers monopetalous.* 497. Bxssta. *Berry* with from 1 to 5 seeds. *Calyx* tetraphyllous. 2. *Flowers mostly letrapelalous.* 498. Rhizophora. *Seed* 1, clavate. *Calyx* qua dripartite and multipartite. *Corolla* quadripartite tetrapetalous and polypetalous. 501. CRAt Aev A. *Berry* unilocular, polyspermOus. *Calyx* quadirifid. 499.; Garcini A. *Berry* sexlocular and octolocular. *Petals* 4. *Calyx* tetraphyllous.
S. *Flowers pentapetalous.*
Rhizophora.
504. Portulaca, *Capsule* unilocular, cut round and trivalve. *Calyx* bifid. *From L.*
Vol. 3. A 503. Peganum. *Capsule* trilocular, polyspermous. *Calyx* pentaphyllous. *Stamina* 15.
507. Klinhovia. *Capsule* qninqучlocular, inflated; cells mouospermous. *Calyx* pentaphyllous. *Nectarium* stamicifcrous. *Germen* pedicellate. 502. Barthamia. *Capsule* trilocular sexlocular and octolocular; cells monospermous. *Nectaria* 5, glandular. *From Gaertn,* 500. Canella. *Berry* unilocular, with 2 and 4 seeds. *Nectarium* urceolate. *Antherae* growing to the outside of

l...
5. *Flo&ers incomplete.* 494. Asarum. *Calyx* superior, trifid and qua drifid. *Capsule* sexlocular. *Obs.* 4752. 495. Bocconia. *Calyx* inferior, diphyllous. *Cap sule* monospermous. 508. Agrimonia. *Petals* 5. *Calyx* quinqucfiil. *Seed* 1 & 2. *L. Order S.* TRIGYNIA. 509. Reseda. *Capsule* unilocular, open. *Pe tats* mostly cloven. *Calyx* partite. *Qbs.* 3775. 510. Euphorbia. *Capsule* tricoccous. *Petals* pel tate. *Calyx* ventricose. *L.* 511-Tacca. *Berry* polyspermous. *Calyx* superior. 512. Menispermum. *Berries* 2 to 6, monospermous. *Calyx* inferior. *Order* 4. TETRAGYNIA. 513. Dichroa. *Berry* qundrilocular, polyspermous. *Calyx* inferior, quadridentatc. *From Lour. Order* 5. PENTAGYNIA. 514. Glinus. *Corolla* none. *Calyx* penta phyllous. *Capsule* quinquelocular. *Order* 6. HEXAGYNIA. 515. Stratiotes. *Calyx* superior, trifid. *Berry* sexlocular. *Petals* 3. *Obs.* 7668. *Order* 7. DODECAGYNIA. 516. SempervivuM. *Capsules* 12. *Petals* 12. *Calyx* duodeciinpartite. *L,* MONOGYNIA, 494. ASARUM. *Calyx* superior, trifid and quadrifid. *Corolla* none. *Ant her ae* growing to the middle of the filaments. *Stigma* sexpartite. *Capsule* sexlocular. *Obs.* 4752. *L—Juss.* 73.

J. ASARUM *renifolium.* Leaves reniform. *Obs,* 8749. In a garden. A. europaeum. *L. suec. n.* 421, in a wood near Hackebarg in Scania; *sp.* 633. *Bot. arr.* 488. *Fl. dan. t.* 633. *Retz, scand. n.* 587, in groves. —*ff'oodv.* ii. 237. *t.* 86. *Smith brit.* 509, found by Dr. Batty near Kirkby Lonsdale in Westmorland; *engl. t.* 1083, found by Dr. Abbot in Berkshire between Henley and Maidenhead.— *Scop, cam. n.* 563, In shady thickets about Idria in Friuli.—*Host* 255. In groves.—*Roth germ.* i. 202; ii. 518. *Poll. n.* 448. In very close shady thickets.—*Turn. Sj Dil/w. guide* 643. Found by Mr. Richardson in Ramskin Martindale in Westmorland; 153, said by Hutchinson to have been found near Keswick in Cumberland; 369, and found by Mr. H utton near Preston in Lancashire. Asarum. *Rait hist.* 207; *tur.* 69. In woods on the side of Mount Jura. —*Dill, ap-Ran sj/n.* J58. Found by Knowlton in a hedge at Chernells Cheverils green near Biachwood, in Hertfordshire. J— *Leigh* 97, in several places in Lancashire.—*Tourn, parts.* 318. In woods.—*VaiU. parts.* 16. *Boerh.* ii. *95.* In Holland.—*Brunsf.* i. 71. *Matth.* 36, Leaves acute.—*Vent. tabl. t.* 6. /. 2, *Guett.* i. 198. In woods.—*Trag.* 64, *repr. in Cord-fol.* 112. *p.* 1. *Fucks.* 9, *fol. ed. cop. in* 10. *c.* 3, *and Bauh. J.* iii. 518. Leaves aente.—*Dalech.* 914. *Dvd.* 354, *repr. /i erf.* ii. 358, *Lob. obs.* 328, *and Ger. by Johns.* 836, *abr. in Park, par,* 532. *t.* 531. /. 6, # *repr. in* A. baccaris, sive baccatus. *Lob. ic.* i. 601; *adv.* 261. In Savoy, Dauphine, Provence, and the Pyrenees. No fig. Asarum. *Cam. epit.* 19, *cop. in* A. vulgare. *Park, theatr.* 266. Stems very short, horizontal, with 2 leaves and I flower. Leaves opposite, at the end of the stem, shining, entire at the margin. Flower 1, between the leaves. Calyx urceolate, coriaceous, brittle, within corollaceous blackish purple and scabrous, green and hirsutulous without; segments ovate, mucronate, the ends index. Stamina inserted into the upper part of the germen. Filaments blackish purple, the part above the insertion of the antherae subulate. Antherae unilocular, 2 to each filament. Germen oval, nearly inferior. 06s. 8749. V. Native of Italy, France, Germany, Sweden, Holland, Berkshire, Hertfordshire, Lancashire, and Westmorland. ASARUM. Leaves. *Pkarm. lond.—Alst.* i. 393, *Berg.* 380. *Blagden, R. in med. facts* iv. 126. *Chom.* 30; *suppl.* 15. *Coste Sf IVUkm. account from in med. comment,* v. 298. *n.* 3. *Cull.* ii. '4$J. 473. *Dale* 79. *Geofr.* iii 129. *Gillibert in med. journ. v.* ISO. *Ileb.* 65. *Hcrm.* 109. *Hill* 639. *Krock. n.* 712. *Lew.* i. 178; *disp. by Dune.* 163. *Linn.* 142. *Mill. Jos.* 56. *Monro* iii. 25. *Murr.* i. 359. *Neum.* ii. 119. *Quar. anim.* 186. P«r.9. i?. i. 110.

Rutty i3. *Sckrod.* 757. Spit/in. 609. *Swirt.* iv. 258. i/nrf. i. 279; ii. 50. *Vog.* 52. 188. *Ware gutta ser.* 114; *in med. soc.* iii. 343, *and account from in chir. rev.* i. 483. *Whytt nerv.* 513. A. curopaeum. *Pharm. edin.—Murr. J.* i. 242. 344. *Pears. R.* i. 174. 222. 2. ASARUM canadense. Leaves reniform, mucronate.
Segments of the calyx patent. *From L. sp.* 633,

R. Sal. & Corn.—*Hort. lew.* i. 124. A. latifolium. *Sal. R. hort.* 344. A. foliis reniformibus mucronatis binis. *Qron. virs, 72r* where Clayton describes the leaves as serrate and not spotted. Asaron canadense. *Corn.* 24. *t.* 25. *cop. in* A. americanum. *Park, theatr.* 266, *Sj* A. canadense, mucronato folio. *Hist. ox. s.* 13. /.

7. /. 4. *ASARUM* canadense. *Bart.* 26. 48. *Coxe* 368. *Schoepf* 72. 3. ASARUM maculatum. Leaves cordate, glabrous. *Obs.* 4753, Specimen gathered in Fothergill's garden. 1. virginicum. *L—//. K.* i. 124. *Lour,* i. 357. *Thunb. jap.* 190. A. foliis cordatis obtusis glabris petiolatis. *Gran. virg.* 72. A. virginianum, pisloloсbiae foliis subrotundis, cv claminis more maculatis. *Pluk. aim.* 53; *phyi, t.* 78. /. 2. A. virginianum, cordato folio maculato. *Hist, ox,* iii. 511. *s.* 17. *t.* 7. row 3. *f.* 3. Leaves triangulari-cordate, acute, entire at the margin, spotted. *Obs.* 4753. *ASARUM* virginianum. *Dale* 79. *Mill. Jos.* 57. Asarum. *Schoepf* 72 495. BOCCONIA. Calyx diph yllous. Corolla none. Style bifid. Cap sule bivalve, monospermous. *L. a Willd. L.* 1, BOCCONIA sinuatifolia.—Leaves oblong, sinuate. *Willd.* B, frutescens. *L. sp.* 634; *a Willd.* ii. 840. *Swartz. obs.* 187. *Jacq. amer.* 146; *Svo,* 184, *Hort. kew.* ii. 125. Bocconia. Browne 244. B. ramosa, sphondylii folio tomentoso. *Trezo sel.*

«4; Chelidonium majus arborcum, foliis quercinis. *Sloane cat.* 82; *hist,* i. 196. *t.* 125. BOCCONIA (misprinted Bocconix.) *Quier in lett.* 83. Cocoxihuitl. *Hern.* 158.
496. ALANGIUM. Calyx superior, permanent, sexdentate and decemdentate. *Petals* 6 and 10. *Berry* unilocular, *From Juss.* 323. *Lam.* 1. ALANGIUM hexapetalum. Petals 6. *From Vahl. symb.* ii.

62. Arbor baccifera maderaspatana. *Pluk. amalth.Qi; phyt. t.* 370. /. 1. KARA ANGOLAM. *Rheede.* iv. 55. *t.* 26. Arbor indica prunifera, fructu umbilicato corticoso persici simili. *Rail hist,* 1483.
£ ALANGIUM decapetalum. Petals 10. *From Vahl, symb.* ii. 61. Grewia salvifblia. *L. JS. suppl.* 409. ANGOLAM. *Rheede* iv. 39. *t.* 17. Arbor indica baccifera, fructu umbilicato rotundo ce rasi magnitudine dicocco. *Rait hist.* 1497.
497. BASSIA. Calyx inferior, tetraphyllous. Corolla octofid to multifid. Stamina inserted into the corolla, in 2 and 3 rows. Berry with from 1 to 5 seeds. *From-Koen. in L, Gaertn. Sf Roxb.* 1. BASSIA Iati'folia. Flowers terminal. Leaves elIiptico-oval. *From Roxb.* i. 20. *t.* 19. MADHVCA. *Hamilt. C. in as. res, i. t. at p.* 300. *Jones ib.* iv. 292;—ii. 351. Mahwah tree. *Hamilt. C. ib.* i. 300.
498. RHIZOPHORA. Calyx quadripartite and multipartite. Corolla tetrapeUlous pentapetalous and polypetalous. Seed 1, very long, fleshy at the base. *From L.* Rheede and *Gaertn.* i. 212.

1. RHIZOPHORA gymnorhita. Calyx of the fruit
multifid; segments incur vate. *From Gaertn.* i.
913. *t.* 45. *L. sp.* 634.
a fusiformis. Seed striate, fusiform. *From*
Mangium celsum. *Rumph.* iii. 102. f. 68.
CANDEL. *Rheede* vi. 57. *t.* 31. 32. *Rai i hist.*
1769. Petals 12.
(¡ cylindrica. Seed striate, cylindric, obtuse. *Front-*
R. gymnorrhiza. *Gaertn.* i. 213 /3,
R. cylindrica. *L. sp.* 635, $
Mangium minus. *Rumph.* ii. 106. *t.* 69.
KARII-KANDEL, seu Kanil-Kandel. *Rheede*
vi. 59. *t.* 33. *Raii hist.* 1770, where for Karil read
Karii.
$ *laevis.* Seed smooth. *From*
R. gymnorrhiza. *Gaertn.* i. 213 y, &
MANGIUM digitatum. *Rumph.* iii. 107. f. 68.
2. RHIZOPHORA Candel. Leaves obtuse. Pedun-
cles bigeminate, longer than the leaves. Fruit su-

bulate. *JL. sp.* 634.
TSJEROU KAN DEL, *Rheede* vi. 63. *t.* 35. *Raii hist.* 1770. Petals 5.
3. RHIZOPHORA *Mangle.* Calyx of the fruit reflex, quadrifid. Petals 4. Stamina 8. From
J acq. am. 141. *t.* 89; *ed. 8vo,* 177, and Rum»
phius's figures.— *L. sp.* 634; *a Murr,* 442.
Gaertn. i. 212. i. 45.
Rh izo phora. *Broicne* 211.
Mangium candelarium. *Rumph,* iii. 108. *t.* 71. 72.
Mangle arbor pyrifera, fructu oblongo tereti, sumrais r inn's radicosa. *Pluk. aim.* 241; *phyt. t.* 204, *f.3.* Mangle pyri foliis, cum siliquis longis, ficu indicae atnnis. *Buuh. J.* i. *b.* 415. No fig.—*Raii hist.* 1772. *Sloane cat.* 155. Caodela americana. *Cat.* ii. *t.* 63. Mangue Guaparaiba. *Pis. bras.* 114. /. 113, repr. in Guaparaiba. *Pis. ind.* 204. MANGLES. *Vog.* 294. Pee Kandel. *Rheede* vi. 91. *t.* 34. *Raii hist.* 1770.
499. GARCINIA. *Calyx* inferior, tetraphyllons. *Petals* 4. *Berry* sexlocular and octolocular. *From L. a Schreb.* 319. 831, *Vent.* iv. 115. *t.* 16. /. 2, # *L.* 1. GARCINIA *sulcata.* Leaves elliptic. Flowers solitary, terminal, nearly sessile. Berries sulcate. *From*
G. Cambogia. *L. a Willd.* ii. 818, from a dried specimen,
Mangostana Cambogia. *Gaerln.* ii. 106. *t.* 105,
Cambogia. *L. amoen. i.* 128. 332, *Sf* Coddam-pulli. *Rheede* i. 41. *t.* 24, *abr. in*
Gumbooge tree. *Brookes* vi. *t. at p.* 86.
CAMBOGIA Gutla. *Z. sp.* 728.—JSToen. ap. *Murr. appar.* iv. 657. *Murr. account from in med. comment, dec. II.* iv. 184. *Lour.* i. 406. (The medical virtues belong to Cambogia Gutta.)
Carcapuli. *Dalech. app.* 13, *cop. in Bauh. J.* i. *a.* i05, *and Park, theatr.* 1635. *Raii hist. 166U* 2. GARCINIA *Mangostana.* Leaves elliptic. Pe# d uncles uniflorous. Berries smooth. *From L. sp.* 635,
Mangostans Garciae. *Garcin in ph. tr. air. by Ifutt.* vii. 632. *t.* 16. /. 1—9, parts

of fructification and a leaf, *Sf*
Mangostana. *Rumph.* i. 132. *t.* 43, which *cop. in*
The Mangostan. *Ellis tnang. t.*
Fructus Mangostan. *Bont.* 115.
Laurifolia javanensis. *Raii hist.* 1662.
Mangostans. *Bavh. J.* i. *a.* 107. No fig.
MANGOSTANA. *Murr.* iii. 525. *Vog.* 295.
G, Mangostana. *Bry.* 199.
Mangustine. *Thunb. trav.* ii. 277.
Mangusteen. *Perciv. Rob. ceyl.* 313.
3. GARCINIA *triflora.* Peduncles triflorous. *From G.* cekbica. *L. sp. 635,* -S
MANGOSTANA celebica, seu Kiras. *Rumph.* i.
134. *t.* 44. 500. CANELLA. *Calyx* trilobate. *Petals* 5. *Nectarium* urceolate. *Antherae* growing to the outside of the nectarium. *Germen* trilocular. *Berry* unilocular. *From Murr. & Swartz.* 1. CANELLA *alba. Murr. ap. L. a Murr.* 443. *Swartz. obs.* 190; *in linn. tr.* ii. 356; i. 96. *t,* 8, *cop. in Woodv.* ii. 318. *t.* 117. *Hort. kea.* i. 125. *Park, theatr.* 1581. No fig. C. Winterana. *Gaertn.* i. 373. *t.* 77. Canella. *Browne* 275. *t.* 27. /. 2. 3. Fructifica tions. Winterania Canella. *L. sp.* 636 ; *fil. sttppl.* 247.
(*Lour.* i. 359, has a berry with 6 cells.) Cassia cinnamomea, sive Cinnamomum sylvestre bai badensium. *Pluk. aim.* 89; *phyt. t.* 160. /. 7. Arbor baccifcra laarifolia aromática, fructu viridi calyculato racemoso. *Shane cat.* 165; *hist.* ii. 87. *t.* 191. /. 2, *cop. in ph. tr. abr. by Lowth,* ii. 665. *t.* 9. *f.* 167; *by Hutt.* iii. 427. *Cat.* ii. #. 50. C. alba quorundam. *Bauh. J.* i. *a.* 461. The bark. (Cassia lignea jaraaicensis, laureolae foliis subcinereis, cortice piperis modo acri. *Pluk. aim.* 89; *phyt, t.* 81. /. 1, has a persistant stylé.) CANELLA. *Lew.* i. 269. Graing. 37. C alba. Bark. *Pharm, fond. edin.*—*Adair in med, comment,* ix. 208. *Chalm.* i. 156. *Cull.* ii. 210. *Dale* 300. *Geqffr.* ii. 174. *Heb.* 240. Hill 669. Lafondgouzi, *account from in chir. rev.* xi. 394. *Lew. disp. by Dune.* 173. *Linn.* 142. *Zo/ig* 705. JlfiV/. *Jos.* 106. Аъиго iii. 37. *Murr.* iv. 566;
J. i. 195. *Pears. R.* ii. 172. *Rutty* 88. ScAoep/ 73. *Wright in med. journ.* viii. 232.
Cortex winteranus. *Alsl.* ii. 31.

Cortex winteranus spurius. *Carth.* iii. 267.
Winter's bark. *Chalm.* i. 137. 149. 181; ii. 115.
Canelle blanche. *Chom.* 548.
501. CRATAEVA.
Petals 4. *Calyx* quadrifid. *Berry* unilocular, polyspermous. *L.* 1. CRATAEVA *religiosa.* Folioles and petals lanceo Iato-elliptic, acute. *From Vahl. symb.* iii. 62.
Forst. G. esc. 45; *austral.* ;. 203. C. inermis. *L. zeyl. n.* 211. NIIR VALA. *Rheede* iii. 49. *t.* 22. Pomifera indica trifolia, fructu pruniformi caudato. *Rail hist.* 1644. 2. CRATAEVA *Tapia.* Folioles ovate, acuminate.
Petals ovato-subrotund, obtuse. Germina globular. *Vahl. symb.* iii. 6. *L. sp.* 637.
Malus americana trifolia, fructu pomi aurantii instar colorato. *Commel. J. hort.* i. 129. /. 67. No fructifications. Separate berries.
Apioscorodon, sive arbor americana triphyllos, allii odore, poma ferens. *Pbk. aim.* 34; *phyt. t. 137. f.* 7. A leaf and 2 seeds.
Tapia arborea triphylla. *Plum. gen.* 22. *t.* 21.
TAPIA. *Marcgr.* 98, *repr. in Pis. bras.* 69. Tapia brasiliensibus. *Raii hist.* 1662. 502. BARTRAMIA. *Petals* 5. *Calyx* pentaphyllous. *Nectaria* 5, glandular. *Capsule* octolocular sexlocular and trilocular, dividing into several parts; cells monospermous. *Obs.* 8738. The account of the fruit from Swartz & *Gaertn.* 1. BARTRAMIA *crispifolia.* Leaves subrotundoovate, sinuose and curled at the margin. *Obs.* 8740. Specimen of leaves gathered ia FothergUTs garden.
Triamfetta Bartramia. *L. sp.* 638. *Burm. N. ind.* 110. Triumfetta Bartramia orientalis. *L. mant.* 391. Agrimooia maderaspatana, folio rotundo singular! sublus incano. *Pet. gas.* 51. *t.* 32. /. 10.
LAPP AGO amboinica laciniata. *Rumph.* yi. 59. *t.* 85. /-« 2. BARTRAMIA *rhotnbifolia.*—*Lezrtes* rhomboidal, the upper lanceolato-ovate. *Swartz f*
Triumfetta rhombifolia. *Szoarts. ind. occid.* ii. 863?
-Triumfetta rhomboidea. *J acq. am.* 147. *t. 90;* 8w, 185? *LAPPAGO* latifolia,

sou serrala. *Rumph.* ri. 59. *t.* 85. /. *A,* a leaf. 503. PEGANUM. *Petals 5. Calyx pentaphyllous and none. Capsule t/ilocular, trivalve, polyspermous. L.* 1.
PJEGANUM *Harmala.* Leaves multifld. Stem herbaceous. *L. a Willd.* ii. 856 j *sp.* 638. 2/brt. *hew.* ii. 126. Harmala. *Boerh-*i. 261. *Clus. hisp.* 425, *repr. in hist.* ii. 135, Docf. 121, *and Ger. by Johns.* 1255, # *co/i.* in Ruta sylrestris syriaca, sive Harmala. *Park, thcatr. m,#*
Ruta quae dici solet Harmala. *Bauh. J.* iii. o. 200, *& abr. in* Ruta sylvestris, flore magno albo. *Hist. ox.* ii. s. 5. f. 14. /. 5. *Raii hist.* 876.

Harmala syriaca. *Lob. adv.* 390. No fig.
RUTA sylvestris. *Dale* 234. *Mill. Jos.* 381;
504. PORTULACA.
Petals 5. Calyx bifid. Capsule unilocular, cut round and trivalve. *L.*
I. PORTULACA *olcracea.* Leaves cuneiform. Flowers sessile. *L. sp.* 638. *Hort. kew,* ii. 127. *a angustifolia.* (Variation.) Leaves narrower. *From authors.*
P. oleracea. *Poll, n.* 449. *Roth germ.* i. 202. On walls and rocks, and in cultivated ground.—*Scop, earn. n.* 564. *Host* 255.

P. foliis cuneiformibus, floribus sessilibus. *Roy.* 473. *Browne* 233. In gardens and cane pieces throughout all the sugar colonies.—*Cutl.* 447. In corn fields in New England.—*Gron. virg.* 73.

P. angustifolia, sive sylvestris. *Vaill. parts.* 163. *Boerh.* i. 220. In Holland.—*Magn. mansp.* 212. In olive grounds, fallow fields, and gardens.—*Sloane cat.* 87. In Jamaica, in sandy barren fields, and sometimes in such as are moist.

P. sativa et sylvestris. *Park, theatr.* 723, *cop. from* i

P. sylvestris. *Dod.* 650, *which repr. in Lob. obs.* 210; *ic.* i. 388, *and Ger. by Johns.* 521. *Rati hist.-039; eur.* 208. In Sicily, Italy, the south of France, and Germany.—*Dalech.* 551. *Matth.* 475. *Fuchs.* 117. c. 39, *cop. in*

P. silvestris minor, sive spontanea. *Bauh. J.* iii.
tfati'de of Sicily Italy, France, Holland. Germany, and America. *PORTULACA* sylvestris. *Dale* 235. *Geoffr. suite* ii, 66.

Poftulaca. *Schoepf* 73. *Spielm.* 64. P. angustifolia, sive sylrestris. *Alst.* ii. 368. *Boecl. up. Herm.* 415. P. oleracea. *Bry.* 87. Purslaine. *Oraing.* 40, *fi latifolia.* (Variation.) Leaves broader than those of *a. From authors.* P. latifolia sativa. *Boerh.* i. 220. In Holland.— *Magn. hort.* 163. *Rati hist.* 1039. P. latifolia, seu sativa. *Sloane cat.* 87. In Jamaica, in rich moist land, especially when in cultivation. Portulaca. *Park. par.* 499. *t.* 501. /. 1. Leaves not broader than in most of the figures of a.—*Trag.* 382, *repr. in* P. sativa. *Cord. fol.* 156. p. 2. *Dalcch.* 551, *cop. from* P. hortensis. *Fuchs.* 117. *c.* 39. P. sativa. *Park, theatr.* 722. No fig.—*Dod.* 650, repr. tn P. domestica. *Lob. obs.* 210; *ic.* i. 388; fl«d C?er. *by Johns.* 521. JV/«««A, 474. P. .hortensis latifolia. *Bauh. J.* iii. 678. (The fig. Menianthes trifoliata.) *PORTULACA. Alst.* ii. 368. Berg. 382. CarfA. i. 334. flfl/e 235. *Krocl: n.* 713. iinn. 143. *Mead mon.* ii. 121. *Mill. Jos.* 357. .fl/«rr. Hi. 354. *Pears. R.* i. 51. *Quar. anim.* 101. ifo/ly 409. Schrod. 654. Spjefoi. 64. Fog. 76. P. sativa. *Geoffr. suite* ii. 64.
VoL. 3.J B

P. oleraeca. *Bry.* 87. *Forsk.* p. xciii. *Lour.* i. 359. P. latifolia, sire sativa. *Chotfi.* 803; *suppl.* 210. *Hcrm.* 410. *y Javescens.* (Variation.) Leaves yellowish. *From memory,* # P. sativa latifolia, foliis flavis. *Boerh.* i. 220. *Magn. hort.* 163. *PORTULACA* sativa latifolia flaveacens, sive foliis aureis. *Boecl. ap. Hertn.* 415.
2. PORTULACA *pilosa.* Leaves subulate, alternate.
Axillae pilose. Flowers sessile, terminal. *L. sp.* 639. *Hort. kew.* ii. i27. P. curassavica, angusto longo lucidoque folio, pro cuinbens. *Commel. J. hort.* i. 9. *t.* 5. P. corassavica lanuginosa procumbens. *Herm. pan* 215. *t.* 215. P. lanuginosa procumbens, vermiculatae foliis, ame ricana, capsulis in summb nonnihil acuminatis.
Pluk. aim. 304; *phyt. t.* 247. /. 7. *Volk.* 341. U 341. *ANACAMPSEROS* supina minor, foliis linearN bus turgidis, floribus summis ramulis confertis, stylo quinquefido. Browne 234. 3. PORTULACA

quadrijida. Bracteae in fours. *Co* rollae quadrifid. Joints of the stem pilose. *L. want.* 73. *Jacq. coll.* ii. 356. From the isle of
Bourbon. PORTULACA linifolia. *Forsk.* 92; *p.* xciii. Portulaca. *Forsk. p.* xcix.
4. PORTULACA *lutea. Forst. G. esc.* 72; *austral.*
». 520.
PURSLAIN. *Hawk.* iv. 148. 505. LYTHRUM. *Calyx duodecimfid. Petals* 6, inserted into the c»lyx. *Capsule* biloenlar, polyspermous. *L.* 1. LYTHRUM *Salicaria.* Leaves mostly opposite, cordatolanceolale. Flowers spicate. Stamina 12 and 10. *Obs.* 1455. On the side of water. —*L. suec. n.* 422; *sp.* 640. *Bot. arr.* 489. *Curt. loruLiii.* 28. *t. Fl.dan.* r. 671. *Smith brit.* 510; *tngl. t.* 1061. L. foliis oblongis acutis, floribus verticiliatis. *L. lapp. n.* 197. Salicaria vulgaris purpurea, foliis oblongis. *Tourn. parts.* 227. *Vaill. paris.* 175. *Dill. ap. Raii syn.* 367. Lysimachia purpurea spicata. *Otr. by Johns.* 476, *cop. in Park, theatr.* 546. *Rati hist.* 1036; *cat. d.* i. 203.
Lysimachia purpurea. *Rati syn. ed.* ii. 211.
Lysimachia purpurea, quibusdam spicata. *Bauh.*
J. ii. 904, (misprinted 902.)
Lysimachia altera: 7»/a«A, 950.
SALICARIA. Pharm. austriaco-prov. 65. *suec.*
—*Berg.* 384. *Dale* 240. *Geoffr. suite* ii. 313. *Linn.* 143. *Quar. anim.* 92. 159. 220. *Vog.* 116.
L. Salicaria. *Ploucq. bibl.* i. 350.
Lysimachia purpurea. *Krock. n.* 714. *Lczc. disp.*
by Murr. iii. 510. *Ploucq. bibl.* i. 422.
Lysimachia spicata. *Rutty* 297.
Lysimachia purpurea spicata. *Mill. Jos.* 279.
Lysimachia vulgaris, flore purpureo. *Haen* i. 226.
357. Lysimachia rubra. *Bang in act. haun.* i. 100. 506 PEMPHIS. *Calyx* duodecimfid. *Petals* 6, inserted into the calyx. *Stamina* inserted into the calyx, in 2 rows. *Capsule* unilocular, cut round near the base, polyspermous. *From Forst. J. Sf G. Sf Juss.* 33il. . PEMPHIS *atidula. Forst. J. St G.* 68. *t.* 34. Lythrura Peraphis. *L. ßl. suppl.* 249. *Forst. G,*

austral, n. 205. MANGJUM porcellanicum. *Rumph.* iii. 126. *t.* 84. ii--'. : 507.
KLINHOVIA. *Calyx* pentaphyllous. *Petals* 5. *Nectarium* campanulate, quinquedentate, growing to the pedicle of the germen. *Stamina* inserted into the nectarium. *Germen* pedicellate. *Capsule* quinquelocular, quinquangular, inflated; celle monospermous. From *L. Sç L. a Willd.* 1. KLINHOVIA *Hospita. L. sp.* 1365. *CATTI-MARUS. Rumph.* iii. 177. *t.* 113.

DIGYNIA.

508. AGRIMONIA. *Calyx* inferior, hypocrateriform; tube contracted at the mouth; limb quiuqnepartite. *Petals* 5, in« serted into the calyx. Seeds 2 and 1, inclosed by the calyx. *Obs.* 335J, and from *L.—Juss.33Q. Vent. tabl. t.* 21. /. 1.

J. AGRIMONIA *Eupatoria*. Calyx hispid. Petals twice as long as the segments of the calyx. Folioles oblongo-elliptic. Spikes pedunculate. *Obs.* 3331, on the sides of fields; and from *Hort. hew.* ii. 129. *L. suec. n.* 423; *sp.* 643. *Bot. arr.* 490. *Curt. lond.* v. 32. *t.* 317. *Smith brit.* 511; *engl. t.* 1335. *Woodv.* iv. 124. *t.* 258. *Mill. J. ill. t. Fl. dan. t.* 588.

Eupatorium. *Cam. epit.* 756. *Fuchs.* 246. c. 92, *cop. in*

A. seu £upatorium. *Bauh. J.* ii. 398. *p.*

A. sive Eupatorium. *Dod.* 28, *cop. in*

A. vulgaris. *Park, theatr.* 594, S? repnin

Agrimonia. *Ger. by Johns.* 712. *Raii syn.* 202. Bracteae 2, rhombic, tridentate, at the base of the calyx. *Obs.* 3351. *AGRIMONIA. Pharm, austriaco prov.* 16 *Alst.* ii. 76. *Berg.* 386. *Carth.* iv. 212. *Dale* 112. *Geoffr.* iii. 46. *Herrn.* 498. *Kroch n.* 718. *Lew.* i. 42; *disp. by Dune.* 328. *Linn.* 143. *MiU. Jos.* 20. *Murr.* iii. 147. *Quar. febr.* 290. 319. 320. 368. 369. 410. 412; *anim.* 56, 594 84. 88. 233. *Rutty* 11. *Schocpf* 74. *Schrod.* 528. *Spielm.* 374. *Vog.* 49.

A. seu Eupatorium. *Chom.* 480; s«/p?. 143.

A. sive Eupatorium graecorum. *Cam. hort.* 7.

2. AGRIMONIA *odorata*. Calyx hispid. Cauline leaves pinnate; folioles oblong, the lower minute. Petals twice, as long as the segments of the calyx. *from Hort. lew.* ii. 130.—*Mill. Ph. diet. n.* 3; *ic.* 10. *t.* 15. *Lob. adv.* 308. Woods near Saintes in France. *Cam. hort.* 7. *Park; theatr.* 594. No fig. ' ' " 509. RESEDA. *Catyx* partite. *Petals* mostly cloven. *Nectarium* glandular, between the filaments and the upper petal and petals. *Capsule* unilocular, polysper. mous, open. *Qbs.* 3775. 3752. *L.* . ". 1. *Leaves entire.*

I. RESEDA *tinctoria*. Leaves lineari-lanceolate, glabrous. Calyces quadripartite. Petals 4. Stigmata 3. 065.3774-On a wall.

R. Luteola. *L.Bot. am* 492. *Smith engl. t.* 320; *hrit.* 512. *Fl. dan. t.* 864.

R. foliis elliptic is obtuse lanceolatis undulatis, calycibns quadrifidis. *Hall. hist. n.* 1058.

Lutum herba. *Dod.* 81, *repr. in*

Luteola. *Ger. by Johns.* 494. Raiisyn. 366.

Lutca Plinii quibusdam. *Bauh. J.* iii. 465.

Antirrhmon. *Trag.* 362.

Pseudostruthium. *Cam. epit.* 356. *Mattk.* 1307.

Petals cuneiform, inserted at the fissures of the calyx, the uppermost the largest; claw of the uppermost turbinate, concave, with the upper margin projecting inwards transversely, those of the rest linear; lamina of the uppermost septemfid quinqueiid and quadrifid, that of the rest tripartite. *Obs.* 3774.

LUTEOLA. *Berg.* 388. *Mitt. Jos.* 277.

Struthium. *Dale* 240.

Flos tinctorius. *Geoffr. suite* iii. 202.

2. *Leaves entire and divided.* 2. RESEDA *lutca*. Leaves pinnatifid. Laminae of the larger petals tripartite, & the upper margin of the claws rising above the base of the laminae. Styles 3. Seeds glabrous. *Obs.* 3752. Specimen gathered in Surry, on chalk.—*L.—Bot. arr.* 493. *Smith engl. t.* 321; *brit.* 513. *JCrock. n.* 72Q. *Jacq. austr. t.* 353. *Bauh. J.* iii. 467.

R. hexapetala, foliis pinnatis undulatis, calyce sexfido. *Hall. hist. n.* 1056.

R. massiliensis, foliis latioribus crispis. *Pluh, aim.* 317; *phyt. t.* 55. /. 4,

R. gallica crispa. *Bocc. sic.* 77. *t.* 41. /. 3.

Rheseda Plinii neotericorum. *Lob. adv.* 76, *repr. in ic.* i. 222, Sf

Rheseda Plinii. *Ger. by Johns.* 277, *Sf abr. in*

Base Dyersweed. *Pet. herb. t.* 37. /. 11.

R. vulgaris. *Rait syn.* 366. *Town, parts.* 137. *Vaill. paris.* 172.

Peduncle and *pedicles* scabrous. *Calyx* scabrous, scxpartite; segments linear, obtuse. *Petals* 6, very unequal, the 2 larger one third longer than the calyx; claws quadrato-oval, obsoletely acuminate at the end, slightly villose at the margin; laminae of a finer texture than the claws, linéate, those of the 2 upper tripartite, lateral segments dolabriform, one third shorter than the claws, intermediate segment linear narrower and as short again as the lateral ones; laminae of the 2 lateral petals tripartite and bipartite, one and 2 segments dolabriform, the rest linear; laminae of the 2 lowermost petals tripartite, linear. Seeds glabrous, glittering, ovate, with a nick in one, of the margins. *Obs.* 3752. RESED4-*Dale* 239. *Geojfr. suite* ii. 209.

510. EUPHORBIA. *Petals* 4 and 5, inserted into the calyx. *Calyx* monophyllous, ventricose. *Capsule* tricoccous. X,.

I. *Fruticose, aculeate.* L.

1. EUPHORBIA *antiquorum*. Mostly leafless, trigonous, articulated. Branches patent. *L. sp.* 646. *Hort. kew.* ii. 133.

Euphorbium antiquorum verum. *Commet. J. hört.* i. 23. *t.* 12.

Tithymalus aizoides triangularis et quarîrangularis articulosus et spinosus, ramis compressis. *Corntnel. Casp. proel.* 55. /. 5.

Euphorbium verum antiquorum; Schadida-Callj, *Rati hist.* 873, *Boerh.* i. 259.

ESULA indica. *Bont.* 153. *Dale* 214. *Rail hist.* 873. Schadida-Calli. *Rheede* ii. 81. *t.* 42. . S. EUPHORBIA *ojficinarum*. Aculeate, naked, mul tangular. Aculei in pairs. *L. sp.* 647. *Hort, hew.* ii. 134. *Mill. Ph. diet. n.* 4. E. aculeata triangularis subnuda articulata, ramis patentibus. *L. ups.* 138. *Roy.* 194. Euphorbium cerei effigie, caulibus crassioribus, spinis validionbus armatum. *Commel. J. hort.* i. 21. *t.* 11, the plant from near Zale. No fructifications.—*Breyn. prodr.* 62. *Boerh.* i. 258. Se6. i. 29. . 19. /. 2. In flower. Tithymalus raauritanicus aphyllos angulosus et spin, osus, ex quo Euphorbium officinarum. *Herm. hort.* 599. From Barbary. Euphorbium vulgo sed falso creditum. *Rati hist.* 872. Euphorbium. *Dod.* 374, repr. in *Lob. obs.* 642, *Sf Ger. by Johns.* 1178, cop. in *Dalech.* 1691, repr. in Euphorbii tenella planta. *Lob. ie.* ii. 25, # cop. in *Stap.* 1057. EUPHORBIUM. *Pharm. austriaco-prov.* 37. *suec.*—*Aht.* ii. 430. *Berg.* 388. *Carlk.* ii. 297. *Chom.* 77. 144. Date 213. «. I. *Fordyce*, ?. /ro. iv. 115. *Geoffr.* ii. 627. *Herm.* 680. *Zea.* i. 420; *disp. by Dune.* 341. Z»w. 144. *Mead mon.* ii. 98. *Mill. Jos.* 193. ik/imro ii. 383. *Murr.* iv. 88. *Neum.* ii. 31. *Ploucq. bibl.* 35. 315. .»««,-/ 187. *ScArorf.* 780. *Spielm.* 482. *Fog.* 324. IPtftf *in ph. tr. abr. by Hutt.* xi, 476. *JVintr. in Mead mon.* ii. 200.

E. officinalis. *Murr. J.* i. 345.

L'euphorbe. *Pom.* i. 268. (t. seems to be E. ca nariensis with racemi of some species of Aloes added.) 3. EUPHORBIA *edulis.* Stem aculeate, leafy, pen tagonal. Peduncles multiflorous, terminal. Flowers without petals. *From Lour.* i. 365.

4. EUPHORBIA *neriifolia.* Stem aculeate; angles obliquely tuberculate. Leaves spatulate. *Obs.* 6852. In Mr. Sitwell's garden.—*L.*—*Hort. Icew.* ii. 134. *Mill. Ph. diet. n.* 5. Euphorbium afrum spinosum, foliis latioribus non spinosis. *Seb.* i. 18. *t.* 9. *f.* 1. No fructifications. Tithymalus aizoides arborescens spinosus, caudice sngulari, nerii folio. *Commel. Casp. prael.* 22. 56. *t.* 6. Ne fructifications. Tithymalns indicus spinosus, nerii folio. *Commel. _ J. hort.* i. 25. *t.* 13. Leaves on the upper part of the stem, smooth, glabrous, with a minute cuspis at the end, lactescent; juice white, exuding copiously when the leaves are separated from the stem, and a small quantity appearing at the costa when broken transversely at the end of a fortnight. *Obs.* 6852. LIGULARIA. *Rumph.* iv. 88. *t.* 40. Ela-Calli. *Jikeede* ii. 83. *t.* 43. *Raii hist.* 1888. 5. EUPHORBIA *Tirucalli.* Unarmed, half bare of leaves, fruticose, filiform, erect. Branches patulous, crowded in a determinate manner. *L. sp.* 649. *Hort. Icew.* ii. 137. *Lour.* i. 366. Ossifraga lactea. *Rumph,* vii. 62. *t.* 29. Tithymalus indiens frutescens. *Commel. J. hort.* i. 27. *t.* 14. Fructifications none. Tithymalus arborescens, caule aphyllo. *Pluh. phyt. t.* 319. /. 6. No fructifications. Tithymalus indicus frutescens. *Boerk.* i. 257. TIRU-CALLI. *Rheede* ii. 85. *t.* 44. *Rait hist.* 1710.

6. EUPHORBIA *Tithymaloides.* Unarmed, fruticose.

Leaves distichous, alternate, ovate. *L. sp.* 649.

Hort. hew. ii. 137. Tithymalus corassavicus myrtifolius, flore coccinco mellifluo. *Herm. par.* 234. *t.* 234, cop. in Tithymalus curassavicus myrtifolius, flore papilion aceo coccinco parvo. *Pluh. aim.* 369; *phyt. t.* 230. /. 2. *Commel. J. hort.* i. 31. *t.* 16. No fructifications. EUPHORBIA Tithymaloides. *Chisholm* 25. *Jacq. amer.* 149. *t.* 92; ii-vo, 188. 7. EUPHORBIA *hypericifolia.* Dichotomous. Leaves serrate, ovali-oblong, glabrous. Corymbi terminal. Branches divaricate. *L. sp.* 650. *Hort. km.* ii. 138. *Swarlz. obs.* 194.

Tithymalus americanus, (misprinted africanus,) sea Pcplis major brasiliensis, flosculis albis. *Commel. Casp. prael.* 60.

Tithymalus americanus, flosculis albis. *Commel. Casp. prael. t.* 10.

Pcplis major brasiliensis, flosculis albis. *Ra-i hist.* 870.

(Cajatia. *Pis. bras.* 102, has only axillary peduncles.) TITHYMALUS erectus acris, parietariae foliis glabris, floribus ad caulium nodos conglomeratis. *Sloan cat.* 82; *hist.* i. 197. *t.* 126. 8. EUPHORBIA *maculata.* Dichotomous. Leaves scrrates oblong, pilose. Flowers axillary, solitary.

Branches patulous. *L. sp.* 652. *Ilort. kew.* ii.

139. *Jacq. hort.* ii. *t.* 186. Leaves oblongo-lin ear. Flowers aggregate, sessile. Tithymalus sive Chamaesyce altera virginiana, foliis crenatis et macula fusca eleganter notatis. *Pluk. aim.* 372; *phyt. t.* 65. /. 8. EUPHORBIA maculata. *Sckoepf7i.* 9. EUPHORBIA *hirta.* Dichotomous. Leaves ser rate at the margin, ovate, acuminate. Peduncles capitate, axillary. Stems pilose. *L. sp.* 651. *Jacq. coll. suppl.* 160. *Ull.f.l.* Tithymalus botryoides zeylanicus, cauliculis villosis. *Burm. J. zeyl.* 223. *t.* 104. EUPHOR-BIA reclinata minor sub hirsuta, foliis serratis opposite, florum fasciculis oppositis. *Browne* 234.

Esula esqulenta. *Rumpk.* vi. 54, *t.* 23. *f.* 2.

10. EUPHORBIA *hyssopifolia.* Dichotomous. Leaves mostly crenate, linear. Flowers fasciculate, terminal. Stem erect. L, *sp.* 651, *Hort. kew.* ii. 139. EUPHORBIA dichotoma erecta tenuis, foliis linearibus, floribus quasi umbellatis terminalibus. *Browne* 235. 11. EUPHORBIA *portulacoides.* Dichotomous. Leaves entire at the margin, oval, retuse. Peduncles axillary, uniflorous, as long as the leaves. Stem erect, *L. sp.* 653.— *Schoepf75.* 12. EUPHORBIA *thymifolia.* Dichotomous. Leaves oblong and oval, mostly serrate. Flowering branches very short. Stems procumbent. *Obs.* 8734. Specimen gathered by Broughton in.Iamaica.—*Obs.* 8736. Specimen from Dr. Wright. —*L. sp.* 651. g *pubescens.* Stems pubescent. *Obs.* 8737. Specimen gathered by Broughton in Jamaica. Tithymalus humilis ramosissimus hirsutus, foliis thy mi serratis. *Burnt. J. zeyl.* 225. *t.* 105. /. 3.

EUPHORBIA thymifolia. *Forsk.* 94. 13. EUPHORBIA *canescens.* Dichotomous.. Leaves obsoletely crenate, roundish, pilose. Flowers solitary, axillary. Stems procumbent. *From L. sp.* 652. *Host* 259. In Littorali, on the sides of roads, and in vineyards and gardens.—*J acq. coll. suppl.* 115. *t.* 2. *f.3.* From Malaga. Flowers pedunculate.

£. dichotoma, foliis crenulatis subrotundis, noribus solitariis axillaribus, caulibus procumbentibus.

All.nic.3l. B. Tithymalus exiguus villosus, nummulariae folio. *Magn. hort.* 197. Chamaesyce villosa major, cauliculis viridibus. *Tourru hort.* 122. Chamaesyce. *Bauh. J.* iii. 667. EUPHOR-BIA canescens. *L. a Reich,* ii. 442; *a Wilid.* ii. 898. *Schreb. ap. Linn.* 230, note. 14. EUPHORBIA *Chamaesyce.* Dichotomous. Leaves roundish, glabrous; margin crenate. Flowers solitary, axillary. Stems procumbent. *L. sp.* 652. *Hort. kew.* ii. 139. *Gouan hort.* 231. In corn #clds and gardens; *monsp.* 174. *Roth germ.* i. 204. In Swabia, on the authority of J. F. Grac lin. E. i'oliis sub-

rotundis obtusis, floribus solitariis in fo. liorum alis. *Guett.* ii. 420. E. dichotoma, foliis crenulatis subrotundis, floribus solitariis axillaribus, caulibus procumbentibus. *All. nic.* 31. A. Tithymalus exiguus procumbens, Chamaesyce dictus. *Boerh.* i. 257. In Holland. Chamaesyce. *Rail hist.* 869. In Sicily, Italy, and the south of France—*Lob. adv.* 154, *repr. in ic.* i. 363. *Clus. hisp.* 441, *repr. in hist.* ii. 187, *Dod.* 373, *and Ger. by Johns.* 504, *and cop. in. Park, theatr.* 195. *Dalech.* 1660. *(Bauh. J.* iii. 667, is E. canescens.).. CHAMAESYCE. *Dale* 212. *Magn. monsp.* 62. 15. EUPHORBIA *Ipecacuanha.* Dichotomous. Leaves entire at the margin, lanceolate. Peduncles axillary, uniflorous, as long as the leaves. Stem erect. *L. sp.* 653.
E. inermis, foliis oppositis, pedunculis uniiloris so litariis longissimis. *Gron. virg.* 74. EUPHORBIA Ipecacuanhae. *Bart.* 26. *Schoepf* 74..';,.'

Ipecacuanha canadensis. *Murr.* i. 523. Tithymalus flore minimo herbaceo. *Clayt. in ph. tr. abr. by Hutt.* viii. 331..,.
16. EUPHORBIA *Peplus.* Umbel with 3 branches;; branches dichotomous above. Involucella ovate. Leaves entire at the margin, ohovate, petiolate. *L. suec. n.* 426; *sp.* 653. *Curt, lond,* i. 35. *t. Wale. t. Sot. arr.*495. *Stnith brit.* 514; *engl. t.* 959. *Kroch n.* 723. Titbymalus parvus annuus, foliis subrotundis non creiiatis, Peplus dictus. *Raii st/n.* 313. Tithymalus rotundis foliis non crenatis. *Tourn. paris.* 234. *Vaill. paris.* 193. *Boerh.* i. 256. In
Holland. Peplos, seu Esula rotunda, *Fuchs.* 578. *c.* 230. (The fig. is E. falcata.) *Bauh. J.* iii. 669. (The fig. is
E. falcata.) Peplus. *Cord. fol.* 106. *p.* 1. (The fig. cop. from
Fuch. is E. falcata.) *Dalech.* 1658. *Cam. epit.* 969. *Dod.* 371, *repr. in ed.* ii 375, Peplus, sive Esula rotunda *Lob. obs.* 197; *ic.* i. 362, *and Ger. by Johns.* 503, # *cop. in* Esula rotunda, sive Peplus. *Park, thealr.* 194. PEPLUS. *Dale* 212. *Rutty* 520. E. Peplus. Cosie # Willem, in med. comment, r. 298. -n. 7. 3/arr. iv. 98.
17. EUPHORBIA *exigua.* Umbel with 3, 4, and 5 branches; branches dichotomous upwards. Petals 4, oval, with 2 horns from below the base. Involncella ovato-ensiform. Cauline leaves linear. *Obs.* 4986. In a corn field.—*L. sp.* 654. *Gouan hort.* 232. About Montpelier.—*Kroch, u.* 725. *Poll. n.* 457. *Host* 260. *Roth germ.* ii. 525. *Jacq. vind.* 82. *Asso n.* 412.
Tithymalus angustifolius saxátil is. *Magn. monsp.* 259.
EUPHORBIA exigua. Corte # fTtfkau ta med. comment, v. 298. я. 8. *Murr.* iv. 98. Native of France, Germany, Holland, Denmark, and Britain. a acutifolia. (Variation.) Cauline leaves acute. *Obs.* 4986. E. exigna acuta. /,. *sp.* 654. *Bot. arr.* 495. *Reth. n.* 351. *JIudi.* 208. *Sibth. ox. n.* 439; *Smith brit.* 515; *engl. t.* 1386. *Fl. dan. t.* 692. *Curt. tend.* iv. 36. . 245. E. inermis, foliis alterrlis lincaribus acutis, umbclla universali trifida, partialibus dichotomis diphyllia. *L. ups.* 143. Tithymalus sive Esula exigua. *Tourn. parts.* 44. *Vaill. parts.* 193. Tithymalus exiguus saxatilis. *Tourn. parts.* 367. *Magn. monsp. t.* 258, inner fig.— *Vaill. paris.* 193. Tithymalus exiguus crectus. *Boerh.* i. 257. In
Holland. Tithymalus miniirius. *Tab. ie.* 505. Esula exigua. *Trag.* 296, *cop. in* Esula minima. *Dalech.* 1656. Esula exigua Tragi. *Lob. ic.* i. 357, *repr. in Ger. by Johns.* 503, $' *cop. in* Tithymalus minimus angustifolius aunuus. *Bauh. J.* iii. 664, # Tithymalus leptophyllos. *Pari: theatr.* 193. *Rail hist.* 868; *sj/n.* 313. *Cam. epit.* 966. Peplis minor. *Dalech.* 1659.
Involucella oblique at the base. *Petals* transversely oval, honeycoloured; horns patent, attenuate, of the same colour as the petals, nearly as long as the petals, inserted into the outside of the calyx. *Capsule* obsolctely tuberculate. *Obs.* 4986. 0 *obtusifolia.* (Variation.) Cauline leaves truncate, cuspidate. *Obs.* 8703. In corn fields near Chesterfield, *a* growing with it.
& exigua retusa. *L. sp.* 654 0. *Gonan hort.* 232 0. Near Montpelier.—*Roth germ.* ii. 525 0. /Trot. «. 725 0.
Titbiraalus exiguus saxatilis. *Magn. monsp. t.* 258,
outer figi
Tithymalus sive Esula exigua, foliis obhisis. *Raii*
hist. 868. *Bat-h. J.* iii. 664. N.p fig.— *Tourn. parts.* 368. *Vailt. parts.* 193.
Seeds ovate, tuberculate, grey. *Obs.* 8700. la Leicestershire. Native of" Italy, Germany, France Leicestershire, and Derbyshire. 18. EUPHORBIA *Lathyris*-- Umbel with 4 branches.
Leaves opposite; margin entire. *L. sp.* 655.
Hort. kew. ii. 140. *Gouan hort.* 232. At Vigan near Montpelier.—*Roth germ.* i. 205. Tithymalus Lathyris. *Scop., cam.* v. 571. Tithymalus latifolius, Cataputia dictus. *Vaill. pa ris.* 193. Annual.—*Boerh.* i. 255. Annual and biennial. Lathyris major. *Raii hist.* 866. Lathyris, *Matth.* 1259. *Cam. epit.* 968. *Fuchs.* 446. *c.* 174, *cop. in* Lathyris, sive CatapUtia minor. *Bauh. J.* iii. 8S0, *and Trag.* 291. *Lob. obs.* 197, *re.pr. in Ger. by Johns.* 503, $
Cataputia minor. *Lob. ic.* i. 363, *cop, in* Lathyris major vulgaris, sive Cataputia minor. *Park.*
theatr. 191, #
Lathyris. *Dalech.* 1657, *and repr. in Dod.* 371.
Native of Italy and France, but probably only naturalised in Germany.
Vol. 3. c *S LATHYRIS. Alst.* i. 442. *n.* 3. *Geoffr. suite* ill. 207. *Plin.* 677. *litt. I. I.* 27. *e.* II.
Cataputia minor..Berg-. 390. *Dale* 210. *Hcrm,* 343. *jftwc. n.* 726. X,mn. 144. *Mill. Jos.* 123.
ATurr. iv. 100. *Rutty* 108. ScftrW. 759. *Spielm.* 480. *Fog.* 174. Tithymalus Iatifolius, Cataputia dictus. *Cfiom.* 24; *suppl.* 12. 19. EUPHORBIA *Apios.* Umbel with 4 branches; brandies biramose. Primary involucella obcordate, the others reniforra. *L. a Murr.* 451; *sp.* 656. *Hort. kea.* ii. 140.
Tithymalus tuberosa pyriformi radice. *Boerh.* I. 256. Tithymafus tuberosa radice. *Clus. hist.* ii. 190, *rt pr. in* Tithymalus tuberosus. *Dod.* 369, *cop. in Daleck,* 1651, *repr. in* Apios vera. *Lob. ic.* i. 364, *Sr Ger. by Johns.* 504, *abr. in* Apios, seu Tithymalus tuberosus. *Parte, theatr,* 195, $ *repr. in APIOS. Lob. obs.* 198. *Raii hist.* 870. *Bauh. J.* iii. 666, *cop. from Daleck.* 1595.—*Dale* 212.
20. EUPHORBIA *dulcis.* Umbel with 5 branches; branches bifid. Involucra ob-

longo-Ianccolate, serrate at (he margin. Involucella ovate, mostly serrate at the margin. Leaves spntulate, mostly obsoletely serrate at the margin towards the end. Capsules verrucose, pilose. *Obs.* 8742. Specimen from M. HerteL—*L. a Willd.* ii. 909; *sp.* 656. *Hort. hew.* ii. 141. *Roth germ.* i. 205; ii. 527. *Jacq. aiistr.* iii. 8. /. 21Si Petals roundish, blackish purple. Tituymalus dulcis. *Scop. earn. n.* 573. Titbymalus nbn acris. *Tourn. paris.* 537. *Vail!. parts.* 192. Tithymalus nbn acris, flore rubro. *Bauh. J.* iii. 673. No fig.—*Raii hist.* 870. On the mountains about Geneva; *eur.* 250. Pitynsa, sive Esula minor altera, floribus rubfis. *Lob. obs.* 193, *repr. in i'c.* i. 358, *cop. in Dalech.* 1654, *repr. in* Esula minor, seu Pityusa. *Oer. by Johns.* 502, # *cop. in* Esula minor altera, purpureis floribus. *Park, theatr.* 192. Esula dulcis-*Trag.* 298, *cop. in Dalech.* 1656. *Leaves,* the lower rounded at the end, the upper rather acute. *Obs.* 8742. EUPHORBIA dulcis. *Coste £ ffillem. in med. comment,* T. 298. *n.* 9. *Murr.* iv. 98.

M. EUPHORBIA *fieiioscopia.* Umbels with 5 branches; branches triramose, dichotomous upwards. Involucella and leaves obovate serrate. *Obs.* 4985. In a corn field.—*L. sp.* 658. *Bot. art.* 497. *Wale. t. Curt. lond.* i. 36. *t. Smith brit,* 516; *engh t.* 883. *Fl. dan. t.* 725.

Tithymalus subrotundis foliis majoribus crenatis. *Boerh.* i. 256.

Tithymalus helioscopius. *Raii syn.* 313. *Cam. epit.* 963. *Matth.* 1253. *Bod.* 367, *repr. in Ger. by Johns.* 498, # *cop. in Park, theatr.* 189, *and Dalech.* 1648. *Fucht.* 770. c. 314, *cop. in*

Tithymalus helioscopius, sive soliscquus. *BaukiJ.* iil. 669. Tithym.ilus helioscopius Matthioli. *Dalech.* 1644.

Serratures of the leaves not expressed. Petats oval. *Obs.* 4985.

EUPHORBIA helioscopia. *Coste and Willem, in met), comment,* v. 298. *n.* 6. *Krocl;. n.* 730.
Tithymalus helioscopius. *llutty* 519.
Tithymalus. *Date 211.*
Esula. *Berg.* 390. il/«rr. iv. 102.

22. EUPHORBIA *verrucosa.* Umbel with 5 branches; branches mostly trifamose; subdivisions biramose. Involucclla ovate. Leaves lanceolate,.villose; margin serrate. Capsules verrucose. *L. sp.* 658.

E. inermis, foliis linearibus, umbella universali trifida triphylla, partialibus trtfidis, propriis dichotomis diphyllis, foliolis subrotundis. *Guett,* i. 263. *Dalib.* 154.

Tithymalus myrsinites, fructu verrucac simili. *Hist, ox. s.* 10. *t.* 3. /. 3. *Vaill. parts.* 192.

Tithymalus verrucosus. *Dalech.* 1650.

EUPHORBIA verrucosa. *Murr.* iv. 105. Tithymalus myrsinites fructu verrucae simili. *Dale* 211.

23. EUPHORBIA *Paralias.* Umbel with 5 and G branches; branches dichotomous. Involucella cordato-reniform. Leaves lanceolate, involute at the margin, imbricate, when cultivated patulous. *Obs.* 4987. Specimen gathered by Mr. Boraston at Teignmouth in Devonshire.—*L. sp.* 557. *Bpt. arr.* 496. *Gort. belg. foed. n.* 411.. *Guett.* ii. 419. *Turn. $ Sower, in linn. tr.v.* 237'. On Portland island.—*Jacj. hort. t.* 188. As cultivated. (*Roth germ.* i. 205, growing at Tubingen; ii. 527, with a multiramose umbel and glabrous capsules is probably a different species.) E. paralia. *Smith engl,* 195; *brit.* 516. Tithymalus paralius ex locis maritimis. *Dod.* 366, *cop. in* Tithymalus paralius Dodonaei et Penae. *Dalech.* 1647, *Sf repr. in* Tithymalus paralius. *Ger. by Johns.* 498. *Matth.* 1252. No fructifications.—*Park, theatr.* 184, *Lob. ic.* i. 354, *cop. in Bauh. J.* iii. 674, *repr. from* Tithymalus paralius ex hortis. *Dod.* 366, *and cop. in.* '

Tithymalus paralius Dodonaei ex hist, purgaut.
Dalech. 1647. Tithymalus paralius Matthioli. *Dalech,* 1643. *Tab. ic.* 593.
Tithymalus maritimus. *Magn. momp.* 255.
Tithymalus paralios. *Cam. epit.* 962. (Tithymalus paralius. *Scop. earn. n.* 581, growing on the sides of roads, with a multifid umbel and glabrous capsules is probably a different species.) *Petals* 4, crescentshaped; anterior margin with 4r and 5 teeth. *Obs.* 7964. Specimen gathered by Mr. Gisborne near Tenby Pembrokeshire.—*Root* perennial. *Stem* 15 inches long. *Capsules* slightly tuberculate. *Obs.* 7963. Specimen gathered by Mr, Watt on the shores of Cornwall. *Native* of the shores of France, Holland, Suffolk, Dorsetshire, Devonshire, Cornwall, and Pembroke *TITHYMALUS* paralius. *Dale* 211.

T, paralios. *Lew.* ii. 437,
T, maritiraus. *Rutty* 518,

24. EUPHORBIA *sylvatica.* Umbel with 5 branches; branches biramose. Involucella perfoliate, sub' cordate, rather acute. Leaves lanceolate, entire at the margin. *L. sp.* 663; *mant,* 395. *Gou, kort.* 234. About Montpelier. *TITHYMALUS* lunato flore. *Raii hist.* 871 J *eur.* 250. *CoL ecphr.* ii. 56. *t.* 57, *cop. in*
T. solvations, lunato flore. *Hist. ox. s.* 10. *t.* 1. roffl 1. /. 3.

25. EUPHORBIA *corollata.* Umbel with 5 branches j branches triramose; smaller branches dichotomous. Involucella and leaves oblong, obtuse. Petals membranaceous. *L. sp.* 658 *I Michaux* ii. 210?

E. biennis, foliis lanceolatis obtusis alternis, ramis floriferis dichotomis, petalis maximis subrotundis. *Gron. virg.* 74?

Tithymalus marianus, angustis rigidis foliis, summo caule ramosus, foliis atque ramulis ad divaricationes ternis. *Pluk. mant.* 182; *phj/t. t.* 446./. 3. Umbel triramose.

TITHYMALUS flore albo. *Clayt. in ph. tr. ahr. by Hutt.* viii. 331. 26. EUPHORBIA *hlbema.* Umbel with 6 branches; branches dichotomous. Involucella oval. Leaves entire at the margin. Branches none. Capsules verrucose. *L. sp.* 662. *Huds* 210. Between Fevershamand Sittingbourn in Kent.—*Smith engl. t.* 1337; *brit.* 520. *Krock. n.* 738. Tithytnalus hibernicus, vasculis muricatis erectis. *Dill. hort.* 387. *t.* 290. /. 374. From the mountainous parts of the province of Munster in Ire« land. Tithymalus hibornicus, Mackenboy dictus. *Rati hist.* 1888. In I re Lind. From a dried specimen. (Tithymalus latifolitis hispánicas. *Bauh. Casp. pin.* 291. *Tab. ic.* 589, *and Park, theatr.* 188, *cop. from* Tithymalus platyphyllos III. *Qus. hist.*

438, found in Valentía; *which repr. in* Platyphyllum hispanicum. *Lob. obs.* 196; *ic.* i.

361, Tithymalus platyphyllos. *Clus. hist.* ii. 190, *Dod.* 368, *and Ger. by Johns.* 500, *and cop. in Dalech.* 1649, has cordate acuminate involuclla.—*Rati hist.* 870.) TITHYMALUS hibernicus. *How 121. Merr.* 118. Лам *syn.* 312 j—*hist.* iii. 666. ê 27. EUPHORBIA *palustris*. Umbel with many branches; primary branches mostly triramosc; se« condary branches biramose. Involucella ovate. Leaves lanceolate. Branches of the stem barren.

L-suec. n. 427; *tp.* 669. *Hort. kew* ii. 145. *Poll. n.* 462, *Roth germ.* i. 207 i ii. 534. *Rupp. ab Hall.* 272. *Jacq. misc.* ii. 314. *Willd. ber. n.* 520. *Host* 266. *Krock. n.* 737. *FL dan. t.* 866.

In the south of Norway. Tithymalus palustris frutioosns, *Tourn. paris.* 368. 537. *Vaill. paris.* 192. *Boerh.* i. 256. In Hot land, Tithymalus magnus multicaulis, sive Esula major. *Bauh. J.* iii. 671. No flg.—*Raii hist.* 864, wheremarked as a native of Britain on the authority of Lobel;—*eur.* 251. About Genera and in Lyonnois between Lyons and Geneva, Ezula major. *Dod.* 370, *repr. in ed.* ii. 374. *cop. in* Esula major. *Dalech.* 1653, # Tithymalus palustris fruticosus, /fist, ox. s.* 10. *t.* 2. roa» 3. *f.* 1, *Sf repr. in* Esula major germanica. *Ger. by Johns.* 501. *Lob, adv.* 151, *repr. in ic.* i. 358, *Si cop. in Park, (heatr.* 188, *&? Dalech.* 1654. Natixe of France, Switzerland, Holland, Germany, and Sweden, EUPHORBIA palustris. *Coste Sc Willem, in med. comment*-v. 298. *n. il..* Esula. *Pharm. suec.-L'mn.* 145. *Vog.* 238. Esula major. *Alst,* i. 442. *n.* 2. *Dale* 210. *Geoffr, suite* iii. 205. *Herrn.* 132. *Mill. Jos.* 191. *Murr,* iv. 105. 28. EUPHORBIA *Cyparissias*. Umbel with many branches; branchesdiçhotomous. Involucra mostly linear. Iiivolucella cordate. Petals crescentshaped and scmioval. Leaves linear, those of the branches twice as narrow as those of the stem. *Obs.* 8229. Specimen gathered in Champagne *L. sp.* 661; *niant.* 394. *Hort, lew,* ii. 145, *Roth germ.* ii. 532. *Gort. belg. foed. n.* 415. *Gouan hort.* 234. Near Montpelier.—*Jaca, austr, t.* 435. *Smith engl. t.* 480.

Tithymalus piiieus. *Rati eur.* 250, Tithymalus cupressinus, sive Humipinus. *L.ob. ic,* i. 356, *repr. in* Tithymalus cupressinus. *Ger by Johns.* 499, *imit, in* Tithymalus Cyparissias repens. *Hist. ox. s.* 10. f, 2. row 1. /. 29, *repr. in* Tithymalus Cyparissias. *Lob. obs.* 192, *and Dad.* 367, *and cop. in Dalech.* 1648. *Scop. earn. n.* 582. *Rait hist.* 867. *Tourn. paris.* 152. *Vaill. parts.* 193. *Matth.* 1254, *cop. in Dalech.* 1644. *Cam. epit.* 964. *Fuchs.* 812, *fol. ed. cop. in* 771, c. 314, *abr, in liauh. J.* iii. 663, *Sf imiU in* Tito/no©-JwsrofwOTof. JVag. 297, *Sf cop. in* Pityusa, sive Esula minor. *Dalech.* 1654. *Calyx,* segments pubescent at tke margin. *Petals* semioval, transverse. *Germen* obsoletely tuberculate, glabrous. *Obs.* 8229.—*Petals* in the barren flowers crescentsbaped, in the fertile flowers semioval. *Obs.* 8759. EUPHORBIA Cyparissias. *Coste Sp Willem. in med. comment,* v. 298. «. 9. 10. Esula minor. *Geoffr,* iii. 444. *Kroch. n.* 734. *Murr.* iv. 103. Tithymalus Cyparissias. *Chom.* 24; *suppl.* 12. *Dale* 211. *Lew.* ii. 438. *Rutty* 519. Tithymalus. *Klebe, account from in chin rev.* vii. 63, *Sf med. rev.* ii. 199, Tithymalus cupressinus I, *Tab, ic,* 594, 29. EUPHORBIA *Esula*. Umbels with many branches; branches bifid. Involucra oblongolanceolate. Involucella cordate. Petals crescentshaped. Leaves oblongo-lanceolate. *Obs.* 8746, Specimen gathered in FothergilFs garden.—*L. sp.* 660; *mant.* 394; *a Murr.* 453. *'Smith engl, t,* 1399. E. inermis, foliis lanceolato-linearibus, involucri universalis foliolis quinis ovato-acutis, partialis semiorbiculatis. *L. ups.lil.* Ezula'minor. *Dod.* 370, *repr. in* Pityusa, sive Pinca officinarum. *Lob. obs.* 192, Tithymalus Pinea. *Lob. ic.* i. 357, *Sr cop. in Park. theatr.* 192, *Sr* Esula minor. *Dalech.* 1653, *Sr repr. in* Tithymalus pineus. *Ger. by Johns.* 499. Tithymalus cupressinus II. *Tab. ic.* 505. EUPHORBIA Esula. *Coste Sr Willem. in med. comment,* v. 298. n.-5. *Murr.* iv. 99. Esula. *Alst.* i-442. *Krock. n.* 735. *Schrod.* 765, Esula major. *Geoffr.* iii. 449. Esula minor. -*Dale* 210. *Herm.* 133. *Mill. Jos.* 192. 30. EUPHORBIA *gerordiana*. Umbel with many branch-

es; branches diohotomous. Involucra ovalilanceolate. Involucella cordate, acute. Petals oval. Leaves lanceolate. *Obs.* 8745. Specimen gathered in Ciiampagne.—*Jacq. ap. L. a Murr.* 454; *austr. t.* 436. Involucella represented as rounded.—*Host* 265,

E. Esula. *Poll. n.* 460,

Tithymalus umbela multifula bifida, inrolucellis triangulari-cordatis, foliis superioribus latioribus. *Ger. Lud.* 540.

Tithymalus amygdaloides angustifolius. *Tab. ic.* 591. *Vaill. parts.* 192.

Tithymallus Myrsinites III angustifolius. *Tab. ic.* 592.

Tithymallus linifolius. *Cam. horl.* 170. On Ibe bunks of the Maine.

Tithymalo cyparissiaesimilis, Pithyusa multis. *Bank. J.* iii. 665. No fig. In Savoy, and near Strasburgh Basle and Mont pel icr.—*Rati hist.* 867.

Alypum. *Cam. epit.* 985, the stem without fructifications, and the fruit, *cop. in*

Alypum Matthioli, tithymalis affine. *Bauh. J,* iii, 676. (The plant in flower *cop. from* Alypum. *Matth.* 1280, is E. spinosa.) TITHYMALUS amygdaloides angustifolius. *Cham.* 24; *suppl.* 12. *Dale* 211. Tithymalus amygdaloides. *Oeoffr. suite* iii. 209.

31. EUPHORBIA *amygdaloides*. Umbels with from 5 to many branches; branches dichotomous. Invol ii cell a perfoliate, orbicular, bifid on each side. Petals crescentshaped. Germen glabrous. *Obs.* 7487. On Needwood forest in Staffordshire be tween Tuthury and Yoxal lodge, plentifully, in flower and fruit. 8 July.—*Obs.* 4988. Specimen gathered in woods near Worcester, in flower.—*L. s/.* 662; *mant.* 394. *Bot, arr.* 499. *Smith engl, I.* 256, just come into flower; *brit.* 520. *Krock. n.* 739,

E. Characias. *Wale. t.*

E. sylvatica. *Poll. n.* 463. *Jacq. austr. t.* 375.

E. inermis, foliis lanccolatis, umbella universal! multifula, partialibus dichotomis, involucris semibi fidis perfoliatis. *Guett.* i. 263.

Tithymalus sylvaticus. *Scop. earn. n.* 572, but tho leaves described as serrulate at the end,

Tithymalus Characias amygdaloides.

Rati hist. 863. In woods and thickets, in England, and on the continent of Europe; *syn.* 312. *Boerh.* i. 255.

Tithymalus sylvaticus, lunato flore, *Tourn. parts.* 155. *Vaill. paris.* 192.

Tithymalus sylvaticus toto anno folia retinens. *Bauh, J.* iii. 671. On the Euganean mountains in Lom bardy, and near Basle, Geneva, and Montbeliard in Franche comte.

Charadas anglicus et francas. *Lob. adv.* 152. No fig.

Stem from If lo 2 feet 3 inches long, terete; the lower half woody, brownish red, glabrous, with the transverse cicatrices of fallen leaves; the upper half green, slightly villoge, with lateral flowering branches from a little way above the lower half to the end. *Leones* slightly villose, those of the lower half of the stem lanceolate, tapering downwards, in some plants acute, in others rather obtuse, those of the. upper half ot the stein successively lanceolatoToblong, oblong, oval, the uppermost emarginate. *Flower tog branches* shorter than the stem, twice dichotomous. *Involucrum* quinquebractcate; bracteae obovate, emarginate, dcflcx. *Umbel* with 5 and 6 branches; branches twice dichotomous. *Involucella* nt the first dichotomy an inch broad, with, segments slightly incumbent rcniform and emarginate; those of the 2nd dichotomy 7 tenths of an inch broad, with segments reniform not incumbent slightly emarginate with and without a very short acumen; those of the 3rd dichotomy 4 tenths of an inch broad, greenish yellow, not incumbent, with a very short; acumen at the end. *Calyx* turbinate, nearly glabrous without, villose within, semiquinquefid; seg. ments erect, obsoletely bifid. *Petals* 4, horizontal, fleshy, greenish yellow, in dried specimens sometimes brownish purple, inserted into the margin of the calyx between its segments; margin entire; lobes. acute, pointing outwards. *Sectaria* numerous, brownish white, ramose, as long as the calyx; segments capillary, very fine. *Pistil* pedunculate; peduncle drcuryate, bent over the margin of the calyx, at the sinus into which no petal is inserted. *oermen* glabrous. *Capsule* stil green, tricoeçous, glabrous, microscopically and obsoleteiy scabrous below. *Seeds* solitary, oval, black, with a white cordate gland at the upper end. *Obs.* 7487. 4988. Specimens in flower and fruit gathered in the woods to the east of Worcester. —*Floral leaves* oblongo-obovate. *Obs.* 6638. In the garden of Mr. S. Shore, who dug up the root on Needwood forest.

TITHYMALUS'*syl*vaticus, lunato flore. *Dais* 211.

32. EUPHORBIA *Characias.* Umbels with many branches; branches dicholomaus. Involucella perfoliate, oval. Leaves pubescent. Petals crescentshaped. Germen villose. *Obs.* 6637. Specimen gathered in Fothergill's garden.—*Obs.* 7486. Specimen from Mr. Hunter's nursery.—/.,. *sp.* 663;.

mant. 394 0. *Jacq. coll.* i. 57; *ic.* 9. *t.* 89. *Gou-*
an hort. 234. Near Montpelier.—*Bot. arr.* 500,
where in 1. the last erase St.—*Smith engl. t.* 442,
just come into flower, from a root found wild 2
years before, but where or by whom we are not informed either there, or in *brit.* 521, where it is.
said on the authority of Mr. Whately to grow in great plenty and undoubtedly wild in the forest of Needwood in Staffordshire, but what Mr. and Mrs. S. Shore and what I found there in great plenty was E. amygdaloides. Tithymalus amygdaloides, sive Characias. *Bauh. J.* iii. 672, the 2 separate branches. (The entire plant *cop. from*

Tithymalus Characias. *Cam. epit.* 960, more resembles E. sylvatica.) About Montpelier.—*Rail hist.* 864. In Italy.

Characias. *Dalech.* 1642, *cop. from f* Tithymalus Clmracids. *Matth.* 1250. (*Park, thcatr* lS6, middlemost *tig. cop. from* Tithymalus Characias legitimus I. Ciusi hist, i'36, tchich repri in Tithymalus Characias I. *Clus. hist.* ii. 188, Tithymalus Characias II. *Dod.* 364, Characias monspelliensiuffi. *Lob. 6bs.* 194 8? Tithymalus Characias monspeliensium. *Ger. by Johns.* 499. is probably £. Characias L. mant394 *ti Raii syn.* 312, found by Plot on the paper mill pool dam in Heywood park in Staffordshire, where I searched for it in vain, is probably E. amygdaloides.) *Stem* villose, the flowering part composed of the umbel and lateral branches cylindric & 5 inches long. *Leaves* lanceolate, rcvolute at the margin, the lower coriaceous, deflex. *Umbel* roundish; branches 14, villose. *Inrolucrum* deflex; bracteae oblong, cuspidate. *Jtroolucella* villose, thin, semibifid on each side; lobes reniformi-ovate, rounded with the costa terminated by a very short cuspis, sometimes emarginate. *Calyx* villose; segments semibifid. *Petals* 4, blackish purple, somewhat crescentshaped; the ends patent and rather obtuse. *Capsule* and its peduncle villose. *Obs.* 6637. EUPHORBIA Characias. *Coste St Willem. in vied, comment, v.* 298. *n.* 12. *Murr.* iv. 98. Tithymalus Characias. *Dale* 211.

511. TACCA. *Calyx* superior, hexaphyllous. *Petals* 6, inserted into the calyx, vaulted. *Stamina* in pairs, in*sated* into the petals. *Berry* dry, hexagonal, polyspermous. From *Forst. J. Sf G. Juss.* 56. . TACCA *pinnatifida.* Leaves ternnte and biternate. From *Forst. G. esc.* 59; *austral, n.* 209; *J. tf G.70. L. jU. suppl.* 251. *Lour.* i. 368. *Gaerln.* i. 43. *t.* 14. Leontice Leontopetaloides. *L. sp.* 448. a *sulcata.* Petiole suicate. From *Forst. G. esc.* », 28. TACCA lltorea. *Rumph.* v. 328. *t.* 114. 19 *latifolia.* (Variation.) Petiole suicate. Segments of the leaves broader thau those of *a.* From T. phallifera. *Rumph,* v. 326. *t.* 113. /. 1. 7 *sativa.* (Variation.) Petiole smooth, spotted. From *G. Forst.* # TACCA sativa. *Rumph.* v. 324. *t.* 112. 9. TACCA *palmata.* Leaves palmate. From TACCA montana. *Rumph.* v. S29. *t.* 115. 512. MENISPERMUM. *Calyx* inferior, hexaphyllous. *Petals* 6. *Pistils* 2 to 6. *Berries* 2 to 6, monospermous. From *Juss.* 285, *Vent. tabl. t.* 14. /. 3, *Sf L.* 1. MENISPERMUM *edule.* Leaves oblong, glabrous. *Vahl. si/mb,* i. 80. CEBATJIA. *Forsk.* J71. 2. MENISPERMUM *peltatum.* Leaves peltate, ob long, acute, subcordate, veined, pubescent underneath. Paniclea axillary, longer than the leave«. *L. a Willd.* iv. 827, from authors. Sinilax

foliis pelfatis cordato-oblongis, floribus minu tissimis et copiosissimis. *Burnt. J. xeyl.* 218. *t.* 101. Convolvuli instar volubilis e coromandel, umbilicatis foliis crassis acuminatis, villosa. *Pluk. phyt. t.* 24. *f.* 6. No fructifications. PADA VALLI. *Rheede* vii. 93. i. 49; 3. MENISPERMUM *rufescens.*—Leaves orbiculatff ovate, acute, quinquenervose, reticulate, tomentose underneath. *Willd.* from authors. Abuta rufescens. *Aubl.* i. 618. *t.* 250. M. Abuta. *L. a Willd.* iv. 828. Abuta scandens. Barreré 1. PAREIRA BRAVA, Root. *Pharm. loni.- Alst.* i. 488. *Berg.* 815. *Carlh.* iv. 111. *Dale* 113. 419. *Gecjfr. in ac. sc. abr. by Southw.* iii. 266. *Helvetius in ph. tr. abr. by Jones* v. part i. 404. *Hill* 599. *Lew. disp. by Dune.* 196. *Linn.* 2G1. *Monro* iii. 197. *Murr.* i. 344. *Neum.* ii. 165. *Ploucq.* ЫЫ. i. 194. *Pom.* 69. *t.* 68.

Root.— *Quarin anim.* 291. *Rutty* 378. *Spielm.* 223.' *Vog.* 221.

Pareira. *Lew.* ii. 186.

Butua. *Geqffr.* ii. 21.

Pareyra brava. *Cham.* 261; мгда/. 86.

4. MEN1SPERMUM *malabaricum.* Leaves cordate, ovate, acuminate, villose underneath. Racemi lateral, *L,-a Willd.* iv. 826, from authors.

PEE AMER,DU. *Rheede* vii. 37. *r.* 19. 20.

5. MENISPERMUM *efispum.* Leaves exactly Cot? date.. Stem quadrangular, curled. *L. sp.* 1468,. probably from ...'!- *FUNIS QUADRANGULARIS. Rumpk.* r. 83. *t.* 44. /. 2. No appearance of-the angles df the stem being; curled..T'.S i. '. '1." ".-.".-.1 6. MENISPERMUM *cordifolium.* Leaves orbiciilato cordate, acuminatopuspidate, septemnervose, glabrous. Racemi longer than the leaves. *J-. a Willd.* iv. 826. CITAMERD U. I*theede* vii. 39. *t.* 21.. 7. MENISPERMUM *cocc»/i/erwn.*--Leaves orbiculatocordate, rotundatO-acuminate, obtuse, mucronate, pubescent underneath, quinquenervose. Cqrymbi shorter 'da the petioles. *Willd.* from a dried specimen. M. Cocculus. *L. a Willd..ir.* 825; *sp.* 1468. *Vent. iabl. t.* 14. /. 3. E—K. Berries 3 together.. if. foliis cordatis retusis. *Gron. orient, n.* 123, cop. from *L. mat. med. n.* 175, apparently from Cocculus officinarum. *Plufc. mant.* 52; *phyt. t.* 345. *fol.* '52. *pi.* 2. with a racemus of reniform berries. Racemus axillary, simple. Tuba baccifera. .*Rumph.* v. 35. *t.* 22. Arbor indica, cocculos officinarum ferens. *Brct/n. prodr.* 45. A leaf gathered iri some of the Dutch gardens. Cocci orientalesi *Ger. ly Johns.* 1548, *cop. in Tab. ic.* 923, *and Bauh. J.* i. a. 348. Berries. (Folium lunatum minus. *Rvtmph.* V. 40. *t.* 25. /. I, referred *to* by Willd. is described as having berries scarcely so large as pepper. Leaves cordato-ovate, acute. VoL. 3. D *r* Arbor aristolochiae foliis, maderaspatana, fructu par vo medicae ad instar convolute *Pink. aim.* 43; *phyt. t.* 13. /. 2, has solitary uniflorous peduncles opposite to the leaves.) COCCULUS JNDJCUS. *Pharm. suce.*—*Linti.* 259. Cocculi indici. *Berg.* 805. *Ploucq. bibl.* i. 256. *Vog.* 271. Cocculus iodus. *Dale* 316. *Mill. Jos.* 143. 4f«гг, i-343. *Neum.* ii. 99 257. Cocculi. *Spielm.* 480. Cocculae. *Schrod, app.* 6. 8. MENISPERMUKT *orbiculatum.* Leaves orbicular, villose underneath. £,. sp. 1468. Cocculi orientalis frutex convolvulaceus, orbiculatis foliis prona parte villosis. *Pink, amalth.* 61; pAyr. f. 384. /. 6. In fruit. CATTU-VALLI. *Rheede* si-127. I. 62. foe Jtnus terminal.

TETRAGYNIA. 513. DICHROA. *Calyx* inferior, quadrideutate. *Petals* 5, lanceolate. *Berry* quadrilocular, polyspermous. From Lour. I. DICHROA *febrifuga.* Leaves lanceolate, opposite Corymbi terminal. *Lour.* i. 369. PENTAGYNIA. 514. GLINUS. *Calyx* pentaphyllous. *Corolla* none. *Nectaria* 5, bifid and trifid. *Capsule* quinquelocular, quinqueyalve, polyspermous. *From L.* 1. GLINUS *lotoides.* Leaves obovate. Stem herba ccous. *Obs.* 8741. Specimen gathered in thp Paris garden.—*L. a Murr.* 455 *sp.* 663. *Locfl,* 145. In Spain.— *Forsk.* 96. *Burnt. N. ind.* 112. *t.* 36. *f.* 1. Alsine lotoides sicula. *Bocc. sic.* Sl. £. 11.

Portulaca baetica, luteo flore, spuria aquatica. *Barrel, t.* 336.

GLINUS. *Forsk. p.* xcix. HEXAGYNIA. 515. STRATIOTES. *Calyx* superior, trifid. *Petals* 3. *Nectaria* many. , *Styles* bipartite. *Berry* sexlocular and octolocu lar. From *Obs.* 7668, *L. a Schreb.* Smith ex*oL*,. 4: *Roth germ.* i. 425. Z. JM. i Differs from Hydrocharis in the fruit being a berry and in stamina surrounded by nectaria. *r* 1. STRATIOTES *aculcatus.* Spathae 2. Leaves erfsiform, aculeate. *Obs.* 7668. Specimen gathered by Mr. VV. Skrimshire junior at Outwell near Wisbeach.

S. Aloides. *L. suec. n.* 479; *sp.* 754. *Bot. arrang.* 564. *Smith engl. t.* 379; *brit.* 579. *Ft. dan. t.* 337. ', S. foliis aloes, semine longo. *Dill.' ap. Rati syn.* 290.

Stratiotes. *L. lapp. n-222. Vent. tabl.* iv. *t.* 6. /I

Aloides. *Boerk.* ii. 132. In Holland.

Militaris aizoides. *Rati hist..*1324; *syn. ed.* ii. 281.

Irfh. ic. i. 375, repr. in Ger. by Johns. 825, *Sf* .Scdi aquatil.is icon cum floribus. *Dad.* 578, *cop. in* Aloe, sive Aizoon palustre. *Bauh, J.ni.* 786, S. aquaticus belgicus-*Stap.* 436, *&r* S. sive militaris aizoides. *Park, theatr.* 1249, *and repr. in Lob. obs.* 204; *adv.* 334. No tig. S. aquaticus. *I)alech.* 1061. , Sedum aquatile, sive S. potamios. *Dod.* 578.

Leaves from 6 to 12 inches long, from 4 to 7 tenths of an inch broad. Scapi 6 inches long, with 1 flower, two-edged, the edge below the larger bractea aculeate. *Bracteae* 2, ovate, opposite, embracing, erect, the ends slightly bowed in, the larger aculeate along the-costa. *Peduncle* 4 times shorter than the bracteac. *Flozccr* projecting beyond the bracteae. *Chh/x* infumlibuHfornt; limb tripartite; segments oblong. *Obs.* 7668. A female plant.—*Scapvs* with several flowers; one of which expanded. *Vatyx* infundibuliform, with reddish dots; tube l£ inch long, cyl'mdric.-*Corolla* with reddish dots. *Nidaria* subulate, shorter-than the -aminai-. .*Obs.* 5421. A male plant. Specimen from Prof. Moench. *ALOIDES. Dale* 198. 2. STRATIOTES *quinquealatus.* Spatha 1, with 5 wings. From S. alismoides. *Smith exot.* i. *t.* 15, (the stamina style and fruit belonging to a var. with narrower ovate leaves,) *L. sp.* 754; *mant.* 405, *Forsk.* 101, Damasonium indicum. *Roxb.* ii. 45. *t.* 185, *8f OTTEL-AMBEL. Rheede* xi. 95. r. 46. 3. STRATIOTES *aroroides.* Leaves ensiform, flat, glabrous. Spatha hoarded at the end. *L. JU. suppl.* 268. ACORUS marinus. *Rumph.* vi. 191. *t.* 75. /. 2. DODECAGYNIA. 516. SEMPERVIVUM. *Calyx* duodecimpartite. *Petals* 12. *Capsules* 12, pob/spermous. *L.* 1. SEMPERVIVUM *tectorum.* Leaves ciliate, those of the shoots patulous. Stamina and pistils *12.* Nectaria cuneiform, caruncnlate. *Hort. hew.* ii. 148. *L. suec. n.* 428; *sp.* 664. *Curt. land.* iii. 29. *t.* 160. *Fl. dan. t.* 601. On roofs of turf.— *Mill. J. ill. t.* Huds. 211. *Smith brit.* 522; *engl. t.* 1320. üoi. *arr.* 502. Sedum majus vulgare. *Rail hist.* 687; sy«. *ed.* ii. 151, on roofs and walls; *eur.* 232, on the summits of Mount Jura and the alps of Savoy and Switzerland.—*Tourn. paris.* 533. *Vaill. parts.* 182. *Boerh.* i. 286. *Bauh. J.* iii. 687, *cop. from*

Sedum majus. *Fucks.* 33. *c.* 10. *Cam. epit.* 854. *Dill. ap. Raii syn.* 269. *Ger. by Johns.* 510, *repr. from*

S. majus alter um, sive Jo vis barba. *Dod.* 127, which *cop. in*

Scdum majus vulgare. *Park, theatr.* 731, *and repr. in*

Aeizoon. *Lob. obs.* 202, *Sf %*

S. majus. *Lob. ic.* i. 373, outer fig.— Inner fig. *repr. from*

Cotyledon altera I. *Clus. hist.* ii. 63, which *cop. in*

Sedum vulgari magno simile. *Bauh. J,* iii. 688.

Sedum. *Trag.* 376.

SEMPERVIVUM. *Berg.* 392. *Geoffr. suite* iii. 11. *Ploucq. bibl.* i. 71.

Sedum majus. *Pharm. austriaco-prov.* 66.—*Dale* 174. *Lew. disp. by Dune* 347. *Linn.* 145. *Mill. Jos.* 406. *Murr.* iii. 350. *Rutty* 478. *Vog.* 83.

Sedum. *Boerh.* 368. *Lew.* ii. 359. *Schrod.* 680. *Spielm* 5S0.

Sedum majus Tulgare. *Chom.* 805; *suppl. 211,*

Houseleek. *Lind hot dim.* 313.

J. *Flowers monopetalous. ill.* Cactus. *Berry* unilocular, polyspermy oua. *Corolla* multipartite. *Obs.* 2953.

2. *Flowers tetrapetalous.* 422. Ca»yo?hylujs. *Berry* monospermou. Ca/j«r quadripartite. 3. *Flowers pentapetalous, inferior.* 526. Chrysobalancs. *Drupe. Nut* sulcate. *Calyx* quinquefid. *L.* 527. Punia. *Drupe* sulcate. *Nut* globu lar, *Calyx* quiuqucpattite 4. *Flowers pentapetalous, superior.* 518. Leptospermum, *Capsule* quadrilocular and quiuquelocular *Calyx* pen taphyllous. *Stigma* orbi ". cutar. *Obs.* 6975.

52/1. Psidium. *Berry* quadrilocular and quin quelocular, polyspermous. *Calyx* quadrifid and quiaquetid. *Petals* 4 end. 5. *Stigma* simple. *Seeds* in a pulp. 523. Myrttjs. *Berry* bilocular and trilocular, *Calyx* quioquefid. *Obs,* 7183. 524. Pcnica, *Berry* multilocular. *Qbs.* 5373, 5. *Flowers hexapctalous, inferior.* 529. Lagerstromia *Capsule* sexlocular quinquelo cular and trilocular. 530. SonXErATiA, *Berry* multilocular, 6. *Flowers polypetalous,* 531. Oncoba. *Berry* unilocular, polysperm ous. *From Forsk.* 7. *Flowers with en operculum,* 520. ErcALYPTuS, *Capsule* quadrilocular, poly sperraou's. 519. Calyptbanthes, *Berry* unilocular, *Order* ?.

T R I GYJ I A.

533. Sbsuvicm, *Calyx* inferior. *Corolla* none. *Capsule* trilocular, cut round, ' i., .:... ' *Order* 3. . I. l..'.. " PENTAGYNIA, ...- 1. *Flowers pentapetalous.* 534. Merpilus. *Berry* pentaspermons,-i.. . *b3o.* Pybus. *Pomum* quinquelocular.

2. *Flowers folypetalous. ..,* ' 537. Mesembbyantbes.; *Petals* in several rows.

Styles 5, 4, and 10. *Capsule* with as many cells as styles; cells polyspermous. f 86. Tetragonia. *Corolla* none. *Drupe* monos« permous. *Nut* with from 3 to 8 cells. *Order* 4. POLYGYNIA. Ф39 3$0£Дй fife& contained within the berrylike tube of the calyx» *Obs.* 8162. 540. Rubtti. *Berry* compound. 538. Spiraea. *Capsules* bivalve. 542. Tormentilla. *Seeds* without aristae. *Petals* 4 and 5. *Calyx* octofid and decemfid. *Obs.* 5866. *Seeds* aristate. *Petals* 5. *Ca lyx* decemfid. *Seeds* aristate. *Calyx* octopartite; segments equal. *Petals* 5 to 8. *Obs.* 7994. *Seeds* placed on a fleshy re» ceptock. *Calyx* decerned. MONOGYNIA. 517. CACTUS. *Corolla* superior, multipartite; segment? incumbent, the inner gradually longer. *Stamina* inserted into the corolla. *Berry* unilocular, polyspcrmous. *Obs.* 2953. 2960. *L.*

Corolla caducous, analogous in structure to thai of monadelphous stamina. *Stem roundish.* From L. 1. CACTUS *Melocactus.* Stem roundish, with from 10 to 18 angles. *From L. sp.* 666, *JJort. hew,* ii. 150, *Sf Smarts, obs.* 198. Melocactus indiae occidentals. *Boerh.* ii. 85. Echinomelocactos. *Bradl.* iv. 9. *t.* 52. *Sloane cat.* 198. *Lob. adv.* 376, *repr. in ic.* ii. 24, *cop. in Bauh. J.* iii. *a.* 93, $ Melocarduus echinatus. *Dalech,* 1449. *Raii hist.* 1467. Get. *by John.* 1177, *repr. from* Echinomelocactos. *Clus. exot.* 93, which *cop. in* Melocarduus americanus. *Park, theatr.* 1627. No fructifications. CACTUS humilis subrotundus sulcatus et coronatus, spinis confertis. Browne 238. 2. Stem angular, erect. From *L. S.* CACTUS *Pitajaya.* Stem triangular. *From L. a Murr.* 459.—*Jacq. amer.* 151 j 8p, 190. 3. CACTUS *repandus.* Stem long, octangular; angles compressed, vaved. Spines longer than the wool. *From L. sp.* 667. *Hort. hew.* ii. 151. Cereus altissimus gracilior, fructu extus luteo intus niveo seminibus nigris pleno. *Sloane cat.* 197 j *hist.* ii. 158. *Trew sel. t.* 14. CACTUS erectus cylindraceus sulcatus tenuior, sum mitate attenuatus, aculeis confertis. *Browne* 238. .... 4. CACTUS *peruvianus.* Stem long, mostly octangu lar; angles obtuse. *From L. sp.* 667. *Hort.-hew.* Ii. 152.. Cereus peruvianus. *Trew in phil. tr. abr. by Reid and Gray* vi. *part* ii. 236; *8c by Hntt.* vii. 441. Cereus erectus, fructu rubro nou spinoso. *Boerh.* i. 293, " Cereus crassissimus, fructu intus et extus rubro. "" *Sloane cat.* 196. Cereus. *Lob. adv.* 453, *repr. in* J)uphorbii arbor cerel effigie, sive Cereus peruvianas vulgi. *Lob. ic.* ii. 23, *8c* Cereus peruvianus spinosus. *Ger. by Johns.* 1179, *8c cop. in* Cereus spinosus. *Dalech.* 1829, Cereus spinosus americanus. *Park, theatre* 1628, *fy* Euphorbii adulta planta. *Stap.* 1057. ' CACTUS cylindraceus erectus sulcatus major summitate obtusus, aculeis confertis.-*Browne* 238.

S. *Branches pendulous.* From Swartz. 5. CACTUS *pendulus.* Branches verticillate, terete, glabrous. *Obs.* 3507. In a garden.—*Swartz. prodr.Tl; ind. occid.* 876. //. *K.* ii. 15S;iiii, 503.,........:,...'.'.. o Hbipsalis Cassutha. *Gaerln.* i. J 37. *t.* 28.

Cassyta baccifera. *Sol. ap. Mill. J. ill.* i.

t. 29.
CACTUS parasiticus inermis apbyllus ramosus pro-
pendens, ramulis gracilibus teretibus striatis.
Browne 238. 4. *Stem creeping, zsith lateral radicles.* From L. 6. CACTUS *flagelliformis.* With 10 angles. *L. sp.* 668. *H. K.* ii. 153. *Cwrt. mag. t. 11.*
Cereus minimus scandens polygonus spinosissimus, flore purpureo. *Ehret t.* 2, 4, *cop. in*
Cereus teres multangularis spinosus articulatus ramosus serpens, flore purpurasccntc noctu diuque aperto, fructu exiguo mbentc. *Treta sel. 6. t.* 30,
Cereus minima serpens americana. *Sloane cat.* 197.
Ficoides americanum, sive Cereus minima serpens americana. *Pink. aim.* 148; *phyt. t. 158. f. 6.*
No fructifications.
Corolla, all the segments pink. *Obs.* 2960. In
Mr. Zachary's garden.
CACTUS cylindraceus sulcatus pusillus repens, aculéis setaceis confertis. *Brotane* 238. 7. CACTUS *triangularis.* Creeping, triangular. *L. sp.* 669. *Hort. hew.* ii. 153. « *ebracteatus.* Fruit without bracteae. *From* C triangularis aphjllus. *Jacq. amer.* 152. *a; Sro,* 19!. C. triangularis scandens. articulatus. *L. ups.* 121. C. debilis brachiatus aequalis triquetrus scandens Vpi repens, spinis brevissimis confertis. *Bзосnс.* 238. Cereus scandens minor trigonus articulatus, fructu suavissimo. *Boer h.* i. 293.
Cereus americainus triangularis radicosus. *Brddt.* i.
4. *t.* 3 No fructifications. Ficus iridica folio triangulatt eririforml profunde canaliculate stellatim aculeato. *Rati hist.* 1466, un der n. 5. *Sloane cat.* 196.
Ficotdes americanum, sive Cereus erectus cristatus, foliis triangularibus profunde canaliculatis. *PluH aim.* 147. *t.* 29. /. 3. No fructifications. Falmacea aut arundinacca pinnata spinosa. *Lob. adv.* 452, *repr. in* Arundinacea pinnata et spinosa exotica planta. *Lob. ic. i.* 54, *Sf* Calamus peruvianus spinosus Lobelii. *Ger. by Johns.* 1179, *Sc cop. in* 'Planta pinnata spinosa. *Park, theatr.* 1629, inner plant; *Sf* Nerii facie arbor.
Daleck. 1831. (The descr. be longs to another plant.) CACTUS triangularis. *Bry.* 183. $ *bracteatus.* Fruit with bracteae. *From*
Melocactus trigonus alius repens, fructu coccineo ex insula Sanctae crucis. *Plum. ic.* 193. *t.* 200. /.
2. CACTUS triangularis foliosus. *J acq:, amer.* 152. (3 *t.* 181. /. 65, fruit; *Sw;* 191.
5. *Stem compressed; internodia proliferous,* 8. CACTUS *Opuntia.* Stem pliant; internodia ovate.
Spines setaceous. *L. sp.* 669. *H. K.* ii. 153. C. compressus articulatus ramosissimus, articulis ova tis, fructu majore. *Gron. virg.* 54. C. brachiatus et articulatus, articulis ovatis coni« pressis, aculeis longissiinis confertis. *Browne* 237.
Opuntia vulgaris. *Mill. Ph. diet.* ». 1. Spinel short. Opuntia folio minore rotundiori et compression.
Mill. Ph. ie. 127. *t.* 191. Ficns indica. *Bod.* 801. *Lob. ic.* ii. 241, *rept. in Get. by Johns.* 1512, *Sf repr. from* Tnne ficifera indorum. *Lob. adv.* 453, *which cop. in* Ficus indica spinosa major. *Park, tkeatr.* 1497, % *abr. in* - '
Opuntia vulgo herbariorura. baka. *J. i.* 154. Bo
«r#. ii. 82. Ficus indica, a greater kind. *Park. par.* 433. *No*
Ficus indica, sive Opuntia. *Ddlech,* 1795.
Ficus indicae fructus. *Dod.* 801, repr. '« *Ger. by Johns.* 1512, $ *cop. in*
Fici indici fructus. *Park, theatr.* 1498. /. 3.
Ficus indica major. *Rati hist.* 1464.
Stem, internodia oval, with tufts of spines disposed in quincunx order. *Spines* setaceous, yellowish brown, nearly one tenth of an inch long. *Flowers* solitary, sessile. *Corolla* longer than the germen, *tall* yellow. Germen obconic, green. *Style* fusiform, strawcoloured, as long as the germen. *Stigma* sexfid. *Obs.* 6677. In Mr. S. Shore's garden. 10 July. OPUNTIA. *Dale* 292. Garden in ph. tr. abr. by *Hutt.* xi. 137. *Murr.* iii. 343. *Schoep/76.* G. Opuntia. *Bry.* 181. Prickly Pear. *Clegh.* 283. 301. *Edzcards west ind.* i. 201.
9. CACTUS *Ficus*—Internodia of the stem ovato-oblong. Spines setaceous. *L.* striis rubris varicgato. *Sloane cat.* 194.
Intro duced into Jamaica from the continent of America;
—*hist.* ii. 152. Ficus indica major laevis sive spinosa, vermiculos proferens. *Pluk. aim.* 146; *phyt. t.* 281. /. 2. CACTUS brachiatus et articulatus subinermis major, articulis oblongis et leniter compressis. *Browne* 237.
12. CACTUS *Pereslia.* Stem terete, arboreous. A culei in pairs recurvate. Leaves lanceolato-ovate. *L. sp.* 671. *Hort. hew.* ii. 155. Pereskia aculcata, flofe albo, fructu flavescente. *Dill. hort.* 305. *t.* 227. /. 294. Mains americana spinosa, portulacae folio, fructu folioso, semine reniformi splendente. *Commel. J. hort.* i. 135. *t.* 70. No fructifications. Portulaca americana latifolia ad foliorum ortum lan ugine obducta, longioribus aculeis horrida. *Pluk. aim.* 135; *phyt. t.* 215. /. 6. No fructifications. Grossulariae fructu majore arbor spinosa, fructu folioso e viridi albicante. *Sloane cat.* 165; *hist.* ii. 86. CACTUS sarmentosus foliatus et spinosus, spinis geminatis recurvis, foliis molUbus ovatis. *Browne* 237. 518. LEPTOSPERMUM. *Calyx* superior, pent aphyllous. *Petals* 5. *Stigma* orbicular. *Capsule* with 5 and 4 cells. *Speds* not winged. *Obs.* 6975. *Smith in lin. tr.* iii. 260.
Closely allied to Philadelphia.
I. *Stamina shorter than the corolla,*
I. LEPTOSPERMUM *scoparium.* Leaves lanceolate and elliptic, mucronate, obsoletely trinervose. Calyces glabrous, deciduous. *Obs.* 7022. In Mr. Philips's garden.—*Smith in tin. tr.* iii. 262. *Forst. J. Sf G.* 72. (misprinted 48) *n.* 6. *t.* 36. *f to I.* Parts of fructification. Philadelphia scoparius linifolius. *Hort. hew.* ii. 156. *Leaves,* upper surface smooth with 3 and some times 5 ribs; ribs sometimes not discernible; lower surface dotted; margin microscopically crenate; costa and sometimes the lateral ribs sericeous. *Capsuics* terminal and lateral, roundish, depressed, with S cells and." valves; dissepiment inserted into the side of the valves. *Seeds* terete, attenuate, flexuose, and curvate, rufous. *Obs.* 6976. Ja Mr. SitwclPs garden, in fruit.—*Leaves,* upper surface glabrous, with 3 and 5 ribs; under surface sericeous at the base and along the middle. *Bracteae,* the outer

sericeous. *Calyx,* phylla semiovafe, obtuse, whitish, membranaceous, with a few greenish dots. *Petals* 5, alternating with the phylla, obovato-subrotund,white. *Filaments* united at the very base, forming a ring round the margin of the germen. *Germen* turbinate, glabrous, the margin surrounded by the calyx, corolla and stamina. *Style* shorter than the stamina. *Stigma* orbicular, green, the margin somewhat angular, permanent. *Capsules* permanent. *Obs.* 7022. MELALEUCA scoparia. *L. JU. suppl.* 343. *Forst. G. austral, n.* 210;—*esc.* 7& 2. LEPTOSPERMUM *lanigerutn.* Leaves obovatooblong and lineaci-lanceolate, mucronate, trinervose. Branches pilose and pubescent. Calyces serrccd-villose; teeth foliaceous, permanent. *Obs.* 6978- Specimen without flowers gathered in FothergiU's garden.—*Smith in lin. tr.* iii. 203.

L. laniger canescens. *Ilort. kcw.* ii. 156.

L. australe. *Sal. R. hort.* 350.

Melaleuca trinervia. *Smith in White, J. toy.* 229.

THE TEA TREE of New South Walt. *White, J. voy.* 229. *t. at p.* 230. No fructifications. The branch and middlemost leaf. ig. CALYFflUNTtfES. *Calyx* superior,-entire. *Corolla* operculiforrtt, orbicular, caducous. *Berry* unilocular. Seeds 1 to 4. *Obs.* 8416. Swartz. ind. occid. 917. 1. CALYPTRANTHES *tuminodord.* Leaves ovali elliptic, acuminate at the end. Panicles lateral. 0658410. Specimen from Di1. Wright from the East Indies. C. caryophyllifolia. *1-. a Willd.* ii. 975, from a dried specimen. Jambolifera pedunculate. *Gaertn. i.* 178. *t, 3G.*

Petals 4. Myrtus Cumini. *JL. sp.* 674. Caryophyllus languescente vi aromaticus malabarien sisy folio et fructu maximo. *Pluk. aim.* 88; *phyt t.* 274. /. 2. Perin-Njara. *Rheede* v. 57. *t.* 29.

Leaves with pellucid very minute dots. *Panicles* on leafy branches. *Calyx* turbinate. *Corolla* whitish, glabrous, inserted into the margin of the calyx, closing the aperture of the calyx, just sensibly rising above it, readily separable from it, when moistened by steeping it in warm water separable into laminae as if composed of several petals, as described by Gaertner. *Obs.* 8416. JAMBOSA ceramica. *Rumph.* i. ISO. *t.* 41. 2. CALYPTRANTHES *jambolifera.*—Leaves ovate, emarginate. Panicles mostly terminal. Stem arboreous. From C. Jambolana. *L. a Willi,* ii. 975, *8f* Jambolana. *Rumph.* i. 131. *t.* 42.

Jamboloins indica, folio arbuti. *Bank- J.* i. *a.* 88. No fig.

Jamboloins. *Acosta, Chr.* 287. No fig. —The account ropr. in *Dalech.* 1873. No fig.—*Park, theatr.* 1636. No fig. JAMBOLONES. *Garc.* 235. *Raii hist.* 1545. Jambolan. *Cool; in Hawk.* iv. 349.

Jambobol. *Thunb. irav.* ii. 273.

520. EUCALYPTUS. *Catyx* superior, permanent, truncate, before flowering covered by an operculum. *Operculum* entire at the margin, deciduous. *Corolla* none. *Capsule* quadrilocular, opening at the end, polypurmous. *From llort. kew. $ Smith. UUerit.*

I. *Operculum conic.* Smith.

1. EUCALYPTUS *robusta.* Operculum constricted in the middle, broader than the calyx. Umbels lateral and terminal. Leaves ovate. *Smith in lin. tr.* iii. 283; *new holl.* 39. *t.* 13. RED GUM of an inferior sort. *Smith new holl.* 41. 2. EUCALYPTUS *retinifera.* Operculum conic, te rete, coriaceous, twice as long as the calyx. Umbels lateral, solitary. *Smith exot.* ii. 49. *t.* 84; *in lin. tr.* iii. 284; *#* in *White, J. toy.* 231. *Andr. rep.* vi. *t.* 400, Metrosideros gurrimifera. *Gaerln.* i. 170. *t.* 34. /. 1.

Bark of the RED-GUM TREE. *White voy.* 231. *t.* with flowers.

2. *Operculum hemispheric.* Smith. 3. EUCALYPTUS *piperita.*—Operculum, mucronate.

Umbels lateral, subpaniculateand solitary. Peduncles compressed. Smaller branches angular. *Smith.*

E. piperita. *Smith new holl%* 42; *in lin. tr.* iii. 286, *Sfin White, J. voy.* 226.

The Peppermint tree. *White, J. toy. t. at p.* 226, the branch with leaves... Leaves ovato-lanceolate, unequal at the base. *Obs.* 5368. Specimen from New Holland.

EUC4L YPTUS piperita. *Pears., R.* ii. 179. 521. PSIDIUM. *Calyx* superior, quadrifid and quinquefid. *Petals* 4 and 5. *Stigma* simple. *Berry* quadrilocular and quinquelocular, polysperniQus. *Frçm Just, L.*

Does it essentially differ from Myrtus? 1, *Flowers sessile.* From

1. PSIDIUM *rubrum,* .teaves glabrous, *from Lour, 1380,* 2. *Peduncles unijlorous,* L. a Gmel.

2. PSIDIUM *pyriferum.* Leaves pubescent under neatb, ovali-elliptic. *Obs.* $350. Specimen ga thercd by Dr. Wright in Jamaica.—*L. sp.* 672 $ *a Murr.* 460. *Hort. kew.* ii. 157. *Lour.* i. 378. *Jacq. obs.* ii. 6. P. fruticosum, foliis ovatis venosis, fructu majori, *Browne* 238. Fruit round. Cujavus surculis et ramis junioribus quadrangulis. *Trew sel. t.* 43. Cujavus domestica. *Humph,* i. 140. *t.* 47. Guaiava alba dulcis. *Commet. J. hört.* i. 121. *t.* 63. Pela, *Jtheede* iii, 31. *U* 34. Guayava. *Raii hist.* 1455. Guayavae arboris ramus. *Clus. hist.* ü. 254, repr. *in Ger. by Johns.* IG 13, *cop.* in Guaiavae arboris ramus et fructus. *Park, ihealr.* 1634, *Sr* Guayava indica, fructu raali facie. *Bauh. J,* i. 0, PSIDJUMpyriferum. *Bry.* 210. *Scfioepf76.* Guava. *Graing.* 37. CO. Z«tg iii-803. Guava tree. *Quier in lett.* 136. *a rubra.* Pulp of (he berries red. *From J.* Bauhine, & Malo punicae atiinis pomifera, flore pentapetalo albo, fructu nullis dissepimentis interstincto ex toto es culento rubro majori. *Sloane cat.* 198. *8 alba.* Pulp of the berries white. *From* Malo punicae affinrs pomifera, flore pentapetalo albo, fructu nullis dissepimentis interstinctp ex toto es culento majore albo. *Ska7ie cat.* 199. Guajava alba acida, fructu rotundiore. *Pluk, aim.* 181; *phyt. t.* 193. /. 4. 3. PSIDIUM *pumilum.* Leaves tomentose underneath, lanceolate. *From L. a Willi,* ii. 957, CUJA VILLUS. *Rumph.* i. 145. *t.* 49. 3. *Peduncles trijlorous,* L. a Gmel. 4. PSIDIUM *pomiferum.* Leaves pubescent under. neath, elliptic. *From* Rum ph. and *L. a Willd.* ii. 958; *sp.* 672; *mant.* 396; *a Murr.* 461. *Ilort. hew.* ii. 157. *Lour.* i. 379. Cujavus agrestis. *Rumph.* i. 142. *t,* 48. Malacka pela. *Rheede* iii. S3, *t.* 35. Section of the fruit, and if I mistake not, the flowers and fruit *cop. in* Guaiava alba, fructu Totundiori. *Plul: aim.* 181 i *phyt. t.* 193. /. 4. Peduncles represented as uni florous and axillary.

PSIDIUM pomiferum.-Bry.-SU.
5. PSIDIUM *guineense*. Leaves ovate, entire, toracntose underneath. *Swarlz. ind. occid.* ii. 881. Cultivated in Hispaniola. M. minor vulgaris. *Lob. obs.* 560, *repr. in ic.* iu 522. CARYOPHYLLUS. *Calyx* superior, quadripartite. *Petals* 4. *Berry* unilocular, monospermous. *From L. a Schreb. SfL.a Willd.—L.*
Eugenia. *L. a Willd.* ii. 956.
1. CARYOPHYLLUS *malaccensis*. Leaves entire at the margin, lanceolate. Peduncles branched, lateral, with mostly 4 flowers. *From* Rumphius, Eugenia malaccensis. *L. sp.* 672; *a Willd.* ii. 959, *Mill. Ph. diet. n.* 1, # *Font. G. esc.* «. 6. Drupe containing 1 nut.—*JJort. tew.* ii. 158. *Smith exot.* ii. *t.* 61. *Andr. rep.* vii. *t.* 458. *a rubens*. Fruit red and white. *From* Jambosa domestica. *Rumph.* i. 121. *t.* 37. Fruit containing in a cavity 1, sometimes 2, and some-' times 3 woody angular nuts and sometimes none. Nati Schambu. *Rheede* i. 29. *t.* 18. Jambos Linschottan. *Bauh. J.* i. a. 117, *cop. in* Jarabos. *Park. theatr.* 1637. JAMBO. *Thunb. trav.* ii. 273. Jamboo. *Cook in Hawk.* iv. 347. Jamboe, (misprinted TamboeJ *Perch. Rob. cei/l.* 314. '
Eugenia Jambos. *Bry.* 250. Jambos alter. *Acosta, Christ.* 287. No fig. *0 niger.* Fruit purplish black. *From* Jambosa nigra. *Rumph.* i. 125. *t.* 38. /. 1. Fruit containing a nut.
Jambos prior Acostae. *Rait hist.* 1478.
Jambos Acostae. *Dalech.* 1872, *cop. in Bauh. J.* i. a. 116. JAMBOS. *Acosta, Christ.* 286.
2. CARYOPHYLLTJS *Jambos*. Leaves entire at the margin, oblong. Peduncles mostly branched and terminal, with mostly 4 flowers. .*From* Rumphius, Eugenia Jambos. *L. sp.* 672; *a Willd.* ii. 959, # *Mill. Ph. diet. n.* 2. *Hort. kess.* ii. 158
Malacca Schambu. *Rheede* i. 27. *t.* 17.
Prunus malabarica fructu umbilicato pyriformi, Jambos dicta minor. *Raii hist.* 1478.
JAMBOSA silvestris alba. *Rumph.* i. 127. *t.* 39. Peduncles sometimes simple, axillary, where a petiole had been inserted. Fruit containing a nut.

Jambu-eyer mauwaf. *Cook in Hawk.* iv. 347.
Jauibo ayer Mauer. *Thunb. trav.* ii. 273.
3. CARYOPHYLLUS *aromatkus*. Leaves entire at the margin. Panicles axillary and terminal, tri chotomous. *From* Willd. and *L. sp.* 735. *Houtt. not. hist.* iii. 3. 44. *t.* 12. /. 1. *Woodv.* ii. 366. *t.* 135. *Mill. Ph. diet. n.* 1. Not cultivated in
England.—*Gaertn.* i. 167. *t.* 33. *f.* 2. Eugenia caryophyllata. *L. a lf'illd.* ii. 965. Hast, account from in med. comment, dec. II. v. 47.
Thunb.. Girofle. *Sonn. nouv. guin.* 196. *t.* 119. Caryophyllus. *Rumph.* ii. 3. *t.* 1. 2. 3. Caryophyllum sylvestre. *Rumph.* i. 12. *t.* 3. *C.* aromaticus indiae orientals, fructu clavato mono pyreno. *Pluk. aim.* 88; *phyt. t.* 155. /. 1.
Garyophylli. *Lob. obs.* 575, *repr. in ic.* ii. 147, & *top. in* Caryophylli indici. *Bauh. J.* i, a. 423, 5r Caryophyllorum effigies spuria. *Park. theatr.* 1578. Caryophylli veri Clusii. *Ger. by Johns.* 1535, *cop. in* Caryophyllorum tormelis genuina effigies. *Park. theatr.* 1578, Sr Caryophyllorum indicorum nova icon Clusii. *Bauh. J.* i. a. 423. Caryophylli. *Cam. epit.* 349. *Clus. exot.* 16, *cap. in* Caryophylli indici, icon alia Clusii. *Bauh. J.* i. a. 424. Caryophylli indici, icon Camerarii. *Bauh. J.* i. a. 424. Caryophylli aromatici. *Dalech.* 1759.
Peduncles branched, terminal, articulated, bracteate. *Bracteae* ovato-subulate, opposite, in 4 rows, falling off before the flowers expand. *Obs.* 5370. Specimen taken in a prize from the Isle of France, in Sir Jos. Banks's herbarium, compared with others from Burmann gathered in the East Indies in 1776, and by Col. Van Preha in 1783, in the same her. barium. CARYOPIIYLLA. *Lew.* i. 291.
Caryophyllum aromaticum. *Monro* iii. 47.
Caryophylli. *Alst.* ii. 268. *Carth.* iii. 493. *Cull.* ii. 203. *Spiclm.* 217. Caryophylli aromatici. *Berg.* 473. *Geoffr.* ii. 389. *Hil-*l455. *Ilerm.* 218. *Linn.* 163. *Mill, Jos.* 118. *Murr.* iii. *333. Rutty* 99. *Schrod.* 557. *Fog.*
Caryophyllus. *Dali* 295.

C. aromaticus. Embryo flower. Volatile oil. *Pharm, edin.—Lew. disp. by* Dune. 221. *Murr. J.* i. 199.
Pears. *R.* i. 95. C. aromatica. Unripe seedvessel, and its essential oil. *Pharm. lond.* Eugenia caryophyllata. *Pears. R.* ii. 179. Clores. *Chdlm.* i. 147: 153. 202; ii. 41. 169. 204. *Fordyce, G. fev.* »U. 253. *Neum.* ii. 204. *Rush* v. 182. Girofle. *Chom.* 400; *suppl.* 124. ANTHOPHYLLI. Fruit. *Pharm. amtriaeo. prov.* 18.—*Berg.* 472. *Carth.* iii. 495. 502. *lierm.* 248. *Linn.* 163. *Murr.* iii. *333. Vog.* 2-16.
P/owcg. *bibl, u* 698. Antophylli. £c/rorf. 558. *Spitlm.* 24S. Antophyllus. *Neum.* ii. 206. OLEUM Caryophyllorum. i/e&. 302v *Und.* i.
319. *Wintr. in Mead mon.* i. 254. Caryophylli essentia. *Ploucq. bibl.* i. 314. Oil of Cloves. *Campet,* account *from in ann. med. lustr. II,* ii. 131. *Darw.* ii. 135. 500. 688. *Und.* i. 314; ii. 59. 4. CARYOPHYLLUS *corlkosus*. Leaves entire at the margin, ovate, acuminate. Racemi corymbose. Filaments very short. *From* EUGENIA corticosa. *Lour.* i. 376. 5. CARYOPHYLLUS *acutangulus*. Leaves crenate.
Peduncles terminal. Berries tetragonous, oblong, angles acute. *From* Eugenia acutangula. *L. sp.* 673, *Lour.* . 375, 8c Eugenia foliis crenatis, pedunculis termiqaniibus, porais oblongis acutangulis, *L-seyl. n.* 190,
Tjeria Samstravadi. *Rheede* iv. 15. *t.* 17.
BUTONICA terrestris rubra. *Rumph.* iii. 181. *t.*
115 Fig. of (he fruit and spike do not accord with the descr.
6 CA.RYOPHYLLUS *raremosus*. Leaves crenate.
Kacemi very long. Berries tetragonous, ovate.
From
Eugenia racemosa. *L. a Murr.* 461; *sp.* 673. *Forst.*
G. austral, *n.* 221.
Eugenia foliis crenatis, pomis ovatis, racemo longissimo. *L. zeyl. n.* 191. BUTONICA terrestris alba. *Rumph.* iii. 181. *t.* 116. Fruit represented as oblong, two-edged, and in p. 182 said not to be tetragonal, but in p.

181, described as quadrate. Samstravadi, seu Caipa-tsjambu. *Rheede* iv. 11. *t.* 6. Fruit sulcate, with 4 angles. 523. MYRTUS. *Calyx* superior, quinquepartite and pentaphyllous. *Petals* 5. Berry bilocular and trilocular; cells with from 1 to 5 seeds. *Obs,* 7183, 7184, *and from Swartz. obs.* 201, *Juss, Sf Gaertn.—L,. — Vent. tabl. t.* 20. /. 1. 1. MYRTUS *communis.* Flowers solitary. Involucrum bibracteate. *L. sp.* 673. *Hort. kew.* ii. 158. *Gaertn.* i. 184. *t.* 38. *a romana.* Leaves ovato-elliptic. *Obs.* 8235. Specimen gathered in Fothergill's garden.— *L. sp.* a. *Hort. kew.* a. 127; M. minor. *Ger. hy Johns.* 1412, *Sr cop. in* M. minor, aculo folio. *Park, iheatr.* 1453, inner fig. MYRTUS minor. *Geo/r.* suite i. J02. M. minor vulgaris. *BvecU ap. Herm.* 445. *Chotn.* 601. ScArorf.-632. 2. MYRTUS *tomenlosa.* Peduncles uniflorous. Leaves triplinervose, tomentose underneath. *H. K.* ii. 159. *Curt. mag. t.* 250. Arbor sinensis canellae folio minorc trinervi prona parte villoso, fructu caryophylli aromatici majoris villis similiter obducto. *JPluk, amalth.* 21; *phyt. t.* 872. /. 1. Branches tomentose, whitish rufous. *Leaves* ovalloblong, glabrous above, tomentose underneath; margin revolute. *Peduncles* opposite, axillary. *Bracteae* ovate, 2 at the end of the peduncle. *Germen* obconic, angular. *Calyx* superior, pentaphyllous; phylla subrotund, incumbent. *Petals* purplish pink, tomentose on the outside. *Stamina* many, inserted into the receptacle, between the calyx and the base of the style. *Obs.* 7183. MYRTUS canescens. *Lour.* i 381.
S. MYRTUS *trinenia.* Racemi mostly terminal. Leaves trinervose, glabrous, ovate, acuminate, *From Lour.* i. 381. Berry unilocular, polyspermous.
4. MYRTUS *caryophyllata.* Peduncles trichetomous, terminal. Leaves obovate and ovato-lanceolate, without dots. Calyces entire. *Swarls. 4bs.* 202. *L. a Murr.* 462; *sp.* 675.
M. foliis obverse ovatis. *L. zeyl. n.* 183. IVjam. *Rheede* v. 53. *t.* 27. Drupe. Donighas. *Herm. zeyl.* 3.
DAM. *Herm. zeyl.* 14. 53.
S. MYRTUS *Pimenta.* Panicles axillary and terminal. Leaves opposite, veined, dotted, lanceolatooblong and oval. Segments of the calyx semiorbicular. *Obs.* 8548. Specimen gathered by Dr. Wright in Jamaica.—*Ilort. hew.* ii. *160. Gaertn.* i. 185. *I.* 38. *L. sp.* 676. *Swarlz. obs.* 202.
Caryophyllus Pimento. *Mill. Ph. diet. n.* 2.
M. foliis alternis. *L. set/1, n.* 186.
M. calyclbus absque appendiculis. *L. cliff.* 501.
Caryophyllus foliis oblongo-ovatis glabris alternis, racemis terminalibus et lateralibus. *Browne* 247.
Amomum quorundam odore caryophylli. *Rail hist.* 1507.
Cambui. *Pis. bras.* 82, *repr. in* Cambuy. *Pis. ind.* 178.
PIMENTO. Jamaica Pepper. Allspice. Berries. *Pharm. lond.—Cull.* ii. 205. Long 702.
Pimenta. *Dale* 296. 421. *Geoffr.* ii. 386. Hill 466. *Linn.* 146.
M. Pimenta. Fruit. *Pharm. edin.— Lets. disp. by Dune.* 264. *Murr. J.* i. 202. *Pears. R.* i. 93; ii. 191. *Wright in med. journ.* viii. 273.
Piper jamaicense. *Alst.* ii. 311. *Berg.* 396. *Lew.* ii. 226. *Mill. Jos.* 349. *Ridty* 394.
Amomum spurium. *Carth.* iii. 515. Amomum. *Herm.* 251. *Murr.* iii. 316. *Neutn.* ii. 207. *Spielm.* 237. *Vog.* 166.
Jamaica Pepper. *Maclean* 143. Monro iii. 222. Piemento. *Hillary* 67. Alspice. .*Rush* v. 182. 188. Poivre de la Jamaique. *Chotn.* 333. *a ovalifolia.* Leaves oblongo-oval. *Obs.* 8548. *Hort.* keio. ii. 160 0 M. arborca aromatica, foliis laurinis. *Sloane cat.* 161. Amomum quorundam, an Garyophyllon Plinii. *Clus. exot.* 17, *repr. in* Amomum quorundam, forte Garyophyllon Plinii. *Gcr. by Johns.* 1610, 5f *cop. in* Amomum aliud quorundam, et Garyophyllum Plinii
Clusio suspicatum. *Park, theatr.* 1567, *Sf* Amomum Clusii. *Bauh.J.* ii. 194
Leaves oval and oblongo-oval. *Petioles* slightly pubescent. *Pedicles* pubescent. *Calyx* quadripartite, limber, pubescent. *Petals* 4. *Germen* pubescent. *Obs.* 8548.
$ *oblongifolia.* Leaves lanceolato-oblong and lanceolate. *Obs.* 5371. Specimen gathered in the garden of Fothergill.—*Hort. lew.* ii. 160 *a* M. Pimenta. *Woodv.* i. 77. *t.* 26, from Sionhouse garden. M. arborea aromatica foliis laurinis angustioribus.
Sloane cat. 161. M. arboroa foliis laurinis aromatica. *Sloane in ph. tr. abr. by Hutt.* iii. 425. No fig.—*by Lowth.* ii. 663. *t.* 9./. 166, *at p.* 776; *hist.* ii. 76. *t.* 191. *f.* 1, the outer branch *cop. in* Caryophyllus aromaticus americanus, lauri acuminatis foliis, fnictu orbiculari. *Pluh: aim.* SS; *phyt. t.* 155. /. 4; *mant.* 39. *Branches* of last year terete, just below the inser tion of the petioles tetragonous; those of the present year quadrangular. *Leaves* opposite, 6 inches long, the lower lanceolato oblong, the upper oblongo-lanceolate. *Panicles* lateral; branches opposite. *Ca« lyx* quadripartite limber, pubescent, tomentose oa the inner side. *Petals* 4, orbicular, with transparent dots. *Obs.* 5S71.—*Berry* bilocular; cells monospermous. *Obs.* 5372. Berries from the shops. 6. MYRTUS *acris.* Peduncles axillary and terminal, corymbose, trichotomous. Leaves opposite, elliptico-oval, convex, coriaceous, veined, dotted. Stem arboreous. Segments of the calyx triangular. *Obs.* 8417. Specimen gathered by Dr. Wright in Barbadoes.—*Szoarlz. ind. occid.* ii. 909. Caryophyllus foliis oblongo-ovatis oppositis, racemis lateralibus et terminalibus. *Browne* 247. Caryophyllus aromaticus indiae occidentals, folio et fructu rotundis dipyrene, seminibus fere orbiculatis planis. *Pluh. aim.* 88; *phyt. t.* 155. /. 3; *manL* 39. The Bayberry tree. *Hughes barb.* 145. *t.* 10 . M. arborea aromatica, foliis laurinis latioribus. *Sloane cat.* 161. (Caryophyllus racemosus. *Mill. Ph. diet. n.* 5, is described as having no aromatic odour.) *Branches* quadrangular, compressed, microscopically tuberculate. *Leaves* opposite, elliptico-oval and oval, glabrous, dull; dots numerous, semitransparent; veins reticulate, the veins near the margin forming a line parallel *to* the margin. *Panicles* axillary, the lower longer than and the upper shorter than the leaves, glabrous; branches alternate and, opposite, patent and horizontal. *Germen* inferior vol.. S.J *f* F nbconic, microscopically tuberculate, glabrous. *Calyx* supe-

rior, quinquepartile, coriaceous, microscopically lubercuiate; segments acute, patent. *Petals b,* orbicular, with transparent dots. *Stamina* inserted into the receptacle between the calyx and the base of the style. *Style* 1. *Obs.* 7184. From Mr. Hunter's nursery.—*Leaves* coriaceous, shining on the upper surface, revolute, veined, dotted, the larger 3f inches long, the smaller 2 inches long. *Panicles* lateral and terminal, shorter than the leaves. ' *Berry* unripe, bilocular, with 8 seeds. 06s. 8417. MYRTUS caryophyllata. *J acq, obs.* ii. 1; *amer.* 8w. 193. 524. PÚNICA. *Calyx* superior, quinquefid and sepfemfid. *Petals* 5. *Berry* multilocular; cells polyspcrmous, in 2 "sets, the upper set consisting of 8, the lower set of 5 cells. *Obs.* 5373. 6839. L. 1. PÚNICA *Granatutn.* Leaves lanceolate and oblong. Stem arboreous. *Obs.* 5373. Specimen from Prof. Jos. F. Jacquin.—*L. sp.* 676. *Hort. lew.* ii. 160. *Woodv.* i. 158. *t.* 58. *Scop. earn, n.* 585. In the mountains near Trieste.—*Host* '271. In Li torn 1 i about Duino and Trieste and at the foot of the mountain Vogliack.—*Lour.* i. 383. *Andr. rep.* ii. *t.* 96. The var. with white corollae.
P. fruticosa major, ramulis crassioribus erectis. *Browne* 239. Cultivated in Jamaica.
Malus púnica sativa, alus simplici flore. *Shane cat.* Punica malus sylvestris. *Rail eur.* 211. In the P. floribus racemosis, foliis deciduis basi antice glan south of France. Malum Granatum. *liumpk.* ii. 94. *t.* 24. /. 1. Malum punicum. *Lob. obs.* $64) *repr. in ic.* ii. ISO, (misprinted 134) *cop. in* Malus punica sativa. *Park, theatr,* 1510, *and repr, in* Malus punica sylvestris. *Ger. by Johns.* 1450. Malus punica. *Dalech.* SOS. *Trag.* 1037. *Rcii hist.* 1462. *Bauh. J. t. a.* 76. *Cam. epit. ISO. Dod.* 782, *repr. m* Malus granata sive punica. *Ger. by Johns.* 1450. Malus grauatus simplici flore. *Park. par. t.* 429.
Malus Granata. Stap. S93.
Mali punicae sive Granatae fructus. *Park, theatr.* 1510. Fruit. Mala punica. *Cam. epit.* 131. Fruit.
Berry multilocular; cells in 2 sets, the upper set consisting of 8, occupying the greater part of the berry, the lower of 5, occupying the lower third or fourth of the cavity; dissepiments membranaceous, reticulate, the areolae transparent polygonal resembling the ends of the cells or a honeycomb, the areolae divided by opaque fibres; columellae 8 above inserted into the sides of the paries of the berry, and 5 below inserted into the lower part of the paries of the berry. No transverse septum discernible between the upper and lower sets of cells excepting the contiguous dissepiments. *Seeds* oblongo-ovate, with many sides, whitish, enveloped with a rosecoloured manysided pellucid pulp, and attached to the columellae by very short pedicles inserted into the nar rower «nd. *Obs.* 6839. GRANATUM. Pomegranate. Rind of the fruit.
Flower called Balaustium. *Pharm. lond.* —*Berg.* 397. Granata. *Cull.* ii. 44. *Dale* 290. *Heb.* 128. *Geoffr.* iii. 791. *Herm.* 217. *Hunt. J. jam.* 2S6. *Linn.* 147. *Mill. Jos.* 218. *Monro* iii. 120 *Murr.* iii. 262. *Quar. anim.* J98. 265. *Rutty* 223. *Schoepf* 77. ScArorf. 598. *Spielm.* 90. *Fog.* 294. Punica. *Aht.* ii. 87. P. Granatum. Pomegranate. Outer rind of the fruit. Double flowers. *Pharm. edin.*— *Bry.* 275. *Lew. disp. by Dune.* 289. *Pears. R.* i. 66; *ed.* ii. 852. P. sive Granata malus. *Vog.* 262. Granata malus. *Lew.* i. 472. Mali granati cortices. *Carth.* ii. 139. *Mead mon.* i. 57. Mala punica. *Mend mon.* ii. 121. Malicorium. *Linn.* 147. *Sauv. nos.* ii. 401. *Schoepf* 77. Pomegranate. *Graing.* 37. *Monro, Don. sold,* ii. 44. Pomegranate tree. *Papin in ph. tr. abr. by Jones* v. parf. ii. 185, '$ *by Hutt.* vi. 53. Grenadier. *Chom*-603. 0 *plena.* Corolla double. *From L. sp.* 19, *and Hort. hew.* 0 Malus punica pleniflora flore majorc. *Sloane cat.* 201. Balaustium romanum seu minus. *Park. par. t.* 429.
Balaustium. *Lob. ic.* ii. 131, *repr. in* Balaustia. *Ger. by Johns.* 1450, *Sf cop. in*
Malus punica sylvestris, sive Balaustium. *Park, theatr.* 1511,
Balaustia hispanica. *Bauh, J. i. a.* 82. Balaustium majus sive cyprium. *Park. par. t.* 429.
f. 6. A flower., BALAUSTIA. *Berg.* 397. *Carth.* ii. 141; *Cull.* ii. 48. *Dale*29. *Geoffr.* iii. 796. *Hill* 437. *Lew.* i. 190. *Mead mon.* i. 57. *Mill. Jos.* 219. i?«*y 53. *Spielm.* 90. Balaustium. */sf.* ii. 87. Balaustiorum flores. *Ilertn.* 610. *Linn.* 147. *Mum.* iii. 262. C?«ar. anfm. 202. 261. *Sckoepf* 77. *Vog. 151.* Balaustines. *Graing.* 60. £//id. ii. 144. Balaustine flowers. *Monro, Don. sold.* ii. 41.
2. PUNICA nana. Leaves linear. Stem shrublike. *L. sp.* 676, from *Mill. Ph. diet. n.* 2. *H. K.* ii. 160. P. fruticosa hnmilior, ramulis gracilibus patent ibus. *Browne* 239, who is doubtful whether to call it a species or var. Cultivated. —Is it not a var. the produce of America? POMEGRANATE. *Graing.* 37. 525. PRUNUS. *Calyx* inferior, quinquefid. *Petals* 5. *Drupe,* nut with slightly prominent sutures. L. 1. Nut smooth. *Flowers racemose.* 1. PRUNUS *virginiana.* Racemi erect. Leaves deciduous, nitid. Petioles glabrous, with from 2 to 5 glands a little below the end. *Obs.* 6468. In a garden, in fruit.—*L. sp.* 677. *Hort. hew.* ii. 163, dulosis. *Gron. virg.* 75. Padus virginiana. *Mill. Ph. diet. n.* 3. Leaves lucid green. Fruit black when ripe. Laurea Cerasus virginiana. *Park. par.* 599. *I.* 597. /6. Branches purplish blackish brown. *Leaves* smooth, glabrous, elliptic and ovali-elliptic, acutely serrate, to 5f inches long, concave, pale green underneath; anterior angles of the axillae of the crista underneath barbate. *Obs.* 6287.—*Leaves* slightly nitid. *Petioles,* glands in the larger leaves mostly below the leaf, one of them very rarely covered by the incumbent base of the leaf. *Flowers* crowded. *Racemi* cylindric, longer than the peduncle, 2 inches long. *Pejtals* orbicular, concave, minutely crenate, just sensibly longer than the tenth of an inch. *Obs.* 6468.—*Berries* red, when ripe purplish black, round. *Obs.* 4106. The same plant with Obs. 6287, & 6468. PRUNUS virginiana. *Bart.* 37. *Coxe* 375.
Cerasus sylvestris. *Schoepf* 77.
Wild Cherry tree. *Rush* ii. 128.
9. PRUNUS *Laurocerasus.* Flowers racemose. Leaves evergreen, with glands underneath. *Obs.* 8238. Specimens

gathered in a garden. Found near a ruin at the foot of Malvern hill on the Herefordshire side below Clutters cave which is to the south of the camp.—*L. sp.* 678. *Hort. hew.* ii. 164. *Woodv.* iv. 73. *t.* 230.

Padus Laurocerasus. *Mill. Ph. diet. n.* 4.
  Laurocerasus. *Raii hist.* 1549. *Boerk.* ii. 246. *Cam. hort.* 86. /. 23. *Park. par.* 401. *U* 399. /. 6. *Clus. pann.* 771, *repr. in hist.* i. 4, *cop. in Bauh. J.* i. a. 420, # Cerasus trapezuntina, sive Laurocerasus. *Park.*
theatr. 1518, *Of repr. in*
Laurocerasi flos. *Ger. by Johns.* 1603.
Laurocerasi fructus. *Ger. by Johns.* 1603.
Lotus secunda. *Dalech.* 849. In fruit.
Leaves with 1 and 2 pairs of glands near the costa towards the base; glands depressed, orbicular. *Obs.* 8238. LAUROCERASUS. *Akerman in new med. journ.* ii. 213. *Berg.* S99. *Cull.* ii. 282. *Dale* 309.
Dane. ii. 682. *Hargens, account from in phys. journ.* iii. 585. *Lew.* ii. 47; *disp. by Dune.* 346. *Linn.* 148. *Madden in ph. tr. abr. by Reid and Gray* vi. *part* iii. 258, *by Hutt.* vii. 468, a«rf *in Mihles ess.* ii. 227. *Murr.* iii. 213. *Ploucq. bibl.* i. 658. *Rogers in phys. journ.* v. 500; *account from in chir. ret.* viii. 84. *Swediaur, account from ib.* x. 489. *Thilenius, account from in phys. journ.* i. 511. *Vog.* 106. *Wurzer, account from in med. rev.* vi. 397; *and phys. journ.* vi. 375; ix. 288. P. Lauro-Cerasus. *Murr. J.* i. 137. Laurel. *Lew. disp.* 376. *Rutty in ph. tr. abr. by Hult.* viii. 297, *and in Mihles ess.* ii. 363..., ?. PRUNUS *Mahaleb.* Flowers corymbose, terminal. Leaves subrotundo-ovate. *Obs.* 8239. Specimen gathered in the Leyden garden.—*L a Murr.* 463; *sp.* 678. *Hort. hew.* ii 164. *Poll. n.* 466. *Roth germ.* i. 211; ii. 539. *Scop. cam. n.* 588. *Host* 272. *Kroch. n.* 752. *Gouan hart.* 239. Near Montpelier.
E 4
  Cerasus silvestris amara, Mahaleb patata. *Rauh. J.* i. *a.* 227. *Raii hist.* 1549; *eur. 91.* In hedges near Grenoble. Vaccinium Plinii. *Dalech.* 255. Macholebum. *Cord. fol.* 205. *p.* 1. Machaleb germanicum. *Park, theatr.* 1518, inner and outer figures. (Mahaleb Matthioli.

Dalech. 154, *cop. in* Macaleb Gesneri. *Ger. by Johns.* 1397, has axillary peduncles.) *Native* of the south of France and Germany, and the Grisons. MAHALEB. *Dale* 309.

4. PRUNUS *hiemalis.* Pedicles aggregate, glabrous.
Leaves oblongo-oval and obovate, abruptly acuminate. Segments of the calyx lanceolate. Stem arboreous. Stipulae with setaceous segments. Fruit subovate. *From Michaux* i. 284.

5. PRUNUS *Armeniaca.* Flowers sessile. Leaves nearly cordate. *L. sp.* 679. *Hort. lew.* ii. 164. Armeniaca. *Boerh.* ii. 242. *Mill. Ph. diet.* ARMENIACA. *Berg.* 407. Armeniaca Malus. *Dale* 301. *Geoffr.* iii. 116. *MilL Jos.* 50. Armeniaca mala. *Spiefm.* 79. P. Armeniaca. *Bry.* 231. *Pears. R.* i. 64. Apricots. *Darw.* ii. 682. *Fordj/ce, G. fev.* ii. *36;* iii. 195. NUCLEI malorum armeniacorum. *Carth.* i. 329. GUMMI pomorum armeniacorum. *Carth.* i. 293. major. Armeniaca Malus fructu majore ex luteo rubescente. *Boerh.* ii. 242.
Malus armeniaca, sive praccocia. *Park. par. t.* 581.
/. 1; *theatr.* 1512, *cop. from* Malus armeniaca. *Dod.* 785, *which repr. in Lob. ic.* ii. 596, Sr Malus armeniaca major. *Ger. by Johns.* 1448. Malus armenia major. *Dalech.* 297. Armeniaca mala majora. *Cam. epit.* 146. *Bauh. J.* i. *a.* 167. *Rati hist.* 1514. B minor. Armeniaca malus fruclu minore ex luleo rubescente. *Boerh.* ii. 242. Malus armenia minor. *Dalech.* 297. Armeniaca malus minor. *Ger. by Johns.* 1449. Armeniaca mala minora. *Cam. epit.* 147. *Bauh. J.* i. *a.* 167. *Raii hist.* 1513. 6. PRUNUS *communis.* Peduncles in threes in pairs and solitary. Leaves elliptico-oval, convolute. *Obs.* 4714. In a hedge.—*Obs.* 1712. In agarden, in spring.—*Huds.* 212. GUMMI prunorum. *Carth.* i. 293. *« spinesceus.* Some of the branches spinescent. Drupes subglobose brownish black. *Obs.* 4714. P. communis insititia. *Huds.* 212. P. insititia. *L. sp.* 680. *Bot. arr.* 508. *Smith brit.* 528. P. sylvestris major. *Bauh. J.' a.* 196. No fig.— *Raii syn. ed.* ii. 30; *ed.* iii. 462. P. sylvestris major, fructu nigro. *Raii hist.* 1528. Leaves ellpitico-obovate, villose

along the costa and veins, 2 inches long and 1 broad. *Peduncles* solitary and in pairs. *Calyx,* segments ovato-subrotund and oblong. Petals ovali-subrotund. Drupes solitary, seven tenths of an inch broad. *Obs,* 6096. 6288. In a hedge. 14 June. 9 Oct. PRUNUS insititia. *Bry.* 242. *Krock.* «. 750. *Spielm.* 95. *With, in bot. arr.* 509. g *damascena.* Branches unarmed. Drupes oval, bluish black. *From memory.* P. domestlca. *L. sp.* 680 0. *Krock. n.* 749. *Woodo.* ii. 235. *t.* 85. *Bot. arr.* 508. *Smith brit.* 527. *Lob. obs.* 595, *repr. in ic.* ii. 176, *Ger. by Johns,* 1497, # Prunus. *Dod.* 193. *Cam. epit.* 163. *Park, theatr.* 1512. JBa«A. *J.* i. *a.* 184. IVag. 1019, *cop. from* P. sativa. *Fuchs.* 403. /o/. ed. Zojca cop. *in 396. c.* 154. Rflii *hist.* 1526. Leaves ovali-elliptic and elliptico-oval, some glabrrus, others villose along the costa and veins, 3 inches long, and 2 broad. *Peduncles* in threes in pairs and solitary. Petals obovate, attenuate at the base. *Obs.* 4712. 6095. In autumn. PRUNA damascena. *Alst.* ii. 315. *Berg.* 405. *Carth.* ii. 187. *Herm.* 398. *Lew.* ii. 246. *Linn.* 150. *Mill. Jos.* 359. *Murr.* iii. 231. ScArod. 656. P. damascena. *Dale* 304. *Rutty US.* Prunella. #«««-. /e6r. 19. Pruna magna dulcia atro-caerulea. *Geoffr. suite* ii. 84. *y gallici.* Similar to (3 but smaller. *From authors,* PRUNUS gallica. Fruit. French Plumb or
Prune. *Pharm. lond.*—Dale 304. *Rutty* 412.. P. domestica. Fruit. French Prunes. *Pharm. edin.*— *Bry.* 237. *Pears. R.* i. 65. 204. Pruna gallica. *Alst.* ii. 315. *Berg.* 405. *Lew.* ii. 246. *Linn.* 149. itfitfit. 05. 359. *Monro* iii. 224. itfarr. iii. 230. Pruna domestica. *Vog.* 261.

Pruna. *Quar. febr.* 19. *Spielm.* 95. *Stoll vied.* i.
127. 134. 144. Prunus. *Ploucq. bibl.* i. 486. Pruna damascena. *Geoffr. suite* ii. 88. Prnna parva dulcia atro-caerulea. *Chom.* 8,, Prunes. *Cull.* i. 254. *Fordyce, G. fev.* ii. 54. *i cerea. L. sp.* (PRUNA catharinae. *Berg.* 405. Pruna coloris cerae ex candido in luteum pallescentis. *Geoffr. suite* ii. 84..«.--i i *maliformis. L. sp.* 680 .:! PRUNA rotunda flava dulcia mali amplitudine. *Geoffr. suite* ii. 85. *t flavescens.* P. fructu ovato maximo fla-

vo. *Geoffr. suite* ii. 84. PRUNA subrotunda flavescentia. *Geoffr. suite* ii. 84. » cereola. *L. sp.* 680 h PRUNA parva ex viridi flavescentia. *Geoffr. suits* ii. 86, S *claudiana.* P fructu majori virescente suavissimo. *Geoffr. suite* ii. 86. PRUNA claudiana. *Geoffr. iuite* ii. 86. i brignolensis.—*L. sp.* 680. o PRUNA brignolensia. *Aht.* ii. 315. *Berg.* 405. *Lew.* ii. 246. *Mill. Jos.* 359. *Murr.* iii. 232. Pruna ex flavo rufescentia, mixti saporis, gratissima. *Geoffr. suite* ii. 85. *Schrod.* 656.
Pruneola. *Linn.* 150.
P. brignolensU–*Vale* 304.
7. PRUNUS Chicasa. Buds aggregate. Peduncles, very short, mostly in pairs. Leaves oblongo-oval, acute and acuminate, serrulate. Calyx glabrous; sogments obtuse. Stem fruticosc. Branches mostly spinescent. Drupe subglobose. *From Michaux. Donn* 114.
P. angustifolia. *Marsh.* Ill, but the leaves are described as lanceolate, and the drupes oval and ovate.
PRUNUS Chicasa. *Michaux* i. 284. 8. PRUNUS maritima. Leaves oval, serrulate, mostly with S glands at the base. Calyces pubescent.
Stem fruticose. Drupe spherical. Nut subrotun do-ovate. *From* Michaux. *Marsh* 112? *Donn* 114? P. sphacrocarpa. *Michaux* i. 284? JBeach or seaside Plumb. *Cull.* 419? PRUNUS sylvestris. *Schoepf* 78. Swamp Plum tree. *Clayt. in ph. tr. abr. by Hutt.* viii. 332.
9. PRUNUS spinosa. Peduncles solitary and in pairs.
Leaves cuneiformi-lanceolate lanceolate and elliptic. Segments of the calyx acute. *Obs.* 4713.
In a hedge.—*L. suec. n.* 432; *sp.* 681. *Bot. arr.*
509. *Woodv.* ii. 233. *t.* 84. *Smith brit.* 528; *Ft dan. t.* 926.
  P. sylvestris. *Rati hist.* 1527; *syn.* 462. *Tourn.*
paris. 129. *Vaill. paris.* 165.. *Boerh.* ii. 241.
Fuchs. 396. c. 154, *cop. in Bauh. J.* i. a. 193,
Dalech. 130, *Trag.* 1016. *Dod.* 741, repr. in
Lob. ii. 176, # Ger-*by Johns.* 1497, # cop. in
Park, theatr. 1033.
Leaves, laminae elliptic, glabrous, serrate; teeth
acute; petioles pubescent. *Obs.* 8078. In a hedge.
81 May. PRUNUS spinosa. *Coste ¿r Willem, in med. com ment.* v. 298. *Pears. R. ed.* ii. 334. 351. P. sylvestris. Fruit. *Pharm, lond.—Cham.* 9; *suppl.* 1, *Cull.* ii. 41. *Lew.* ii. 247; *disp. by Dime.* 287. Pruna sylvestria. *Mill. Jos.* 360. *Monro* iii. 225. *Paisley in ann. med. lustr. II.* i. 420. Prunellus sylvestris. *Dale* 305. Acacia germanica. *Akt.* ii. 478. *Kroch, n.* 751. *Mill. Jos.* 360. *Rutty* 4. *Schrcd.* 524.
Acacia nostras. *Berg.* 408. *Geoffr.* ii. 718. *Linn.*
150. *Murr.* iii. 234. *Spielm.* 414.
Acacia. *Vog.* 229. 269.
Blackthorn. *Lind hot clim.* 314.
Sloes. *Darw.* ii. 710. 715.
ACACIARUM flores. *Vog.* 143.
LYCIUM. *Schrod.* 725.
10. PRUNUS pumila. Peduncles aggregate. Leaves obcuneato-lanceolate, serrate, glabrous. *Obs.* 8077.
In Mr. Wilkinson's garden.—*L. mant.* 75; *a*
Murr. 463. *Duroi obs.* II. //ort. ¿ею. ii. 165.
Michaux i. 286.
(P. sylvestris humilior, fructu rubro praecociori et minori, radice reptatrice. *Gron. virg.* 76, not this plant, which Clayton would have s tiled a Cerasus.)
Stem fruticose, 4 *feet* long, grafted on a cherry stock. *Branches* crowded. *Leaves* green, paler underneath; teeth glandular, the lowermost at the base on each side rounder. *Petioles* glabrous, somewhat shorter than the breadth of the leaves. *Pedun' cles* 4 together, somewhat shorter than the laminae of the leaves. *Calyx,* segments oblong, obsoletely serrate, defies. *Peta's* obovate, emarginate. *Drupe* when unripe oval, acute. *Obs* 8077.—*Drupe* when ripe full red, not distinguishable from a tolerably good cherry in flavour or appearance, which induces me to believe that this is the natural state of P. Cerasus, and that
л is the naturalised offspring of what the Romans introduced into Europe. *Obs.* 8760. In the nursery of Mr. Boughton at Lower Wick near Worcester.—*Peduncles* in pairs. *Obs.* 8761. Specimen gathered in the Utrecht garden. CERASUS canadensis. *Mill. Ph. diet. n.* 5. II.
PRUNUS Cerasus. Umbels on short peduncles.
Leaves oblongo-elliptic. *Obs.* 6291. In Mr. S.
Shore's pleasure ground spontaneously.—*Huds.* 213. *Smith brit.* 526. *Kroch, n.* 748. Cherry tree. *Tourn. noy.* ii. 166. About Cerasonte in Anatolia. CERASUS. *Pharm, suec—Akt.* ii. 273. *Boecl. ap. Herrn.* 377. *Geoffr.* iii. 285. *Lew disp. by Rolher.* 135. *Vog.* 293. Cerasa. *Carth.* i. 329. 435. *Herrn.* 377. *Lew.* i.
443. *Ploucq. bibl.* i. 661. *Schrod.* 560. P. Cerasus. *Bry.* 235. Cherry. *Fordyce, W. fev.* i. 189. 206; iii. 194. *Rush* ii. 241. Cerisier. *Chom.* 816. GUMMI cerasorum. *Carth.* i. 293. *Monro* ii. 439. *Rutty* 228. *Syielm.* 82. *Vog.* 320. *a* avium. Glands near the end of the petioles. Drupes black, of the size of the nut of *(S Obs.* 6291. P. Cerasus avium. *Huds.* 213. P. avium. *Sibtk. ox.* 154. *Bot. arr.* 507. Cerasus nigra. *Mill. Ph. diet. n.* 2.
The wild black Cherry tree. *Evel. by Hunt.* i. 181.
t. Cerasus silvestris, fructu nigro. *Bauh. J.* i. 220. *Raii syn.* 463. In hedges in Suffolk.— *Vaill. parts.* 32. Cerasus nigra. *Ger. by Johns.* 1505. *Mill. Ph. diet. n.* 2. *Leaves* when young pubescent underneath along the cost a and veins. *Obs.* 6291. CERASUS nigra. *Dale* 307. Cerasa nigra. *Pharm. austriaco-prov.* 28.— *Lew. disp.* 376; *by Dune.* 346. *Linn.* 149. *Mill. Jos.* 127. *Murr.* iii. 209. P. avium. *Bry.* 233. *Krock. n.* 747. Cerasus major ac sylvestris, fructu subdulci nigro colore inficiente. *Chom.* 366. Black Cherry. *Darm.* ii. 682. *Lew.* i. 444. & Corone. Drupe somewhat larger than that of *a. From* Black Coroun. *Mill. Ph. diet,* who says the drupe is a little rounder than that of 9.
P. Cerasus *t. Smith brit.* 527. About Bergh Apton in Norfolk, and in Hertfordshire.
y rubra. Petioles mostly with glands

near the end.
Drupe red, 4 tenths of an inch broad. *Obs,* 6711.

In a hedge at Cutthorp near Chesterfield. 5 Aug.

. —*Obs.* 7134. In a hedge in the Bythrops near
Chesterfield. P. avium. *L. sp.* 680. P. Cerasus. *Bot. arr.* 507. *Sibth. ox.* 155. *Huds.* 213 a&i. *Smith brit.* 526 a j3 *y*
Cerasus sylvestris, fructu rubro. *Bauh. J.* i. 220.
Raii syn. 463. Cerasus sylvestris septentrionalis, fructu parvo serotino. *Raii cat. ed.* ii. 62, from the itin. of Johns, who found it on the banks of the Tees near Bernard castle in the bishopric of Durham; *syn.* 463.64G7 in fruit.—*Petioles,* glands mostly a little below the leaf. *Obs.* 6286. Specimen from Dr. Heise.
Cerasus sylvestris septentrionalis anglica, fructu rubro parvo aerotino. *Raii hist. 1539.*

Cerasus sylvestris, fructu minimo cordiformi. *Raisyn.* 463. About Bury and Manchester in Lancashire, Stockport in Cheshire, and Hosgill in Westmorland. *Petioles* with 2 glands I gland and without.
Obs. 6711.—*Leaves,* the lowermost teeth on one and sometimes on both sides glandular. *Petioles* without glands. *Drupe* unknown. *Obs.* 7134. *i acidula.* Drupe round, red; pulp easily separating from the nut. *From memory.*
P. Cerasus aproniana (misprinted caproniana.) *' L. tp.* 679.

Cerasa acida rubella. *Bauh. J.* i. 221. No fig.

Cerasus foliis ovato-lanceolatis. *L. i/ps.* 125 &

Cerasia. *Lob. obs.* 592, *repr. in ic.* ii. 170, *£?*

Cerasus vulgaris. *Ger. by Johns.* 1502, *and cop. in Park, theatr.* 1517. *Mill. Ph. diet. n.* 1.

Kentish Cherry. *Mill. Ph. diet.*
Cerasa aproniana. *Plin.* 371. *l.* 15. *c.* 25.
CERASUS rubra. *Dale* 307.
Cerasa rubra. *Berg.* 402. *Linn.* 149. *Mill. Jos.* 128. *Murr.* iii. 205. *Rutty* 114. *Schoepf* 78. *Vog.* 250 *0*

Cerasa acida. *Spielm.* 74. *Quar. febr. S&l. '.*
Cerasa rubra acida. *Lew. disp. by Dune.* 346.
Census sativa, fructu rotundo rubro et acido. *Chom.*
Red Cherries. *Lew. disp.* 123.
t aquosn. P. Cerasus Juliana. *L. sp.* 679
E CERASUS fructu aquoso. *Vaill. parts.* 32.—
Chom. 816.
(*maialis.* Petioles sometimes with glands at the end.
Lowermost teeth of the leaves sometimes glandular. Drupe round, of a uniform red, the pulp separating without much difficulty from the nut.
Ol/s. 6712. In a garden. The account of the fruit from memory.
May Duke Cherry. *Mill Ph. diet.*
Leaves when young pubescent underneath along
the costa and primary veius. *Obs.* 6289. —*Petioles* frequently with a gland at the end, one on each side.
Obs. 6712. *n cordiformis.* Drupe white and red; pulp whitish, adhering to the nut. *From memory.*
P. Cerasus dulcis. *L. sp.* 679.

Ccrasa hispanica. *Lob. ic.* ii. 170, *re. pr. in*
Cerasus hispanica. *Ger. by Johns.* 1502, *&j cop. in*
Cerasa duracena oblonga. *Bauh. J.* i. 221.
Cerasus hispanica, sive alba. *Park. par. t.* 573. *f.3.*
Cerasus major, fructu cordato maguo. *Raii hist,* 1538.
White heart Cherry. *Mill. Ph. diet.*
CERASA dulcia. *Spielm.* 81. S'*nigra.* Drupe similar in shape to that of », reddish black; pulp blackish red. *From memory.*
Cerasus cordata. *Park. par. t.* 573. *f.* 7.
Smaller Lacure or hart Cherrie. *Park; par.* 572.
Black heart Cherry. *Mill. Ph. diet.* CERASA nigra. *Rutty* 114. *Fog.* 250 *a*
Black Cherries. *Lew. in Neum.* ii. 234; *disp,* 123.
VoL. 3. G i *aulvmnalis.* Dnipe round, small, blackish red, somewhat acrid, bitterish, ripening late. *From Duhamel* quoted by Berg.

Agriot Cherry. *Park. par.* 572.
CERASA autumnalia. *Berg.* 403. *serótina.* Drupe blackish red, roundish. *From memory.*
P. Cerasus austera. *L. sp.* 679.
Cerasa acida nigricantia solidiora, tardius maturescentia. *Bauh. J.* i. 221. CERASA acida nigricantia. *Dale* 308.
Morello Cherries. *Ltw. in Nemn.* ii. 234; *disp. 123.*
Cerasus nigra. *Berg.* 402.
12. PRUNUS *nigra.* Umbels sessile, solitary, with few flowers. Leaves deciduous, ovate, acuminate. Petioles with 2 glands. *Hort. hew.* ii. 165.
P. borealis. *Michaux* i. 286.
BLACK CHERRY TREE. *Cull.* 449. 2. *Nut with cavities on the outside.* 13. PRUNUS *Padus.* Flowers racemose. *Obs.* 6467. In a hedge between Fossbrook and Cheadle in Staffordshire, in fruit, on gritstone.—*Hort. lew.* ii. 162. *L. sure. n.* 431; *sp.* 677. *Light/.* 253. *Bot. arr.* 506. *Smith brit.* 526; *engl. t.* 1383. *Scop. earn. it.* 589. *Poll. n.* 465. *Roth germ.* i. 211. *Gort. belg. foed. n.* 418. *Huds.* 213. *Fl. dan. t.* 205. *Krock. n.* 746.
Padus avium. *Mill. Ph. diet. n.* I.
Padus foliis annuis. *L. lapp. n.* 198.
Cerasus racemosa sylvestris, fructu non eduli. *Boerh.*
ii. 244.
Pseudo ligustrum. *Dod.* 765, *repr. in*
Ccrasus avium nigra et racemosa. *Ger. by Johns,*
J504. *Rati hist.* 1549; *syn.* 463. *Warn, woodf.* 31.
Cerasa racemosa. *Dolech.* 312.
Padus. *Dalech.* 312, *cop. in*
Cerasus racemosa putid.i, Padus Tbeopfarasti dicta.
Park, theatr. 1518, #
Cerasus racemosa quibusdam, aliis Padus, *Bank. J.*
i. *a. 22%.* Serraturcs of the leaves represented as ciliae. Nut rough. Cerasus racemosa rubra. *Ger. by Johns.* 1504, *cop. in* Cerasus avium racemosa. *Pari: theatr.* 1517, may be P. rubra. Cerasus avium racemosa. *Park. par. t.* 573. *l.* 9, in fruit, *ratty* be P. rubra.
Branches lightish brown, with oblong cicatrices; young branches pubescent below, glabrous above. *Leaves* when the plant is in flower elliptic, acuminate,

acutely serrate, mostly cordate at the base, one half sometimes a little longer than the other, pale green on both sides; costa pubescent below next the substance of the leaf and more especially so at the superior axillae of the lateral costae; when the plant in fruit elliptico-oval, glaucous underneath. *Petioles* with *2 glands at the end, one on each margin, contiguous to the leaf, one of them generally covered by the incumbent base of the longer half of the leaf. Petals obovato-subrotund. Drupe* purplish black, shining, not unpleasantly astringent; pulp green, rather thin; nut oval, slightly acute at each end. *Obs.* 6606. In flower in a hedge row between Bakewell and Edensor in Derbyshire, on gritstone.—*Obs.* Native of Germany, Dauphine, Holland, Scandinavia, Scotland, Cumberland, Westmorland, Lancashire, Yorkshire, Derbyshire, Staffordshire, Norfolk, Cambridgeshire, Essex, and Kent. PAD US. *Berg.* 401. *Dale* 309. *Murr.yi.lHL* P. Padus. *Coste # Willem. account from in med. iomment.* v. 298. *Krock. n.* 746. *With, in hot. arr. ed. IV.* iii. 446. 14. PRUNUS *Pertica.* Leaves serrate, lanceolate.
Flowers sessile. Nut roundish. 06?. 6266. In a, garden.— Amygdalus Persica. *L. sp.* 676. *Hort. hew.* ii. 161. *Woods,* iv. 71. *t.* 239. *Lour.* i. 386.-.. Mains pi'rsica. *Park, theatr.* 1513. *Bauh. J.* i. a. 157. *Dod* 78t, *repr. in* Persica alba. *Ger. by Johns.* 1447. Persica. *Cam. epit.* 144. Persica rubra. *Cam. epit.* 145. PERSICA. *Pharm. austriaco-prov.* 55.—*Alst.* ii. 365. *Berg.* 413. *Lew.* ii. 192; *ditp. by Ro thcr.* 215. *Linn.* 147. *Murr.* iii. 241. *Schoepf* 77. *Spielm.* 224. *Vog.* 149Amygdalus Persica. *Bry.* 220. *Coste Sf Willem. in med. comment,* v. 298. Peach. *Bishop in med. facts* viii. 122. *Boulduc in acad. set. air. by Souths),* iii. 229. *Fordyce, G. fev.ii.* 36; iii. 195. 196; *W. fev.* 135. *Monro, Don. sold.* i. 354. *White, R. in med. rev.* iv. 81. Mains persica. *Carth.* iv. 231. *Chom.* 11; *suppl.*. 2. Gfofr. iii. 798. /fc/fty 383. *Schrod.* 644.
Persica mains. *Dale* 301.

Persica mata. *Mill-Jos.* 338. *Spielm.* 94.
NUCLEI malorum persicorum. *Carth.* i. 329.
Persicorum nuclei. *Hcrm.* 381. *Vog.* 259.
GUMMI pomorum persicorum. *Cartk.* i. 293. *a lanuginosa.*—Fruit downy. *llort. kew. a*
Mala persica. *Park. par.* 580. *t.* 581. /. 3 to 6:
Mains persica. *Park, theatr.* 1513. *Raii hist.* 1515..
Leaves lanceolate; teeth acute. *Flowers* sessile,. solitary. *Germen* downy. *Obs.* 6266. *$ acuminata.* Drupe downy, acute. *From*
Malus persica Melocotonea. *Park. par. t.* 581. /. 2.
Persica hispanica, Melocotonea quibusdam. *Bauh. J.* i. a. 162. No fig—/fan Am. 1515. 7 *glabra.* Drupe glabrous. *Ilort. kew. &. L. sp* 676 e Nucipersica. *Park. par.* 582. *t.* 581. /. 9. 10; *theatr.* 1516. /?ai'J Ais«. 1516.
Leaves lanceolate; lowermost teeth generally glandular. *Obs.* 7332. In a garden. NECTARINE. *Fordj/ce-G. fev.* iii. 195; *W. fev.* 135. 15. PRUNUS *Amygdalus.* Leaves serrate, lanceolate. Peduncles shorter than the calyx. Nut ovate. *Obs.* 6268. In a garden. Amygdalus communis-*L. sp.* 677. *Ilort. kew.* ii. 161. *Woodv.* ii. 230. *t.* 83. *Gou. hort.* 239. In corn fields and vineyards near Montpelier.—*Lour.* i. 386. Amygdala. *Lob. obs.* 569, *repr. in ic.* ii. 140 *and cop. in*
Amygdalus. *Park theatr.* 1515. *Dod.* 798, *repr. in Ger. by Johns.* 1445. *Trag.* 1089. Amygdalus dulcis et amara. *Bauh. J.* i. a. 174. Amygdalus sativa, t'ructu majori. *Mill. Ph. ic.* 19. *t.* 28. /. 1. « *amara.* Kernel bitter. *Obs.* 6268.—*L. y. Hort. kew.* 8 Petioles often with *2 glands at the end. Flowers* solitary and in pairs. *Calyx* hypocrateriform; tube lined on the inside with a glandular yellow nectariferous coat. *Corolla* whitish pink. *Obs.* 6268. AMYGDALA amara. Bitter Almond. Kernel. Pharm-lond.—*Berg.* 410. *Linn*-148. *Monro* iii. 12. Amygdalae amarae. *Alst.* ii. 250. *Cull.* ii. 239. *Herm.* 289. *Lew.* i. 78; *dup. by Dune.* 139. *Murr.* iii. 256. Ploucq. bibl. i. 359. *Rutty* 23. *Schrod.* 531. *Spielm.* 112. *Fog.* 245. A. amara. *Chom. suppl.* 33. fla/e 302. *Geoffr.* iii.

83. #«/ 480. MM. *Jos.* 33. Bitter Almond. *J)arw.* ii. 682. Hufeland, *account from In phys. journ.* vi. 378. *Phys. journ.* xi. 94. Pieore, *account from in med. rev.* ii. 286. *P dulcis.* Kernel sweet. *From* the shops.—*L. $. Hort. lew-a* AMYGDALA dulcis. Sweet Almond. Kernel. *Pharm. lond.*—*Berg.* 400. *Linn.* 148. *Monro* iii. 12. Amygdalae dulces. *Alst.* ii. 250. *Carth.* i. 323. *Cull.* i. 297. *Fordyce, G. pract.* 235. *Herm.* 369. *Lew.* i. 75. *Murr.* iii. 250. *Mead man.* ii. 57. *Pears. R. ed.* ii. 292. *Rutty* 23. *Schrod.* 531. *Spielm.* 112. &o// *med.* iii. 298; apA. ». 825. *Und.* i. 355. *Fog.* 245. *Wintr. in Mead mon.* i. 265. 276. *Leaves,* lowermost teeth glandular. *Petals* pink, obovato-oblong. *Obs.* 6269. AMYGDALUS nana. *Lew. disp. hy Dune.* 328. *Thunb. jap.* 199! 3. *Specific character unknown.* 17. PRUNUS *americana. Marsh.* 111. 526. CHRYSOBALANUS. *Calyx* quinquefid. *Petals* 5. *Style* lateral. *Drupe. Nut* quinquesulcate. *Swarls. obs.* 203. *L.* 1. CHRYSOBALANUS *Icaco. L.,p.* 681 . *Jacq. amer. 8vo.* 194. *Hort. Icew.* ii. 166. Chrysobalanus. *Browne* 250. *t.* 17. *f.* 5 CHRYSOBALANUS *Icaco. Bry.2U.* cells monospermous. *Seeds* villose. *From L. a Willd.*
Touroulia. *Aubl.* 1. TOUROLIA *solitaria.* ROBINSONIA *melanthifolia. L. a Willd.* il. 999.
529. LAGERSTROMIA. *Calyx* sexfid. *Petals* 6, inserted into the calyx. *Capsule* sexlocular quadrilocular and trilocular; cells polyspermons. *From Roxb. Hort. kezc. § L. a Schreb.* 361. 833. *L.* 1. LAGERSTROMIA *pliciflora.* Stamina equal. Petals obovate, plaited. *From L. rcginae. Roxb.* i. 46. *t.* 65. *Bonn* 70. Ii. Flos reginae. *Retz. obs,* v. 25. ADAMBOE. *Rail hist.* 1902. 2. LAGERSTROMIA *hirsuta.* Petals flat. Panicle corymbose, terminal. Leaves oblong, pubescent. *L. a Willd.* ii. 1178. KATOU ADAMBOE. *Raii hist.* 1902. 530. SONNERATIA. *Calyx* sexfid. *Petals* 6, subulate. *Berry* multilocular; cells polyspermous. *From L. fil.* and 1. SONNERATIA *aeida. L. JU. suppl.* 252.
Rhizophora caseolaris. *L. sp.* 635.
MANGIUM caseolare. *Rumph,* iii. 111. /. 73.
74. 75.

531. ONCOBA. *Petals* many. *Calyx* monophyllous. *Berry* unilocular, polyspermous. *Forsk.*
1. ONCOBA *spinosa. L. a Gmel.* ii. 828. ONCOBA. *Forsk.* 103. *p.* xctii.
532. ORYGIA. *Petals* 5. *Calyx* diphyllous. *Capsule* unilocular, trivalve. *From L. a Gmel.* 1. ORYGIA *portulacifolia.* Leaves alternate, cuneiform, glabrous. *Forsk.* 103. *p.* xciii. TRIGYNIA. 533. SESUVIUM. *Calyx* quinqucpartite, coloured. *Corolla* none. *Capsule* ovate, tnloculur, cut round, polyspermous. 1. SESUYIUM *Portulacastrum. L. sp.* 684. *Hori. kew.* ii. 172. *Swartx. obs.* 204. Crithruus indicus. *Rumph.* vi. 165. *t.* 72. /.. 1Aizoon. *Browne* 241. Portulaca aizoides maritima procumbens, iiorc par pureo. *Sloane cat.* 88; *hist.* i. 204. SESUVJUM Portulacastrum. *Schoepf* 79. PENTAGYNIA. 5S4. MESPILUS. *Calyx* quinquefid and quinquedentate. *Petals* 5. *Berry* wiih from 1 to 5 seed-. *Obs.* 3749. L. 1. MESPILUS *calycina.* Calyx longer than the corolla. Flowers solitary. *Obs.* 3331. la a garden. M. germanica. *L. sp.* 684. *Hori. litre,* ii. 172. *Bot. arr.* 515. *Smith brit.* 530; e»g/. f. 1523. *Poll. n.* 474. On a mountain between Hartenberg and Durckheim on which are the ruins of a monastery.—*Host* 275. In Istria, Litorali, and the south of Carniola,—*Qou. hort.* 242. Near Montpelier. —*Willd. bcr. n.* 529. In a forest.—*Reich, franc. n.* 322. *Roth germ.* i. 214. In forests in Hesse and Saxony;— ii. 546. Always spinose iu its native state.— *Pall. ross. i. t.* 13. /. 1. *Gaertn.* Ii. 43. *t.* 87. Native of Italy, France, and Germany. MESPJLA. Al$t.ii.m.
Mesp'ilum. i/erm.442.
Mespilus. *Berg.* 417. *Dale* 289. *Herm.* 442.
Linn. 151. *Mill. Jos.* 295. il/wrr. iii. 200. *Rutty* 326. ScArod. 625. *Fog.* 266. Mespili. *Spielm.* 106. M. germanica. *Bry.* 205. *Krock. n.* 758. *Pears. R.* i. 15. 63. M. vulgaris. *Geoffr. suite* i. 49. Neflier. Cjiom. 620. « *lancifoϊa.* Leaves lanceolate. 06s. 3331. In a garden.—*L. sp, a* M. germanica stricta. *Hort. kew.* ii. 172. M. sylvestris. *Mill. Ph. diet. n.* 1. M. foliis lanccolatis. inlegerrimis subtus tomentosis, calycibus fructus prominentias. *Guett.* i. 296. M. germanica, folio lauriuo non serrato, sive M. sylvestris. *Tourn. paris.* 496. *Vaill. paris.* 126. *Boerh.* ii. 256. Mespilus. *Raii eur.* 181, in herlges near Viterbo ia
Tuscany; syn. 453. Found by Dubois in all the hedges about Minehiville, (or according to Dr.
Smith Minshull in Cheshire.)—*Dod.* 789, repr. in *Lob. obs.* 591; *ic.* ii. 166, & M. sativa. *Ger. by Johns.* 1453. M. setania. *Dalech.* 334. Rhamnus bavaricus. *Dalech.* 142. M. vulgaris. *Cairi. epit.* 154. *Pari. par. t.* 569. /. 3 *theatr.* 1422. *Bauh. J.* i. a. 69. *Raii hist.* 1460. Leaves acute, serrate from about the midway to the end. *Obs.* 8240. Specimen gathered in the Paris garden. & *oblongifolia.* Leaves lanceolato-oblong. *Obs.* 3331.
In a garden.—*L.sp.*-8 ...
M. germanica diffusa. ITort. kew. ii. 173.
M. germmica. *Mil!. Ph. diet. n.* 2.
M. italica, folio laurino non serrato. *Vaill. parts.* 127.
M. folio laurino major. *Boerh.* ii. 256. M. domestica. *Lol. ic.* ii. 166, repr. in M. sativa altera. *Ger. by Johns.* 1453, 8ƒ cop. in
M. maxima sativa. *Park, theatr.* 1422. Mespilus. *Trag.* 1014.
Leaves crenato-serrate; portions of the margin entire. *Ohs.*3331. *Leaves* entire at the margin, oblong, 2 inches broad. *Obs.* 5765. Specimen gathered in the garden of Fothergill.
2. MESPILUS *japonica.* Without spines. Leaves oblong, serrate at the end, tomentose underneath. *Thunb. jap.* 206. Crataegus Bibas. *Lour",* i. 391. Arbor sinice Pi-pa dicta, foliis castaneae haud absi milis. *Pluk. amaltlu* 26; *phyt. t.* 371. /. 2. Bywa. *Kaempf.* 800. MESPILUS japonica. *Thunb. trav.* iv. 89. 90; iii. 214..'.' '.'" 3. MESPILUS *Pyracantha.* Leaves serrate, elliptic.
Corymbi compound. *Obs.* 3748. In a garden.
—*L. sp.* 685. *Hort. kew.* ii. 172. M. spinosa, foliis lanceolato-ovatis crenatis, calycibus fructus obtusis. *All. nic.* 180. *Guett.* i. 297. Uva ursi. *Dalech.* 134. M. spinosa, pyri folio. *Boerh.* ii. 257. Pyracantha quibnsdam. *Bauh. J.* i. b. 51, who remarks that the engraver had omitted the flowers and the hollow at the end of the berries.
Oxyacantha Theophrasti. *Ger. by Johns.* 1604, cop. from
Pyracantha. *Park. par.* 604. *t.* 605. /. 2. *Rati hist.* 1459; cur. 211. About Florence and elsewhere in Tuscany.— *Lob. adv.* 438, cop. in
Paliurus alter peregrin us. *Lob. ic.* ii. 179, #
Rhamnus tertius Dioscoridis. *Lob. ic.* ii. 182. (The names of this and the preceding synonym belong to other species.) *Calyx* quinquedente. *Styles* 5. *Obs.* 3748.
Native of Italy, Provence, and the neighbourhood
of Estampes. PYRACANTHA. *Dale* 290. *Geoffr. suite* i. 56.
4. MESPILUS *rubra.* Leaves cunciformiovate, crc nate, glabrous, crowded at the ends of the branches. Racemi terminal, glabrous. *From* CRATAEGUS rubra. *Lour.* i. 391. 5. MESPILUS *grossularifolia.*— Leaves cuneiformiovate, serrate, somewhat angular, villose underneath. Branches spinose. *L.*
Crataegus foliis cuneiformi-ovatis serratis sub angu latis subtus villosis, rainis spinosis. *Gron. virg.* 76. M. caroliniana, apii folio, vulgari similis, major, fructu luteo. *Trew. sel. t.* 17. M. virginiana, grossulariae foliis, fructu rubro mi nore. *Pluk. aim.* 249; *phyt. t.* 100. /. 1. CRATAEGUS tomentosa. *L. sp.* 682,— *Schoepf* 79.
6. MESPILUS *Oxyacantha.* Leaves obovato-rhom bic, semitrifid; segments serrate. Styles 2. Berries dispermoua. Seeds rugose on the inner sid«. *Obs.* 6683. Specimen from Prof. Jos. F. Jacquin. —*Obs.* 8097. In a hedge between Heanor and Codnor in Derbyshire. Just come into flower 20 May, on the same day with M. monogyna. Proba« bly not indigenous.—*Gaertn.* ii. 43. *t.* 87. Crataegus Oxyacantha. *L. suec. n.* 434; *sp.* 683. A specimen in the Linnaean herbarium.—*Host* 274. *Poll. n.* 472. *Roth germ.* ii. 543. *J* αc*q. αustr.* Ⅲ. *t.* 292. /. 2.
Crataegus Oxyacantha major. *H. K.* ii. 170 *β. Bot. arr.* 512. *β*
M. sylvestris, foliis trifidis splendentibus. *Vaill. paris.* 127.

M. apii folio, sylvestris, spinosa, folio et fructu majore. *Dill. ap. Raii syn,* 454? Found by James Sherard in the hedge of an orchard at Gadingtim in Northamptonshire, and by Merret in Ricot park and elsewhere in Oxfordshire.

Oxyacantha vulgaris, seu Spinus albus. *Bauh. J. i. b.* 49, descr. including M. monogyna. *Flowers* somewhat larger than those of M. mono gyna. *Petals* S to 4 tenths of an inch long. *Obs.* 8097.
CRATAEGUS Oxycantha. *Kroch n.* 755. 7.
MESPILUS *monogyna.* Leaves pinnatifido-incise; segments serrate towards the end. Style 1. Berry monospermous. Seed smooth. *Obs.* 3117. In hedges, and on Malvern hill in Worcestershire pretty high up the sides of the hill.—*Specimen* in the Linnaean herbarium, without a name.
M. Oxycantha. *Smith brit.* 529 *a. Scop. earn. n.*

Crataegus monogyna. *Bot. arr.* 511; iii. *123. Reiz. . scavd. n.* 607. *Sibtk. ox.* 156. *Host* 274. *J acq. $ minor. L. sp. y austr.* iii. *t.* 292. /. 1. Crataegus Oxycantha. *Fl. dan. t.* 634. *In* wild pastures. —*Huds.* 214 *a. Gort. belg. foed. n.* 422. *Wale. t.* The Hawthorn. *Evel.by Hunt.* - ii. 94. *t.* 7, at *p.* 92..rr.V.
Crataegus Oxycantha vulgaris. *//. K.* ii. 170.
M. apii folio, sylvestris, spinosa, sive Oxyacantha.
Rati hist. 1458; *syn.* 453. *Tourn. parts.* 495.
Vaill. parts. 127. *Boerh.* ii. 256.,.:?,£. Cynosbatos. 2rag. 984,.:!...rraviy-.i, Oxyacantha. *Dalech.* 136. Z.06. ic. ii. 200, cop. i« Spina appendix vulgaris. *Park, theatr.* 1025. Oxyacanthus, sive Spina acuta. *Dod.* 738, *rrpn in* Oxyacanthus. *Ger. by Johns.* 1327. liaii hist. 1458. Oxyacantha vulgaris, seu Spinus albus. *Jianh. J.* i.
6 49, (misprinted 44,) the descr. comprehending
M. Oxycantha; (The fig. is M. Oxyacanthai). Oxyacantha spinosa, minore folio.. *Barrel.* 125./.
563. *Pedicles* villose at the end. *Calyx,* rube villose; segments triangular,-horizontal, glabrous. *Corolla* 6 tenths of an inch broad; petals 2 J long. *Obs.* 3117. OX YACANTHA. *Geoffr. suite* i. 53. Spine

ajba. *Dale* 290. *Mill. Jos.* 422. *Rutty* 491. Epine blanche. *Cham, su'ppl.* 175. ,, 1: . MESPILUS *Azarolus.*—Leaves mostly trifid, pubescent; segments obtuse, subdentate. Segments of the calyx ovate. *IFi/ld.* Crataegus Azarolus. *L. a Willd.* ii. 1007; *sp.* 683. *Ilort. keze.* ii. 171. *Gou. hort.* 241. In corn fields and vineyards near Montpelier.
M. orientalis, apii folio subtus hirsuto, fructu magno luteo. *Poc.* ii. 189. *n.* 60. *t.* 85. In Palestine. M. Aronia veterum. *Bauh. J. i. a.* 67. M. folio laciniato, spinosa, fructu majore esculento.
Rati hist. 1458. M. apii folio laciniato. *Magn. monsp.* 176; *hort.* 135. *Boerh.* ii. 256. M. Aronia. *Lob. adv.* 443. No *fig.—Dod.* 789. *repr. in Ger. by Johns.* 1454, *8f cop. in* M. Aronia, sive neapolitana. *Park, theair.* 1423. M. prima. *Matth.* 252. CRATAEGUS Azarolus. *Clegh.* 22. Azerole. *Gepffr. suite* i. 55. Araroles. Robins, in *ph. tr. abr. by Jones* v. 143. M. Aronia. *Dale* 290. 9. MESPILUS nirca. *Marsh.* 90. 535. PIRUS.

Ca/yx quinquefid. Petals 5. Pomum inferior, with from 2 to 5 cells. *Obs.* 2714. *Gaertn.*

Pyrus. *L. .* PIRUS *Cydonia.* Flowers solitary. Leaves entire at the margin. From *L. sp.* 687. *Hort, kew.* ii. 176. *Woodv.* ii. 221. *t.* 79. *Reich, franc. n.* 1000. In hedges near Frankfort.—*Gou. hort.* 243. On the borders of fields and forming hedges near Montpelier.—*Host* 277. In 1 stria and Austria, in vineyards and hedges and on the sides of roads.— *Lour.* i. 394. *Jacq. austr. t.* 342. Pomum round.

Cydonia. *Boerh.* ii. 247.
Vol. 3.J a COTONEA. malus fructu minori. *Geoffr.* iii. 367.
Mala cotonea minora. *Chom.* 606. V major. *L. sp.* 0 COTOSEA malus fructu rrnjori. *Geoffr.* iii. 367.
Mala cotonea majora. *Chom.* 606.
2. PIRUS *japonka.* Peduncles solitary. Leaves cu neiform, crenate, glabrous. From *Thunb. Jap;* 207.
Malus japonica. *Andr. rep,* vii. *t.* 462. Buke. *Kaempf. amoen.* 844.
P YR US japonica. *Thunb.*
3. PIRUS *Malus.* Peduncles crowded. Leaves ser rate, elliptico-oval, acuminate. *Obs.* 2714. In a garden.—*H. K.*

n. 175 . *L. sp.* 686. *a rubra.* Leaves glabrous. Petals 7 tenths of an inch long. Poma of the size of small cherries. *Obs.* 7768. In Mr. Martain's nursery. Stem 3 to 10 feet long. Leaves stil villose at the margin; upper surface glabrous, not shining. *Stipulae* lineari-subulate, 2, inserted into the petiole a little above the base. *Flowers* corymbose. *Obs.* 7768. fi *jlava.* Leaves glabrous. Petals an inch long. Poma of the size of large cherries. *Obs.* 7767. la Mr. Martain's nursery. Pyrus Malus *g* II. *K.* ii. 175. Pyrus prunifolia. *Willd. phyt.* i. 8. *n.* 96. *Leaves* elliptico-oval, acuminate, smooth, unequally serrate, when young serrulate, glabrous, not nitid as in *y* when young. *Peduncles* crowded. *Styles* united below into a solid cylinder, villose below. *Obs.* 2715. In a garden.—*Stem* 4 to 10 feet long. *Leaves* glabrous, slightly shining. *Petioles* pubescent above near the base. *Stipulae* lineari-subulate, inserted into the petiole, 2, opposite. *Flowers* corymbose. *Obs.* 7767. CRATAEGUS cerasi foliis, floribus magnis. *Mill. Ph. ic.* 179. *t.* 269. *y sylvestris.* Leaves glabrous. Fruit acid, acerb, about the size of a chesnut. *Obs.* 5753. *L. sp. a. Huds. a. Krock. n.* 761. *Lour.* i. 393. *Bot. arr.* 517. *a. Smith engl. t.* 179; *brit.* 531. Malus sylvestris, sive agrestis. *Rait hist.* 1448. Mai us sylvestris, fructu valde acerbo. *Vaill. paris.* 124. Mains sylvestris. *Raii syn.* 452. In woods and hedges.—*Ge-: by Johns.* 1461. *Petals* scarcely unguiculate, 5 tenths of an inch long. *Styles* united at the base, villose below. *Obs.* 5753. Specimen gathered in a hedge. MALA sylvestria. *Lea. dhp.* 171. Poma sylvestria. *Schrod.* 653. Pom ura sylvestre. *Murr.* iii. 177. Malus sylvestris. *Dale* 288. *Mill. Jos.* 283. *Rutty* 303. Malus agrestis. *Geoffr.* iii. 789. VERJUICE. *Biss. ess.* 185. *Bromf.* ii. 68. *Mill. Jos.* 283. *Ware epiph.* 28; *ophth.* 51. Crab juice. *Darw.* ii. 219. 710. 715.
y sativa. Leaves villose underneath. Fruit more or less sweet. *Obs.* 2714. In a garden. Pyrus Malus. *Mill. J. ill. t. Huds.* 217 (3. *Bot. arr.* 517 (3 Pyrus foliis serratis, pomis basi concavis. *L. ups.* Malos sativa. *Raii syn.* 451. *In* orchards and hedges; *hist.* 1445. Malus. *Bauh. J. i. a.* 1 *Dod.* 777, *repr. in* Mains

carbonaria, longo fructu. *Ger. by Johns.* 1459. Mala Dioscoridis. *Lob. obs.* 590, *repr. in ic.* ii. 165, # Malus carbonaria. *Ger. by Johns.* 1459. Malus, sive Pomum. *Boerh.* ii. 249.. *Leaves* slightly rugose, when young shining above and villose underneath, unequally serrate, mostly obovato-oval. *Petals* from 7 tenths of an inch to an inch long; ungues from 1 to 1 tenth of an inch long. *Styles* villose below. *Obs.* 2714. MALA dulcia. *Spielm.* 92. Malum. *Spielm.* 76. Poma. *Heb. 3.* 280. *Ploucq. bibl.* i. 623. *Quar. anim.* 261. *Stoll med.* iii. 447. Poma domestica. *Schrod.* 652. Malus. Da/e288. Malus sativa. *Geoffr.* iii. 774. *Mill. Jos.* 282. *Rutty* 303. Pvrus Malus. *Bry.* 290. *Pears. R.* i. 67. *Schoepf* 79. Apples. *Clegh.* 189. *Cull. clin.* 68. *Fordyce, G. fev.* ii. 36; iii. 195. 196; *W. fev.* 206. *Lind seam.* 20. *Monro, Don. sold.* ii. 185. i?«sA i. 113.241; iii. 285; v. 120. *Trott.* ii. 163. *Und.* i. 322. MOLOSSES. *Dudley in ph. tr. abr. by Reid 8f Gray* vi. *part* iii. 320; *St by Hutt.* vi. 618. CYDER. *Dam.* ii. 125.217.218.245. *Dwight, account from, in phys. journ.* i. 286. *Fordycei W. fev.* 220. *Geach. in med. tr.* ii. 243. *Mudge ib.* 246. *Lempr.* ii. 174. 178. 191. *Lind seam,* 20. *Pears. R.* i. 105. *Rush* ii. 70. 241; iii. 293. *Sims, James epid.* 22. 28. *33.* J *renetia.* POMUM renetium. *Berg.* 418.-rubelliana. POMUM rubellianum. *Murr.* iii. 177. *i borsdoifiana.* POMA borsdorfiana. *Phurm. austriaco-prov.* 58. Poiuaborstorfiaua. *Quur. febr.* 19. Poma borsdorphiensia. *Linn.* 152. Poraura borsdorfianum. *Berg.* 418. *Vog.* 261. Pomum borsdorphianum. *Murr.* iii. 177. 4. PIRUS *Pulheria.* Flowers corymbose. Leaves serrate, tomentose underneath. *From L. vmnt.* 244. *Roth germ.* i. 215; ii. 549. *Ilort. kem.ii.* 175. PIRUS Pohvilleriana. *Bank. J.* i. *a.* 59. 5. PIRUS *communis.* Flowers corj'mbose. Leaves el liptico-oval; margin serrate. *O's.* 2716. In a garden.—*L. sp.* 686. *Smith brit.* 531. *Huds.* 216. *Lour.* i. 393. *Bot. arr.* 516. S6tA. or. n. 451. *P. Achras. Gaertn.* ii. 44. f. 87. a *spinosa.* Branches spinose. *From authors.*

Pyrus communis. *L. succ. n-*436. Po//. n. 477.

On Mount Donnersbcrg, and on rocks in woody mountains near Steinbach in the Palatinate.—*Gou. hort.* 242. Near Montpelier.—*Roth. germ.* i. 214; ii. 548. *Scop. earn. n.* 598. Pyrus sylvestris. *Magn. monsp.* 215. In the hedges of vineyards.— *Vaill. paris.* 166. *r*

Piraster, sen P. sylvestris. *Bauh. J.* i. *a.* 57. No *fig.* In Switzerland in mountainous situations, in

Germany France and Italy in woods hedges and borders of fields. Pyraster, seu Pyrus sylvestris. *Rati syn.* 452, in woods and hedges; *hist.* 1451. Pyrum strangulatorium rnajus. *Ger. by Johns.* 1458. PYRUS sylvestris. *Ratty* 419. ß *inermis.*—Branches without spines. *Obs.* 271 G. 8629.

In a hedge, a young tree, probably a seedling. Pyrus communis. *Smith engl. t.* 1784. *IIuds.*216 *ß. Bot. arr-*516 *ß. L. sp. & to c* Pyrus foliis serratis, pomis basi productis. *L. vps.* 130. Pyrus satiya. *Rati syn.* 452. In orchards and hedges. —*Banh. J.* i. *a.* 35. *Boerh.* ii. 247. *Vaill. paris.* 166. Pyrus. *Rali hist.* 1450. *Dalech.* 308. *Dod.* 788, *repr. in* P. superba, sive katherina. *Ger. by Johns.* 1456. Pyra Dioscoridis. *Lob. obs.* 590, *repr. in ic.* ii. 165,

Pyrum strangulatorium majus. *Ger, by Johns.* 1457.

(The name and descr. belong to я.) Pyra. *Matth.* 251. PYRUS. *Berg.* 419. *Dale* 288. *Geoffr. suite* ¡i. 123. *Kroch, n.* 760. *Mill. Jos.* 365. *Schrod.* 658. Pyri. *Spielm.* 109. Pyrus sativa. *Rutty* 418. Pyrus communis. *Bry.* 276. *Pears. R.* i. 67. Pears. *Fordyce, G. fev.* iii. 195. 196; *W. fev,* 159. 167. 206. *Monro, Don. sold.* ii. 185. PERRY. *Pears. R.* i. 105. 6. PIRUS *coronaria.* Flowers corymbose. Leaves cordate, inciso-serrate, angular, glabrous. *From H. K.* ii. 176. *Bartr. W. trav.* 396. PYRUS-MALUS coronaria. *Marsh.* 118. 7. PIRUS *sanguisorbifolia.* Flowers corymbose.

Leaves oval, serrate. *Obs* 5757. Specimen gathered in the garden of Fothergill. Pyrus Amelanchier. *L. JU. suppU* 256. *Host* 276.

Roth germ. i. 314. In the Hartz forest and Fran conia. Mespilus Amelanchier. *L. sp.* 685. *Hort. kezo.* ii. 173. *Scop. earn. n.* 595. *Jacq. austr. t.* 300. Crataegus fructu nigro. *Vaill. parts.* 43. M. folio rotundiori, fructu nigro subdulci. *Tourn. parts.* 4&b. *Vaill. paris.* 127. Fruit quinqutlo cular; cells monospermous.—*Boerh.* ii. 257. Vaccinia alba. *Ger. by Johns.* 1416, *repr. from* Vitis idaea III. *Clus. pann.* 81, *which repr. in hist,* i. 62, *and the branch in flower cop. in Park. theatr, li*5!, outer fig.—Inner fig. *cop. from* Amelanchier. *Lob. obs.* 608, *which repr. in ic.* ii. 191. Raii cur. 61. On mountains near Genera and bordering the Rhine.

Hamamelis Athenaei latiorc folio. *Dalech.* 203.

Hamamelis Athenaei angusto folio. *Dalech.* 203.

Diospyros. *Bauh. J.* i. *a.* 75. No *tig.*— *Raii*

hist. 1461. *Native* of Italy, France, Switzerland, and Germany. DJOSPYRUS. *Dale* 289. 8. PIRUS *lemcifolia.* Flowers corymboso-racemose.

Leaves 6errate, oblongo-elliptic, cuspidate, *Obs,* 7362. In a garden.

Mespilus canadensis. *L. sp.* 685. *Ilort. lew.* ii.

173. (Mespilus inermis, foliis subtus glabris obverse ova tis. *Gron. virg.* 54, is probably P. arbutifolia examined when the leaves were nearly or quite glabrous.) *Leaves* very thin, oblongoelliptic and ovali-elliptic, rounded at the base, at first pubescent, becoming glabrous before the petals are fallen off. *Petioles* without glands. *Calyx* glabrous without, pubescent within. *Petals* lanceolate and lanceolato-oblong. *Germen* roundish, the greater part invested by the calyx. *Obs.* 7362. Going out of flower. 10 May. PYRUS Botryapium. *Ehrh. ap. L. JU. supply ro*5. 9. PIRUS *ovalis.* Flowers corymboso-racemose. Leaves subrotundo-elliptic, acute, glabrous. Petals obovate. Gcrmina and calyces pubescent. *Obs.* 5764. Specimen of racemi and young leaves gathered by Dr. Cutler in New England.— *L. a Willd.* i. 1014. PYRUS. *Cutl.* 450. 2. *Leaves divided.* 10. PIRUS *septiloba.* Leaves septeralobate; lowermost lobes divaricate. *Obs.* 4411. Specimen gathered on the edge of the cliff at Clarktonleap near Worcester, and in woods in Worcestershire, on red clay.

Pyrus tormina! is. *Smith brit.* 532. *L. a Willd.* ii. 1021. *Ehrh.*

Crataegus torminalis. *L. sp.* 681. *Bot. arr.* 511. *Smith engl. t,* 298. Leaves not well done.—*Roth germ.* ii. 543. *Gou. hurt.* 241. Near Montpelier. —*Host* 274. *Poll. n.* 471. *Ft. dan. t.* 798. *Jacq. amir, t* 443. *Mart. cant.* 11.-Crataegus folio laciniato. *Tourn. paris.* 425. A fruit containing pepins. *VaiU. paris.* 43. *Boerh.* ii. 248. ' Mespilus apii folio, sylvestris non spinosa, sive Sorbus torminalis. *Rati hist.* 1457; *syn.* 453. The wild Service tree. *Evel. by Hunt.* i. /. *al p.* 176. Sorbus torminalis vulgaris. *Park, theatr.* 1420, *cop. in* Sorbus torminalis. *Bauh. J.* i. *a. G3.—TJicyd in in ph. tr. abr. by Jones v. part* ii. 122; *and by Hult.* vi. 20. Near Brecknock.—*Cam. epit.* 162.

Edw. G. glean, i. 2. *t.* 212. In fruit.— *Dod.* 791, *repr. in Lob. obs.* 614; *ic.* ii. 100, *Ger. by Johns.* 1471, Sorbus torminalis Plinii. *Clus. hist.* i. 10. Sorbus torminalis. *Trag.* 1010, *repr. in Cord. fol.* 176. *p.* 1, *Sf cop. in* Crataegus Theophrasti. *Dafech.* 99, 332. Natixe of Italy, France, Germany, and England as far north as Oxfordshire Worcestershire Cambridgeshire and Suffolk. SORBUS torminalis. *Dale* 290. *Geojfr. suite* iii. 111. *Mill. Jos.* 419. Crataegus torminalis. *Bry.* 160. 11. PJIIUS Aria. Corymbi compound. Leaves elliptico-oval, doubly serrate and inciso-pinnatifid, tomentose underneath. Styles 2. Poma bilocular. *Obs.* 6060. In the shrubbery at Chatsworth in Derbyshire.—*Smith brit.* 534. *L. a lfilld.* ii. 1021. *Ehrh.*

Crataegus Aria. *L. suec. n.* 455; *sp.* 681 *a. Bot. arr.* 510. *Fl. dan. t.* 302. *Mill. J. ill. t.* Huds. 214. Chiefly in mountainous situations and on calcareous soil.—*Host* 274. *Gou. hort.* 240. Near

Montpelier.—*Sibth. ox. n.* 448. Woods and hedges in calcareous soil — *Fl. dan. t.* 302. Sorbus Aria. *Crantz austr.* ii. 86. *t.* 2. /. 2. Mespilus Aria. *Scop. earn. n.* 591. Mespilus alni folio subtus incano, Aria Theophrasti dicta. *Raii syn.* 453Crataegus folio subrotundo serrato. *Vaill. parts.* 42.

Boerh. ii. 248.
Aria. *Dalech.* 202.
The Whitebeam tree. *Evel. by Hunt. t. at p.* 175.

Sorbus alpina. *Bauh. J.* i. *a.* 65.
Aria Theophrasti. *Lob. adv.* 435, *repr. in ic.* ii.

167, *8f Ger. by Johns.* 1327, $ *cop. in* Sorbus sylvestris, Aria Theophrasti. *Park, theatr.* 1421. Sorbus svlvestris anglicus. *How* 117. *Rati hist.* ii.

1459; *praef. p.* v. Sorbus Aria cognominata. *Clus. hist.* i. 9. No fig.

—*HowU6.* Poma cylindrico-oval, scarlet, dotted; dots scattered, white; valves of so loose a texture as scarcely to be distinguished from ihe pulp. Seeds 2 in each cell, seldom more than 1 in a pomum coming to perfection, obovate, flat on one side, convex on the other. *Obs.* 6060.

Native of Europe from Italy to Lapland. ARIA. Da/e289.

Crataegus Aria. *Bry.* 160.
Crataegus. *L. lapp. n.* 199.
3. Leaves pinnate. L. a Gmel. 12. PIRUS aucuparia. Folioles oblong, distinct from the petiole, serrate. *Obs.* 87.58. Specimen gathered in Cumberland.— *Gaertn.* ii. 45. *t.* 87. *Smith brit.* 533.

Sorbus aucuparia. *L. lapp. n.* 200; *suec. n.* 435; *sp.* 683. *Vail!, paris.* 189. *Boerk.* ii. 248. Бог.

arr. 513; iii. *p.* cxxiii. *Smith engl. t.* 337. 1 *Bauh. J.* i. *a.* 62. *Gou. hort.Zil.* Near Monr pelier.—*Mill. J. ill. t. Crantz, austr.* ii. 88. *t.* 1. /. 4. Pomura.—Я. *dan. t.* 1034. Mespilus aucuparia. *Scop. earn. n.* 593. Sorbus foliis pinnatis. *Guelt.* i. 299. Sorbus sylvestris, foliis domesticae similis. *Raii hist.* 1457; iyn. 452. Ornus. *Dod.* 822, rfpr. *in* Sorbus sylvestris, sivc Fraxinus bubula. *Ger. by Johns.* 1473, ' S¡*cop. in* Sorbus silvestris alpina. *Lob. obs.* 544, *which repr. in ic.* ii. 107, $ *cop. in* Sorbus torminalis. *Dalech.* 99, *Sf* Ornus, sivc Fraxinus sylvestris. *Park, theatr.* 1419, but without the flowers. Sorbus sylvestris. *Malth.* 263. *Cam. epit.* 161. *Da J tech.* 332. The Quicken tree. *Evel. by Hunt.* i. *t. at p* 211. Panicles fastigiate. *Obs.* 3116. A planted tree. Native of Europe from Italy to Lapland. SORBUS aucuparia. *Berg.* 415. *Kroch, n.* 756. *Linn.* 151. ¿/«гг. iii. 203. *Vog.* 267. S. sylvestris. *Geoffr. suite* iii. 107. Oruus. *Date* 289. 13. PIRUS Sorbus. Folioles ovato-oblonsr, dentatoserrate;

margin contiguous to the petiole. *Obs.* 3115. In the forest of "Wire in Worcestershire, where there are regular falls of wood.—*Gaertn.* ii. 45. *t.* 87. SORB US. *Dale* 289. *Geoffr. suite* iii. 104. *Mill. Jos.* 419. *Rutty WO. Schrod.* 685.

Sorba. S/iiwot. 109.

Sorbus domestica. *Berg.* 416. *Bry.* 214. *Kroch. n.* 757. *Fog.* 267. *a obovata.* Pomum obovate. *Obs.* 3115.

Pear Service. *Edw. G. glean,* i. *1.1.* 211, the separate pomum.

Pyrus domestica. Sm*h engl. t.* 350; *brit.* 532.

Sorbus domestica. £. *sp.* 684." J5o. zrr. 514, where at 1. 11 from the bottom read mountainous parts of Cornwall and Staffordshire. R. syn. In the middle of a thick wood in the forest of Wire near Bcwdley in Worcestershire, one mile from Mopson's Cross between that and Dowles brook. St.— *Mill. Ph. diet. n.* 2, who says that it must be grafted upon a pear stock.—*Reich, franc. n.* 999. About Frankfort.—*Roth germ.* i. 214. About Erford, Frankfort on the Main, Frankfort on the Oder, Nauenburg, and Tubingen.—*Cranlz. austr.* ii. 87. *t.* 2. /. 3. Pomum.—*Jacq. austr. t.* 447. *Host* 275. About Tillages and vineyards.— *Cam. epit.* 160. *Matth.* 261. *Asso n.* 430. *Lob. adv.* 416. No fig.—*obs.* 544, *repr. in ic.* ii. 106,

Sorbus. *Dod.* 791, *Ger. by Johns.* 1471, Sr

Sorbus legitima, *Clus. hist.* i. 10, *and abr. in Park, theatr.* 1420. I*Jzcyd in ph. tr. abr. by Jones* v. *part* ii. 118; *and by Hutt.* vi. 20. On Y Vann uwch deni a mountain near Brecknock.

Sorbus. *Dalcch.* 330. *Fuchs.* 554. *c.* 220, *cop. in*

The apple Service. *Edw. G. glean,* i. 1. .811. la fruit.

5S6. TETRAGON I A. Calyx tripartite quadripartite and quinqnepartite. *Corolla* none. Drupe inferior. Nut with from 3 to 8 cells. *Hort, kew. L. I* 1. TETRAGONIA quadricornis. Fruit with 4 horns. Leaves deltoideo-ovate. *Obs,* 8368. Specimen gathered for me by Murray in the GoUingen garden.

T. expansa. *Murr. ap. L. a MurrAGl. Hort-kew.* ii. 178. *Thunb. in tin. tr.* ii. 335 *Haw. misc.* 119.

Demidovia.tetragonoides. *Pall. hort. t.* 1.
TETRAGONIA haliraifoUa. *Font. G. esc.* 67. 537. MESEMBRYANTHES. *Calyx* superior, pentaphyllous and tetraphyllouf. *Petals* numerous, linear. *Capsule* fleshy, poly spermous. *Obs.* 5835.
Mesembryanthemum. *L. Vent. tabl. t.* 19. /. 3. 1. *Corolla while.* L.
1. MESEMBRYANTHES *nodiflorus.* Leaves rather, terete, alternate, obtuse, ciliate at the base. *L. sp.* 687. *Hort. kew.* ii. 178. *Woodv.* 387. *Haw. mes.* 118; *misc.* 54. Kali floridum repens neapolitanum. *CoL ecphr.* ii. /. 73, *cop. in Park, theatr.* 1285. SODA. *Murr.* iv. 286.
Souda. *Berg.* 182..
2. MESEMBRYANTHES *crystallinus.* Leaves o vate, papulose. Flowers sessile. Phylla ovate, acute. *Obs.* 8216. In a garden.—*L. fil. suppl.* 259. *Hort. kew.* i. 179. *Gou. hort.*213. *Haw. tnes.* 113: *misc.* 43. Ficoides africana, folio plantaginis undulato micis argenteis adsperso. *Boerh.* i. 291. *Flowers* not expanded. *Calyx* pentaphyllous; 2 outer phylla foliaceous, trilobate, lobi-s nearly equal, middlemost segment acute; 3rd phyllum bilobate, oblique, inner segment acute; 2 inner phylla obtuse with a macro projecting from the under surface below the end. *Obs. 82)6.* 20 Oct. MESEMBR YANTHEMUM*crystalliniim. Murr.* vi. 128. *Wendt, account from in phys. journ.* vi. 371. 2. *Corolla yellow.* L. 3i MESEMBRYANTHES *edulis.* -Leaves triquetrous, acute, straight, without dots, connate; sides equal; keel subserrate. Stem twoedged. *L.* MESEMBR YANTHE M UM *edule. Haw. mcs.* 392; *misc.* 76.—*L. sp.* 695. POLYGYNIA. 538. SPIRAEA. *Calyx* inferior, quinquefid and septemfid. *Petals S. Capsules* several, bivalve, containing from 1 U3 seeds. *Obs.* 3889. L.
1. SPIRAEA *luberosa.* Leaves interruptedly pinnate, glabrous; folioles oblong. Calyces septemfid segments rounded. *Obs.* 3889. Specimen gathered near Worcester.—*Sal. R. hort.* 36£.
S. Filipendula. *L. sp.* 702. *Bot. arr.* 518. *Smith engt. t.* 284. *Fl. dan. t.* 635.

Oenanthe. *Fuchs.* 542. *c.* 214, *cop. in* Daucus pratensis Dalechampii, folio millefolii. *Bauh. J.* iii. *b.* 9, (the name and descr. belonging to Sison verticilla-tum,) *Sf abr. in*
Filipendula. *Trag.* 883. *Bauh. J.* iii. *b.* 189. (The fig. is Sison verticillatum.) *Raii syn.* 259. *Dod.* 56, *repr. in Ger. by Johns.* 1058,
Oenanthe. Filipendula. *Lob. obs.* 420; *ic.* i. 729, ..
Filipendula vulgaris. *Clus. hist,* ii. 211, *8f cop. in*
Filipendula major. *Park, theatr.* 435.
Filipendula, Oenanthe multorum. *Dalech.* 782.
Filipendula minor. *Park, theatr.* 435.
FILIPENDULA. *Berg.* 422. *Dale.* 163. *Geoffr.* iii. 469. *Mill. Jos.* 197. *Murr.* iii. 118. *Rutty* 200. *Schrod.* 590. *Spielm.* 266. *Vog.* 238.
S. Filipendula. *Krock. n.* 765. *Linn. am.* v. C7.
Filipendula vulgaris, an Molon Plinii. *Chom.* 213.
Saxifraga rubra. *Linn.* 152.
2. SPIRAEA *contorta.* Leaves interruptedly pinnate, hoary underneath; folioles ovate. Calyces qui.icluetid; segments acute. *Obs.* 3891. In wet meadows. VoL. 3. . *1*
S. Ulmaria. *L. suec. n.* 440; *sp.* 702. *Curt. lond.* v. 33. *t.* 340. *Fl. dan. t.* 547. *Bot. arr.* 519. *Smith brit.* 536. *Gou. hort.* 245. Near Montpelier.
Filipendula. *L. lapp. n.* 201.
Ulmaria. *Raii hist.* 623; *syn.* 259. *Boerh.* i. 295. *Bauh. J.* iii 488.
Rcgina prati. *Dod.* 57, *repr. in Ger. by Johns.* 1043, *Sf cop. in*
Ulmaria vulgaris. *Park, theatr.* 592. ULMARIA. *Berg.* 424. *Chom. Vll.* Dale 163. *Geoffr. suite* iii. 382. *Krock. n.* 766. *Lew.* ii. 474; *d&p.* 263. *Linn.* 153. *A/tV/. Jo.* 458. *Murr.* iii. 120. *J?w/y* 550. *Schrod.* 703. Fog;. 244.
Barba caprae. *Pharm. austriaco-prox.* 22.. 3. SPIRAEA *trifoliata.* Leaves ternate; folioles serrate:, nearly equal. *Obs.* 6994. Specimen gathered in the garden of Fothergill.—*L. sp.* 702. *Ilort. kew.* ii. 200. *Curt. mag. t.* 489.
Filipendula foliis ternatis. *Gron. virg.* 55. *Roy.* 529. *Filaments* very short, inserted info the upper part of the calyx on the inside, at different heights. *Obs.* 7182. From Mr. Hunter's nursery.
SPIRAEA trifoliata. *Bart.* 26. *Coxe* 377. *Schoepf* 80.

Ipecacuanha virginiana. *Murr.* i. 523.
Ulmaria americana. *Dale* 421. *col.* 1. *par.* 1.
' 539. ROSA.
Petals 5. Cafyu; inferior, hypocrateriform; tube con traded at the mouth; limb quinqueparfite. *Berry* unilocular, polyspermons, formed from the tube of the calyx. *Obs.* 8162. L.
1. *Segments of the calt/x entire.*
R. macrostylis.
1. ROSA *moschata.* Tube of the calyx ovate, villose.
Peduncles villose. Stem and petioles aculeate.
Folioles oblong, acuminate, glabrous. Panicles multiflorous. *Hort. kern.* ii. 207. *Mill. Ph. diet. n.* 13. R. moschata minor, flore simplici. *Bauh. J.* ii. 45. *Raii hist.* 1474. R. moschata, flore simplici. *Lob, ic.* ii. 207, *repr. in* R. moschata, simplici flore. *Ger. by Johns.* 12G5.
R. damascena. *Dalech.* 125. ROSA moschata. *Dale* 293. *Geoffr. suite* ii. 235. R. moschata simplici flore. *Chom.* 13; *suppl.* 4. 2. ROSA *caroliniana.* Tube öf the calyx globular, hispid; segments entire and 3 and 1 with a single appendage. Peduncles hispid and glabrous. Stem mostly with prickles at the base of the leaves; internodia sometimes with numerous softish prickles. Petioles sometimes prickly. Folioles elliptic. *Obs*-5996. In a gardi-n.—*Obs.* 5997. Specimen gathered by Or. Cutler in New England.— *Michaux* i. 295.
ROSA Carolina. *Duroi obs.* 21. *II. K.* ii. 203. *L. sp.* 703.—*Schoepf* 81. Rosa. *Cutl.* 451. 2. *Three of the segments oj the calyx pinnate.* R. Carolinian». 3. ROSA *macrostylis.* Styles united, as long as the stamina. *Obs.* 2564. In hedges.
R. arvensis. *L. Bot. arr.* 521. *Smith engl. t.* 188.
R. sylvestris altera minor, flore albo nostras. *Raii syn.* 455.
R. sylvestris altera, flore albo nostras. *Vaill. parís.* 173.
R. sylvestris, folio glabro, flore plane albo. *Bauh. J.* ii. 44.
Peduncles hispid, mostly aggregate, sometimes in
twos and solitary. *Calyx,* tube ovate.

Obs. 2564.

—*Phyila* without pinnae. *Obs.* 6049. In a field.

A second set of flowers. Sept.

HOSA arvensis. *Mitsching, account from in phys. journ.* iii. 271.,3 (Variation.) *Huds.* 219. Peduncles sometimes solitary. *Obs.* 5009.

R. alba. *Wale. t.*

R. canina sylvestris, único flore et fructu. *Dill. ap. Raii syn. indicul. pl. 9,* from James Sherard's herbarium.

4. ROSA *villosa.* Tube of the calyx globular, mostly hispid. Peduncles hispid. Stem and petioles aculeate. Leaves and younger branches villose. *Obs.* 8147. In Mr. Thomson's nursery.—*L. suec. n.* 1295; *sp.* 704; *mant.* 399; *a Murr.* 474. *Roth germ.* ii. 556. *Hort. kcxa.* ii. 203. *Bot. arr.* 523 *a. Lightf.* 261. *Retz. obs.* i. 19. я. 55. *Gov. hort.* 245. Near Monfpelicr.—*Smith engl. t.* R. sylvestris, fructu majorc hispido. *Rati syn.* 451. Observed by Dale in hedges. R. sylveitris poraifera major nostras. *Raii syn.* 455. In the mountainous parts of Yorkshire and

Westmorland. R. porao spinoso, folio hirsuto. *Bauh. J.* ii. 38.

Found by Cherler on Mons Calcar, and on the de clivitics of Hortus Dei.— *Magn. monsp.* 223. R pomifem major. *Park. par.* 420. *t.* 419. *f y,*

Berry oval.—*Raii hist.* 1472.

Peduncles aculeate and hispid; aculei numerous crowded straight; hairs globular at the end. *Obs.* 8147.—*Berries* hispid, red. *Obs.* 6149. In Mr. Wilkinson's garden. ROSA villosa. *Spielm.* 425.

i. ROSA *cerdipetala.*—Tube of the calyx ovate, hispid. Peduncles hispid. Stem hispid, aculeate. Petioles glandular. Folioles ovate, serrate, pilose underneath. *Duroi.*

R. centifolia. *Duroi obs.* 26. *L. sp.* 704. (*Wood-c.* iii. 379. *t.* 140, is more like R. provincialis.)

R. centifolia batavica. *Clus. hist.* i. 113, *repr. in*

R. provincialis, sive damascena. *Ger. by Johns.* 1261.

R. multiplex media. *Boerh.* ii. 252. *n.* 28.

(R. damascena. *Iob. obs.* 618, *repr. in ic.* ii. 206,

R. alba. *Ger. by Johns.* 1260, has too many and too strong prickles on the stem, and the segments of the calyx are entire.) ROSA centifolia. *Pharm. edin.— Lew. disp. by Dune.* 296. *Murr. J.* ii. 56.

R. rubra. *Linn.* 153. *Quar. anim.* 232.

R. damascena. *Pharm, suec.—Berg.* 426. *Kroch. n.* ПЪ, Rosae. *Quar. anhn.* 96.

Ö. ROSA *galfica.* Tube of the calyx subrotundo-turbinate, with glandular hairs at the base Peduncles hispid. Stem and petioles hispid and aculeate. Folioles ovali elliptic, slightly villose underneath; margin with glandular hairs. *Obs.* 8536. In a garden—-*L. sp.* 704; *mant.* 399. *Horl. hew.* ii. 205. *Woodv.* iii. 382-*t.* Ml. *m officinalis—Hort. kew.* ii. 205 *a Stem* 2 feet long, erect, wi(h few or no aculei below. *Folioles* glabrous above. *Style* compound, as long as the shorter stamina. *Obs* 2536.

Rosa. *Cam. epit.* 98, the inner of the 2 upper figures.

R. rubra. *Bauh J.* ii. 34.

R. intense rubens. *Cam. horl.* 143. No fg.

R. purpurea sanguínea. *Lob. adv.* 446. No fig.

Rosa. *Dalech.* 424.

R. anglica rubra. *Park. par.* 412. No fig.

Petals cuneiforini-obcordate, 1 inch 8 tenths long, 2 inches 1 tenth broad, obscurely marbled with lighter and dark shades of purplish crimson. *Obs.* 2536. ROSA gallica. Petals. *Pharm. edin.—Leva. disp. by Dune.* 296. *Murr. J.* i. 217; ii. 55. *Pears. R. ed.* ii. 354.

R. rubra. Red Rose. Petals. *Pharm, lond.— Alst.* ii. 206. *Berg.* 428. *Carth.* iv. 240. *Cull.* ii. 34. *Dale* 293. *Fordyce, G. pract.* 207; *fev.* iv. 182. *Heb.* 27. 281. 357. *Kroch n.* 776. *Lew.* ii. 277. ЗИП. *Jos.* 376. *Murr.* iii. *166. Pringle* 139. *166. Rutty* 432. *Und.* ¡i. 64. *Fog.* 149 Rosac rubrae. *Fordyce, G. pract.* 153. *Herrn.* 613.

Mead mon. i. 57. 14 t. *Quar. febr.* 238. 240. *Schrod.* 663. *Spielm.* 423. *Wintr. in Mead mon.* i. 212. 233. Red Rose. *Aitk. midw.* 136. Жояго iii. 237. *Und.* i. 133. 144. Rose. *Monro, Don. sold.* ii. 44. *Reíd, T. phth.* 289. *Und.* ii. 62. Rosae. *Rogert in act. haun.* i. 189. 7.

ROSA *provincialis.* Tube of the calyx turbinate, with glandular hairs. Peduncles and petioles with prickles and hairs. Folioles oval, glandular below. *Obs.* 2492. In a garden.—*Mill. Ph. diet. n.* 18. *Duroi obs.* 19. *H. K.* ii. 204. ROSA rubra, seu provincialis. *Geoffr. suite* ii. 240.

R. pallida. *Dale* 293. *n.* 4.

R. purpurea. *Vog.* 149.

Roses de Provins. *Chom.* 608.

Branches green, not rorid as in R. alba; smaller branches acuteate. *Fo/ioles* elliptico oval, acute, somewhat conduplicate, whui&h green above, greenish whitish underneath; serrutures not glandular, slightly villose, margin above brownish red. *Peduncles* with glandular hairs. *Calyx,* tube obovate, attenuate below, contracted at the neck; hairs short. *Corolla* semidouble. *Berries* oblongolufbinate, hispid, scarlet. *Seeds* oval, angular, bony, 3 tenths of an inch long, 1 to 3 fertde, the rust abortive. Accords with R. provincinlis and R. gallica in calyx and peduncles. *Ohs.* 2513. ROSA damasoena. Damask Rose, Petals. *Pharm, lond,—Jlst.* ii. 206. *Dale* 292. *Lew.* ii. 275 i *disp. by Dune.* 296; *by Rother.* 226. *Linn.* 154. *Mill. Jos.* 375. *Monro* iii. 236. *Murr,* iii. 157.

R. pallida. *Dale* 293. *n* 3,

Rosae pallidae. *Uenn.* 588. *Quar, febr,* 120. 137,

Schrod. 663. *Spklm.* 424,

R. purpurea. *Vog.* 140.

R. rubra pallidior. *Chom,* 12; *supph* 3, Damask Rose, *lordyce, G. fev.* ii. 54.

SYRUP of Roses. *Und.* i. 22. 54. 55,

ROSE WATER. *Und.* ii. S3.

I. ROSA canina. Tube of the calyx oval, mostly glabrous. Peduncles glabrous. Stem and petioles aculeate. Aculei recurvate. Iolioles glabrous on the upper and under surfaces. *Obs.* 8162. In hedges.—*L. suec,* «. 441; *sp.* 704; *mant.* 399. *Wale. t. Curt. lond.* v. 34. *t.* 299; *mat-med. t* 15. *Fl. dan. t.* 555. *Duroi obs.* 23. *Woodv.* iii. 377. *t.* 139. *Bot. arr.* 523. *Smith brit.* 540; *engl. t.* 992. *Trag.* 986, Bedeguar on the lowpr branch; *abr. from*

Rosa. *Fuchs.* 626. c. 255, *which cop. in*

K. candida plena ct semiplena. *Bauh.*

J. ii. 45, (name and descr, belonging to R. alba.) R. sylvestris, incarnato flore. *Boerh.* ii. 152. R. sylvestris inodora, sive canina. *Park: theatr.* 1017. *Rati hist.* 1470 i *syn.* 454. R. canina inodora. *Ger. by Johns.* 1270. (The fig. R. spinosissima.) R. sylvestris vulgaris, flore odorato incarnafo.
Tourn. paris. 527. *Vaill. part's.* 172. *Magn. monsp.* 222. R. sylvestris alba cum ruborc, folio glabro. *L. lapp. n.* 202. *Bauh. J.* ii. 43, *cop. from* Rosae sylvestres. *Cam. epit.* 99, the 3 lower figures. R. sylvestris. *Tab. ic.* 1088. *Dod.* 186. *Peduncles* aggregate, short. *Bracteae* elliptic and lanceolate, serrate, 2 to each peduncle, opposite; teeth globular at the end, with globiferous hairs interposed. *Berry* stil green, smooth, glabrous, oval and obovate, about as long as the peduncles. *Caly.r,* limb stil permanent, deflex, as expressed in the uppermost berry in Fuchs. *Obs-*8162. Aug. 16. CYNOSBATUS. Dog Rose. Fruit called Hips. *Pharm. lond.*—*Berg.* 429. *Hill* 510. *Kroch n.* 777. *Lew.* ii. 279. *Linn.* 154. *Monro* iii. 86. *Ploucq. bibl.* i. 640. *Schoepf* 81? *Vog.* 265. Cynosbatos. *Cull.* i. 252. *Murr,* iii. 172. *Rutty* 161. *Schrod.* 579. Cynosbati. *Spielm.*435. R. caninn. Fresh fruit. *Pharm. edin.*—*Bry.* 168. *Dale* 292. *Lew. disp. by Dune.* 297. *Mill. Jos.* 376. *Pears. R.* i. 68. R. sylvestris. *Alst.* ii. 206. *Berg.* 429. *Krock. n,* 777. *Murr.* iii. 172. ScAoep/ 81?
Rosae rubrae vulgares. *Spielm.* 425.

R. sylvestris vulgaris, flore odorato incarnato. *Chern.* 607; *suppl.* 173. *Vog.* 145. BEDEGUAR. *Berg.* 429. *Kroch. n.* 777. *Mill. Jos.* 377. *Murr.* iii. 172. *Schoepf8lt* Cynosbati fungus. *Vog.* 303. 10. ROSA *alba.* Tube of (he calyx oval and turbinate, hispid and glabrous. Peduncles hispid. Stem and petioles aculeate. Leaves glabrous above, pubescent underneath. *Obs.* 6424. In a garden. *L. sp.* 705. *llort. I;ew.* ii. 208. *Retz. obs.* iii. 34. *n. 62.* R. candida plena et semiplena. *Bauh. J.* ii. 44. (The fig. K-. canina.) 0 *plena.* Corolla double, before it is expanded having a tingle of orange white. *Obs.* 6-124. *L. 0. H. K.*
R. alba vulgaris major, flore multiplied *Magn. hort.* It *J*R. alba flore pleno. Boerh. ii. 251. R. alba. *Tab. ic.* 1083. *(Ger. by Johns, repr. from* R. sativa. *Dod.* 186, which repr. in R. damascena. *Lob. obs.* 618; *ic.* ii. 210, *and cop. in Pari: theatr.* 1017, has the segments of the calyx entire.) *Branches* glabrous, without aculei. *Flowers* paniculate. *Peduncles* terminal, mostly with 2 opposite branches at the base, branches uniflorous. *Bracteae* lanceolate, serrate, opposite, 2 at the base of each peduncle. *Calyx,* tube hispid at the base hispid on one side hispid and nearly glabrous. *Stamina* and *pistils. Obs.* 6424. ROSA alba. *Alst.* ii. 206. *Berg.* 431. *Carth.* iv. 242. *Dale* 293. *Krock. n.* 778. *Linn.* 154. *Murr.* iii. 175. Rosaealbae. *Schrod.*663. *Spielm.* 424. R. alba vulgaris major. Fog. 149. 540. RUBUS. *Calyx* quinquefid. *Petals* 5. *Berry* compound. *Obs.* 8188. *L.* 1. *Stem* herbaceous. L. J 1. RUBUS *Chamaemorus.* Leaves lobate. Stem without prickles, uniflorous. Segments of the calyx ovate. *From Smith brit.* 545. Observed by Mr. Lambert on Axedge a hill near Buxton in Derbyshire.— *L. suec. n.* 449; *sp.* 708. *Huds.* 221. On mountains in Caernarvonshire, Yorkshire, Lancashire, Westmorland, and Cumberland.— *Lightf.* 266. *t.* 13, *at p.* 266. *Bot, arr.* 528. *Retz. obs.* i. 20. *n.* 59, who was informed by O.cder that the roofs of the male plants are distinct from those of the female.— *Fl. dan. t.* 1. Smith engl.t. 716.
R. caule unifolio et uniflovo, foliis simplicibus. *L. lapp.n.208.i.5. f.* 1.

Chamaemorus cambro-britanica. *Park, theatr.* 1014.

Chamaemorus. *Raii hist.* 653; *syn.* 260, whereat k 9 from the bottom for 1630, read 1368. On Pendle, Ingelborough, and Hincklehaugh.—*Pennaeus ap. Clus pann.* 118, *repr. in hist. i.* 118, *and Ger. by Johns.* 1273, # *cop. in*

Chamaemorus anglica. *Park, theatr.* 1014, 4,

Rubo itinea minori atTinis, Chamaemorus. *Bauh. J.* ii. 62.
Vaccinia nubis. *Ger. by Johns.* 1420.
Native of Scandinavia, Siberia, Caernarvonshive, Derbyshire, Lancnshire, Yorkshire, Westmorland, Cumberland, and Scotland.

CHAMAEMORUS. *Pharm. suec.*—*Carth.* i. 435. *Dale* 323. *Linn.* 156. *Murr.* iii. 156. *Schoepf* 82.
R. Chamaemorus. *Berg.* 435. *Bry.* 170.
2. RUBUS *trifidus.* Leaves inciso-frifid, glabrous.
Stem unarmed. *L. a Willd.* ii. 1089.— *Thunb. r V'* 3. RUBUS *arcticus.* Leaves ternate. Stem without prickles, uniflorous and biflorous. *Obs.* 8193.

Specimen gathered in a garden.—*L. suec. n.* 448; *sp.* 708. *Smith brit.* 544; *engl. t.* 1585, from a garden.—*Hort. ken.* ii. 210. *Curt. mag. t.* 132. R. caule unifloro, foliis ternatis. *L. lapp. n.* 207. *f* 5. *f.* 2. A variation with crenate petals. *Native* of Scandinavia, the isle of Mull, and North America. *Leaves* hirsutiolous at the margin. *Petioles* and *petiolules* pubescent. *Stem* biflorous. *Obs.* 8193. Two specimens. RUBUS arcticus. *Pharm. suec.*—*Berg.* 434. *Bry.* 171. *Lew. disp. by Dune.* 346. *Murr.* iii. 153. Baccae norland icae. *Linn.* 155, 4. RUBUS *saxatilis.* Leaves ternate. Flowers co rymbose. *Obs.* 6302. In Monsal dale near Ashford in Derbyshire.—*L. suec. n.* 447; *sp.* 708; *a Murr..* 476. *finds.* 221. In Yorkshire, Cumberland, and Westmorland.— *Lightf.* 265. *PL dan. t.* 13-1. *Bot. arr.* 528. *Roth germ.* ii. 565. *Smith brit.* 544. *Jacq. vind.* 245. *Ger. by Johns.* 1273, *repr. from* R. saxatilis alpinus. *Clus. pann.* 116, which repr. in hist. i. 118, *St cop. in Park, theatr.* 1014. R. caule repente annuo, foliis ternatis. *L. lapp. n.* 206. R. alpinus humilis. *Bauh. J.* ii. 61. *Boerh.* ii. 60. Chamaerubus saxatilis. *Raii syn.* 261; *hist.* 654. *Root* woody, horizontal. *Stems* herbaceous, woody at the base, erect, simple, angular, aculeate, hirsute, 5 to 8 inches long; *aculei* attenuate, not pungent, scattered. *Shoots* 15 to 20 inches long, declinate and then procumbent. *Leaves* ternate, hirsutulous; folioles deltoideo-ovate, unequally serrate, the lower halves of the lateral ones larger than the upper halves. *Petioles* aculeate, slightly villose, mostly longer than the leaves. *Stipulue* oval elliptic linear and-subulate, sometimes bifid. *Corymbi* with from 2 to 4 flowers, mostly solitary, sometimes 2 together. *Peduncles* aculeate, villose. *Petals* white, obovatolanceolate, some-

what longer than the calyx. *Stamina* as long as the calyx. *Pistils* 5. *Obs.* 6302. *Native* of the mountains of Switzerland, Germany, North Wales, Derbyshire, Lancashire, Yorkshire, Westmorland, Cumberland, and Scotland. CHAMAERUB US. *Dale* 323. R. saxatilis. *Krock. n.* 788. *L. am.* i. 346. 2. *Stem frutescent.* L. 5. RUBUS *moluccanus.* Leaves cordate, slightly lobate. Stem aculeate, decumbent. *L. a Murr.* 475; *sp.* 707. *RUBUS moluccus ktifoiius. Rumph.* v. 88. *t.* 47. /. 2. 6. RUBUS *quinquelobus.* Leaves quinquclobate. 06. 5236. Specimen gathered by Dr. Cutler in
New England. R. odoratus. *L. sp.* 707. *Hort. kew.* ii. 210.
Curt. mag. t. 333. *Boerh.* ii. 60. *Mill. Ph. diet. n.6.* R. caule inermi multifolio multifluro, foliis palmatis. *L. ups.* 133. *It.* foliis digitatis denis quinis ternatisque, caule in ermi. *Cut I.* 452. VIRGINIAN FLOWERING RASPBERRY. *Mill. Ph. diet.* 7. RUBUS *occidentalis.* Leaves ternate, tomentose underneath. Stem aculeate. Petioles terete. *L. sp.* 706; *a Murr.* 475, where for temis read ternatis. —*Hort. kew.* ii. 209. *Mill. Ph. diet. n.* 5. R. caule suberecto leviter aculeato, foliis ternatis, fructu nigro. *Gron. virg.* 78. RUBUS occidentalis. *L. am.* vi. 345. *Schoepf* 81. . 8. RUBUS *parvifolius.* Leaves ternate, tomentose un derneath, Stem hirtose, aculeate. Petioles aculeate. Prickles recurvate. *L. sp.* 707. Found by Osbeck in India. RUBUS moluccus parvifolius. *Rumph.* v. 88. *t.* 47. /. 1. 9. RUBUS *caesius.* Leaves ternate and quinato-pin nate, hirsutulous and tomentose underneath. Stem aculeate, terete. Petioles aculeate. Fruit rorid. *Obs.* 8192. Specimen gathered near the plaister stone pits at Chelaston in Derbyshire, on clay.— *L. suec.* n 445; *sp.* 706. *Bot. arr.* 526 *a. Poll. n.* 489. *Roth germ.* ii. 563. *Scop. carn. n.* 612. *Smith brit.* 542; *engl. t.* 826. *Gou. hort.* 247. Near Montpelier.
R. caute aculeato reflexo perenni, foliis ternatis. *L. lapp. n.* 205.
R. caule aculeato, foliis ternatis. *Gron. virg.* 78.
R. repens fructu caesio. *Goody, in Ger. by Johns.*

1271. No fig.—*Tourn. paris.* 528. *Vaill. paris.* 174. *Boerh.* ii. 60. In Holland. R. minor, fructu caeruleo. *Bauh. J.* ii. 59. *Rati hist.* 1640; *syn.* 647.
R. tricoccos. *Park, theatr.* 1015. No fig. *Native* of Europe.
RUBUS caesius, *Bry.* 169. *Krock. n.* 786. *L. am.* vi. 345. *Spielm.* 96. R. repens. *Rvtty* 437. Chamaebatos. *Dale* 323. 10. RUBUS *corylifolius.* Leaves ternate and quinato-pedate, hirsutulous underneath. Stem and petioles aculeate. *Obs.* 7535. Near Chesterfield, on gritstone.—*Smith brit.* 542; *engl. t.* £27. *Reth. ed.* ii. *n.* 424.
R. fruticosus. *L. suec. n.* 444; *sp.* 707. *Bot. arr.* 528. *tar.* 3. *Poll. n.* 490 *a. Roth germ.* ii.
564. var. 1. R. caesius major. *Woodw.* in *bot. arr.* 526. *r* R. foliis quinato-pinnatis ternatisque, caule hispido. *L. ups.* 133 *β* R. quinqueíidus subtus glabcr. *Doody ap. Jlcüi sgn.* 467. R. minor, Chamaerubus sivc Huniirubus. *Park. theatr.* 1013. *Leaves* pale green and slightly hairy underneath; cauline leaves with 5 folioles; folioles petiolate, oval, acuminate, larger upwards, the terminating foliole very much resembling the leaf of Cory lus Avellana; leaves of the flowering branches ternate; lateral folioles petiolate. *Peliolules* of the lowermost pair of folioles a tenth of an inch long, inserted into the lower margin of the petiolules of the middlemost pair a little above their base; those of the middlemost pair 5 and 6 times longer than those of the lowermost pair; that of the terminating foliole nearly thrice as long as those of the middlemost pair. *Calyx* reflex. *Corolla* when gathered yesterday white, to day fleshcoloured white, lanceolato-oblong, slightly villose. *Obs.* 7535. RUBUS. See the medical references under R. fru ticosus. 11. RUBUS *frulicosus.* Leaves ternate, and quinaiopedate, tomentose underneath. Stem and petioles aculeate. *Obs.* 8189. Specimen gathered at Areley in Worcestershire.—*L. a Reich,* ii. 534, where we read vel sublus alba et tomentosa, but from what work of Linnaeus I cannot discover.—*Bot. arr.* 527. *a. Smith brit.* 5i3; *engl. t.* 715. *Reich,*

franc, n. 332. *Scop. cam. n.* 613. *Abb.* 112. *Poll. n.* 490 *e. Roth germ.* ii. 564. *Lour.* i. 398. *Mill. Jos.* 379. *Monro* iii. 240. *Murr.* HI. I5L, *Pears. R.* i. 68. *Piepenbring, account from in phys. journ.* iii. 271. *Rutty* 437. *Quar. fcbr.* 03. 122. 381. *Sckrod.* 667. *Spielm.* 96.. *Vog.* 262. Raspberries. Jbnfyce, *W. fev.* 167. *Reid, T.phth.* 289. « ruber. Fruit red. 0 &5. 6188. R. idaeus. JDorf. 731, repr. in X,o6. Oj. 619; 'e ii. 212, anrf G«r. 6y *Johns.* 1272, # ofrr..1 *Park. par.* 557. . 559. /. 1,4" »«r«. i« II. idaeus spinosus, fructu rubro. *Bauk. J.* ii. 59. *Boerk.* ii. 60. *Rati kist.* 16t0; sy». 467.-In Wales, and (he north of England, and observed by
Dillenius in Stoken Church woods in Oxfordshire. R. caule erecto hispido, foliis ternatis. *L. lapp. it.* 204. R. idaeus spinosus. *Dalech.* 123. *Tourn. parts,* 528. *Vaill. parts.* 174. Chamaebatus, sen R. idaeus alter. *Trag.* 973, *cop. in Dateck.* 424.
Native of Lapland, Sweden, Germany, of France as far south as Franehe compte, Scotland, the north of England, Yorkshire, Derbyshire on gritstone and limestone, Wales, the north of Worcestershire near Kidderminster on gravel, Warwickshire on gravel, Oxfordshire, Bedfordshire, Cambridgeshire, and Norfolk-. ' x RUBUS idaeus spinosus. Ckom. 817. $ albus. Fruit yellowish white. In gardens.—*Hort hew.* ii. 209 0. *L. sp.* 706 i. *Rolk gerpi.* fi. 56S. *var.* 2. R. idaeus spinosus fructu albo. *Boerk.* ii. 60. *Bauk, J.* ii. 59. *Rati hist.* 1640.
F. vesca. *Gou. hort.* 247. Near Montpelicr. *Host* 282. Woods and pastures—*Roth germ.* ii.
568. *Bot. arr.* 529. *Smith brit.* 546; *engl. t.* 1524. *lfuds.22l.* Potent ilia vesca. *Scop. earn. n.* 625. F. flagellis reptans. *Guett.* i. 287. F. vulgaris. *Vaill. parts.* 55. *Magn. monsp.* 99; *hort.* 80. *Boerh.* i. 41. In Holland.—*L. lapp.* ». 209. Fraga altera. *Dod.* 661, *repr. in* F. et Fraga major subalba. *Lob. ic.* i. 697, *8f* F. et Fraga. *Ger. by Johns.* 997, *if cop. in* Common Strawberry. *Pet. herb. t.* 40. /. 7. Fragaria. *Raii hist.* 609; *syn.* 254. *Dalech.* 614. Fraga vulgaris. *Park. par. t.* 527. /. 6. & alba. Fruit roundish, white. *From memory.*—*L*» *sp.*

a; suec. 0; lapp. a. Bot. arr. i. Jluds. i F. vulgaris, fructu albo. Vaill. paris. 55. Boerh, iL 41. Magn. hort. 80. y conica. Fruit ovate, acute..From memory, F. vesca. Poll. n. 191. Krock. n. 789, var. found in the higher mountains. Fragaria. Trag. 500, rcpr. in Fragula. Cord. fol. 173. p. 2. F. major et minor. Fuchs. 808. c. 328, cop. in T. ferens fraga rubra. Bauh. J. ii. 394, representing this and var. $ Alpine Strawberry. Mill. Ph. diet. n. 1. var. the 2nd. i dioica. Flowers dioicous. From memory. F. muricala. Mill. Ph. diet. n. 3. Hauboy Strawberry: v ''' F. vesca pratensis. L. sp. 0. Hort. kew. 0. Jluds. 22? y No place of growth mentioned.

F. fructu parvi pruni magnitudine. Vaill. parts 55. Boerk. ii. 42. Magn. hort. 80. F-et Fraga. Dod. 661, repr. in Lob. obs. 396; ic. i. 697; F. et Fraga subalba. Oer. fcy Johns. 997, and cop, in F. vulgaris. Pari: tkeatr. 758. Fraga bobemica maxima. Park. par. t. 527. /. 7. F. major fcrtilis, seu bohemica maxima. Jiaii hist. 609. i virginiana. Fruit roundish, scarlet. From memory.— Hort. kew. $ In Carolina and Virginia. F. virginiana. Mill. Ph. diet. n. 2. Rait hist. 609. F. virginiana, fructu coccinco. Boerh. ii. 42. F. flagellis reptatricibus. Gron. virg. 78. Virginia Strawberry. Park. par. 528. No fig.

Native of North America from Carolina to Newfoundland. n chiloensis. Chili Strawberry. L. sp. y. Hort. kew. y In South America. F. chiloensis. MiU. Ph. diet. n. 4. 9 Ananas. Pine Strawberry. Hort. kew. c In Surinam.-simplicifolia. Leaves, excepting the lowermost and the 2 lowermost, simple. Obs. 3011. F. monophylla. L.—-H. K. ii. 212. Curt. mag. t. 63. Fruit conic. 2. FRAGARIA pinnatifolia. Leaves pinnate, Obs. 4674. Specimen gathered on a common near Congleton in Cheshire, in fruit. "., Comarum palustre. L. suec, n. 463; sp. 718. Bot, err. 540. Smith brit. 556; engl. t. 172. Fl dan. t. 636. Potentilla palustris. Scop. earn. n. 617. Comarum. L. lapp. ». 214. Pentapbyllon rubrum palustre. Lob. ic. i. 691, re pr. in Quinquefblium quartern. Dod. 117, ¿i Pentapbyllum rubrum palustre. Ger. by Johns. 987. Raii syn. ed. ii. 140.-"_

Pentapbyllon palustre. Cam. hört. 120. Cord. fol. 96, cop. in ...-..

Pentaphyllon, vel potius Ileptaphyllum flore rubro.

Ben/h. J. it. 598. c. (Purple marsh Cjnqueíbil. Pet. herb. t. 41. /. 1, is cop. from Ger. by Johns, 987. /. 2, which is a rig. of Potentilla recta.), v COMJRUM palustre, firopk. ii. я. 811. t. 14. » tenuifolia. Leaves thin, green underneath. Obs. . 6756. t Specimen from an herbal formed in lingland. Penta phylloides palustre rubrum.. Dill. ap. Hait gyn. 256. Petals lanceolate, more than half as long as the smaller segments of (he calyx. Obs? 8756. B crassifulin. Leaves tbickish, somewhat glaucous an» derneatb. Obs. 8757. v Specimen from Dr. Heise. Pentaphyllum palustre rubrum, crassis et villosis í'o liis, h несип m et bibernicum. Raii syn. 256. Doodi/ ap. Raii syn. éd. ii. 312.

Irish marsh Cinquefoil. Pet. herb. t. 41. f. 2.

Pilais obovaté, acute, more ithan half as long as the smaller segments of the calyx. Obs. 8757.—. Petal's lanceolate. Obs. 8758. Specimen gathered in Saviile's garden.

Fragaria silvestris minime vesca, sive sterilis. Lob,. ic i. 698, repr. in Fragaria minime vesca, sive sterilis. Ger. by Johns. 998, St abr. in Barren Strawberry. Pet. herb. t. 40. /. 8. Fragaria' non fragifera, vel non vesca. Bauh. J. ii, 395. Native of France, Germany, and Britain. FRAGARJOIDES. Dale 160. 3. TORMENTILLA reptans. Leaves quinate. Stem creeping. Obs. 180. On dry banks. Potentilla reptans. L. suec. n. 456; sp. 714. Curt. load. i. 37. t; mat. med. t. 14. Wale. t. Bot. arr. 534. Smith brit. 551. Gou. hort. 249. Near Monk. pelier.— Woodv. i. 160. t. 59. Quinquefolium majus repeos. Tourn. parts. 31. Vaill. parts. 167'. Boerh. i. 40. In Holland. Pentaphyllum vulgatissimum. Park, theatr, 398. iiflft' hist. 611; yn. 255. Quinquefoliam majus luteum, puchs. 596, c. 239, cop. in Pentaphyllum, sive Quinquefolium vulgare repens. Bauh. J. ii. 397. Quinquefolium luteum majus. Dalech. 1264. Quinquefolium majus. Dod. 116, repr. in Quinquefolium, sive Pentaphyllum vulgare. Lob. obs. 393,

Quinquefolium vulgare. Ger. by Johns. 987, Sr Pentaphyllon majus, flore subluteo interdum albo. Lob. ic. i. 690, (the name belonging to T. recta,) and cop. in Pentaphyllum majus, Iuteo flore vel albo, Parle. theatr. 396. 543. GEUM. Calyx decemfid; every other segment smaller. Petals 5. Seeds aristate. Hort. Acs. L, 1. GEUM urbanum. Aristae uncinate, glabrous. Flowers erect. Caulme leaves ternite tripartite and trifid. Petals at long as the calyx. Obs. 4650. In hedges.— Hort. kew. ii. 218. L. suec. n. 460; tp. 716. ffoodv. iv. 126. t. 259. Smitk brit. 554; engl. t. 1400. Bot. arr. 537. Curt. loud. ii. 36. t. 113. Wale. t. Fl. dan. t. 672. Gou. hort. 250. Near Montpelier. —Poll. n. 501. Buchhave in act. haun. i. 124. 141. t.

Geum. Guett. i. 288.

Caryophyllata vulgaris. Tourn. par-s. 254. Vaill. paris. 30. Lob. obs 396, repr. in ic. i. 693, cop. in Park, theatr. 136, fruit ill done, and the radical leaves pinnate instead of subrotund; cop. with corrected fruit in .

Avens. Pet. herb. t. 40. /. I, and repr. in . Caryophyllata Dod. 137, and Ger. by Johns. 994.

Rati hist. 606; syn. 253. Caryophyllata Matthioli. Dalech. 686. Caryophyllata hortensis. Fuchs. 380. c. 145. Caryophyllata vulgaris, flore parvo luteo. Bauh. J. ii. 398. /. (The fig. Anemone Hepatica.) Caryophyllata. Trag. 67. Petals oval. Styles terminal, as observed by Gmelin. Aristae formed of the part of the style belaw the joint, the upper half having fallen oir. Obs 4650. Native of Europe as far north as Sweden. CARYOPHYLLATA. Pharm. austriaco-prot. Srt.—Alst. i. 404. Berg. 445. Carth. iv. 99. Dale 160. Geoffr. iii. 263. Herm. 169. JKrock. n. 807. Lew. i. 394; disp. by Rother. 131; by Dune. 342. Liim. 157. A//W. Jo. 117. Murr. iii. 122. Jtetty 99. Schrod. 558. SpiWm. 247. Fog. 96. 217.

G. urbanum. Bang in act. haun. i. 99. 109. 253. 296. Buchhave ib. 119; and account from inmed. comment, dec. II. iv. 43; vii. 119. Callisen in act. haun. i. 422. Mezajun. ib. ii. 28. 32. Pears. R. ed. ii. 386. Perciv. Rob. of Dublin in phys. journ. xviii. 557. 436. Ploucq.

bibl. i. 484. *Ranoe in act. haun,* i. 333. 454. *Vog. the son, account from in phys. journ.* i. 191.

Geum. *Bang in act. haun.* i. 241. 249. 261. 297. Caryophyllata vulgaris. *Chom.* 463; *suppl.* 140.

2. GEUM *rivale.* Aristae uncinate, villose. Flowers nodding. Receptacle of the fruit pedunculate. Petals cuneiform, retuse. *Obs.* 6333. In Langwit li woods near Bolsover in Derbyshire, on limestone.—*Obs.* 8247. Specimen gathered by Dr. Cutler in New England.—*Hort. kea.* ii. 218. *L. lapp. n.* 216; *suec. n.* 461; *up.* 717. *Bot. arr.* 538. *Smith engl. t.* 106; *brit.* 554. *Fl. dan. t.* 722. *Roth germ.* i. 224. *Gou. hort.* 250. Near Montpelier.—*Lightf.* 274.
Caryophyllata rivalis. *Scop. earn. n.* 629.

Caryophyllata aquatica, flore nutante. *Boerh.i.* 43.

Cariophyllata septentrionalium rotundifolia papposo flore. *Lob. ic.* i. 694.

Caryophyllata montana I. *Clus. pann.* 434, *repr. in hist,* ii. 103, *and*

Caryophylkta montaria purpurea. *Ger. by Johns.* 995. *Park, theatr.* 137. *Rati hist.* 607; *syn.* 253. J

Caryoph'yllata montana Dalechampii; *Dalecft.* 686. CaryophVltita sylvestris. *Fuchs.* 380. c. 145. Ftowers' rmick larger than those of G. urbauuiu and more inclining to saffron colour.

Stem 16 inches long with 1 and 2 flowers. *Radical leaves* pinnate, rarely simple; terminal rbliole re'niform, incise; lower folioles ovate, very small, from 1 to 3 pairs; *cauline leaves* simple. Ci,,x partitodeoemfid, brownish red. *Corolla* somewhat shorter than the calyx, straw-coloured. 06s. 6333.—*Stem* with several flowers, to 2 feet long. *Cauline leaves* ternate. *Petals* of a purplish reddish hue. *Obs.* 5793. From near Ilam, and gathered in Monsal dale Derbyshire on the banks of a brook, and in a thicket high up the sides of the adjoining hill, on limestone. *Native* of the south of Francie, Germariy, Scancrt.navia, Scotland, the north of England, Wales, Derbyshire, Warwickshire, Oxfordshire, Bedfordshire, Cambridgeshire, Norfolk, Essex, and New England. GEUM rivale.

Berg. 447: *Buchhdve, account from in wed. comtrtbtt.* xiv. 45. *Murr.* iii; *132.* G. palostrc.' *Ixio. disp. by Dune.* 342. *Linn.* 158. G. flotib'us nutantibus, fructu bblongo.'ariBtis plumo sis. *Cutl.* 454. J. GEUM *virgManum.* Aristae uncinate, glabrous. Flowers erecf. Cauline leaves ternate, the upper lanceolate.' Petals shorter than the calyx *Mort. hew.* ii. 217. *L. sp.* 716.
GEUM. Gron, %itg. 79,—ScAoep/83, E...:...!..

JW4. DRYAS. d(yxoctopartite; segments distinct. *Plat&5-to* 8. Seeds aristate. *Obs.* 7994. *Hort. kew.* ii. 219. i..;.,.;-;..
::.. vc; ...'.-,.'.. -. I '.ii i' '...:i.. '..',l. I.; *PflYAS.pctopetala: U sua. n.* 662; *sp.* 717. *Bot.. art.* 53d. *Ligbtf.* 274, On mountains in Breadalbanc, Rossshire, Argyleshire, and the isle of *Sky.—Pall, reise* iii. 733. *Fl. dan. t.* 31. *Penn. hcbr. t. 33, at p.* 285. *Smith brit.* 555; *engl. t.* 451.

Dryas. *L. lapp. n.* 215.

Caryophyllata alpina chamaedryos folio. *Rati hist.* C08. On Thuiri the highest summit of Mount Jura, and on the Alps of Carinthia; and a specimen gathered between Gort and Galloway in Ireland; *syn.* 253. Found by Lhwyd on mountains near Sligo in Ireland, and on all the higher mountains of Scotland.— *Boerh.* i. 43.

Chamaedrys III alpina, cisti flore. *Clus. pann.* 611. *repr. in*

Chamaedrys III, seu montana. *Clus. hist.* ii. 351, *and*

Tcucrium alpinum, cisti flore. *Ger. by Johns.* 659, *and abr. in*

Germander Avens. *Pet. herb. t.* 40. /. 6.

Chamaedris montana frutescens durior. *Lob. adv.* 209, repr. *in*

Chamaedrys montana durior. *Lob. ic.* i. 495. *f.* 1. No fructifications.—/. 2 in fruit *cop. in*

Chamaedrys spuria montana, cisti flore. *Park, theatr.*

Chamaedrys montana. *Dalech.* 1164. *Petals* 5. *Leaves* acute. *Calyx,* segments not incumbent, as in the genera most nearly nearly allied to it. *Petals* 8, when dry tawny. *Ubs.* 7994.—*Leaves* obtuse. *Obs.* 7995. Specimen gathered in the Edinburgh garden.

CHAMAEDRYS alpina, flore fragariae albo. *Bank. J.* iii. *b.* 290. On Mount Thuyri near Geneva, and on the mountains of the Grisons and the Engadine. (The fig. Salvia pratensis.) 161 *Class* 13. POLYANDRIA. *Order* 1. MONOGYNIA.
.. 1. *Flowers monopetalous.* 545. Acacia. *Legumen.* Corolla quinqncful. *Calyx* quinquedentate. 2. *Flowers ietrapetalcus.* L. 551. Chelidonium. *Capsule* unilocular'. *Calyx* diphyllous. *Obs.* 4018. *Capsule* unilocular. *Calyx* polyphyllous. *Capsule* semimultilocular, opening by pores underneath the permanent stigma. *Calyx* diphyllous. *Obs.* 5315. *Berry* unilocular. *Calyx* bipartite, deciduous. *Berry* unilocular. *Calyx* tetraphylVous. *Seeds* in two rows. *L.* 555. Clusia. 552. Papaveb. 554. Mammea. 548. Actaea. 547. Cambogia. *Berry* unilocular, crowned by the style and stigma. *Calyx* tetraphyllous and hexaphyllous. *Petals* 4 and 6. *Receptacle* tetragoirous. 546. Cafparis. *Berry* unilocular, pedicellate, corticose. *Calyx* tetraphyllous. 560. Calophyllum. *Drupe. Nut* globular. *Ca lyx* tetraphyllous. 559. Orias« *Drupe. Nut* with 8 furrows. *Calyx* quadrifid. 3. *Flowers pentapelalous.* L. 569. Cist us. *Capsule. Calyx* pentaphy» bus; 2 of the phylla smaller. *L.* 570. Corcho в us. *Capsule* quinquelocular. *Ca lyx* pentaphyllous, as long as the corolla, deciduous. 561. Tilia. *Capsule* quinquelocular, mon« os per rao us. *Calyx* pentaphyllous. *Obs.* 4033. 564. Algia. *Drupe* orbicular. *Nut* uni locular. *Calyx* truncate *From Lour.* 563. Microcos. *Drupe. Nut* trilocular. *From L. a Willd.* 565. EbΛEocAnpüs. *Drupe. Nut* tuberculate. *Pc» tais* lacerate. 562. Grecia. *Berry* quadrilocular. *Calyx* pentaphyllous and quinqué« 1. *Flowers pentapelalous.* 593. RAnUNCULuS. *Seeds* many. *Calyx* pentaphyllous. *Petals* with a nectanuin al the base. *Obs.* 3450. 586. Uyaria, ' fiMseveral, pedicellate. *Ca lyx* triphyllous. 587. ftf«L0PQuM,. *Merries* several.. *Sefds* dis .-.'.! C;'.pe,red. Ca/yr triphyllous, jProm Xowr.

3. *Flowers polypetalous.* 584. Nelumbium. iV«s monospermous, immersed in a truncate receptacle. *Calyx* tetraphyllous and pentaphyllous.

594. Ficahia. *Capsules* monospermous. *Ca lyx* triphyllous. *Petals* 8 to 11, with a nectarium at the base. *Obs.* 4501.

595. Tbollius. *Capsules* polyspermous. *Calyx* triphyllous, as long as the corolla. *Neetaria* obsubulate. 065.4896.

585. Michelia. *Berries* many, polyspermous. *Calyx* triphyllous. *Petals* 15.

4. *Flowers incomplete.* 598. Hydrastis. *Petals* 3. *Berry* compound. *From L.* 591. Thalictrtjm. *Seeds* without a tail. *Petals* 4 and 5. 590. Clematis. *Seeds* aristate. *Petals* 4, 5, and 6. 597. Caltha. *Capsules* 4 to 17, polysperm 4 545. ACACIA.. *Calyx* quinquedentate. *Corolla* quinquefid. *Legitimen. From L. a Willd.* iv. 1049. Male and female flowers sometimes interspersed.

X.

1. *Leaves bipinnale. Spines and aculei stipular. Spikes elongate.* From L. a Willd. 1. ACACIA *trispinosa.* "Spines in threes, the intermediate one bent back. *From*

Mimosa Senegal. *L. sp,* 1506. *Ilort. hew.* iii. 442.

A. Senegal. *L. a Willd.* iv. 1077.

Mimosa spinis geminatis distinctis, foliis duplicator pinnatis, partialibus utrinque quiñis pluribus. *L. vps.* 146.

Mimosa spinis geminatis, foliis duplicato-pinnatis, partialibus utrinque quiñis. *Roy.* 471.

Mimosa spinis geminatis distinctis, foliis duplicator pinnatis, particularibus utrinque quinis pluribus.

L. mat. med. n. 261... GUMMI senegalense. *Cod. med. p.* lvii.—*Le&.i.* 480. ..

Gummi Senegal. *Phartn. austriaco-prov.* 67.—*Berg.* 831. *Linn.* 266. *Murr.* ii. 414. Gummi Senega. *Carth.* i. 289. *Cull. din.* 305.

Gcoffr. ii. 577. *Monro* ii. 439.

Gummi arabicum. *Lew. disp. by Dune.* 344.

Spieltn. 458.

A. siliquis compressis. *Dale* 343.

2. ACACIA *Catechu*. Spines in pairs, rc-curvate. . Leaves and foliations multi-jugate. Petiole with a gland at the insertion of each pair of foliations and below the lowermost pair. Flowers spi-cate. *From* Kerr and L. fil. *L. a Willd.* iv. 1079.

Mimosa Catechu. *L. JU. suppl.* 439. *Donn* 130.

Roxb. ii. *t.* 175.

Catechu. *Kerr in med. obs.* v. 151. *t.* 4, *cop. in Woodv.* ii. 183. *t.* 66.

Lycium Garciae, sive Cate. *Bauh. J.* i. *b.* 61. No fig.—*Rait hist.* 1628. CAT-ECHU, commonly called Terra japonica. In spissated juice. *Pharm. lond.*—*Boul-duc in ac. sci. abr. by Southw.* Hi. 265. *Cull.* ii. 42. *Geoffr.* ii. 72. i/iV/784. *Hull phlegm.* 281. *Lind seam.* 275.-lm. 267. *Ploucq. bibl.* i. 248. @w«r.

/eAr. 43. 79. 209; *anim.* 158. 202. 222. 229. *Und.* i. 360, ii. 121. 207. 210. Fog. 331. *Wortmuller, account from in med. comment,* vii. 265. Mimosa Catechu. Extract of the wood. *Pharm. edin.*—*Lew. disp. by Dune.* 255. *Murr. J.* i. 218; ii. 31. *Pears. Jt. ed.* ii. 348.

Succus japonicus. *Alst.* ii. 480.

Terra japonica. *Blane* 491. *Carth.* ii. 142. *Ckalm.* ii. 169. *Dale* 270. *Ilerm.* 721. *Home, F. cUn.* 822. *Hunt. J. jam.* 236. *Lew.* ii. 420. *Lind seam.* 275 *Mead mon.* ii. 266. 3/'//. *Jo.* 47. J?H/ty 514. *Spielm.* 217..Afe'um. ii. 56. Moan) it. 399. *Pringle28l.* .c,y.:.' .'J

Terra Catechu. *Berg.* 880. *Caflisem-fa act. haun.* i. 421. *Chom.* 452. /«rr. ii. 415. .--.'. ..'.. 0 Lycium indicum. *Dale* 313. '-. 2. *Leaves bipinnate. Spines and. aculei stipular..'. Spikes globular.* L. a Willd.

3. ACACIA *farnesiana.* Spines setaceous, distinct. Leaves quinquejngate and qc-tojugate; foliations multijugate. Spikes mostly sessile. Petioles with a gland below the foliations. Lcgumina terete. *From L. a H'illaiv.* 1083, " v Mimosa farnesiana. *L. sp.* 1506. *Horf.* Areal, iii.

Mimosa spinis geminis distinct is, foliis duplicato-pinnatis, parlialjbus utrinque octo. *L. ups.* 146. r

A. indica, foliis scorpioidis legumi-nosae, siliquis fuscis teretibus resinosis. *Boerh.* ii. 56.,

A. americana. *Sloane cat.* 152.

A. americana farnesiana. *Park, theatr.* 1548.

AC4CIA indica farnesiana. *Rait hist.* 97T. —*Dale* 343. Seissaban. *Sonnini* i. 316.

.. 4. ACACIA *arabica*. Spines in pairs. Leaves trijugate and quadrijugate; folia-tions multijugate; folioles linear, acute, contiguous. Petioles pubescent, with a gland below the foliations. Lcgumina Gum arabic. *Cfialm.* i. 90. 174; ii. 120. *Cuff. cUn.* 305. 308. 315. *Darw.* ii. 31. 466. 749. *Denm.* i. 270; ii. 522. *Fordyce, G. fev.* iv. 119. *Home, F. din.* 66. 135. 322. 324. *Hull phlegm.* 281. *Monro, Don. sold.* 274. *Pott* iii. 93. *Pringle* 273. 279. *Reid, T. phthis.* 155. *Und.* i. 355. Gomme arabique. *Chom.* 825; *suppl.* 214. ACACIA. *Chom.* 638. *Lew.* i. 13. A. vera. *Pharm. austriaco-prov.* J5.—*Gtoffr.* ii. 716..Les). *disp.by Rother.3. Linn.266. Mutt.* ii. 404. ScArorf. 523. *Vog.* 335. Acaciae succus. 4/ri. ii. 478. *Carth.* iv. 295. *Jferm.* 723.. *Monro* ii. 438. Acaciae succus acgy pti-acus. *Spielm* .411. . 546. CAPPARIS. *Ca-lyx* tetraphyllous, coriaceous. *Petals* 4. *Stamina* long. *Berry* covered with a bark, unilocular, pe' dunculate. *L. .'ii .*

1. *Stipulae spinescent.* L. a Willd.

I. CAPPARIS *spinosa*. Peduncles uniflor-ous, solitary. Stipulae mostly spinose. Leaves deciduous. Capsules oval. *From L. sp.* 720, and J. Bauhine.— *Hort. hew.* ii. 221. *Curt. mag. t.* 291. *fVoodv.* Iv. 42. *t.* 228. Cappares. *Lob. adv.* 281. No fig. On the coasts of Spain Tuscany and the south of France. *Native* of the south of Europe, or possibly only naturalised, the authors cited mentioning it as grow-ing in the vicinity of towns. CAPPARIS. *Pharm. austriaco-prov.* 26,—*Alst.* $. 370. *Berg.* 449. *Dale* 394. *Geoffr.* iii. 250. *Herm.* 213. *Lew. disp. by Rother.* 127. *Lirm.* 159. *Mill. Jos.* 108. *Murr.* ii. 305. *Rutty* 92. *Schrod.* 553. *Spielm.* 47. *Fof.* 233. C. spinosa. *Bry.* 148.

C. spinosa, fructu minore, folio ro-tundo. *Chotn.* 221; *suppl.* 70. a *oblusifo-lia.* Leaves emarginate and obtuse. *Obs.* 8248. Specimen gathered in a garden. C. spinosa, fructu minore, folio rotuudo. *Magn. tnonsp.* 48. *Boerh.* ii. 71. Cap-paris. *Trag.* 967. *All. nic.* 121. On old walls. C. spinosa et non spinosa. *Bauh. J.* ii. 63. C. retuso folio. *Lob, obs.* 359, *repr. in ic.* i. 635, *and* C. rotundiore fo-lio. *Get. by Johns.* 895, *and air. in .* C. spinosa, folio rotundo. *Park, theatr.* 1023, inner 6g.—*Raii kist.* 1629; *em.* 83.

On walls and rubbish in Rome Sienna and Florence. *Leaves* subrotundo-oyal, the lower of a branch, emarginate, the upper »bsoletely emarginate with a minute cuspis. *Obs.* 8248.—Leaves elliptico-oval. *Obs.* 8249. Specimen gathered by Mr. Boraston on the walls of Florence. 6 *acutifolia.* Leaves acute. *From authors.* C. ovata. *L. a Willd.* ii. I IS I. *Desf.* Capparis. *Dalech.* 155. *Dod.* 734, *repr. in* C. folio acuto. *Lob. obs.* 359, *repr. in ic.* i. 634, *Ger. by Johns.* 895, *and cop. in* Dalech. 155, *and* C. spinosa folio acuto. *Park, theatr.* 1023. Inner fig.—*Magn. monsp.* 48. In vineyards and on walls.

2. CAPPARIS *Badueca.* Peduncles uhiflorous.-Leaves perennial, ovato-oblong, crowded in a determinate manner, naked. *L. sp.* 7'20. *BADXTKKA. Raii hist. 1630.* ,f '''' ..'. '.,'".. I' '' 3. CAPPARIS *cynophatlopliora.* Peduncles multiflarous, terminal. Leaves elliptic, obtuse, glabrous.

Glands axillary. Leaves oval, perennial. Fruit cylindric, torulose. *From L. a ff'i'l..* ii. 1136; *a Murr.* 488; *Sf sp.* T21; *mant.* 401. *Szoartz. obs.* 209. Breynia fruticosa, foliis oblongis obtusis. *Browno* 246. *t. 21. f.* 1. Acaciis affinis arbor siliquosa, folio subrotunrlo singu lari, flore stamineo albido, siliqua tereti ventricosa cujus interior tnnica est muscosa et eleganter mU niata. *Shane cat.* 153. CAPPARIS cynophallophora. *Wright in med. journ.* viii. 233.

Stalagrailis. *L. a Schreb.* n, 1585.

I. CAMBOGIA *solitaria.*

Gottaefera vera. *Koen. ap. Murr. appar.* iv. 655.

In Siam and Ceylon.

Stalagmitis cambogioides. *L. a Willd.* iv. 980.

GAMBOGIA. Gum resin. *Pharm. lond.-Alst.* ii. 432. *Biss. ess.* i. 188. *Cull.* ii. 542. *Dune. cases* 33t. *Jteb.* 190. *Lew,* i. 450; *disp. by Dure.* 308. *Mill. Jos.* 209. *Monro* ii. 427.

Neum. H. 29. *Rutty* 216. *Wintr. in Mead* i. 277. Cambogium. *Dale* 326. (The botanical authors referred *to* treat of Garcinia sulcata.) C. Gutta. *Murr. J.* i. 276. 380. *Pears. R.* i. 198. *Woodt,* iv. 165. Stalagmitis cambogioides. *Pears.*

R. ii. 259. Gumrai Gutta. *Berg,* 461. *Brookes nat. hist.* vi. 86. *Carth.* ii. 463. *Geojfr.* ii. 678. *Hill* 776. JArfU 161. *Feg.* 325. Gummi Guttae. *Beck, account from in phys.journ.* xi. 434. *Murr.* iv. 106. 654; *ap. commentat. gott.* be. 175, *and account from in med. comment,* xiv. 180. *Pears. R.* i. 198. *Ploucq. bill,* i. 657. *Quar. anim.* 155. *Spielm.* 614. Gutta Gamba. *Ilcrm.* 684. Ghitta Jemou. *Schrod.* 781. Gamboge. *Campet, account from in ann. med. Iustr. II.* ii. 130. *Ferriar* i. 67.92; ii. 154. *Fordyce, G. in tr. impr.* ii. 332. *Rush* iii. 245. 249; iv. 89. Gomme-guite. *Chom.* 72. . 548. ACTAEA. *Petals* 4. *Calyx* tetraphyllous. *Berry* and *capsule* unilocular, polyspermous. *Seeds* semiorbicular. *Obs.* 8250. 4140. L. 1. ACTAEA *corymbosa.* Flowers corymbose. Fruit a berry. *Obs.* 8250. Specimen gathered in Fo.-thergill's garden.

A. spicala. *L. sp.* 722. *Hort. kern.* ii. 221. *л nigra.* Berries black. *From authors.—L. sp. a.* A. spicata. *L. suec. n.* 464. *Scop. earn. n.* 633. . *Host* 289. *Poll. n.* 503. *Gou. hort.* 251. Near

Montpelier.—*But. arr.* 546. *Smith brit.* 562. *Fl. dan. t.* 498. *Huds.* 238. In a wood near Clapham in Yorkshire.

A. caule inermi. *L. lapp. n.* 217. '

Actaea. *Dalib.* 152.

Christophoriana vulgaris nostras, raccmosa et ramosa.

Boerh. ii. 62. Christophoriana. *Raii syn.* 262, to whom it was shewn by William in Haselwood woods in York. " shire, and found by Newton Lawson and Richard' son in Mathani Cove near Settlc in Yorkshirc.— *Dod.* 397, *repr. in* Clus. *hist.* ii. 86, *Sf Ger. by Johns.* 979, *Sf cop. in* Chrisiophoriana vulgaris. *Park, theatr.* 379. Napellus racemosus. *Dahch.* 1747. Aconitum racemosum, A. quibusdam *Bauh, J.* iii. 660. *Calyx* caducous; phylla oblongo obovaf e. *Pc tals* unguiculatc, one third shorter than the calyx; laminae elliptic, thrice as long as the ungues, triplinervose. *Obs.* 8250. *Native* of Germany, France, Scandinavia, and the north-west quarter of Yorkshire, a district consisting of limestone and gritstone mountains, and found at Tborparch in the plain below on limestone. ACTAEA spicata. *Krock.* ii.

n. 812. *0 alba.* Berries white. *Hort. kew.* ii. 221. £. *L. sp.* p ACTAEA spicata. *Schoepf85. Native* of North America. 7 *rubra.* Berries red. *Hort, kew. y* ACTAEA. *Cutl.* 454. 2. ACTAEA *racemosa.* Flowers racemose. Fruit dry. *Obs.* 4140. In a garden.—*L. sp.* 722. *Hort. kew.* ii. 221. *Michaux* i. 308. *Calyx* tetraphyllous, caducous; phylla whitish, Bubrotundo-obovate, concave. *Petals* or *Neciaria* 4, minute, unguiculate, deciduous; white; laminae ovali-cuneiform, with two horns at the end fleshy; horns irregularly curved. *Stamina* as large as the petals, white. *Germen* ovate, unilocular, polyspermous. *Obs.* 8765. In a garden. ACTAEA. *Grofi. virg.* 79.—*Bart.* 9. *Berg.* 430. *Linn.* 159. ScAoep/85. *Vog.* 215. 549. SANGUINARIA. *Petals* 8. *Calyx* diphyllous. *Capsule* unilocular. *Obs.* 7758. *L.* 1. SANGUINARIA *canadensis. L. sp.* 72J. *Gron.*

virg. iil 80; *ed.* i. 57. *Hort. kew.* ii. 222. *Curt,*

mag. t. 162.

Chelidonium maximum acaulon canadense. *Rati*

hist. 1887.

VoL. 3. 31

Ranunculus virginiensis albus. *Park, theatr.* 320. Chelidonium maximum cauadense acaulon. *Corn,* 212. SANGUINARIA. *Bart.* 28. Coxc376. *Cull.* 455. *Schoepf* 86. Bleeding root. *Mather in ph.. tr. abr, by Jones* V. *part* ii. 160; *8j by Hutt.* vi. 86. « *minus.* Petals from 6 to 8 tenths of as inch long'. *Obs.* 8260. Specimen gathered by Dr. Cutler in New England. Sanguinaria. *Cutl.* 455. S. minor, florc simplici. ' '*Dill. hort.* 335. *t.* 252. *f.* 326. '' ' *fi major.* Petals from 1 inch 1 tenth to 1 inch 4 tenths long. *Obs.* 7758. In Mr. Knowlton's garden. S. major, flore simplici. *Dill. hort.* 335. *t.* 252. *f.* 325.

Leaf septemlobate, trincrvate, rorid; lobes cuneiform, the middlemost mostly semitrifid, segments obtuse and rounded; lateral lobes trapeziform, obtusely crenate. *Scapus* uniflorous. *Bractea* I, transversely oval, sessile, white, inserted about two thirds from the base of the scapus. *Petals* white, lanceolato oblong, concave, unequal in breadth. *Capsule* elliptic, tetragonous; sutures pubescent, prominent. *Seeds* round, inserted into the sutures, in 2 and *2* rows. *Obs.* 7758. 550. PODOPHYLLUM. *Petals 0. Calyx* triphyllous. *Berry* unilocular, crowned by the stigma. *L.* 1. PODOPHYLLUM *peltatum.* Leaves peltate, partite. *Obs.* 8251. Specimen gathered in Fothergill's garden.—*L. sp.* 723; *a Murr.* 489. *Ilort. kew.* ii. 222. , Anapodophyllum canadense Morini. *Boerh.* ii. 72.

Anapodophyllum canadense. *Cat.* i. *t.* 24.

Leaves 2, at the end of the stem, scarcely peltate, partite to near the base. *Flower* at the junction of the petioles. *Obs.* 23S4. *POD OPH YLL UM. Schoepf* 86.

P. peltatum. *Bart.* 31. S7. 40. *Coxe* 374.

Anapodium. *Dule* 421. *col.* 1. *par.* 1. 551. CHELIDONIUM. *Calyx* diphyllous. *Petals* 4. *Capsule* linear, bivalve and trivalve. *Obs.* 4018. *L.* 1. CHELIDONIUM *Glaucium.* Peduncles uniflorous. Capsule bdocular, bivalve. Stem glabrous. *Obs.* 7544. Specimen gathered by Mr. Boraston on the sea beach at Teignmouth in Devonshire.— *Obs.* 7545. In Saville's garden.—*L. sp.* 724. *Krock. n.* 814. *Fl. dan. t.* 585. *Bot. arr.* 548. *Smith engl. t.* 8. Glaucium luteum. *Scop. earn. n.* 635. *Smith brit.* 563. Glaucium flore luteo. *Tourn. parts.* 336. In old sand pits at the end of the plain of Bercy.— *Vaill. paris.* 81, between Bercy and Charenton. Papaver sylvestre corniculatum. *Trag.* 123. Papaver corniculatum, *Fuchs. fol.* 520, *cop. in* 504. c. 198, %

Papaver corniculatum luteum. *Bank. J.* iii. 398. *Raii hist.* 857; *syn.* 309. Perennial. Found by Richardson among rocks near the summit of Gribgogn a lofty mountain near Llanberris.

Papaver corniculatum majus. *Dod.* 445, who says it sometimes continues for several years; *repr. in*

Papaver corniculatum flavo flore. *Clus. hist.* ii. 91,

Papaver corniculatum flore luteo. *Ger. by Johns.* 367. Papaver corniculatum luteum. *Park, theatr.* 262. Papaver cornutum. *Dalech.* 1712.

Leaves, the lower pinnatifid, the uppermost sinuate. *Germen* scabrous. *Obs.* 7546.—*Capsules,* those in which the valves separating from the dissepiment glabrous, those which entire scabrous. *Seeds* nearly reniform, reticulate; meshes disposed in semicircles. *GLAUCIUM. Schoepf* 87. *Vog.* 102. Papaver cornutum. *Geoffr. suite* i. 314. Papaver corniculatum. *Dale* 209. Papaver corniculatum majus. *Chom.* 240. Papaver corniculatum luteum. *Newton in ph. it. abr. by Lowth.* ii. 642; *by Hutt.* iv. 295. 2. CHELIDONIUM *umbelliferum.* Flowersr umbellate. *Obs.* 401.8. In hedges near houses. C. majus. *L. suec. n.* 465 on rubbish; *sp.* 723. *Wale. t. FL dan. t.* 542. *Bot. arr.* 547. *Smith brit.* 563. *Asso n.* 453. On rubbish.—*Gou. hort.* 252. Corn fields and sides of roads.—*Host* 289. In hedges, and on the borders of woods. —*Scop, earn. n.* 634. On the sides of roads, and on rocks. —*Roth germ.* i. 228. In hedges, and on walls and rubbish.—*Lour.* i. 402. *Woodv.* iv. 134. *t.* 263. *Raii hist.* 858. *Dod.* 48, *repr. in Ger. by Johns.* 1069, *Sf cop. in C.* majus vulgare. *Park, theatr.* 617. *Tourn. parts.* 15. *Vaill. paris.* 35. *Boerh.* i. 305. In Hoi. land. C. majus. *Fuchs.* 821. *c.* 332, *cop, in* Chelidonia. *Bauh. J.* iii. 482. Chelidonion majus. *Trag.* 107. Papaver corniculatum luteum, Chelidonia dictum. *Jtaii syn.* 309. *Capsule* unilocular. *Obs.* 4018. *CHELIDON1UM. Alst.* i. 407. *Ploucq. bibl.* i. 34. 176. 228. 234. 244. 253. 289. 481. 606. C. majus. *Pharm. suec. austriaco-prov.* 29.—*Berg.* 431. *Dale* 210. *Geoffr.* iii. 309. *Krock. n.* 813. *Lew.* i. 328; *disp.* 124; *by Dune.* 340. *Linn.* 160. *Mill. Jos.* 132. *Murr.* ii. 300. *Quar. anim.* 173. i&ittylSl. *Schoepf* 86. *Schrod.* 562. Sp/efoi. 557. Fog-. 59. 233. *lVendt, account from in phys. journ.* xi. 139, *and chir. rev.* xi. *part* ii. 27. C. majus vulgare. *Chom.* 414; *suppl.* 127, Chynlen, *Berg.* 908. /«rr. vi. 153. 552. PAPAVER. *Petals* 4. *Calyx* diphyllous. *Capsule* semimuUilocular, opening by pores underneath the stigma. *Obs.* 5315. *L.* 1. *Capsules* glabrous. *L.* 1. PAPAVER *amplexicaule.* Calyces glabrous. Leaves amplexicaul, incise. *Obs.* 942. In a garden.

P. somniferum. *L. sp.* 726. *Hort. hew.* ii. 224.

Bot. arr. 552. *Smith brit.* 568, in corn fields and on rubbish, scarcely indigenous; *engL t. 1399. Huds.* 231. Corn fields.—*Gou. hort.*253. Near Montpelier.—*Reich, franc. n.* 313. On the sides of roads, the refuse of gardens. P. capsula, flore, folio lato glabro pallido, maximis.

Boerh. i. 279.

Papaver. *Trag.* 122...

P. sativum. *Rati hist.* 853. *Fuchs.* 502. c. 197, *cop. in.* i

P. silvestre. *Dalech.* 1711, peduncles improperly represented as hirsute; *Sf* Hypecoum siliquosum. *Bauh. J.* ii. 899. Peduncles glabrous. (The name and descr. belong to

Hypecoum.) *Filaments* dilated upwards, cuspidate at the end. *Obs.* 942. *Native* of the old continent, naturalised in the southern parts of Europe, and seminaturalised in England. PAPAVER somniferum. Capsule, and its inspissated juice. *Pharm. edin.*—*Krock. n.* 821. *Lew disp. by Dune.* 270. *Murr. J.'.* 117; ii. 54. *Pears. R.* ii. 216. 239; *ed.* ii. 333. 349. 489. Papaver. *Boerh.* 359. *Cels.* 239. /. 4. c. 24. *Ploucq. bibl.* i. 72. OPIUM. *Pharm. lond.*—*A ashore in act. haun.* i. 162. *Abernethy, account from in Und.* ii. 75. *Adair in vied, comment,* ix. 211. *Aitk.* 118. 125. 127. 128. 134. 154. 174. 210. *Alst.* ii. 455, *and in med. ess.* v. 93. *Atkins, in phys. journ.* viii. 50; xi. 516. *Awsiter in med. mus.* i. 473. *Babington in med. commun.* i. 219; *med. rec.* 117. 132. *Barlow in phys. journ.* ii. 107. *Barllet ib.* xii. 3. *Bedd. in med. facts* v. 17. *Berg.* 453. *Berlinghieri, account from in med. rev.* viii. 324. *Blair, account from in ckir. rev.* v. 149. *Blanc* 394. 404. 408. 412. 422. 454. 455. 475. 478. 482. 490. 504. 522. 533. 540. *Boerh. aph. n.* 1402. *Brandreth in med. comment, dec. II.* vi-S83, *repr. in new med. journ.* i. 229. *Bree* 250. 251. 252. 254. 258. 278. 284. 285. 287. 190. 291. 311. 323. 350. 354. 372, *and account from in chir. rev.* vii. 280. *Brera in ann. med.* iii. 192. *Bromf.* i. 132. *Brown* i. 108. 150. 151. 181. 198. 225. 231. 232. 241. 253. 265. 282. 285. 320. 349. 357; ii. 15. 290. *Callisen in act. haun.* i. 421. *Cappel-account from in med. rev.* iv. 44. *Carth.* ii. 526. *Cayley in phys. journ.* xv. 337. *Chalm.* i. 10.1. 102. 108. 119. 120. 129. 156. 158. 165. 203. 212; ii. 28. 40.

46. 156. 166; *in med. obs.* i. 104. *Chaxasse in med. comment*, ix. 374. *Chiarenti, account from in phys. journ.* ii. 467, and *chir. rev.* iv. 566. *Chiarugi, account from in ann. med.* iii. 194. *Chir. rev.* ix. 159. *Chish.* 159. 172. 176. 272. *Chom.* 775. *Clark, James, account from in ann. med.* ii. 167, 178; *J. long 'coy.* i. 176. 182. 184; ii. 398. *Clegh.* 250 to 252. 254. 255. *Clephanc in med. obs.* i. 53. *Clerk in phys. ess.* iii. 121. *Cole in phys. journ.* vii. 55. *Collier ib.* v, 164. *Cooper, account from in chir. rev.* xi. 333. *Copland in med. facts* iv. 118. *Coste in med. journ.* ix. 7. *Cox, account from in chir. rev.* xi. 300. *Crawford, J. in Troll,* ii. 96. *Crossfield in new med. journ.* i. 360. *Crowther in phys. journ.* ii. 512. *Crumpe, account from in ckir, rev.* i. 324. 389, *Cull,* ii. 224; *clin.* 79. 83. 91. 158. 276. 283. 300. 306. 308. 312; *pract. n.* 1198. 1221. 1397. 1434.1445. 1471.1480.1541.1571.1828. *Currie, James in Rollo* 147; *W. account from in med. rev.* vi. 64. *Dallas in ann. med.* iii. 324. *Dancer, account from in med. rev.* vii. 504. *Darw.* ii. 16. 23. 29. 31. 41. 43, 44. 47. 52. 65 *p* 68. *71.* to 73. 78. 79. 87. 99. 100. 102. 108. 111. 114. 117. 118. 125. 127 *to* ISO. 132. 133. 135 *to* 138. 144. 152. 153. 155. 157. 160. 162. 182. 185. 198. 203 *to* 205. 208. 209. 216. 217. 222. 223. 245. 251. 252. 256. 262. 269. 273. 277. 292. 298. 302. 304. 308. 310. 314. 324. 327. 329. 331. 33L 336. 337.341.344 *to* 346. 359 *to* 362. 392. 441. 449. 460. 462. 479. 487. 489. 494. 495. 497. 500. 501. 506. 514. 516. 522. 524. 529. 535, 678. 706. 710. 7i6. 721. 722. 724. 725. 731. 745. 748. 749. *Varies in phys. journ.* xvi. 496. *Daws, in lett.* 290. 292. *Denm.* 1. 176. 272. 275; ii. 422. 476. *Dickins.* 177. *Dobs, in med. mus.* i. 62. *Docker in phys. journ.* iii. 102; vii. 258. *Dune. F. account from ib.* ix. 184. *Falcon, in med. soc.* ii. *2H3. Farr in med. obs.* iv. 92. *Fergus, account from in med. rev.* vii. 136. *Ferr.* i. 18. 174. 175; iii. 89. *90. Fordyce, G. fev.* i. 203; ii. 60. 145. 150; iii. 2S4; v. 81. *93.102;* vi. 28. 40; *pract.* 152. 154. 156. 208. 297. *330.* 360. 361; *W. fragm.* 20. *Fotherg. J. in med. obs.* vi. 79. *Foule, account from in med. rev.* iv. S47. *Founiier, account from ib.* vi. 400.

Foal. R. in çontrib. 517, *and account from in aim. med.* iv. 161. *Gassner, account from in phys. journ.* xiv. 524. *Geoffr.* ii. 687. *Glosler in med. comment,* i. 72, *Goodie. W. in phys. journ.* iii. 442. *Graing.* 41. 44. 51. *Grant, Alex, in med. journ.* v. 1. 130. *Hamilt. James, jun. in. ann. med.* v. 339; *Mob. of Ipsw. in med. journ.* v. 75. 190; *Rob. pf Lynn in med. comment,* ix. 195. *Hammick in fontrib.* 383. *ffasl. insan.* 147. *Henry, T. in phys. journ.* ii. 103. *Hey, account from in chir. fev.ix.* 71. *Heb.* 5. 6. 13. 48. 55. 61. 64. 79. 87. 88. 90. 92. 95. 121. 128. 164. 168. 184. 194. 204. 207. 214 *to* 216. 227. 233. 236. 262. 305. 309. 314. 321. 334. 346. 347. 349. 352. 374. 415, *Herm.* 624. *Hill* 779; *G. in phys. journ.* ix. I53: x. 532; xi. 436. *Hillary* 192. *Home, Ever rard account from in ann. med.* iii. 55, *and chir, rev.* xi. 416; *F. din.* 50.88.200. 321. *Hope in phys. journ.* iii. 413. *Huck in med. obs.* iii. 326, *Hufeland, account from in med. rev.* ii. 453, *Huggan in phj/s. journ.* ii. *S33;* iii. 57. 539, *Hull phlegm.* 217. 221. 276. 280 *to* 285. 294. 333, *Hume in lett.* 231. 239. *Hunt, account from in chir. rev.* x. 243. *Hunt. J. ven.* 46. 79. 89. 118, 231. 234; *in Pringle* 275; *J. jam.* 252. 259, 260. 261. *Jacks. H. account from in chir, rev,* xTiii. 62; *Rob. fev,* 258. 261. 273. 319. 321; *Jam.* 224. 226. 236. 278. 283. 333; *account from in chir. rev.* x-437. *Jacobs, account from in med. rev.* viii. 169. *Jo/ inst. James account from in chir. rev.* ii. 360. 365. *Josse in ann. med.* iii. 259. *Kinglake in phys. journ.* y. 437. *Kirkl, apopl.W.* 93. *96.* 98. 99 *to* 124. 140. 144. 154, 169. 178. 180. *Knebel, account from in phys. journ.* iv. 83. *Kok, account from in med. rev,* vi, 405. *I. afondgouzi, account from in chir. rev.* xi, 394. *Lassus, account from in phys. journ.* Y« 491. *Latham, account from in chir. rev.* iii. 410. *Leigh, account from in mcd. comment, dec. II.* i. 397. *Lempr. U.* 178. 180.181.215.217.222. 225. 227. 228. 229. 26S. *Lew.* ii. 161. *Lind hot dim.* 26. 281.318; *seam.* 260. 261. *Linn.* 161. *Macgregor, account from in chir. rex.* xi. 50. *Mackie in med. comment, dec. II.* x. 304. *Maclean* 125. 144. 163. 168. 169; *account from in ann. med.* ii. 202, *and med. rev.* v. 171. *Macleish in*

ann. med. ii. 408. *Marcus, account from in phys. journ.* ix. 269. 270. 271. 306. *Mason in med. obs.* vi. 19. *Mather in med. facts* iv. 102, *May* 14. 28. 46. 59. *Med. comment,* x. 361. *Meadmon.* ii. 56. 152. *Mease* 114, *and account from in phys. journ.* viii. 88. *Michaelis in med. commun.* i. 307; *account from in med. rev.* iv. 150, *and phys. journ.* viii. 442. *Mihles ess.* i. 302. *Milne, account from in chir. rev.* x. 495. *Monro* ii. 400; *sold.* i. 351.356; ii. 92.9S-.245. 254. *Mos.* 223. 490. *Mossman in phys. jiwrn.* x. 16. *Murr.* ii. 215; *J.* i. 318. *Mursinna, account from in phys. journ.* vi. 280. *Neum.* ii. 40. *Oberne in phys. journ.* x. 39. *Odier in med. comment.* yi. 352. *Pears. J. in med. obs.* vi. 246; *med. commun.* ii. 56, *and account from in ann. med. lustr. II.* i. 270, 8c *med. comment, dec. II.* vi. 217. *Peart inf.* 17. 20. 23. 33, *St account from in phys. journ.* viii. 472, *Sf chir. rev.* x. 289. *Perch. T.* i. 421; ii. 195. 342. *Perfect, account from in med. rev.* vii. 42. *Ploucq. bibl.* i. 79. 124. 131. 194. 221. 249. 265. 268. 308. 316. 533, ' 336. 351. 353. 357. 370. 425. 462. 464. 485. 495. 501. 506. 516. 520. 524. 543. 548. 559. 566. 574. 587. 620. 644. 696. 699. *Pop, account from in chir, rev,* x. 393. *Portal, account from in phys. journ.* iv. 570. *Pott* iii. 96. 97. 302. 361. *Power, G. account from in chir. rev.* x. 15'4. *Pringle* 132. 144. 152. 166. *Quar. anim.* 21. 90. 92. 93. 109. 206. 218. 221. 228 232. 234. 251. 254. 263266. 282; *febr.* 36. 40. 43-59. *60.* 126. 135. 136. 173. 286. 287. 308. 356. 366. 382. 392. 402. 404. 408. *Quierin lett.* 126. 132. 174. 181. *Reid, J. in phys. journ.* x. 345. *ReiUy in Trott.* ii. 129. 142. *Remmett, account from in med. comment.* ii. 19. *Richt. account from in chir. rev.* i. 94. *River, obs. I.* 1. c. 12. *Roberts, jail fev.* 373. *Rollo* 27. 102. 112. 378. 401. *Rush* i. 115. 136. 145. 195. 201; ii. 287. 320; v. 176. 180 *to* 182. 188; *account from in chir. rev.* viii. 369; xii. *part* ii. 39. *Rutty* 364; *8f in med. obs.* iii. 232. *Sabatier, account from in arm. med.* iv. 202, *Sf med. rev.* iv. 51. *Schonheyder in act. haun.* i. 168; ii. 445, *c account from in med. comment. dec. II.* viii. 141. *Schrod.* 728. *Schumacher, account from in phys.*

journ. vii. 81. *Seaman, ac count from ib.* iii. 574, *Sf chir. rev.* vii. 486. *Sibbern $ Winsl. in act. haun.* i. 425. *Sims, James, epid.* 2t. 46. *Smith, E. in ph. tr. abr. by Lowth.* ii. 643; *by Hutt.* iv. 101, *and in Mihles ess.* i. 185, *which repr. in Med. mus.* i. 142. *Spielm.* 516. *Steidele account from in journ. de med.* lxxxv. 104. *Stichel, account from in med. rev.* i. 573. *Stone account from in chir. rev.* xiii. 180. *Stoll aph. n.* 82. 235. 372. 715; *med.* ii. 149. 235. 283. 284. 287 *to* 292; iii. 13. 4Q. 149. 153. 264. 272. 285. 286. 318. 324. 420. 423. *Szeiet. account from in med, journ.* iv. 146, *Tainsh in phys. journ.* v. 539, *Sr chir. rev.* viii. 86. *Thomas, account from in med. rev.* viii. 103. *Thuessink, account from in journ- de med.* Ixx. 515, *Sr med. comment,* x. 146. *Trotter, account from in chir. rev.* iv. 11, 14; x. 286. *Und.* i. 44. 190. 193. 318. S31. *Unzer, account from in phys, journ.* ii, 169. *Urvins ib.* iii. 228. *Valentine, account from in chir. rev.* xi. 240. *Vaume, account from ib.* iii. 392. *Vog.* 332. *Ward in phys. journ.* i. 441; ii. 6; vi. 431. 478; vii. 124. 341.497; viii. 324. 388; ix. 335; xi. 111.538. *Ware epiph.* 28; *ophth.* 50.53. *Warner, W. in phys. journ.* vii. 305. *Washbourn in med. rev.* ii. 199. *Wavell in med. rec.* 142. 151. *Weber in phys. journ.* x. 435. 501. *Whately ulc.* 52. 64. 118, *Sf in med. obs.* vi. 331. *White, W. of Bath in phys. journ.* vi. 387; viii. 16. *Willan lond,* 180. 326. *Willick A.* 339. *Willis, &c. in ph. tr. abr. by Jones* v. *part* L 357, *by Ilntt.* iv. 634, *Sr in Mihles ess.* i. 302. *Wilson, C. in phys. journ.* xi. 145. *Wintr. in Mead* i. 167. 207. 246. 269; ii. 244. 248 *to* 250. 255. 262. *Wright in enn. med.* ii. 357. *Yeats in ann. med. lustr. II..* iii 394. *Young opium* 30 *to* 157,

Jjlxtractum thebaicum. *Fordyce, G. pr.* 308. 328. *Hillary* 160. *Mead mon.* i. 131. 132. 136. *Pringle* 208. 271. 273.

Laudanum. *Quar. febr.* 209. *River, obs. I.* 1. *c.* 63. *Stoll med.* i. 63. 127. 134. 139. *Syd.* 423.

TINCTURA Opii. *Brown, W. account from in thir. rev.* x. 281. *Clark, J. long toy.* 394. *Crawford, J. in Trott.* ii. 92. *Darw.* ii. 195. 234. 731. *Denm.* ii. 35. 474. *Heb.* 13. 90. 91. 131. 132. 135. 148. 152. 153. 160. 161. 274. 282.322, S28. 337. 357. 360. 367. 40.5. *Hull caes.* 347, 351. *Okes in phys. journ.* xyi. 575. *Und.* i. 159. 161. 170; ii. 40. 145. 152. *Wright in ann. med.* ii. 368. *Yates, account from in med. rev.* i. 342.

Tincture of Opium. *Darw.* ii. 196. *Gapper in phys. journ.* vi. 17, *Hoven, account from in med. . rev.* ii. 363. *Lempr.* ii. 124. 125. 192. *Taylor sea wat.* 66. *Warren in Blane* 532. *Willan land.* 284. 294.

Tinctura Ihebaica. *Biss. ess.* 163, *Bromf.* i. 14*Brown* i. 278. 327. *Clarkson in phil. coll.* i. 69. *Daniel in med. journ.* v. 183. *Darw-*ii. 200. *Hunt. J.ven.* 88; *jam.* 113. 118. 225. 237. *Lind hotclim.* 2t&; *seam.* 249. 276. *Macaulay in med. obs.* ii. 132. *Monro, Don. sold.* i. 4. 310. *Noble, account from in chir. rev.* x. 399. *Paterson ix, Pringle* 269. *Perciv. T.* ii. 405. *Petrie in med. tr.* iii. 165. *Ploucq. bibl.* i. 316. *Pringle* 162. 164. *Ware epiph.* 16. 40; *ophth.* 46. 56. 59. 75 o 85. 89. 95. 98. 128. 133. 150. 152. 157; *account from in med. journ.* i. 118, *Sf chir. rev.* T. 81. *Wintr. in Mead* i. 253. 277.

Laudanum liquidum. *Bang in act. haun.* i. 109. *Quar. febr.* 79. 93. 126. *Ranoe in act. haun-*i. 38. *Syd.* 423.

Liquid Laudanum. *Cull. din.* 279. *Fowl, T. art.* 90. 115. i?«««A.i. 152; iii. 293.

Laudanum..Ba«g *in act. haun.* i. 109. *Bassan in Blane* 528. B/o«c 484. 533. *Brown* i. 193. 361 *to* 364; ii. 162. 168. *Campet, account from in onn. med. lustr. II.* ii. 132, *Chalm.* i. 83. 129. 136. 140. 192. 202. 214; ii. 155. 159. 166. *Clegk.* 227. 229. *Cull. din.* 91. 92. *Darw.* ii. 27. 48. 51. 136. 138. 145. 185. 187. 188. 302. *Denm.* ii. 511. *Drummond, T. in med. comment, dec. II.* iv. 300. *Fordj/ce. G. pr.* 161. 187; *W. fen.* 165; *fragm.* 39. *Kausch, account from in med. rev.* iv. 191. *Lempr.* ii. 161. 180. 191. 19S. *Mos.* 487. 489. *PeHeton, account from in phys. joum.* ii. 482. *Perciv. T.* i. 356. *Pole in med. soc.* ii. 373. *Prtngle* 152. *Rush* i. 152; iii. 229. 288. 298. 303: iv. 101; v. 121. *Und.* i. 110. 117. 131. 134. 135. 185. 205. 2o: ii. 42.58. 190. *Vaugh. W. in med. soc.* ii. 130. *Wright in med. facts* vii. 13; *6(ann. med.* ii. 349., v

PULVIS opiatus. *Heb.* 94.. ELIXIR paregoricum.. *Mead mon.* i. 117. CONFECTIO opiata. *Geach, account from in med. rev.* i. 589. ELECTUARIUM Dioscordion. *Quar. febr.* 93. THERIACA Andromachi. *Daws, in lett.* 280. 290....

Theriaca. *Pringle* 306. 317. 410.

OPIATA. *Aaskow in act. hatm.*i. 309. *Fordyce, W. fragm.* 25. 70. 73. 91. *Heb.* 251. *Hoffm.* i. 78. *Quar. anim.* 35. 48. 114. 132. 158. 167. 281. 290. 295. 310; *febr.* 278. 283. 331. 425. *Stoll aph. n.* 320. 448. 829; *med.* ii. 37. 183; iii. 295. Opiates. *Aitk.* 141. 143. 150. 158. 160.161.175. 193. 202 *to* 204. 206. 209. *Blane* 390. 392. 424. 454. 455. *Brown* i. 268. 347. 349. *Chalm.* 3. 85. 90. 129. 189. 190. 205; ii. 35. 37. 79. *Clark, James account from in ann. med.* ii. 180, *Sf chir. rev.* iv. 289; *J. fev.* 28; *long voy.* 260. 396. *Cull. pr. n.* 231. 233. 299. 375. 395. 468.487. 570. 680. 581. 620. 648. 693. 802. 923. 924. 1066. 1083. 1424. 1461. 1503. *Darw.* ii. 69. 73. 235. 717. 723. 725. 742. 743. 748. *Denm.* i. 172. .254.268.335; ii. 270. 335. 397. 418.516.520. *Dickins.* 207. 208. *Fordyee, G. pr.* 173. 178. 236. 314. 323; TV. *fev.* 219. *Hall, R. in ami. tried,* iv. 339. *Hamilt. Rob. of Lynn, account from in chir. rev.* ix. 553. 555. *Hillary* 95. 209. 232. *Home, F. din.* 50. 55. 66. *Hull caes.* 244. *Hunt. J. ven.* 90. 91. 108. 164; *jam.* 128. 228. 235. 239. *Huxh. fev.* 37. 50. *Lind hot dim:* 92. 244. 261; *seam.* 202. 302. *Maegregor in ann. med.* iii. 343. *Monro, Don. sold.* i. 258. 289. 347. 373. 365; ii. 112. 170; *G. in hit.* 271. *Mos.* 215. *Paisley in ann. med. lustr. II.* i. 419. *Perciv. T. in Mease* 163, *Pringle* 232. 263. 266. 272. 274. 279. 284. 318; *app.* p. cviii. *Qukr in Ictt.* 145. *Rush* ii. 135. 242. 243. *Turn. tib.* 100. *Willan load.* 166. " Paregorica; *Quar. anim.* 49. 199; *febr.* 285. 320. Anodynes. *Blane* 422. *Mos.* 484. nigrum.

—Seeds brown. *Berg. mat. med. n.* 287. «. *L. sp.* (3. *Hort. fcew.* (3 P. somniferum. *Mill. Ph. diet. n.* 8. P. nigro semine sylvestris. *Magn. monsp.* 197.

On burnt up spots on Mount Capouladon. P. tortense, semine nigro, sylvestre Dioscoridis, nigrum Piinii. *Boerh.* i. 279. P. nigrum sativum. *Dod.* 442, *repr. in Lob. ic.* i. 274, *cop. in Dalech.* 1710, # *repr. in* P.

sativum nigrum. *Ger. by Johns.* 369. '
PAPAVER nigrum. *Berg.* 453. *Dale* 209.
Geofft. suite i. 325. *Lew.* ii. 179. *Linn.*
160. *Mill. Jos.* 330. *Murr.* ii. 215. *Rutty*
377. *Fog.* 164. :
P. sativum nigrum. *Schrod.* 640.

P. hortense, nigro semine, sylvestre Dioscoridis, rite grum Plinio. *Boccl. ap. Herm.* 437. *Chom.* 77K *P album.*— Seeds whiter *Berg, mat, med. n.* 287 & *L, sp. a. Hort. lew. a*

P. somniferum. *fVoodv.* iii. 503. *t.* 185. Ts

P. album. *Mill. Ph. diet. n.* 9, who observes that a capsule from which Opium had been extracted in Turkey was of a different shape from those of this species.—*Bduh. J.* iii. 590, Cultivated in gardens, and not unfrequently in fields, especially the smallest kind with a pale purple or blue corolla, and which is frequently seen as a weed in gardens.

P. spontaneum sylvestre et hortense. *Lob*-ic. L 274, *cop. in Daleck.* 1710, *and reft, in*

P. sylvestre. *Ger. by Johns.* 370. (mispr. 400.) *JRaii syn.* 308.!

P. spontaneum sylvestre. *Raii hist.* 854.

P. sativum Matthioli. *Dalech.* 1708. Peduncles erroneously represented as hirsute.

P. sativum. *Lob. obs.* 142, *repr. in*

P. album sativum. *Lob. ic.* i. 272,

P. sativum tertium. *JDod.* 442, #

P. sativum album. *Ger. by Johns.* 869, $ *cop. in*

P. sativum simplex nigrum. *Park, theatr.* 366.

P. simplex album sativum. *Park, theatr.* 365.

PAPAVER album. White Poppy. Capsule. *Pharm. lond.*—*Berg.* 453. *Blane* 395. *Boerh. aph.* «. 976. *Dale* 208. *Fordyce, G. pract.* 278. 279. *Heb.* 259. *Lew.* ii. 179. *Linn.* 160. *Mill. Jos.* 328. *Monro* iii. 193. *Murr.* ii. 215. *Sloll med.* iii. 149. *Swiet.* iii. 44. *Und.* i. 187. *309;* ii. 69. *Vog.* 164. *Willan lond.* 301.

P. sativum. *Carih.* i. 335. *Spielm.* 515..j.

P. borterise. *Rutty* 376.

P. sativum album., *Schrod.* 640.

P. hortense semine albo, sativum Dioscoridis, album Plinio. *Boecl. ap. Herm.* 437. *Chom.* 771.

Papaver. *Fordycet G. pract.* 207. *Herm.* 436.

Poppy. *Arnol in med. ess.* v. 90. *Blane*395. 485. 486. CAo/m. i. 102; ii. 36. 46. 106 121. 129. *Cull. clin.* 233. *Denm.* i. 74. *Home, Ever, ac count from in ann-med.* iii. 55. 56. *Hull phlegm.* 274. 295. *Perch. T.* ii. 405. *Ware epiph.* 40; *ophth.* 50. 51. 157.

"White Poppy. *Pringle* 137. 278. *Und. i.* 44. 102, 117. 123.318.323.

DIACODIUM. *Quar. febn* 287. 319. 320. Diacodion. *Wintr. in Mead mon.* ii. 250.

Syrupus Diacodion. *Fordyce, G. pr.* 256. 280.

Syrupus e Meconio. *Hillary* 90. *Pringle* 164. *Reidi T. pht/iis.* 177. 192. *Syd.* 426.

Syrup of White Poppies. *Und.* i. 44. *Vaume, account from in chir. rev.* iii. 399.

Syrup of Poppies. JB/ane395 2. PAPAVER Rhoeas. Capsules turbinato-obovate. Stem with many flowers. Peduncles with horizons tal hairs. Leaves bipinnatifid. *Obs.* 1576, In corn fields.—*L. sp.* 726; *suec. n.* 468. *Huds.* 230. *Lightf.* 279. *Woodv.* iii. 512. *t.* 186. *Kroch. n.* 820. *Curt. lond.* iii. 32. *t.* 215. J3*of. am* 551. *Smith brit.* 567; »gf. r. 645. *Lob. obs.* 143, *repr. in Get. by Johns.* 371, (mispr. 401,) *cop. in Park, theatr.* 366, # "?»"."

P. erraticum. *Dod.* 444.

P. laciniato folio, capitulo breviore glabro, annuum, Rhoeas dictum, *hail syn.* 308, VOL. 3. »

P. erraticum, inajus, foia; Dioscoridi Theophrasto Pli nio. *Tourn. paris.* 123. *Vaill. parts.* 156. P. erraticum alterum. *Fuchs.* 516 *fol. ed. cop. in* 500. c. 197. Argemone. *Trag.* 120. P. erraticum prinuin. *Fuchs.* 514. *ed. fol. cop. m* 500, r. 197, P. Rhoeas minus. *Dalech.* 439, # P. erraticum rubrum campestre. *Bauh. J.* iii. *b.* 395. The unexpanded flowers represented erect, the artist possibly conceiving the peduncles to be nodding in consequence of their having been faded. P. Rhoeas prius. *Dalech.* 438.

Corolla reddish scarlet. *Filaments* capillary, attenuate. *Stigma* convex; margin deflex, crenate; segments incumbent, roundish 8 and 9. *Obs.* 1576. RHOEAS. *Linn.* 160. *Murr.* ii. 212. *Quar.febr.* 43.

78. 287. 308. P. Rhoeas. *Berg.* 460. *Carlk.* iv. 248. *Spielm.* 520. *Swiet.* iv. 44. P. rubrum. *Dale* 209. *Mill. Jos.* 331. P. erraticum. Red Poppy. Petals. *Pharm. lond.*

—*Alst.* ii. 461. *Boulduc in ac. sc. dbr. by Southw.* iii. 282. *Geoffr. suite* i. 317. *Ilerm.* 609. *Lew.* ii. 183; *disp. by Dune.* 270. *Monro* iii. 192.

Murr. ii. 212. *Schrod.* 641. *Vog.* 118". 553. ARGEMONE. *Petals* 5 and 6. *Calyx* diphyllous and tripfayllous. *Capsule* unilocular, polyspermous, semivalvular. *L. a Cruel. L.* 1. ARGEMONE sexvalvis,—Capsules sexvalve. Leaves spinose. *L.* A. mexicana. *L. a Murr.* 490; *sp.* 727. *Hort» hem.* ii. 225. *Curt. mag. t.* 243. *Boerh.* i. 280. Argemonc. Browne 244. Papaver spinosum. *Bauk. J.* iii. *b.* 297. *Clus. hist.* ii. 93, *repr. in Ger. by Johns.* 371, (mispr. 401,) *$ cop. in* Papaver spinosum americanum. *Park, theatr.* 366. ARGEMONE mexicana. *Wright in med. journ.* viii. 225.

Glaucium. *Dale* 210.

Papaver spinosum. *Schoepf* 87.

Thistleseed. *Grain'g.* 9. 24. 35.

554. MAMMEA. *Petals* 4. *Calyx* bipartite, deciduous. *Berry* tetraspermous and trispermous. *From L. a Schreb.* # *Vahl. L.* 1. MAMMEA obtusifolia.— Leaves very obtuse, striate. Peduncles short. Berries tetraspermous. *Vahl.* Mammea. *Mill. Ph. diet.*

M. foliis ovalibus nitidis, fructu subrotundo scabro. *Browne* 249.

Malus persica maxima, foliis rotundioribus splendentibus glabris. *Sloane cat.* 179.

Arbor indica, Mamci dicta. *Raii hist.* 1665,

Mamei folium. *Dalech.* 1836.

MAMMEA americana. *L. a Willd.* ii. 1157; *sp.* 555. CLUSIA. *Calyx* imbricate; phylla from 4 to 16, opposite. *Petals* 4 to 6. *Stamina* 5 to many. *Style* none. *Stigma* peltate, with from 4 to la radii. *Capsule* unilocular, polyspermous, with from 4 to 12 valves. *Juss. L., Flowers* not unfrequently abortive from some imperfection in the antherae or pistil. *From L. and Juss..,.* 1. CLUSIA rosea. Leaves without veins. Petals 6. *L. sp.* 1495.— *Schoepf* 153. 2. CLUSIA /lava. Leaves without veins. Petals 4. *L. sp.* 1495. *H.*

K. iii. 432. Terebinthus folio singulari non alato rotundo succu lento. *Sloane cat.* 167. CLUSIA. *Browne* 236. *556.* AEGLE. *Petals* 5. *Cafyx* inferior, quinquelobate. *Style* short. *Stigma* oval. *Berry* decemlocular; cells polyspermous. *From Corr. in lin. tr. r.* 222. 1. AEGLE Marmelos. *Corr. ib.* 223. *Roxb.* ii. *23. t.* 143.
Cucurbitifera trifolia spinosa medica, fructus pulps cydonii aenuila. *Pluk. aim.* 125; *phyt. t.* 170. N. latea minor. *Dalech.* 1009. Leaves too acute.
/5. Cncurbitifera trifolia indica, fructus pulpa cydonii aemula. *Raii hist.* 1665. Covalira. *Rheede* iii. 57. *t.* 37. Bilacus. *Rumph.* i. 197. *t.* 81. CRATEVA Mannelos. *L. sp.* 637.—*Bry.* 192. Marmelle. *Thumb, trav.* iv. 179. Bilra. *Jones in as. res.* ii. 349? NYMPHAEA lutea. *Carth.* iv. 84. *Dale* 238. *Herrn.* 174. *Lea.* ii. 154. *Mill. Jos.* 318-*Rutty* 355. *Schrod.* 637. Spe/m. 462. Fog. 241. *With, in hot. arr.* 555.
N. lutea major. *Alst.* i. 484,
Nenuphar luteum. *Geqffr. suite* i. 205.
2. NYMPHAEA a#i. Calyx tctraphyllous, about as long as the corolla. Leaves cordate; margin entire. *Obs.* 4838. In a pool.—*L. suec. n.* 470; *sp.* 729. *Fl. dan. t.* 602. *Bot. arr.* 555. *Smith engl. t.* 160; *brit.* 570. *Ran hist.* 1320; sy«. 368. JDorf. 575, repr. *in Lob. obs.* 324; *ic.* i. 595, o«d Ger. *by Johns.* 819, # *cop. in* N. alba major vulgaris. *Park, thealr.* 1251.
N. calice tatrapbyllo, corolla multiplie!, £. /epp.
и. 219.
Leuconymphaea, N-alba major. *Boerh.* i. 281. In
Holland.
N. alba imjor. *Tourn. paris.* 507. *Vaill. paris.*
145. *Magn. monsp.* 188.
N. candida. *Luchs.* 555, «?. /o/, cop. t« 520. c. 204, zVflg. 69ti, *whir h repr. in*
N. alba. *Cord. fol.* 99, *p, I, %* cop. *in Bauh. J.* iii. 7ЧО. Leaves too acute.
N. major alba. *Dalech.* 1008.
N. latea majer. *Dalech.* 1009.
(N. foliis integerrimis cordatis, calyce tetrapbyllo,.
corolla multiplici. *Gron. virg.* 81,

N. ioliis cordatis integerrimis, calyce quadrifido.
Cutl. 456, 4
N. alba major. *Shane cat.* 120, will probably prove
N. odorata Hort. kew. ii. 227.
Native of Europe from Italy to Lapland, and possibly of America from the West Indies to New England.
NYMPHAEA alba. *Berg,* 463. *Carth.* iv. 84. *u Dale* 238. *Kroch, n.* 823. *Lew.* ¡i. 154; *disp.* ' 186. *Linn.* 162. *Mill. Jos.* 317. *Murr.* iii. 532. *Rutty* 355. *Sclwepf* 87. *Schrod.* 637. *Vog.* 154, 240. N. alba major. *Herrn.* 174. Nymphaea. *Alst.* i. 483. *Herrn.* 611. *Spielm.* 462. Nenuphar album. *Geoffr. suite* i. 202. 3. NYMPHAEA Zoíki. Calyx tetrapbylloug. Leaves cordate, dentate, glabrous; lobes approximate. *From L. a Willd.* ii. 1153; *sp.* 729.
N. foliis amplioribus profunde crenalis subtus areolars. *Browne* 243.
N. indica, ílore candido, folio in ambitu serrato. *Sloane cat.* 120.
N. alba major altera, sive Lotus aegyptia. *Park, theatr.* 1251, *cop. in*
Lotus aegyptia. *Stap.* 450.
N. alba major aegyptiaca, sire Lotus aegyptia. *Rati hist.* 1321.
NYMPHAEA Lotus. *Bry.* 12. Jone *in as. res,* iv. 293. 559. GRIAS, *Petals* 4. *Calyx* quadrifid. *Stigma* sessile, cruci form. *Drupe. Nut* with 8 furrows, L. probably from Browne.
. 1. GRIAS cauliflora. *L. sp.* 732. Swarts, *obs.* 215.
Drupe with 8 furrows. Nut oblong,.;,. Calophyllum. *Browne* 245.
GRIAS cauliflora. *Bry.* 251,
1. CALOPHYLLUM Inophyllum. Leaves oval; *L. sp.* 732. Bintangor maritima. *Rumph.* ii. 211. /. 71. PONNA. *Rait hist.* 1525. 2. CALOPHYLLUM Calaba. Leaves ovate, obtuse.
L. sp. 732. Jbcç. amer. erf. 8то, 346. *Swartz. obs.* 216. Arbor altissima, foliis oblongis nitidissimis ncrvosis.
Broome 37%. .. г: «
Mali persicae mameyae dictae folio longiorc arbor maxima, cortice sulcato cinéreo amaro. *Shane cat.* 180.. i ' Tsjerou-Ponna. *Raii hist.* 1537. BASTARD MAMMEE. *Long* 835.
561. TILIA. .'. Л. .i--.. *Calyx* pentaphyl-

lous. *Petals* 5. *Capsule* globular, with 5 cells and 5 valves, opening at the base. *Seeds,* seldom more than one coming to perfection. *Obs.* 4033. L.
I. TILIA *barbata.* Flowers without nectaria. Leaves cordato-ovale; axillae of the veins underneath barbate. *Obs.* 297. In an avenue. T. europaea. *Smith brit.* 571; *engl. t.* 610. *L. spy* 733. *Fl. dan. t.* $53. *Light/.* 280. In walks and avenues. The Lime tree. *Erel. by Hunt.* i. 195. *t. at p.* 194. The Linden tree and its seed. *Le Pluche not. del. üt.$li ....*
Tilia. *Dod.* 826, *repr. in*
T. foemina Theophrasti. *Lob. obs.* 606; *ic.* ii.
188, *cop. in* T. foemina major. *Park, theatr.* 1407, *Sf* T. foemina. *Park. par. t.* 609, /. 1, *and repr. in Ger. by Johns.* 1483. *Tab. ic.* 983. *Cam. epit.* 93. *Dalech.* 89. *m hirsutula.* Upper surface of the leaves hirsutulous. *From J. Bauh.* & *Scop.* T. europaea communis. *Hort. kew.* ii. 229 T. europaea *L. suec. n.* 471. *Gou. hort.* 254.
Near Montpelier.—MM. *Ph diet. n.* 2. T. platyphyllos. *Scop. cam. n.* 641. Tilia. *L. phil.* 259. T. foemina, folio majore. *Vail I. paris.* 192. *Magn. hort.* 166. *Boerh.* ii. 230. T. foemina. *Fuchs.* 818. *c. 331, imit. in* T. sativa. *Trag.* 1110, # T. vulgaris platyphyllos. *Bauh. J. i. b.* 133. *Rati hist.* 1694, not a native of Britain; *syn.* 473. In public walks and squares. —*Magn. monsp.* 254. In the fissures of rocks on Mount Capouladou.
Native of Carniola, Silesia, the Palatinate, France, and Sweden. TILIA. *Pharm. austriaco-prov.* 71. *&uec.—-Alst.* ii. 238. *Berg.* 467. *Cartk.* iv. 234. *Chmn.* 358; *suppl.* 110. *Geoffr. suite* iii. 196. *Herm.* 592. *Krotk; n.* 824. £«». ii. 436; tfrsp. fly *Mother.* 257V.Lin. 162. jtfi'tf. Jiw. 438. *Monro* iii. 281. il/«rr. iii. 527. *Ploucq. bibl.* i. 433. *Rutty* 518. SfcArorf.692;.Spfrfm. 348 Fog. 122. T. foemina. Z)a/e *330. fi parvifolia.* Leaves glabrous on the upper side. *Obs.* 297. *Sal. W.* 91. *Hort. kew.* ii. 229 y (where parviflora is probably a misprint for parvifolia.)late, staminiferous. *Pericarpium* cut round, polyspermous. L. T. parvifolia. *Smith engl. t.* 1705.
T. europaea. *Poll. n.* 510. *Roth germ,* ii-587. *Abb. n.* 390. In woods in Bed-

fordshire, rare.— *JReth. n.* 388, White wood near Gamlingay in Cambridgeshire.

T. cordata. *Mill. Ph. diet.* B. 1. In woods in many parts of England.

T. ulmifolia. *Scop. cam. n.* 642.

T. foenaina folio minore. *Magn. hort.* 196. *Boerh.* ii. 230. *Vaill. parts.* 192.

T. folio minore. *Bauh. J.* i. *b.* 137. (The fig. of the seminal leaves belongs to «) In the woods of the Pays des Vosges in Loraine and in Silesia.— *Rait hist.* 1695; *syn.* 473. In woods and hedge in Essex and Sussex, and observed by Lister in Lincolnshire.

T. nlmifqlia, semine bexgono. *Dill. ap. Raii syn.* 473. Observed by Merret at Whitstable and Darking in Surry.— *Rupp. ab Hall.* 100.

T. sytvestris. *Trag.* 11U. No fig.

Leaves obliquely and obsoletely truncate at the
hase, acuminate, from 3 to 3 inches long. *Obs.* 297.

Native of Carniola, Silesia, the Palatinate, Loraine, Sussex, Essex, Oxfordshire, Worcestershire in Hurcot wood near Kidderminster) and in woods on both sides oi the Severn between Kidderminster and Worcester, Bedfordshire, Cambridgeshire, Lincolnshire, and in a hedge near the eastern extremity of the Marklands, a common near Clown in Derbyshire. TILIA focmiaa folio minore. *Cod. tned. p.* cxvii» —*Dale* 330. 562. GREUIA. Petals 5. Nectaria 5. *Calyx* ppntaphyllous and quinquedentate. *German* on a columnar receptacle. *Berry* quadrilocular. *Obs.* 5571, *Sf from L.* 4 *L. JU.* 1. *Calyx pentaphyllous.* 1. GREUIA orientalis. Flowers solitary. Leaves sublanceohte. *L. sp.* 1367. //. *K.* iii. 314. *FRUTEX* baccifer malabaricus, fructu plano-rotundo piloso tetrapyreno. *Rati hist.* 1624.

"!j/ ' ' -il..'..,
. x;.

563. MICROCOS.

..., Ca/yx pentaphyllous. Petals 5-Nectarium none. *Drupe. Nut* trilocular. Z,. a WiYW. Z» 1. MICROCOS *paniculata. L. sp.* 733. Grewia Microcos. *L. a Murr.* 827. *SCHAGERI COTTAM. Raii hist.* 1553. -mil ni ami 564. AUGIA. . *n* '.. Petals 5. *Calyx* inferior, truncate. *Drupe* orbicu

ar. 1. AUGIA *sinensis.* From Zo«r. i, 411. 565. ELAEOCARPUS. *Petals* 5, hcerate. *Antkerae* with 2 valves at the.-end. *Calyx* pentaphyllous. *Drupe* with a curled nucleus. *L.*

"... . ' ' 1. ELAEOCARPUS *serrata.* Leaves alternate, lanceolato-elliptic, serrate. Racerai axillary. *L. a Willd.* ii. 1169; *sp.* 734. *Retz. obs.* iv. 27.. Leaves obovate. Specimen gathered by Koenig in India. Olea sylvestris malabarica, fructu dulci. *Raiihitt.* 1546. GANITRUS. *Rumph.* iii. 160. *t.* 101.

2. ELAEOCARPUS *integrifolia.* Leaves entire at the margin. Racemi axillary. From *L. a Willd.* ii..,1170.-.....;.. GANI-TRUM oblongum. *Rumph.* iii. 163. *t.* 102. S. ELAEOCARPUS *copallifera.* Leaves entire at the margin. Panicle terminal. From *Ret2. obs.* iv.
' 27,4-L.o *Willd.* ii. 1170..
Vateria indica. *L. sp.* 734.

Amygdalae affinis indica, fructu umbilicato, nuclea nudo cortice pulvinato trifido tecto. *Rail hist.* 1482.

COPAL orientale. *Schreb. ap. Linn.* 285. 1. LECYTHI9 *Ollaria.* Leaves sessile, cordato-ovate, mostly entire at the margin. *L. a Murt.* 494; *sp.* 734. NUCIFERA brasiliensis, cortice fructus ligneo quatuor nuccs continente. *Rati hist.* 1677.

2. LECYTHIS *minor.* Leaves petiolate, lanceolate, serrate. *L. a Murr.* 494.—*J acq. amer.* 8w, 210. 567. XYLOPIA. *Calyx* tridentate and quinquedentate. *Petals* 6. *Capsule* unilocular, monospermous. From Browne. *L.* (*Juss.* 284, *Sf L. a Schreb. n.* 946, has a triphyllous calyx, and from 2 to 15 gennina and cap sules.) 1. XYLOPIA *glabra.* Peduncles mostly uniflorous.
Fruit glabrous. *L-sp. 1367.* XYLOPICRUM foliis amplioribus nitidis ovatis, petiolis brevibus, fructibus glabris. *Browne* 251.
Bitter wood. *Lows* 819.

a 568. THEA. *Calyx* triphyllous to hexaphyllous. *Petals* mostly 6. *Capsule* tricoccous. *Obs.* 5727, *and from L, 9s Lour,* 1. THEA *cochinchinensis.* Flowers solitary, terminal.
Calyces triphyllous to peataphyllous. Petals 5.
From *Lour.* i. 413.

2. THEA *sinensis.* Peduncles uniflorous. Calyces pentaphyllous and hexaphyllous. Petals 6 to 9.

Obs. 5727. Specimen gathered in Chelsea garden, and from L. & Lour. THEA. *Alst.* ii. 233. *Baldaeus, account from in ph. tr. abr. by Hutt.* i. 690. *Dale* 321. *Fordyce, G. pract.* 207. *Heb.* 201. 371. *Herm.* 500. *Lew.* ii. 427; *disp. by Rother.* 256. *Linn.* 16S. *Mill. Jos.* 434. *Pears. R.* i. 97; *ed.* ii. 289. *Pechlin, account from in ph. tr. abr. by Hutt.* iii. 119. *Spielm.* 430. *Wintr. in Mead mon.* i. 257. Thee orientale. *Pharm. austriaco-prov.* 71. Thee. *Ploucq. bibl.* i. 286. *Schrod. app.* 10. *Vog.* 86. The. *Chom.* 262. *Geoffr.* ii. 274. Tea. *Conradi in phys. journ.* i. 51. *Cult. pr. n.* 1198. 1241. 1399. *Fotherg. J. in med. obs.* vi. 122. 131. *Letts, account from in med. rev.* ii. 188. *Neum.* ii. 142. *Nisbet, account from in med. rev.* vi. 416. *Perciv. T.* i. 85. *Rusk* ii. 78. *Rutty* 510. T. vera. *Carth.* iv. 171. *a grandifolia.* Leaves obovato-clliptic. *Obs.* 8620, In Mr. Sitwcll's garden.

T. viridis. *L. sp.* 735; *mant.* 402. *Sal. W.* 90.

Donn 70. *Forst. J. in Osb.* ii. 353.

T. canton iensis. *Lour.* i. 414.

Thea. *Letts, diss,* 2£. *t. f, I* in flower and fruit;

f. 2 in leaf from a plant in Kew garden. —*Woods.* iv. 116-*1.* 256, from the garden of Mr. Liptrap. T. grandifolia. *Sal. R. hort.* 370.. T. Bohea laxa. *Hort. kezc.* ii. 230. *Leaves* of last year 4 inches long, of the present year 2 long. *Obs.* 8620. June 1. THEA viridis. *Berg.* 471. *Bry.* 131. *Murr.* iv. 226. Green Tea. *Ailk.* 136. *Denm.* i. 103. $ *parvifolia.* Leaves lanceolato-elliptic. *Obs.* 5727. T. parvifolia. *Sal. R. hort.* 370. T. Bohea. *L. sp.* 734; *mant.* 402. *Thunb. trav.* iv. 91. *Forst. J. in Osb.* ii. 352. *Sal. W.* 90. *Bonn* 70.

T.. Bohea stricta. *Hort. kezo.* ii. 231.

Leaves cmarginate, *3* inches long. *Calyx* pentaphyllous; phylla incumbent. *Petals* 6. *Obs.* 5727.—*Petals* 7. *Capsule* with 1 seed, the other 2 cells having proved abortive. *Seed* roundish, smooth, glabrous, with 4 depressions at the base, 4 tenths of an inch broad. *Obs.* 7269. In a garden. THEA Bohea. *Berg.* 469. *Bry.*

130. T. Bohe. *Murr.* iv. 225. 3. THEA *oleosa.* Peduncles triflorous. *From Lour.* i. 414. 569. CISTUS. Petals 5. Calyx pentaphyllous, 2 of the phylla smaller. Capsule with 1, 5, and 10 cells, and 3, 5, and 10 valves. *Obs.* 3978. *L. a Gmel. L.* 1. Exstipulate shrubby. L. 1. CISTUS *viscosus.* Leaves lanceolate, trinervose, smooth above, tomentose underneath. Petioles united at the. base, sheathing. *Obs.* 2905. In a garden.. '.. C. ladaniferus. *L.—//. K.* ii. 591. *undulatus.* Leaves undulate. *Hort. hew.—Curt. mag. t.* 112. C. Ledon I. *Clus. hisp.* 156, *repr. in Ger. by Johns.* 1286, *Lob. ic.* ii. 120, *Sf* C. Ledon I, angustifolius. *Clus. hist.* i. 77, *and cop. in* C. Ledum I. *Dalech.* 233, C. Ledon, flore macula nigricante notato. *Bauh. J.* ii, 8, # C. Ledon angustifolium. *Park, theatr.* 663. Ledi species. *Dalech.* 231.. CISTUS ladaniferus. *Tilesius, account from in phi/s. journ.* xi. 240. 2. CISTUS *ladaniferus.* Leaves oblongo-lanceolate, petiolate, ribless, rough. Phylla ovate, acuminate. *From* C. cretensis. *Jacq. ic.* i. 10. *t.* 95; *coll.* i. 80. C. creticus. *L. sp.* 738; *mant.* 403. *Hort. hew.* ii.234. *(Wbodv.* ii. 249. *t.* 91 is C. hybridus.— *Regn.* not the plant.) C. ladaniferus erectus creticus, flore purpureo. *Tourn. voy.* i. 59. C. ladanifera erotica. *Tourn. cor.* 19. *Buxb.* iii. 34. *t.* 64. /. 1. Ladanum creticum. *Alp. exot.* 89. *t.* 88. Corolla much smaller than in the other figures. . VOL. 3. o LADANUM. Labdanum. Resin. *Pharm. lond. —Alst.* ii. 214r. *Berg.* 476. *Carth.* iii. 348. *Chom.* 634. *Cull.* ii. 195. *Geoffr.* ii. 539. *Hetm.* 6T5.'. *ffiinSS. Lew. disp. by Dunci* 196. *Lftm.* 164.
Mbfeftf ik 361. *Mutt,* Hi. 514. *Ntui.* ii. 21.
ScArocf. 723. *Spielm.* 315. Fog. 327. fad. i.
200. ' "
Labdanrtfft. *Lew.* ii. 29. Afr7/. Jo. 252. *Quar. febr.* 92. 275. 288. 292. *Rutty* 260. tftd. i. 133. C. Ukdanifera. *Dale* 232. J!
C. creticus. *Pears. R.* ii. 174.
#... 3. CISTUS *monspeliensis.* Leaves sessile, lanceolate, trincrvose. Flowers racemose. *Obs.* 3438. In Mr. Hunter's nursery.—*L. sp.* 737. J/drt. keW. ii. 233. ..

Ledum. *Dalech.* 230. i.L"
Ledon V. *Clus. hist.* i. 79, *repr. in* Ledon narbonense, cum Hypocisto. *Lob. ic.* ii.
119, C. Ledon, cum Hypocistide. *Get. by Johns.* 1287. CISTUS ladanifera, sive Ledum monspeliense an gusto folio nigricans. *Bauh. J.* ii. 10. 2. *Exstipulate. Stems syffruticosc.* L. 4. CISTUS *Helianthemum.* Leaves lanceolato-oblong, tomentose underneath; margin slightly revolute; hairs of the upper side in pairs. *Obs.* 3978. Near Plaisley in Nottinghamshire, on limestone.— *L. tuec. n.* 472; *sp.* 744. *Bot. arr. 5od. Curt, iond.* v. *36. t. Wale, t. Fl. dan t.* 101. *Smith engl.* 1.1321. Helianthemum vulgare. DUl. *ap. Raii syn.* 341. *Park, theatr,* 656.
Chamaecistus vulgaris, floreJuteo. *Rajii syn. ed..* 202. , ' ' ' Chamaecistus I. *Clus. hist.* i. 73, *repr. in* Helianthemon, *Lob. ic.* ii. 117, $' Helianthemum album germanicum. *Ger.br/Johns,* 1283, the name belonging to another var. *and cop, in* Helianthemum vulgare flore luteo. *Bank. J.* ii. 15.
Tourn. parts. 93. *Vaill. paris.* 90.
Ilyssopus campestris, *Trag,* 221, *rqpr. m* Helianthemum. *Cord-fol.* 89. *p,* 2.
Helianthemum, give Flos solis. *Dalech.* 860.
Panacea Chironium, sive Flos solis. *Dalech.* 740.
*Calyx-*2 outer phylla nearly thrice as short as the inner, oblong, green, opaque, resembling bracteae; the 3 inner ovate, membranaceous, with 4 prominent green ribs, the left hand margin membranaceous, the right hand margin almost bordered by one of the ribs. *Obs,* 6301. HELIANTHEMUM vulgare. *Geoffr;* iii. 546. Panax Cbiroaium. J3fe233. 570. CORCHORUS. Corolla pentapetalous. *Calyx* pentaphyllous, deciduous. *Capsule* with from 2 to 5 Yalves and 2 to 5 cells. *From L. Sf Juts,* 1. CORCHORUS *olitorius.* Capsules oblong, ventricose. Lowermost serratures of the leaves setaceous. *L. sp.* 746; *mant.* 665. *Hort. kew.* ii. 240. Corcoros Plinii. *Lob. obs.* 269, *repr. in ie.* i. 505, *and*
Corchoros. *Ger. by Johns.* 676, *Sr cop. in*

Melochia sive Corchorus. *Park, theatr.* 309; the
capsule and seeds *cop. from* Corcorus. *Cam. hort.* 47. *t.* 12. The capsule and seeds *cop. in* C. sive Melochia. *Bauh. J.* ii. 982. CORCHORUS olitorius. *Bry.* 123. 2. CORCHORUS *capsularis.* Capsules roundish de pressed rugose. Lowermost serratures of the leaves setaceous. *L. sp.* 746. GANJA sativa. *Rumph.* v. 212. *t.* 78. /. 1. 3. CORCHORUS *japonicus.* Capsules round, gla brous. Leaves doubly serrate. *Thunb. ap. In a. Murr.* 501 *i—trav.* iii. 216. 571. ELEPHANTUSIA. Calyx and corolla none. Stamina numerous. Style quinquefid and sexfid. Drupes several, monospermous. *From L. a Willi.*
Male flowers on a distinct plant, *lb.* 1. ELEPHANTUSIA *acaulis.* Stem none. *From* ELEPHANTUSIA raicrocarpa. *L. a Wittd.* iv.
1157. 2. ELEPHANTUSIA *caulescens.* With a stem. *From* ELEPHANTUSIA macrocarpa. *L. a WML* iv. 572. DELPHINIUM. *Calyx* pentaphyllons, coloured; uppermost phyllum with a spur. Petals 4 and 1. Siliquae 3 and I, *Obs.* 5906. L. 1. Siliqua 1. 1. DELPHINIUM *diffusam.* Branches patent. *Obs.* 5921. In a garden.
D. Consolida. *L. suec. n.* 475; *sp.* 748. *Bot. arr.* 560. *Smith brit.* 577. *Gou. hort.* 258. Near Montpelier.—*Host* 295. *Scop. earn. n.* 651. *Asso n.* 476. *Roth germ.* i. 230. *Abb. n.* 394. Corn fields near Bedford, rare.—*Northumb. guide* i. 51. On the ballast hills of Tyne and Wear,.— *Fl. dan. t.* 683.
D. segetum, llore caeruleo. *Dill. op. Rail syn.* 273 478. Found by James Sherard amongst com in Swaffham field in Cambridgeshire, and by Dillenus between Blackheath and Kit ham in Kent. -*Tourn. paris.* 432. *Vaill. paris.* 46. *Boerh.* i. /
D. simplici flore purpureo-caeruleo, vulgare. *Rail eur.* 115. Amongst corn in Italy, the south *of* France and Germany.
Consolida regalis. *Cam. epit.* 521. *Fuchs.* 28. c. 8, *cop. in*
Consolida regia. *Trag.* 569,
Consolida regalis flore rainore. *Bauh. J.* iii. *a.* 210, *and* Anthemis eranthemos, site Coilsolida tegalis. *Dalech.* 970. Cuminum sylvestre II. *Matth.* 760, *cop. in*

Cuminum silvestre alterum. *Dalech.* 698. Flos regius. *Dod.* 252, *repr. in* Consolida regia, sive ealcaris Flos recentiorum. *Lob. obs.* 426; *ic.* i. 739, # Consolida regalis sativa. *Ger. by Johns.* 1082. *Tab. ic.* 63. Flos regius sylvestris. *Dod.* 252, *repr. in* Consolida stgetum regia, strigosior rota. *Lob. obs.* 427; *ic.* i. 739, $ Consolida regalis sylvestrfs. *Ger. by Jdftns.* ¥08$. Consolida regalis arvensis. *Tab. ic.* 62. *Rati hist.* 70S. *t.* majus, sive vUlgare. *Park. pat.* 276. *Rati hist.* 708. D. fibre simplici. *Parle, par. t.* 279. /. 3. Fumaria, quae Split dicitur. *Bauh. J.* iii. *a. 203.* (The descr. Fumaria lutea.) *Calyx* blue. *Corolla* blue, monopetalou; *Obs.* 5907. Specimens gathered in corn fields in Champagne. *Native* of Europe from the south' to Sweden, and of Kent, Suffolk, Cambridgeshire, and Bedfordshire. DELPHINIUM. *Mill Jos.* 174. Consolida regalis. *Berg.* 479. *Carth.* iv. 243. *Dale* 179. *Krock. n.* 831. *Linn.* 165. *Matt;* iii. 31. *Spierm.211. Vog.* 145. Calcatrippa. *Pharm. austriaco-prov.* 25. ---iS'cArod. 552.

Pied d'alouette. *Chom.* 422; *suppl.* 131.

2. *Capsules* 3. L. 2. DELPHINIUM *elatum.* Petals 4, 2 with a spur; the other 2 bifid; segments unequal. *Obs.* 5905. In a garden.—//. *K.* Li. 243. *L. sp.* 749. D. neetariis diphyllis labellis bifidis apice barbatis, foliis trilobis incisis, caule erecto. *Mill. Ph. ic.* 167. *t.* 250. /. 2. D. nectariis diphyllis labellis bifidis apice barbatis, foliis iucisis, caule erecto. *L. ups.* 151. *GmcL sib.* iv. 187.;t. 75. Aconitum lycoctonum, flore delphinii. *Besl. kort. aest. ord.* 1. *fol.* 11. Aconitum lycoctonum, flore delphinii I silesiae. *Clus. hist.* ii. 94, *repr. in* Aconitum lycoctonum hirsutum, flore delphinii. *Gen by Johns.* 973, *cop. in* Aconitum lycoctonum cacruleum, calcari magno. *Bank. J.* iii. 657. Stem rorid. *Leaves* fisso-partite; segments 7 to 3, incise. *Calyx* blue. *Petals,* the spurs of the 2 upper sheathed by the spur of the uppermost phyllum of the calyx; laminae trapeziform, brownish black, sometimes purple at the end, and sometimes with yellow hair; 2 lowermost bifid, the lowermost segment smaller; limb with yellow hairs. *Obs*

5905. DELPHINIUM elatum. *Kroch n.* 833. 9. DELPHINIUM *Staphisagria.* Nectaria 4, shorter than the petal. Leaves palmate. *From L. a Murr.* 503; *sp.* 750. *Hort. hew.* ii. 244. *Gou. hort.* 259. Near Montpelier.—*Woodv.* iii. 417. *t.* 154. D. platani folio, Staphisagria dictum. *Boerh.* 1.

301. Staphisagria. *Magn. monsp.* 246. *Rati hist.* 705; *eur.* 240. *Dod.* 362, *repr. in Lob. obs.* 393; *ic.* i. 689, *and Ger. by Johns.* 495, *and cop. in Park. iheatr.* 223. *Dalech.* 1629, *cop. in Bauk. J.* iii. 641. /. 2. /. 1, *cop. from Fuchs.* 745. *c.* 302, *which cop. in Trag.* 902. STAPHISAGRIA. Stavesacre. Seeds. *Pharm. lond.* —*A 1st.* ii. 376. *Berg.* 480. *Geoffr. suite* iii. 121. *Ilerm.* 329. *Hill* 543. X,«t. ii. 388; *disp. by Dune* 217. *Z.inn.* 165. *Monro* iii. 275. *Neum.* ii. 97. *Rutty* 196. *Schoepf* 89. *ScArorf.* 687. 776. *Fog.* 181. Staphis agria. *Chom.* 77. 134; s«pjp/. 46. *Da/e* 179. *Dora,* ii. 57..*Hefi.* 106. 338. *ilfiff. Jos.* 424. *Murr.* iii. 32. *Spfe/m.* 488. Stavesacre. *Und.* ii. 16. 169. 573. ACONITUM. *Calyx* pentaphyllous, coloured; upper phyllum vaulted. *Petals,* the 2 upper tubular, pedunculate. *Siliquae* 2 and 5. *Obs.* 4934. Z. 1. *Capsules* 3. L. 1. ACONITUM *galeriflorum.* Leaves palmate; segments muli ti;!. Uppermost phyllum as long again as the lateral phyila. 0s. 4932. In a garden. A. Lycoctonum. *L. suec. n.* 476; *sp.* 750. *Kroch. n.* 834. *Ja-q. austr. t.* 380.

A. foliis paliuatis uulufiuis villosis. *Gmel. sib.* iv. 188.1.81.

A. Lycoctonum, flore luteo. *Besl. hort. aest. ord. l.fol.* 11. A. II. *Cam. epit.* 827.

A. Lycoctonon luteum majus. *Dod.* 436, *repr. in* A. luteum ponticum. *Lob. ic.* i. 677, *Get. by Johns.* 970, # A. Lycoctonon vulgare, luteo flore. *Clus. hist,* ii. 94, $' *cop-in* A. luteum ponticum scrotinum. *Park, theatr. 3l2t Sf abr. in* A. flore albido, sive A. luteum ponticum. *Parlc. par.* 214. *t.* 219. /. 2. A. folio platani, flore luteo pallescente. *Bauh. J.*

Hi. 652. ACONITUM ponticum. *Dale* 180. *L. lapp. n.* 221.,.

2. ACONITUM *Napellus.* Leaves ternate, shining; folioles laciniate; segments ensiform. Upper phyl lum convex, some-

what longer than the lateral phylla. Spur of the uppermost petals very short; limb rounded, erose and semibifid at the end. *Obs.* 4934. In a garden.—*Koelle aconit.* 14. *t.* the best representation of it.—*L. suec.* 477; *sp.* 751. *Hort. kern.* ii. 245. *fttoraeus ap. act. stochh.* i. 41. *t.* 2. Branches too diffuse.—*Blackw. t.* 561. *Mill. J. ill. t. Regn. t. Zorn t.* 49. *fVoodv.* i. 16. /. 6. *Garid.* 7. *t.* 2.—*(Jacq. ft.* iv. 42. *U* S81, is A. neomontanum.) A. caule simplici, spica densa, petiolis unifloris, casidis mucrone brevi. *Hall. hist. n.* 1197. Napelius minor. *Riv. pent. 1.*129. A. caeruleum, sive Napellus. *Rob t.* 13. *Knott. herb. t. E. Boerh.* i. 300.

Napellus verus caeruleus. *Lob. adv.* 301. On the

Alps in the country of the Grisons. No fig.—*Lob. ic.* i. 679, *repr. in Ger. by Johns.* 972, 8f A. Lycoctouon VI, Napellus verus. *Clus. hist.* ii.

96, who found it on Snealben; *cop. in* Napellus caeruleus. *Med. mus.* i. *t.* 8, *at p.* 515, *repr. in* Napellus verus. *Lob. obs.* 387, *cop. in Park.theatr.* 314, *abr. in par. t.* 219. /. 3, *Sf repr. in* Napellus. *Dod.* 439. (*Spal.* the smaller fig. is A. Cammarum with which it is probable Storck made at least his first trials on himself.—*Cam. epit.* 836 is more like A. Cammarum.) A. magnum, purpureo flore, vulgo Napellus. *Bauh. J.* iii. 655. Near Montbeliard in Franche Comte. Napellus arborescens. *Besl. hort. aest. ord. 1. fol.* 12.

Petals 5 and 8, violet purple; S and 5 lowermost subulate, shorter than the filaments; 2 uppermost unguiculate, very long, horizontal; limbs of the two uppermost tubular, ending behind in a short obtuse apur, and anteriorly in a cuneiform recurvate segment; ungues canaliculate, attenuate. *Obs.* 4934. — *Calyx.*, upper pbyllum an inch long, rather lowly fornicate, the point being considerably nearer to the apex of the fornix "than to the base. *Petals,* 2 uppermost wiguiculate; limb oblong, glabrous. *Obs.* 4934. Examined when dry. *Native* of Stiria, Switzerland, France, Sweden, and Siberia. ACONITUM. Leaves. *Pharm. land. $ td. noviss.* —*Berg.* 481. *Gebel, account from in*

phys. jotkrn. tv.-164. *Herz, account ib.* i. 385. *Murr.* iii. 5. *Spielm.* 503.
Napellus. *Bacon, Vincent in ph. tr. abr. by Hutt.* vii. 642, *and in Mihles ess.* ii. 279, *which republ. in med. mus.* iii. 233. *Dale* 180. *Geoffr. suite i.* 115. *Krock. n.* 835. *Ploucq. bibl.* i. 69. 128. 333. 454. *Schoepf.* 89, on the supposition that the American plant is this species. Napellus caeruleus. *Wilmer quoted in med. journ.* i. 340. A. Napellus. *Brera, account from in phys. journ.* i. 71. *Mufr. J.i.* 128; ii. 20. *Pears. R.* ii. 229. Aconite. *Mann, case of in phys. journ.* xi. 226. 8. ACONITUM *neomonlanum.* Leaves ternate, shining; folioles laciniate; segments ensiforra. Pistils 3. Pedicles pubescent. Upper phyllum convex, somewhat longer than the lateral phylla. Spur of the uppermost petals very short; limb retuse. *Obs.* 7924. Specimen from Prof. Jos. F. Jacquin.-- £. *a Willd.* ii. 1236, but he characterises the pedicles as glabrous though Jacquin describes them as villose.
A. Cammarum & *L. sp.* 751.

A. Napellus. *Jacq. austr.* iv. 42. *t.* 381, descr. and fig. *cop. in*

A. sive Napellus officinarum. *Spal.* IS. *t.* the larger plate.

Napellus flore minore. *Riv. pent. t.* 130.

A. Lycoctonum tertium. *CUis. pann.* 408, on the top of Neuberg mountain in Stiria; *repr. in*

A. Lycoctonon quintum, neubergense. *Clus. hist.* ii. 96, A. purpureufn neubergense. *Ger. by Johns,* 973, *if top, in*

A. purpureum aliud. *Park, theatr.* 314, Sj

A. Lycoctonum, oapello simile, neubergetlse, foliis latioribus, florc purpureo. *Bauh. J.* iii. 657. Calyx, uppermost phylluin an inch long. *Petals,* 2 uppermost unguiculate; limb oblong, ciliate. *Obs,* 7924.

ACONITUM neomontanum. Root. *Pharm. edin.* —*Lew. disp. ly Dune.* 126, who gives as synonyms A. Cammarum and tauricum, which are distinct species. Fie adds that it is cultivated in our gardens. It may in botanic gardens, but the plant cultivated in our flower gardens is A. Napellus.— *Pears. R.* ii. 229.

Napellus. *Pharm. austriaco-prov.* 51.— *Neum.* ii. 105. *Schreb. ap. Linn.* 165.

A. Napellus. *Pears. R.* i. 244.

A. sive Napellus. *Storck transl. in Med. mus.* i. 515.

Aconitum. *Aik. in Lew.* i. 28. *Collin obs.* ii. 130. *Fordyce, W. fragm.* 75. *Med. journ.* ii. 297; T. 87. *Monro* iii. 7. *Murr.* iii. 5. *Quar. anim.* 277. *Stall med.* i. 140; ii. 365; iii. 167.
2. Capsules 5. L. 4. ACONITUM *Author a.* Segments of the leaves linear. *L. sp.* 751. *Itort. kew.* ii. 245. *Scop. earn. n.* 655. *Host.* 297. *Krock. n.* 838. *Jacq. austr. t.* 382. A. salutiferum, seu Anthora. *Mill. Ph. ic.* 8. *t.* 12. Anthora, sive Antiphtora. *Besl. hort. aest. ord.* I *fol.* 12. Anthora, sive Antithora. *Cam. epit.* 837. Anthora. "*Park. par.* 215. *t.* 219. /. 4. *Dod.* 440, *repr. in Lob. obs.* 385, $ *ic.* i. 677; *cop. in Park. theatr.* 318, *Sf repr. in* ". 'il! Anthora vulgaris. *Cltts.* ii. 96, # Anthora, sivesA. salutiferum. *Ger. by Johns.* 696. Antithora flore luteo aconiti. *BauJt. J.* iii. 660. .Leases pedate; segments pinnatifid; lesser segments ensiform. Corolla dipetalous, fuscous; upper lip of the petals recurvate, obtuse; lower lip declinate, the lamina obcordate. *Obs.* 8355. Jn Mr. Knowlton's garden. 20 Sept.' ANTHORA. .Berg. 484. *Chom.*311. *Dale* ISO. *Geoffr.* ii. 9. *Lew.* i. 93. *Linn.* 166. *Mill. Jos.* 42. *Murr.* iii. 29. *Schrod.* 536. *Vog.* 231. 5. ACONITUM Cammarum. Leaves ternate, dull; folioles laciniate, ensiformi-triangular. Pistils 5. Pedicles glabrous. Upper phyllum convex, twice as long as the lateral phy Ma. Spur of the uppermost petals recurvate; limb emarginate, shorter than the faux. *Obs.* 6138. 6139. Specimens from Prof. Jos. F. Jacquin.—*Hort. hew.* ii. 246. *Jacq. austr.* v. 11. *t.* 48k. *L. sp.* 751 *y* apparently from
A. Lycoctonum sextum. *Clus. pann.* 412, who found it on Judenberg the highest mountain in Stiria; *repr. in* ,,!

A. Lycoctonon nonum Judenbergense. *Clus. hist.* ii. 97, £

A. maximum judenbergense. *Ger. by Johns.* 973, *Sf cop. in*

A. Lycoctonum, flore maximo. *Bauh. J.* iii. 659.

A. caeruleo-purpurcum, flore maximo, sive Napellus

IV. *Boerh.i.* 301.
Leaves, segments crowded. *Calyxt* uppermost
phyllum an inch long, the end horizontal, half way between the end of the sacklike process and the base. *Petals,* 2 uppermost unguiculate; limb oblong, glabrous. *Obs.* 6138. 4CQNITUM Cammarum. *Hall, account from in chit. rev.* vi. 364. *Krock. n.* 837. *Pears. R.* ii. 229. 574. PAEONIA.
Calyx pentaphyllons. *Petals* 5 and more. *Germina* 2 to 5. *Style* none. *Capsules* polyspermous. *From Juss. L. a Gm. Sf L.*

I. PAEONIA officinalis. Folioles oral, oblong, elliptic, and lanceolate. *Obs.* 8125. 5735. 5734. In a garden.—*L. sp.* 747. *Hort. hew.* ii. 241. *Gou. monsp.* 266. *Lour.* i. 419. *Scop. cam. n.* 650. *Host* 294. In Carniola and Littorali.

Paeonia. *L. ups.* 149. *a elliptica.* Leaves glabrous; folioles entire, oval ovali-elliptic and elliptic. *Obs.* 5735. Specimen gathered in the garden of Fothergill.—*Z. Sp. 0; vps.* 149 *a*

P. corallina. *Rett. obs.* iii. *n.* 65.

P. mas. *Cam. epit.* 657, but the folioles lanceolate. —*Boerh.* i. 294. *Tab. ic.* 784. *Dod.* 194, *repr. in Lob. ic.* i. 684, *Ger. by Johns.* 980, *and cop. in Park, theatr.* 1381, $ *Bauh, J.* iii. 492. *Park, par. t.* 343. /. I.

P. mas cum semine. *Lob. ic.* i. 685, *repr. in Ger. by Johns.* 980.

P, folio nigricaate splendido, quae mas. *Maga. hort.* 151. P. mas Matthioli. *Dalech.* 856.., P. mas Dalechampii. *Dalech.* 856.

Stem 20 inches long, erect, flexuose. *Leaves* bternate, glabrous; the lateral petioles sometimes with 5 folioles; folioles oval, acute, the terminal foliole sometimes bipartite. *Petioles* nearly terete, slightly canaliculate along the upper side. *Flowers* terminal, solitary. *Pistils 3. Gambia* after flowering, brownish white, tomentose, patulous. *Obs.* 8135. In the garden of Miss Wood who informed me that the root was tuberous. „ PAEONIA mas. *Dale* 175. *Geoffr. suite* i. 299. *Mill. Jos.* 325. *Sckrod.* 651. Paeonia. *Pharm. austriaco-prov.* 54. *suec.*—*Alst.* i. 485. *Berg.* 477. *Biss. ess.* 169. *Carth.* iv. 81. 236. *Herm.* 176.

435. *Horne-F. din.* 196. *Krock. n.* 830. *Lew.* ii. 175; *disp. by Dune.* 345; *by Rother.* 212. *Murr.* iii. 37. *Ploucq. bibl.* i. 426. *Spielm.* 514. *Vog.* 204. P. folio nigricante splendido, quae mas. *Chom.* 359. Peony. *Neum.* ii. 137. 3 *lancifolia.* Leaves glabrous; folioles lanceolate. *Obs.* 8112. Specimen gathered in the Paris gar den.—*L. sp. a; ups* B P. officinalis. *L. a WUld.* ii. 1221. *Woodv.* iv. 91. *1.* 247. *Retz obs.* iii. 35. *n.* 67. P. foeminea. *Mill. Ph. diet. n.* 2.,
P. communis vel foemina. *Magn. hort.* 151; *monsp.* 197. In woody tracts near Montpelier.—*Boerh.* i.294. P. foemina prior. *Dalech.* 856. P. foemina vulgatior. *Bauh. J*, iii. 492, *cop. from* Paeonia. *Fuchs.* 203. c. 75, *which imit. in Trag.* 581, *which repr. in* P. foemina. *Cord. fol.* 135, *p.* 2. *Cam. epit.* 658.
Lob. ic. i. 682, *repr. in Ger. by Johns.* 981, *Sf* P. femina altera. *Dod.* 195, # *cop. in* Dalech. 857. PAEONIA foemina. *Alst.* i. 486. Date 176. *Geoffr. suite* i. 302. ЛШ. *Jos.* 326. Monro iii. 192. *Schrod.* 651. ' -;
Paeonia. *Berg.* 477. /Term. 608. *Linn.* 164. Mwrr.
iii. 37. *Spielm.* 514. Fog. 154. 170. P. communis, sive foemina. *Boecl. ap. Herrn.* 177. *Chom.* 359. y *hirsutula.* Leaves slightly hirsute underneath. Fo« Holes oblongo-elliptic, mostly cloven. *Obs.* 6296.
In Mr. Watson's garden. P. foeminea with double flowers. *Mill. Ph. diet. я.* 2. P. foemina altera. *Boerh.* i. 294. P. femina prior. *Dod.* 194, *repr. in* P. promiscua seu neutra. *Lob. ic.* i. 683, P. promiscua. *Gcr. by Johns.* 982, *⫪ cop. in* P. faemina vulgaris, flore simplici. *Park, theatr.* 1380. P. promiscua Vormarii, folio latiore. *Bauh. J.* iii.
493. Stem 2 feet 4 inches long, erect, with scattered minute hairs, obsoletely angular. *Leaves* alternate, dull, glaucous underneath; foliotes tripartite, bipartite, and entire, undulate. *Petals* the outer cuneiform, 2 inches long, the inner linear. *Germina* 2, and 3, tomentose. *Obs.* 6296. PAEONIA. *Berg.* 477. î *kermesina.* Leaves glabrous, somewhat shining above; foliolesoblongo-lanceolate,entire, semitrifid, and semibifid. 06s. 5733. In a garden.

Paeonia *y L. tips.* 149.
P. foeinina, flore pleno rubro majore. *Boerh.* i. 295.
Mag», *hart.* 152. P. foemina multiplex. *Tuh. ic.* 784. Paconiac feminae multiplex flos. *Dod.* 195, *repr. in* P. femina polyanthos. *Lob. ic.* i. 681, *cop. in Da lech.* 85», *repr. in* P. femina multiplex. *Ger. by Johns.* 981, *and cop. in* P. faemina, flore pleno purpureo. *Park, theatr.* 1380. P. faemina vulgaris flore pleno rubro. *Park. par.* 341. *t.* 343. /. 3. P. flore pleno rubro. *Iiauh. J.* iii. 493. No fi». Stem solid, flcxuose, tough. *Leaves* alternate, biternate. *Pistils* 2, silky, shining, whitish. *Stigmata* crimson. Probably a distinct species. *Ulis.* 5733. PAEONIA officinalis. *Alst.* i. 486. Paconia. *Dale* 176. Peony. *Neum.* ii. 137. *t edulis.* Leaves shining on both sides. *From* Amman. & P. albiflora. *Andr. rep.* i. *t.* 64. PAEONIA edulis. *Sal. R. par.* ii. *t.* 78. P. lácteo flore, foliis utrinque viridantibus et splendentibus. *Amm.* 77. C *alba.* Corolla white, double. *Obs.* 6675. In Mr. S. Shore's garden. P. foemina polyanthos flore albo. *Ger. by Johns.* 982. P. albo flore pleno, sire polyanthos alba foemina. *Bauh. J.* iii. 494. *you* 3.? P. foemina-polyanthos flore albo. *Tab. ic.* 785.
PAEONIA flore albicante. *Dale* 176.
576. AQUILEGIA.
Calyx pentaphylloüs, coloured. *Petals* 5, ending below in a nectariferous spur. *Nectario* 10, membranaceous, between the stamina and the pistils. *Capsules* 5, distinct. *Obs.* 4867. L. 1. AQUILEGIA vulgaris. Stamina as long as the petals. Folioles of the loaves at the base of the upper branches entire. *Obs.* 3442. Specimen gathered on Soustons-roch near Shelsley in Worcestershire, but near a cottage.—*Obs.* 4867. On a common near Skegby in Nottinghamshire, and in Langwith woods in Derbyshire.—*I. suec. n.* 478; *tp.* 752. *Hort. kea.* ii. 247. *Asson.* 478. 577. NIGELLA. *Calyx* pentaphyllous, coloured. *Petals* 5, bilabiate, unguiculate. *Pistils* 5, 10, and 1 with 5 styles. *Capsules* from 5 to 10 distinct and with several cells. *Obs.* 5904. L. 1. *Styles 3 to 5.*
L NIGELLA *satita.* Capsules muricate, roundish. Leaves pubescent. Plrylla el-

liptic. *Obs.* 7557. In Mr. S. Shore's garden from seeds gathered in
Russia.—*L. sp.* 753. *Roth germ.* i. 232, in com fields in Saxony; ii. 594. *Ilort. kew.* ii. 249.
Kroch n. 843.
N. flore minore simplici candido. *Boerh.* i. 283.
Mêlant h i um hortense priraum. *Fuchs.* 488. c. 193,
cop. in
Me Ian tía uni calycc et flore minore, semine nigra et
lúteo. *Bauh. J.* iii. *a.* 208. Mclanthium sativum. *Cam. epit.* 551. Melanthium. *Dod.* 301, *repr. in G er. by Johns.* 1084, Melanthium, sive N. romana odora. *Lob. obs.* 427; *St ic.* i. 740.
N. romana sativa. *Park, theatr.* 1375, middlemost fig. (N. pistillis dcnis corolla longioribus. *Mill. Ph. ic.* 125. f. 187. /. 1, is N. orientalis.) *Stan* 2 feet long, erect, pubescent, branched at the end. *Calyx* greenish white; phylla elliptic, acute. *Petals* 8, several times shorter than the calyx, tubular at the base; limb erect, bilabiate; upper lip subulate, lower lip bipartite, one third longer than the upper lip; segments lineari-lanceolatc, obtuse, yellowish white with a transverse blue line about the middle. *Pistil* as long as the corolla, green. *Germen* tnrbinato-oval, quinquedentate, with whitish pellucid granules. *Styles* 5, erect, green. *Obs.* 7557. Sept. 18. NIGELLA. *Pharm, austriaw-prov.* 52.—*Alst.* ii. 364. *Berg.* 486. *Carth.* iii. 450. *Dale* 237, *Herrn.* 302. *Lev. disp. by Dune.* 344. *Linn.*-167. *Mill. Jos.* 314. *Murr.* iii. 35. *Neum.* ii.
194. *Rutty* 348. *Schrod.*636. *Spielm.* 284. *Vog.* 164...
N. arvensis cornuta. *Chom.* 239; *suppl.* 81.
Melanthion sativum. *Geoffr. suite* i. 188
2. NIGELLA *unguiculata.* Pbylla unguiculate. *Obs.*
7558. Specimen from Prof. Jos. *F*, Jacquin.
N. arvensis. *L. sp.* 753. *Roth germ.* ii. 594. *Hort. kew.* ii. 249. *Krock. n.* 842. *Raii eur.* J88. la Germany, Italy, and the south of France, in corn fields.
Melanthium sylvestre alterum. *Cam.*

epit. 553.

Melanthium sylvestre. *Fachs.* 489. c, 133. *Dod.* 301, *repr. m ed.* ii. 303; % *Ger. by Johns.* 1084, a flowering branch *cop. in*

N. sylvestris floribus nudis. *Park, theatr.* 1375, inner fig. and the whole *cop. in*

N. arvensis, cornuta. *Hist. ox. s.* 12. *t.* 18. row 1. /. 1. *Tourn. paris.* 348. *Vaill. parts.* 144, *Magn. monsp.* 187. *Garid.* 328. *t.* 73, *at p.* 332.

Melanthium silvestre, sive arvense. *Bauh. J.* iii. a. 209. The fig. Hypericum perforatum.) MELANTHIUM. *Dale* 237.

Melanthion sylvestre. *Geoffr. suite* i. 186.

W". _.,..

578. REAUMURIA.
Cotyx pentaphyllous. Prtafc 5. *Capsule* quinqueleeular, quinquevalve, polyspermous. 2»

1. REAUMURIA *vermiculata.* Leaves subulate, semiterete. L. a *Wittd.* ii. 1249; p. 754.

Sedum minimum arborescens vermiculatum. *Lob.*
obs. 206, *repr. in ie* i. 3s0, #

r

Vermfculdris fruiex minor. *Ger. ly Johns.* 523, and some of the lower branches *cop. in*

Vcrmiculis fruticosa altera. *Park, theatr.* 731, inner fig.

Sedum Mculum maritimum vermienlatnm. Pore saxifraghe albae, scinine villoso. *jftaii ear.* 234. *Bocc. sic.* 6. *t.* 4. C, d, e, f, *cop. in*

Sedum maritimnm, flore albo, v-IIoso semine. *Hist, ox. s.* 12. *t.* 9. /. 6.

Kali vermiculatum, albo et amplo sedi rosei flore. *Barrel, t.* 868.

Kali arabum prrmum genus. *Da'eck. app.* 19, *cop. in*

Calt arabum. *Bauh. J.* iii. 702. *Ran hist.* 212.

SODA. *Murr.* iv. 287.
Souda. *Berg.* 182.
1 .',.: POLYGYNIA, 579. DRIMYS. *Calyx* trilobate. *Petals* 6 and 12. *Germina* clavate. *Style* none. *Berry* obovate. L. JSL suppl. 43. *Ford. J. Sf G.* 83. *t.* 42.

Wintera. L. a *Murr.* 507, where at 1. 4. fox clavata read obovata.. 1. DRIMYS. *lFinteri.* Pistils 3. Peduncles with mo-

fly S flowers. *From IVUld. £ Forst. J. Sf G.* 84. *t.* 42. /. *m*—%; *and in nov. act. ups.* iii. J81. L. JU. suppl. 269.

Winterana aromatica. *Sol. aimed. obs.r.il.t.1 cop. in* Wintera aromatica. *TVoodv.* iv. 192. *t.* 257. *Murr. ap. L. a Murr.* 507. L. a *Willd.* ii. 1239. Periclymenum rectum foliis laurinis, cortice acri aromatica. *Sloane in ph. tr. n.* cciv. 922. *t.* 1; *cop. in abr. by Lorzth.* ii. 666. *t.* 9. *f.* 168. 169, *at p.* 776; *by Hutt.* iii. 587. Winteranus cortex. *Clus. exot.* 75, *ill cop. in Park. theatr.* 1652, # Cortex winteranus acris, sive Canella alba. *Batfh. J.* i. a. 460. Laurifolia magellanica cortice acri. *liaii hist.* 1801. CORTEX WINTERANUS. *Aht.* ii. 32. *Dale* 296. *Hcrm.* 198. *Hill* 668. jtftf/. *Jos.* 155. Zeeo.

ii. 480. *Linn.* 168. Jtfarr. iv. 557. *Spielm.* 3C3. *Vog.* 297. Cortex winteranus verus. *Carth.* iii. 260. *Geoffr.* ii. 177. Cortex Winterani, Berg-. 381. Wintera aromatica. Winter's bark. Bark *Pharm. edin.—Lew. disp. by Dune.* 324. Winterana Canella. *Monro* iii. 289; iv. 29i. Winterana aromatica. *Pears. R.* ii. 201.

: . 580 DILLENIA. *Calyx* pentaphyllous. *Petals* 5. *Capsul&s* polyspermous, connate, full of pulp. L.

I. DILLENIA *speciosa.* Leaves oblong, rotnndatoacute, denticulate. Peduncles uniflorous. *Thunb. in tin. tr.* i. 200. In Java.—*Smith exot.* i. *t.*

D. indica. L. sp. 754.
Syali/a. *Rheede* iii. b9. *t.* 38. 39.

J), elliptica. *Thunb in tin-tr.* i, 200, *from* SONGIUM. *Rumph.* ii. 140. *t.* 45. Leaves in the fig. elliptico-lanccolate, but described as very broad at the end. Arbor indica, flore max i mo, cui multae innascuntur siiiquae. *Rati hist.* 1707.

2. Ditj-enia *serrata.* Leaves elliptic, acute, serrate. Peduncles tnilorous. *Thunb. in tin. tr.* i, 201, *from* SANGIUS. *Rumph.* ii. 142. *t.* 46. *Bank. J.* i. a. 485, with additional figures of the fruit. ANISUM stellatum. *Pharm. austriacoprov.* 18. *suec.—Berg.* 487. *Carth.* iii. 445. *Lew.* i. 91; *disp. by Dune.* 342. *Linn.* 16S. JMurr. iii. 562. *Neum.* ii. 175. *Spielm.* 240. *Vog.* 274.

Anisuin chinense. *Jlcrm.* 273.
AniMim indicum. *Dale* 177. *Geoffr.* ii. 469.

Zingi..d/s. ii. 3:20.

B. ILLIC1UM *floridanum.* Flowers rd. *M rr. ap. L. a Mnrr.* 507, *from L. mant.* 395. *Curt. mag. t.* 439. Jlort. faw. ii. 250. *Ellis in ph. tr. abr. by Hutl.* xiii. 87. /. 2. *A to LL* Leaves laticeolato-elliptic, slightly acuminate, slightly veined. *Peduncles* near the ends of the branches, among and shorter than the leaves, sometimes 2 together. *Petals* numerous, linear and ensiform, brownish red. *Pistils* 13 and 14, in a circle. *Obs.* 7035. From Mr. Philips's garden. AN J SUM stellatum floridanum. *Schoepf* 91.

r I q. 582. LIRIODENDRUM. *Calyx* triphvllous. *Petals* 6. *Capsules* monosperii-ous ami dispermous, imbricate. *From Juss. L.* 1. LIRIODENlRUM *truncatifolium.*—Leaves lobate.
Liriodendron Tulipifera. / *sp.* 755. *Hort. hea.* i. 250. *Curt mag t.* 275. L. foids angulatis tru r iLs *Trew. sel.* 2. *t.* 10. Tulipitera arbor vi.gmiaaa. *Herm. hort.* 612. r

Tulipifera virginiana, tripartito accris folio, media lacinia velut abscissa. *Pluk. aim.* 379; *phyt. t.* 117. f. 5; *t.* 248. /. 7. *Cat.* i. . 48. Tulipifera caroliniaua, foliis productioribus magis angulosis. *Pink. aim.* 379; *phyt. t.* 68. /. 3. Arbor tulipifera virginiana tripartito aceris folio, media lacinia vrlut abscissa. *Rail hist.* 1798. LIRIODENDRON. *Schoepf* 90. Liriodendron Tulipifera. *Coxe* 373. *Marsh.* 78.

Murr. i. 552. Rush in tr. ph. colt. i. 183, *and account from in med. comment, dec. II.* ix. 158. Populus sive Tulippa arbor. *Clayt. in ph. tr. abr. by Hutt.* viii. 332.
583. MAGNOLIA. . *Calyx* triphyllous. *Petals* 6 and 9. *Capsules* unilocular, bivalve, monospermous. *Obs.* 5467. *Juss.* 281. L.

I. MAGNOLIA *grandiflora.* Leaves perennial, oblong. Petals obovate. //. *K.* ii. 251. L. *sp.* 755.

M. foliis Ianceolatis persisfentibus, caule erccto arboreo. *Mill. Ph. ic.* 115. *t.* 172.

M. altissima, flore ingenti candido. *Cat.* ii. *t.* 61. *Trew sel. t.* 33. 35. MAGNOLIA altissima. *Chalm.* i. 65.

2. MAGNOLIA *glanca.* Leaves glaucous underneath. *Obs.* 5467. In Crome garden.— L. *sp.* 755. *H. K.* ii. 251. M. lauri folio subtns albicante. *Cat.* i. *t.* 39. *Trcto*

sel. t. 9. Dili. hort. 207. *t.* 168. /. 205. Laurus tulipifera, foliis subtus ex cinereo aut argenteo purpurantibus. *Rati hist.* 1798. Laurus tulipifera, baccis calyculatis. *Rati hist.* 1690.

In Compton's garden. *Leaves* ovali-elliptic, sericeous underneath. *Obs.* 5407. MAGNOLIA glauca. *Bart.* 46. *Schoepf* 91.
Marsh. S3. 3. MAGNOLIA acuminata. Leaves ovato-oblong, acuminate. *L. sp.* 756. *H. K.* ii. 25 1. M. fiore albo, folio majorc acurainato baud albicante. *Cat. app. t.* 15. v...ici: MAGNOLIA acuminata. *Humphreys in med, comment, dec. II.* vi-ii. 445. *ScJioep/9L* ."-. i" " .'....n ;;; u. .; "i..'!, 'j..!;,m.i .."'.. .'if-' '.. I .-. .(. i.. »:. 584. NELUMBIUM. *Calyx* tef raphyllous and penlaphyllous. *Corolla* polypetalous and pentapetalous. *Nuts* monospermous, crowned by the style, immersed in A truncate receptacle. *L. a Willd. Juss.* I '.. -. . r. *1*, NELUMBIUM *sprciosum.* C»rolla polypetalous.
J weaves peltate, orbicular, entire at the margin.
From L. a Mild. ii. 1258. Nelumbo micifera. *Gaertn. i.* 79. c. 19. Nymphaea Nelumbo. *L. sp.* 730. *Hort. ket$.* ii. 227. *Lour.* i. 416. *Thvnb. jap.* 223. « muricati'm. Peduncles and petioles muricate. *From L. a Willd* ii. 1258. a Nymphaea indica major. *Rumph.* vi. 164. *t. 13.* Cyauius Nelumbo. *Smith exot.* i. 59. *t.* 31. 32.
N. speciosum. *Bot. mag. t.* 903. *A. B.* Nymphaea indica, Faba aegyptia dicta, flore incarnato. *Herm. par.* 205. *t.* 205. Nymphaea fabifcra, indiac pdudibus gaudens, foliis umbilicatis amplis, pediculis spinosis, florc roseo purpureo. *Pluk. aim.* 267. *t. 322.* Nymphaeac species. *Bont.* J28. Tamara. *Rheede* xi. 59. *t.* 30. Corolla pink. Bem-tamara. *Rheede* xi. 61. *t. 31.* Corolla white. Fabae aegyptiae affinis. *Ger. by Johns.* 1552, *cop. in* Fabae aegyptiae fructus. *Park theatr.* 374, $ Fructus valde elegans, Faba forte aegyptia Dioscori dis. *Bauh. J.* iii. 775. Faba aegyptia. *Rati hist.* 1322. *Stap.* 446. Umbilicus aquaticus maximus chinensis. *Hyde ap. hist. ex.* iii. 620. 5. 15. *t.* 4, from a Chinese book.
Leaves. NYMPHAEA Nelumbo. *Bry.* 337. *Pall, account from in phys. journ.* iii. 273. Faba aegyptia. *Dale* 239. *ft glabrum.* Peduncles and petioles glabrous. *From L. a Willd.* 0 NYMPHAEA Nelumbo. See *a.* 7 *quadrifidum.* Calyx quadrifid. *From L. a Willd.*
Nymphaea Nelumbo. *Walt.* 155.
Nymphaea foliis orbiculatis peltatis subtus radiatis fructu obverse conico, seminibus majoribus nidi lantibus. *Browne* 243. NELUMBO. *Schoepf 8S.* ..
585. MICHELIA. *Calyx* triphyllous. *Petals* 15. *Berries* many, polyspermous. *From L. Sf* Rumph. 1. MICHELIA. Champaca.—Leaves glabrous. *From* Rumph. and *L. sp.* 756. *Osb.* i. 141. Cook in Hawk. iv. 353. *Lour.* i. 425. Sampacca. *Rumph.* ii. 199. *t.* 67. Flos indicus, Champacca dictns. *Bont.* 140. CHAMPAC4M. *Rheede* i. 31. (.19. *Rati hist.* 1641. 2. MICHELIA *Tsiampaca.*—Leaves when young sericeous underneath. *From* Rumph. # *L. mant.* 78.
M. euonymoides. *Burtn. N. tad.* 124.
SAMPACCA silvestris. *Rumph.* ii. 202. *t.* 68.
Tjampaka. *Thunb. trav.* ii. 273.
586. UVARIA. *Calyx* triphyllous. *Petals* 6. *Stamina* inserted into a fleshy receptacle. *Berries* several, pedunculate. *Seeds* 1 to 6. *From Roxb. Juss.* 283, and *L.* 1. Petals equal. 1. UVARIA *ntylanica.* Leaves entire at the margin. Peduncles uniflorous, solitary. Berries oblong, polyspermous. *From* Rumph. *L. sp.* 756; *a Wlld,* ii. 1261. *Lour.* i. 426. Funis musatius. *Rumph.* v. 78, *t.* 42. NARUM-PANEL. *Rheede* ii. 11. *t.* 10. (mis engr. 9.)
FruL x baccifer, fructu ad singulos flores multiplici. *Raii hist.* 1636.
S. UVARIA cerasoides. Leavrs entire at *the* margin, Berries monospwmous. Antherae sessile, with & and *5* sides, truncate. *From Roxb.* i. 30. *t.* 33.
3. UVARIA odorata. Leaves ovato-lanceolate. Pe duncles uniflorous, solitary. Petals mari-lancolate, very long. *L. a Willd.* ii. 1262, probably from CANANGA. *Rumph. ii.* 195. *t.* 65. Cook in Hawk. jv. 353. 4. UVARIA ligularis. Leaves ovate, acute. Peduncles multiflorous, solitary. Petals linear, acute, very long. *L. a Willd.* ii. 1263, probably from CANANGA silvestris secunda sive angustifolia. *Rumph.* ii. 198. *t.* 66. /. 2. Peduncles quinqueflorous and uniflorous. 587. MELODORUM. .'''' ' ' ''' '-. *Calyx* triphyllous. *Petals* 6, triangular. *Berries* many. *Seeds* dispersed. *From Lour.* 1, MELODORUM *fruticosum.* Leaves lanceolate, glabrous. Stem fruticose. *Lour. i.* 430. 588. ANONA. *Calyx* triangular tripartite and triphyllous. *Petals* 6 and 3. *Berry* pplyspermous. *From Swarlz L. Sf Juss. Rumph.*
Annona. *L.* 1. ANONA *Iripetala.* Leaves ovali-elliptic, villose underneath, pubescent above. Petals 3, lanceolate, coriaceous, tomentose. *Obs.* 8052. Specimen ' from Lonsborough garden, without fructifications. —*Hort, kezo.* ii. 252.
Annona Cherimola. *Mill. diet. n.* 5.
A. foliis ovatis acutis, flore albido ungue purpureo, fructu coniformi tuberoso nigricante. *Trew. set.* 16. *t.* 49. /. a, 6, c, e, *g,* h, i, *f, d, k.—cop. from*
Guanabanus perseae folio, flore intus albo exterius virescente, fructu nigricante squamato, vulgo Cherimolia. *Feuill.* iii. 24. *t.* 17.
Annona. *Brought, hort.* 485.
CHIRIMO YA. *Edw. Bryan west ind.* i. 200. 2. ANONA *sqzeamosa.* Outer petals lanceolate, inner minute. Leaves elliptic and oblong, nearly glabrous. Fruit covered with obtuse tubercles. *Obs.* 5598. Specimen of a branch in flower and of a berry, gathered by Broughton in Jamaica.—*Hort. kezo.* ii. 253. *L. sp.* 757; *mant.* 405. Swartz. *obs.* 221. Jacq. *obs.* i. 13. *t. G. f. I; amer. ed. 8vo,* 216. *Lour.* i. 427.
Annona foliis oblongo-ovatis undulatis venosis, flori bus tripetalis, fructibus mamillatis. *Browne* 256.
A. tuberosa. *Rumph.* i. 138. *t.* 46, has acute scaUs.
A. foliis odoratis minoribus, fructu conoide squammoso parvo dulci. *Sloane cat.* 205; *hist.* ii. 168. . 227. In fruit.
Atamaram. *Rheede* iii. 21. *t.* 29.
A. indica, fructu ex viridi luteo cortice squamato aspero, nucleis nigricantibus parvis. *Pluk. aim.* 31; *phyt. t.* 134. /. *3.* Branch and 2 separate seeds. Pomitera indica, fructu conoide squamoso viridi. *Raii hist.* 1650.
Leaves slightly pubescent. *Obs.* 5598.

ANNONA squamosa. *Bry.* 178. *Wright in med. journ.* viii. 224. 3. ANONA *reticulata*. Outer petals lanceolate; inner minute. Leaves oblongo-lanceolate, acute, glabrous. Fruit ovate, reticulata-arcolate. *From H. K.* ii. 253. *L. sp.* 757, *Szcartz. obs.* 222. *Jacq. obs.* i. 14. *t.* 6. *f.* 2; a berry; *amer. ed. 8vof* 218.
Annona foliis oblongis undulatis venosb, fructibus areolatis. *Browne* 256.

A. maxima, foliis oblongis angustis, fructu maximo luteo conoide coriice glabro in arcolas distinco. *Sloane cat.* 204; *hist.* ii. 167. /. 226, has fruit with the appearance of distinct scales.—*Cat.* ii. *t.* 86.

Anona. *Rumph.* i. 136. *t.* 45.
ANNONA reticulata. *Bry.* 177. *Wright in med. journ.* viii. 224.
Custard Apple. *Perciv. Rob. ceyl.* 315.
. 4. ANONA *mucosa*. Leaves oblong. Areolae of the fruit elevated. Outer petals connate at the base. *Jacq. amer. 8vo,* 219. . 5. ANONA *palustris*. Three inner petals as short again. Leaves ovale, glabrous. Fruit areolate. *From Swartz obs.* 223 *Sf L.*
Annona uliginOsa, foliis nitidis ovatis, fructibus areolars odoratis. *Browne* 256.

A. aquatica, foliis laurinis atrovirentibus, fructu minore conoide luteo cortice glabro in areolas distinct©. *Sloarie tat.* 205; *hist,* ii. 169.fi 228/. 1. Two seeds.

A. americana, juxta fluviorum ripas innascens, pyriformi fructu. *Pluk. aim.* 32; *phyt. t.* 240. /6. Two seeds and a branch without fructifications.

ANNONA palustris. *Wright in med. journ.* viii. 224. 6. ANONA *muricata*. Three inner petals as short again. Leaves ovali-lanceolate, glabrous, acute. Fruit muricate. *From II. K.* ii. 252, *and Swartz obs.* 220. *L. sp.* 756; *mant.* 405. *Jacq. obs.* i. 10. *t.* 5; *amer. 8vo,* 214. Annona foliis oblongo-ovatis nitidis. *Browne* 255. A. maxima, foliis iads splendentibus, fructu maximo viridi conoide tuberculis seu spinulis innocentibus aspero. *Sloane cat.* 203; *hist.* ii. 166. *t.* 225. Guanabanus fructu molliter aculeato. *Plum. gen.* 43; *ic.t.* 143. /. 1. Anona. *Comm. hort.* i. 133. *ti* 69. No fructifica tions. A. indica, fructu conoide viridi squamis veluti acu leato.

Pluk. aim. 32; *phyt. t.* 135. /. 2. Branch aiui 2 separate seeds. A. indica latifolia, fructu squamoso aspero. *Pluk, aim. 31; phyt. t.* 134. /. 2. No fructifications. Aratichu Ponhe. *Marcgr.* 93.

Anona. *Comtnel. J. hort.* i. 133. f. 69. . V ' VOL. 3.J « Guanabanus fructu e viridi lutescente molliter aculeate *Plum. ic. t.* 143. /. 1. *ANNONA* muricata. *Bry.* 177. *Wright in med. journ.* viii. 224:. 7. ANONA *glabra*. Leaves lanceolato-ovate. Fruit somewhat conical, glabrous. *L. sp.* 758. A. maxima, foliis latis, fructu maximo luteo conoide cortice glabro. *Cat.* ii. *t.* 64. *ANNONA* glabra. *SchoepfM.* 8. ANONA *triloba*. Petals several, ovate. Leaves elliptic, acute, glabrous, Flowers pendulous, cam panulate. Calyces ovate. Berries from 2 to 4. *From Hort. Kew.* ii. 254, Catesby and Michaux. *L. sp.* 758. *Mill. Ph. diet.* ». 8. Orchidocarpum arietinum. *Michaux* i. 329. A. foliis lanceolatis, fructibus trifidis. *Mill. Ph ie.* 23. *t.* 35. A. fructu lutescente laevi scrotum arietis rcferente. *Cat.* ii. f. 85. A. aquatica, foliis lauriuis atro-virentibus, fructu mi nore conoide luteo cortice glabro in areolas dis tincto. *Sloane cat.* 205; *hist.* ii. 169. /. 228, / I. A. americana juxta fluviorum ripas innascens, py riformi fructu. *Plul: aim.* 32; *phyt. t.* 240. /.6. *ANNONA* triloba. *Bart.* 30. *Coxe* 367. 9. ANONA *asiatica*. Leaves lanceolate, glabrous, shining, lineate. *L. sp.* 758. *Vahl, symb.* iii. 73. A. glabra. *Forsl:* 102. *t.* 15. *ANNONA* asiatica. *Lour.* i. 428. 589. ANEMONE. *Calyx* none. *Petals* 5 lo 15. *Capsules* many, monospermous. *Obs.* 5170. L. 1. Involucrum resembling a calyx. 1. ANEMONE *triloba*. Leaves trilobate; lobes rounded. *Obs.* 7952. Specimen gathered by Dr. Cutler in New England.

A. Hepatica. *Michaux* i. 319. var.
A. foliis trilobis integerrimis. *Cud.* 458. *Gron. oirg.* 84.
Involucrum, bracteae oval, as long as the petals. *Obs.* 7952. ANEMONE Hepatica. *Schoepf92.*
American plant. *Reneaume in ac. sc. abr. by*
Southa. iii. 286? 2. ANEMONE *Hepatica*. Leaves trilobate; lobes acute. *Obs.* 3444. In a garden.—*L. suec.* ». 480; *sp.*

758. *Fl. dan. t.* 610. In woods. *Hort.* Xea. ii. 254. *Poll. n.* 515. *Roth germ.* i. 235.
Scop. earn. n. 658. *Host* 299. *Krock. n.* 815, *Cou. hort.* 261. Near Montpelier. Involucrum, bracteae 3 and 4, shorter than the petals. *Obs.* 5552. HEPATICA nobilis. *Pharm. austriaco-prov.* 41.
—*Berg.* 488. *Chom.* 501. *Geoffr.* iii. 554. *Lew.* i. 493. it'nn. J68. *Mill. Jos.* 227. A/«rr. iii.
102. *Spielm.* 381. *Fog.* 130. Epatica nobilis. *Schrod.* 585. Trtfolium aureum. *Vale* 158. el *a caerulea*. Corolla blue, single. *Obs.* 3414. In a garden.—*H. K.* ii. 254 *a*
Hepatica trifolia caeruleo flore. *Boerh.* i. 30.

Trifolium hepaticum flore simplici. *Raii hist.* 580. On Mount Wasserfall near Schaffhausen in Switzerland.

Trifolium hepaticum, sive trinitatis Herba, flore caeruleo. *Magn. monsp.* 271. *Bauh. J.* ii. 389, *repr. in*

Caryophyllata vulgaris, flore parvo luteo. *Bauh. J.* ii. 398. /. (The name & descr. Geum urbanuin.)

Trifolium aim-ura. *Dod.* 569, *cop. in*
Hepatica nobilis, sive trifolia simplex. *Park, theatr. 1368, Sf repr. in*
Hepaticum trifolium. *Lob. obs.* 496; *ic.* ii. 34, *8f Ger. by Johns.* 1203. *Raii eur.* 143. About Turin SchafThausen and Geneva.

Herba trinitatis. *Dalech.* 1274.
Hepatica nobilis. *Trag.* 519, *repr. in*
Epimediuin. *Cord. fol.* 93. *p.* I.
Native of the south of France, of Germany, and
Sweden. *0 rubens*. Corolla pink. *Obs.* 5552. In a garden. —*Curt. mag. t.* 10. //. K. ii. 254 *y*
Hepatica trifolia rubra. *Clus. pann.* 765, in the forest of Vienna; *repr. in Ger. by Johns.* 1203, &
Hepatica rubra. *Lob. ic.* ii. 34, *Sf cop. in*
Trifolium hepaticum, sive trinitatis Herba flore rubro. *Bauh. J.* ii. 390.
Hepatica flore rubro simplici. *Park. par.* 1.221 2. Seeds caudate. From L 3. ANEMONE *patens*. Leaves digitate, multlfid. *L. sp.* 759. *jflort. kew.* ii. 254. *Roth germ.* ii. 603, on the authority of Bergen. Pulsatilla patens. *Mill. Ph. diet.*

n. 4. Corolla whitish yellow. ANEMONE patens. *Krock. n.* 846.

4. ANEMONE *Pulsatilla.* Leaves bipinnate. Petals straight. *L. sp.* 759. *JBot. arr.* 565. *Willd. her.* 186. *Ft. dan. t.* 1,53. *Krock. n.* 848. *Smith ens;l. t.* 51, on Newmarket heath; *brit.* 580. *Reth.* 208. *t.* Petals patent, but only 9 tenths of an inch long, at Bartlow Cambridgeshire. — *Roth germ.* ii. 603. Petals after flowering not unfrequently slightly recurvate.

Pulsatilla vulgaris. *Mill. Ph. diet. n.* 1. The places of growth cop from

Pulsatilla folio crassiore et majore flore. *Dill, ap. Rait syn.* 260, who inserts the places of growth given in *ed.* ii, and adds that it had been found by Richardson in dry mountainous pastures near Led stone hall near Pontefract. about 7. miles north pf Pontefract in a limestone country.—*Tourn. paris.* ISO. Plant acrid.— *Vaill. paris.* 166.

Pulsatilla purpurea caeruleave. *Bauh. J.* iii. 409. Root acrid. '',

Pulsatilla. *Bod.* 430, *repr. in*

Pulsatilla vulgaris dilutiore flore. *Clus. hist.* i. 246,

Pulsatilla vulgaris. *Lob. ic.* i. 281, and *Qer. by Johns.* 385, *cop. in Park, theatr.* 341, #

Pasque flower. *Pet. herb. t.* 40. /. 10, *Sr abr. in*

Pulsatilla anglica purpurea. *Park. par.* 1.201. *f.. h* (The descr. A. pratensis,) *6f cop. in*

Pulsatilla vulgaris flore dilutiorc. *Hist. ox. s.* 4. *t.* 26. /. 1.

Scapus 6 inches long, erect, villose. *Involucrum* villoso-sericeous, shining; hairs yellowish white. *Flower* oblique. *Corolla* half as long again as the involucrum, glabrous within, without villoso-sericeous, with yellowish white shining hairs, extending beyond (he ends of the petals; petals 5, elliptico-Ianccolate, straight, acute, some emarginate and entire, from 1 inch 5 tenths to I inch 7 tenths of an inch, long, patent, the points of the most distant petals being 2 inches from each other, twice and a fourth, longer than the stamina. *Pistils* half as long as the corolla. *Obs.* 7033. Specimen from Prof. Jos. F. Jacquin, on (he label of which it is said to be the Pulsatilla officinarum vulgaris, but not that of Storck, and the flowers are said to appear before the leaves. Storck says the plant is not acrid. If Storck made this observation on a recent plant, what many medical authors have treated of as A. Pulsatilla, most have been A. pratensis. None of my dried specimens are acrid. Some leaves of what Dr. Coyte cultivates for A. Pulsatilla and which when recent 4 years ago were highly acrid are now perfectly mild.—*Scapus* 6 inches long, villose, acrid. *Involucrum* multipartite, villose, erect, sheathing the scapus at the base; segments some deeply pinnatifid, others simple, setaceo-linear. *Peduncle* shorter than the involucrum, villose. *Corolla* violaceo-purple, sericeo-villose on the outside, glabrous within, somewhat shorter than the invotucrum, as long as the peduncle, catnpannlate; petals 6, ovali oblong, obtuse, 1 inch 2 tenths of an inch long, the ends slightly recurvate. *Stamina* erect, half as long as the corolla. *Antherat* yellow, beginning to discharge their pollen. *Pistils* somewhat longer than the stamina. *Obs.* 8065. la the garden of Mr. Knowlton, who says that the corolla is patent for a few honrs in a fine day after rain. PULSATILLA. *Dale* 164. *Geoffr. suite* ii. 114 *Lim.* 169. *Vog.* 136. Pulsatilla folio crassiore, et majore Hore. *Chom.* 135. 5. ANEMONE campaniβora. —Leaves bipinnate. Ends of the petals reflex. *L.*

A. pratensis. *L. sp.* 760; *mant.* 406. *Fl. dan. t.* 611. *Spal.* 18. *f.* Petals an inch long.—*Hort. Jcew.* ii. 255. *Willi, ber.* 186. *Roth germ.* ii. 604. *Krock* ii. я. 849. *t.* 15. *Sibth. ox.* 169. On "Which-wood forest, near Cornbury quarry, and Burford downs in Oxfordshire. He says it appeared to be different from a plant from Gogmagog hills Cambridgeshire cultivated in the Oxford garden.— *Woodv.* iii. 400. *t.* 148.

Pulsatilla pratensis. *Mill. Ph. diet, n,* 2.

Pulsatilla vulgaris. *Rati cat. ed.* i. 255; *ed.* ii. 216. On Gogmagog hills, on the left of the highway leading from Cambridge to Havcrill, just at the top of the hill; and also about Hildersham, 6 miles from Cambridge; and on Barnake heath not far from Stamford in great plenty, and on Southrop common adjoining thereto.

Pulsatilla anglica purpurea. *Park, par* 199. descr. (The fig. A-Pulsatilla.)— *Raii syn. ed.* i. 93; ii. 144, observing that in his former works misled by Gerarde he had erroneously referred it to Pulsatilla vulgaris instead of

Pulsatilla vulgaris, saturaliore flore. *Clu-s. hist.* i. 246, *cop,,* in *Hist. ojc. s.* 4-*t.* 26. /. 2, repr, *in*

Pulsatilla altera icon. *Dad.* 430,,

Pulsatilla flore clauso. *Lob. ic.* . 283, $" Pulsatilla flore minore. *Ger. by Johns.* 386, and one

of the flowers *cap. in* i.!-.'i.-.

Pulsatilla rubra Swertii. *Pari. par. t.* 201, *f.,*4.

Pulsatilla flore clauso caeruleo. *Banff, j. Hi.* 4J0.

No fig. (

Herba venti. *Trag.* 413, just come into flower, with *the* radical leaves fully grown, Petals reflex at the end. PULSATILLA nigricans. *Pharm. austriaco prpv.* 59——*Berg.* 489. *Cull.* ii. 215, *Lew. disp.* ., l-*by Dune.* 329; *by Rother,* 222. ij/«rr. iii. 93. , Pulsatilla. *Lew. ji.* 252. *Vog.* 156, who considers it the produce of A. Pulsatilla, but as Willdenow ip ber. speaks of A. Pulsatilla as rare and A. pra tensis as common, I suspect that it was this latter-,,; species which the Prussians made use of.-rfFare *ophth.* 178.

Pulsatilla nigra. *Ploucq. bibl.* i. 230, '. ' 2. Seeds without a tail. From L.

6. ANEMONE nemorosa Leaves ternate, in threes, petiolate; folioles incise. Stem uniflorous. Petals oval. *Obs.* 7324. In a wood.—*L. sp.* 762. *Curt. lond.* ii. 38. *t. Fl. dan. t.* 549; *Bot. arr.* 566. *Smith engl. t.* 355; *brit.* 581. *Krock. n.* «5d.

A ne mono ides nemorosa alba vern a. *Vaill. paris.* 12. Ranunculi quarta species candida. *Fuchs.* 166. c, 57, *cop. in*

Ranunculus phragmites albus vcrnus. *Bauh. J.* iii. 412. *Tourn. paris.* 125, A. quinta. *Dod.* 432, *cop. in* Wood Anemone. *Pet. herb. t.* 40. /. 9, *&?* Ranunculus nemorosus al-

bus simplex. *Park, theatr.* 325, *Sr repr. in ,..*
Ranunculus sil varum. *Civs. hist.* i. 247, *Sf,*
A. nemorum alba. *Ger. by Johns.* 383. *Rail syn.*
259..'... /.".;. '","'.' ' i?oo terete, horizontal and erect.: *Radical leaf* solitary, ternate; *petiole* filiform, with a furrow-on the upper side. *Stem* nearly twice as long as the radical leaf. *Caulinc leaves* as large again as the radical leaves; folioles rhombeo-elliptic; margin sericeous. ' *Obs.* 7324.—*Receptacle* of the fruit globular, with angular cavities. *Obs.* 6325, ANEMONE. *Rutty* 27. *Vog.* 93. Anemonoides. *Dale* 163. Ranunculus nemorosus. *Geoffr. suite* ii. 170. Ranunculus albus. *Pharm. suec—Berg.* 491. *Lew. disp. by Dune'* 329. *J Ann.* 169. *Murr.* iii. 91, Ranunculus phragmites purpureas yel albus vermis.
Clwm. 653, . i.'i.; *r,* .. '',.-....'...i.. M 590. CLEMATIS. *Calyx* none. *Petals* 4, 5, and 6, S«fc caudate. Jrorn *L. Sr Murr.* "'"''''
I. CLEMATIS *sinensis*. Leaves pinnate; folioles 5, entire at the margin. Petals lineari-lanceolate; inner margin, tomentose. *From*
    C. chinensis. *Retz. obs.* if.' 18. «. 53. . 2, $ CLEMATIS sinensis.-Lour. i. 422.
2. CLEMATIS *Flammula*. Leaves pinnate; folioles of the lower leaves incise, of the uppermost entire.
Petals oblong, longer than the stamina. *Obs.* 8755.
    Specimen gathered by Mrs. Thomas in a garden near London.—*L. a Murr.* 512; *sp.* 766. *Hort. hew.* ii. 260. *Host* 304. *Gou. hort.* 262; *monsp.* 155. *Roth germ.* i. 232; ii. 596. C. caespitosa. *Scop. cam. n.* 671. C. caule scandente, foliis pinnatis trilobatis. *Hall. hist. n.* 1143. Clematitis maritima repens. *All. nic.* 122. Clematitis, sive Flammula repens. *Magn. hort.* 59.
Garid. 120. Flammula. *Rupp. ab Hall.* 68. In thickets.—*Dod.* 400, *repr. in* C. altera urens, vulgi Flammula. *Lobf obs.* 316; *k.l* 627, *Sr* C. urens. *Gcr. by Johns.* 888, $ *cop. in* C sive Flammula scandens tenuifolia alba. *Bauh. J.* ii. 127. *Magn. movsp.* 70. Flammula Dodonaei. *JJalech.* 1171. C. urens I. *Tab. ic.* 882. (C. urens II. *Tab. ic.* 883 is a plant with simple leaves.) *Panicle* terminal, folia ccous. *Petals* semi transparent pubescent. *Obs.* 8753. Specimen from Dr. Heisc.—*Panicle* terminal, leafless. *Petals* semitransparent, glabrous, pubescent at the margin, yellowish white. *Obs.* 8755. CLEMATIS altera mens, vulgi Flammula. *Lo$.* . *adv.* 276. No fig. 3.
CLEMATIS *Vitalba*, Leaves pinnate,-foliole ovate & cordate. Petioles scandent. Petals oblong, coriaceous, just longer than the stamina. *Obs.* 5191. 8754. Specimens gathered in Worcestershire on the west side of the road between Powick and the Old hills on the descent to the first brook, between Powick and Malvern, and between Hanley Castle and Upton, all on gravel. 16. Aug. I have seen also a specimen gathered by Dr. WinBtftnley between Froceter in Gloucestershire and the next stage on the road to Bath.—*L. sp.* 766; *am.* vi. 52. At Harderwyk in Holland.—*Reich, franc. n.* 352. *Bot. arr.* 568. *Smith brit.* 583; *engl. t.* 612. *Krock. n.* 859. *Huds.* 238. Oa calcareous soil. C. caule scandente, foliis pinnatis ovato-lanceolatis, petalis coriaceis. *JIall. hist. n.* 1142. C. seu Viorna vulgi. *Best. hort. aest. ord.* 6. *foU* 5. Vitis nigra II. *Tab. ic.* 892.
C. latifolia, seu Atragene quibusdam. *Bauh. J.* ii. 125. The figures represent the 2 variations.—*Rail sj/u.* 258; *hist.* 620. *Petals* tomentose. *Oht.* 8754. Native of Ita'y, France, Switzerland, Germany, the Low Countries, Holland, Kent, Essex, Bedfordshire, Buckinghamshire, Oxfordshire, Gloucestershire, and Worcestershire as far north as "Worcester. VITALBA. *Mutt.* vi. 120. Clematis. *Vos,.* 98. Viorna. *Geoffr. suite* iii. 327. Atragene. *Dale* 162. Herbe au gueux. *Chom.* 651; *suppl.* 182. *a integrifdlia.* leaves mostly entire at the margin. *Obs.* 5191. *L. sp.* 766 *a. Roth germ.* ii. 595 *a* C. Vitalba foliis mums dentatis. *Poll. n.* 521. C. Vitalba. *Jacq. austr.* iv. *t.* 308. C. Vitalba with entire leaves. *Mill. Ph. diet. n.* 4. C. caule scandente, foliis pinnatis ovato-lanceolatis, petalis coriaceis. *Hall. hist. n.* 1142. Clematitis sylvestris latifolia, foliis non incisif.
Tourn. paris. 72. *Vaill. paris.* 39. Vitis nigra. *Fuchs.* 97, *fol. ed. cop. in* C. lat-
ifolia integra. *Bauh. J.* ii. 125, *8f* Plain Travellers-joy. *Pet. herb. t.* 40. *j.* 12, *and abr. in.,*
Vitis sylvestris. *Trag.* 818. C. tertia. *Cant. epil.* 697., ' Viorria. *Ger. by Johns.* 885. (The fig. is *S)* $ *serratifolia*. Folioles serrate. *From authors.—L. sp.* P -' C. Vitalba with indented leaves. *Mill. Ph. diet. n.* 4, who observes that this variety is the most com'» mon. C. Vitalba. *Curt. lond.* iy. 37, *t.* 244. In chalky soil. ' C. foliis pinnatis, foliolis cordatis inaequaliter inciso crenatis. *L. cliff.* 225. Clematitis sylvestris latifolia. *Tourn. paris,* 72, *Vaill. paris.* 39. *Boerk.* i. 46. Vitalba. *Dod.* 399, *repr. in* ' Vibrna. *Lob. if.* i. 626, *Ger. by Johns.* 886, *Sr* Atragene Theophrasti. *Clus. hist.* i. 122, *Sr cop. in* C. sylvestris latifolia, slve Viorna. *Park. theatr.* 383, who observed it in Buckinghamshire, Bedfordshire, Essex, and Kent. C. latifolia dentata. *Bauh. J.* ii. 125, *Sr* Travellers-joy. *Pet. herb. t.* 40. /. 11.
Vitis sylvestris. *Dalech.* 1408.
    "i '..; " '.'.
.CLEMATIS *erecta*. Leaves pinnate; folioles entire at the margin, lanceolato-ovate. Stem erect. Petals 5 and 4. *Obs.* 7987, Specimen gathered 2. THALICTRUM *jlavum*. Folioles euneiformi-oblong, trifid. Panicle coarctate, erect. Stem furrowed. 06s. 4556. Specimen gathered on the banks of the Severn below Worcester.—*L. suec. n.* 488; *sp.* 770. *Fl. dan. t.* 939. *hot. arr.* 569. *Smith engl. t.* 367; *brit.* 585. *Krock. n.* 864.
T. nigricans. *Jacq. austr.* v. *t.* 421.
    T. pratense. *L. lapp.* a. 224.
    T. sive T. Jnajus. *Raii hist.* 403; *syn.* 203.
    T. majus, siliqua angulosa aut striata. *Boerk..* i. 44. *Tourn. paris.* 308. *Vaill. paris.* 191.
    T. nigrius, caule et seraine striato. *Bauh. J. Hi.* 486.
THALICTRUM. *Boerk. i.* 68. *Dale* 112. *Geoffr. suite* iii. 172. *Murr* iii. 107. *Vog.* 228. 3. THALICTRUM *Cornuti*. Flowers dioecious. Fo lioles ovate, trifid. Panicles terminal. *Hort. hew.* ii. 262. *L. sp.* 768.
T. canadense minus. *Boerh.* i. 45.
T. canadense. *Com.* 186. *t.*
THALICTRUM Comuti. *Schoep/93.*

4. THALICTRUM *purpurascens*. Folioles tripartite.
Stem twice as long as the leaves. Flowers cernuous. *L. sp.* 769 *i—Schoepf93.*
5. THALICTRUM *mojus*. Folioles trifid and multi fid, glaucous underneath. Flowers cernuous. Panicle diffuse. Flowering branches axillary, in twos and threes. *Obs.* 8768. Specimen from Prof. Jos. F. Jacquin, and from *Jacq. ap. L. a Murr.* 513; *austr. v. t.* 420. *Smith brit.* 585; *ngl.* t. 611.

T. speciosissimum glaucum, semine et caulc striate.
Bauh. J. iii. 486. *Raii hist.* 403. T. majus fia v um, staminibus lute is, vel glauco folio. *Boerh.* i. 44. *Rupp. ab Hall.* 69. T. magnum. *Dod.* 58, *cop. in* T. majus vulgare. *Park, theatr.* 264, & *repr. in* T. BÏve T. majus. *Get. by Johns.* 1251. PSEUDO-RHABARBARUM. *Dale* 112. 592.
ADONIS. *Calyx* pentaphyllous. *Petals* 5 to 15. *Capsules* monospermous, numerous. *Obs.* 6612. L. 1. ADONIS *erosipetala*. Petals 6 *to* 10, oborate, erόse. Heads of fruit oblongo-ovate. *Obs.* 2876. In a garden.
A. autumnalis. *Smith engl. t.* 308; *brit.* 586. *L. sp.* 771; *mant.* 407; *a Murr.* 514. *Curt. lend.* ii. 37. *t.* 135. *Bot. nrr.* 571, where erase Plant with one flower, an error *cop. from L. a Reich*, ii. 651, *which repr. in L. a Wiild.* ii. 1304, Reichard baring inserted from L. mant. 407, an observation relating to A. vernalis under A. autumnalis.—*Huds.* 239. In Kent frequent j and found *by* Watson near Acton..

Adonis. *L. ups.* 156/3. *Cam. epit.* 647.

A. annua. *Mill. Ph. diet. n. .* In fields of wheat by the side of the Medway, between Rochester and Maidstone.—*Gou. hort.* 264. Near Montpelier.

A. hortensis, flore minore atro-rubente. *Boerh.* i.

A. receatiorum. *Magn. monsp.* 5»
Ranunculus foliis anthemiclis, florc minore atro rubente. *Magn. hurt.* 168. Ranunculus arvensis, foliis chamaemeli, flore minore atro-rubente. *Tourn. parts.* 523. *Vdill. parts.* 170. Fids A. flore rubra. *Park. par.* 293. *t.* 291. /. 5. In corn fields in many places in England—*Rati eur.* 126. In-corn about Leghorn, and about Montpelier.—*Ger. by Johns.* 387, who gathered it in the west of England; *repr. from* Eranthemum. *Dod.* 260, *which abr. in* A. flower. *Pet. herb. t.* 39. /. 8, *and repr. in* Flos A. vulgo. *Ctus. hist.* i. *336,* A. recerrtiorum. *Lob. obs.* 150, *and* Flos Adonis. *Lob. ic.* i. 283. *Raii hist.* 596; *cat.* 116, who observes that he never saw it in Britain; —*syn.* 251. Found by James Sherard between Stonechurch and Qucenhithe. A. sive Anthemis. *Dalech.* 970, *tepr. in* Chamaemelum silvestre. *Dalech.* 1344. (Theseparate flowers and fruit A. aestivalis.) Flos A. vulgo, aliis Eranthemum. *Bauh. J. in.. a.* 125..'(The figures probably A. aestivalis from the obovato-oblong petals.) *Native* of Italy, France, Kent, the neighbourhood of London and. Dublin, Norfolk, and Gloucestershire. FLOS ADONIS. *Dale* 159.

'.'.. . U t. ADONIS *.cernalis.* Petals about 12, lanceolate.— Head of fruit ovate. *Obs.* 6612. In a garden.— *L. suec. n.* 492; *sp.771. Hort. kea.* ii. 264. *Curt. mag. t.* 134. *Scop. earn. n.* 678. *Poll. n.* 526. *Gou. hort.* 264. Near Montpelier.—*Host* 306In Austria and Hungary.—*Krock. n.* 867. ". Pseudo-helleborus niger. *Best. hort. hyem. fol.* 4 *imit. in* A. hellebori radice, buphthalmi flore. *Mill. Ph. ic.* 9. *r.* 14. *f.* 1.
Buphthalmum. *Dod.* 261, *repr. in* Buphthalmum, sive Helleborus niger fcrulaceus. *Ger. by Johns.* 746. # *cop. in* Helleborus niger ferulaceus. *Park, theatr.* 213.
Pseudoelleborus, sive Consiligo. *Dalech.* 1638.
Helleborus niger ferulaceus, sive Buphthalmum.
Park. par. t. 291. /. 6.
Elleborus niger verus. *Tragi* 406, Buphthalmum Dodonaei, aliis Consiligo tenuifolia.
Bauh. J. iii. 637. *Raii hist.* 597. Stem branched from the base. *Leaves* laciniate, the lowermost on short membranaceous petioles, those above sessile. *Calyx* yellowish green, villosulous; phylla lanceolate) obsoletely serrate towards the end. *Corolla* bright yellow, as long again as the calyx; petals 15, obsoletely serrate towards the end. Gcr*miria* microscopically pubescent. *Obs.* 6612.
Native of the south of France, Carniola, Hungary,
Germany, and the isle of Ocland on the coast of
Sweden.

HELLEBORUS niger teriuifolius, buphthalmi
flore. *Carth.* ii. 415. *Schrod.* 761. Vseudo-Helleborus niger. *Dale* 159. 8. At)ONIS *capensis.* Leaves biternate; folioles sub cordate. *L.f.1. suppl.* 272. Imperatoria ranunculoides africana enneaphyllos, Iaserpitii lobatis foliis rigidis margine spiuosis.
Pluk. aim. 198; *phyt. t.* 95. /. 2, Vot. 3 r RANUNCULUS aethiopicus, foliis rigidis, floribus ex luteo-virescentibus. *Comm. J. hort.* i. 1.*t.* 1. Calyx quinquepartite. Petals 5.

4. ADONIS *vesicatoria.* Leaves biternate; foliolec serrate. Petals many, linear. *Obs.* 8769. Specimen gathered in Fothergill's garden.
A. capensi9. *L. a Murr.* 514; *sp.* 772.
Knowltonia rigida. *Sal. R. hort.* 372. *Bot. mag. t. 115.*
Christophoriana trifoliata hirsuta, foliis scabris, flore sulphureo rariore. *Burtn. J. afr.* 145. *t.* 51. Calyx pentaphyllous. Petals many.
ADONIS vesicatoria. *L.jil. suppl.* 272.
593. RANUNCULUS. *Calj/X* pentaphyllous. *Corolla* pentapetalous. *Nee taria* 5, inserted into the base of the petals. *Capsules* monospermous, not opening. *Obs* 3450. L, 1. Leaves undivided. L. 1. RANUNCULUS *Flammula.* Leaves lanceolate, petiolate, denticulate. Stem declinate. *Obs.* 283.
On the side of Kinson pool near Stafford.—*L. sp.* 772. *Lightf.* 288. *Bot. arr.* 571. *Smith engl. t.* 387; *brit.* 587. *Fl. dan. t.* 575. *Curt. lond.* vi. *t.* 37. 11. longifolius, palustris, minor. *Tourn. paris.* 135, R. ilammcus minor. *Rail sj/ n.* 250. R. longifolius, aliis Flammula. *Bauh. J.* iii. 864, with leaves representing the varieties, as entire at the margin, and serrate. (The 5 lower leaves elliptic ovate and oval, arc I suspect It. parnassifo lias.) *Leaves)* margin remotely and irregularly serrate dentate and nearly entire. *Petals 3* tenths of an inch long,

and nearly as much broad. *Obs.* 283. *FLAMMULA. Dale* 159. *Krock. n.* 869. *Lew.* ii. 262. *Murr.* iii. 86. R. Flammula. *With, in bot. arr.* iii. *p.* exxiv. R. longifolius, aliis Flammula. *Vog.* 115. *m denticulatus.* Leaves denticulate. *Obs.* 283. *Wale. t.* R. longifolius palustris minor. *Vaill. parts.* 168. Flammula Ranunculus. *Dod.* 429, *repr. in* R. flammeus minor. *Ger. by Johns.* 961, and a branch *cop. in Park, iheatr.* 1215, right hand figure. Ranunculi species duodecima laevibus foliis. *Cord. fol.* 121. *p.* 2. & *serratus.* Leaves elliptico lanceolate, serrate. *Obs.* 4347. On the side of Kinson pool near Stafford.— *L. sp.* 773 3 R. palustris, serratus. *Vaill. paris.* 168. Flammula R. folio serrato. *Dod.* 429, *repr. in* R. flammeus, serratus. *Ger. by Johns.* 962, *abr. in* Small Spearwort. *Pet. t.* 39. /. 6, *and* a branch *cop. in* R. flammeus minor folio serrato. *Park, theatr.* 1215, left hand fig. Ranunculi species duodecima serratis foliis. *Cord. fol.* 121. p. 2. A leaf.

2. RANUNCULUS *salkifolius.* Leaves lanceolate, nearly sessile. Stem erect. *Obs.* 271. On the margin of Kinson pool near Stafford.

R. Lingua. *L. sp.* 773. *Bot. arr.* 572. *Smith engl. t.* 100; *brit.* 588. *Fl. dan. t.* 755. *Kroch, n.* 871.

R. flammeus major. *Raii syn.* 250. *Ger. by Johns.* 961, *cop. in Park, theatr.* 1215, *and* Great Spearwort. *Pet. herb. t.* 39. /. 5. "

R. longifolius palustris major. *Town. pans.* 524.

Vaill. paris. 168. *Rupp. ab Hall. 101.* R. longo folio maximus, Lingua Plinii. *Bauh. J.* iii. 865. Stem 2 feet 10 inches long, branched above, gla brousbelow, hirsutulousabove; hairs mostly adpressed, some patent, yellowish. *Branches* erect. *Leaves* acute, ebsoletely dentate at the margin, microscopvcally sericeous, not shining, with minute whitish dots, the lower a foot long; hairs distinct. *Peduncles* hirsutulous; hairs adpressed and patulous, yellowish. *Petals* yellow, obovate, 7 tenths of an inch long, 6 tenths of an inch broad. *Seeds* in a globular head, ovate, somewhat acuminate, compressed; inner margin more acute than the outer. *Obs.* 7166.

RANUNCULUS flammeus. *Dale* 159. R. longifolius. *Rutty 4Sl.* 2. *Leaves divided.*
3. RANUNCULUS *Thora.* Leaves reniform, subtrilobate, crenate; that on the stem sessile; those near the flowers lanceolate. Stem with mostly 2 flowers. *L. sp.* 775. *Hort. hem.* ii. 266. *Scop, earn. n.* 685. *Host.* 309. *Jacq. vind.* 249; *austr. t.* 442. *Kroch, n.* 874. R. folio cyclaminis, radicc asphodeli major. *Boerh.*

Tora major. *Cam. epit.* 825, flowers of the outer fig. and the inner fig. *cop. in* Thora folio cyclarainis. *Bauh. J.* iii. 650, with added leaves. Tora valdensium. *Dalech.* 1735. Thora valdensium. *Clus. pann.* 372. No fig. Thora valdensis. *Rati hist.* 591; *eur.* 248. On the highest summits of Mount Jura near Thuiri. — *Ger. by Johns.* 966. *Dod.* 440, *repr. in* R. grumosa radice. *Clus. hist.* i. 239, *8f* Thora montis Baldi sive sabaudica. *Ger. by Johns.* 966. Phthora valdensium. *Lob. ic.* i. 604, *repr. in* Pthora valdensium montis Baldi. *Clus. hist.* i. *239.* Phtora valdensium, et Thora. *Lob. adv.* 263, *imit. in* Limeum alterum duplici folio. *Dalech.* 1739. Limeum pardalianchis genus imo tantum folio. *Da lech.* 1738. Tora minor. *Cam. epit.* 826, *cop. in* Aconitum Pardalianches, seu Thora minor. *Park. theatr.* 317. *THORA. Dale* 159. Thora valdensis. *Lew. disp.* 146. Aconitum Thora. *Woodv.* 435. Root found among Gentian. *Brocklesby in ph. tr. abr. by Hutt.* ix. 488.
4. RANUNCULUS *sceleratus.* Lower leaves palmate j the uppermost digitate. Fruit oblong. *L.* J«*ec. n.* 499; *sp.* 776. *Bot. arr.* 573. *Curt. lond.* ii. 42. /. *Fl. dan. t.* 571. *Smith brit.* 590; *engl. t.* 68-1,
R. sylvestris I. *Dod.* 423, *repr. in* R. palastris, rotundiore folio. *Lob. obs.* 382; *ie.i.* 669; *cop. in* R. palustris sardonius laevis. *Park, theatr.* 1215; *Sf repr. in* R. palustris rotundifolius. *Ger. by Johns.* 962.

Roii hist. 585. R. palustris. *Raii syn.* 249. R. aquaticus, sive Apium risus. *Fuchs.* 165. *c.* 57, *cop. in* R. palustris, flore minimo. *Bauh. J.* iii. 858, *and imit. in* Apium aquaticum. *Trag.* 93. R. I, Matthioli. *Dalech.* 1027. *RANUNCULUS* sceleratus. *Coxe* 376. *Schoepf* 93. R.

palustris. *Dale* 158. *Geojj'r. suite* ii. 176, *Kroch. n.* 876. *Murr.* iii. 82. R. palustris apii folio laevis. *Rutty* 421. 5. RANUNCULUS *aquatilis.* The leaves under water with hairlike segments, those floating on and out of the water lobate tripartite and ternate. *Obs.* 4348. Specimen gathered near Worcester.—*L. suec. n.* 509; *sp.* 781. *Bot. arr.* 577. *Scop. cam. n.* 681. *KrocIc. n.* 887. *RANUNCULUS* aquatilis. *Poll. n.* 539. *Pull. in lin. tr.* v. 18. *loiatus.* (Variation.) The leaves which float on the water lobate. *Obs.* 4350. Near Worcester. R. aquatilis albus. *Bauh. J.* iii. 781. (The word tenuifolius belongs to the name in the adjoining column.) *Leaves,* upper in one plant lobate, lower and uppermost hairlike. *Petals* 3 tenths of an inch long. *Stamina* many. *Receptacle* pilose; hairs attenuate, as long as the germina. *Obs.* 5775. In a pool, the sides of which dried up. $ *trifidus.* (Variation.) The leaves which float upon the water trifid and lobate. *Obs.* 5705. Specimen gathered by Mr. Hollefear in Worcestershire.

R. aquatilis. *L. a. Huds. a. Bot. arr. a. Dod.* 576, *repr. in Ger. by Johns.* 829. *Raii syn.* 249. *Smith engl. t.* 101.

R. heterophyllus. *Willd. ber.* 190. *Sibtk. ox.* 175.

R. foliis inferioribus capillaceis, superioribus peltatis. *L. lapp. n.* 231.

R. aquaticus, folio rotundo et capillaceo. *Tourn. paris.* 524. *Vaill.* 170. y *circinatus.* (Variation.) Leaves with hairlike segments; the ends forming a circular outline. *Obs.* 5707. Specimen gathered by Withering near Birmingham.

R. aquatilis. *L.* ». *Huds.* %. *Bot. arr. & Willd. ber.fi*

R. circinatus. *Sibth. ox.* 175.

R. aquaticus capillaceus. *Tourn. paris.* 298.

R. aquatilis capillaceus. *Vaill. paris.* 170.

R. aquaticus albus, circinatis tenuissime divisis foliis. *Pluk. aim.* 311; *phyt. t.* 52. /. 2.

R. aquatilis omnino tenuifolius. *Bauh. J.* iii. 781, the word tenuifolius misplaced in the adjoining column.— *Raii syn.* 249.

Millefolium, sive Maratriphyllon flo-

re et seminc ranunculi aquatici, hepaticae facie, *Ger. by Johns.* 827.
Petals S tenths of an inch long. *Stamina* many. *Receptacle* pilose j hairs as long as the germioa. *Obs.* 5775. Gathered on the side of a pool, wher© the water had been dried up, growing amongst *a.*
Millefolium aquaticum cornutum. *Bauh. J.* iii. 784.
R. aquaticus albus, circinatis tenuissime divisis foliis, floribus ex alis longis pediculis innixis. *Rati syn.* 249. *Vaill. parts.* 171. $ *capil/aceus.* (Variation.) All the leaves with hairlike segments; segments diverging, the ends;unning an irregutar outline. *Obs.* 5706'. Specimen lathered near Worcester.
R. aquatilis. *L. y. Jtuds. &. Bot. arr. y. Sibth. ox.* 175. *lViUd. ber. a.*
R. Trichophyllon aquaticus medioluteus. *Col. wphr.* i. 315.
R. alter aquaticus feniculaceus *Tpx-oipuMav. Cot.* ec*phr. i. t.* 316.
Alga prima. *Trag.* 687. No fig. *c Jlwciatilis.* Leaves with hair'ike segments; segments parallel. *Obs.* 5708. Specimen gathered on shoals in the Severn above Worcester.
R. aquatilis. *L. 3". Huds. y-Bot. arr.* 578?. *Fl. dan. t.* 376.
R. fluviatilis. *Willd. ber.* 191. *Sibth. ox.* 176.
Ranunculo sive polyanthemo aquatili albo affine, Millefolium maratriphyllon fluitans. *Bauh. J.* iii. 782. *Rati syn.* 250.
R. aquatilis albus fluitans, peucedani foliis. *Tourn.* ' *par is.* 524. *Vaill. pans.* 171. Petals 3 to 7 tenths of an inch long. *Obs.* 5708.
6, RANUNCULUS *abortivus.* Radical leaves cordate, crenate; cauline leaves ternate, angular. Stem mostly triflorous. /,, *sp*, 776. *Bonn* 138,
R. fuliis radicalibus cordafis crenatis, cauliuis digitals petiolatis. *Roy.* 490.
R. foliis radicalibus cordatis crenatis, caulinis ternatis angulatis, caule subtrifloro. *Gron. virg.* 86.
R. virginianus, parvo flore, molliori folio. *Herm. hort.* 514. *Boerk.* i. 32. «. 18.
RAXUVCULUS abortivus. *Schoepf93.*
Ranunculus. *Push* i. 31.
R. tbliis radicalibus subrotundo-crenatis, caulinis digitals dentatis, caule multifloro. *Cutl.* 458.
7. RANUNCULUS *acomtifolius.* Lower leaves ter« nate; lateral-'oiioles bipartite; intermediate foliole partite; segments lanceolato-elliptic, incise, serrate. *Obs.* 3448-Specimen gathered iu Fothergill's garden.—*Scop. earn. n.* 680. *L. sp.* 776. *JfJost* 310. *Hort. kets.* ii. 267. *Roth germ.* ii. 613. *Poll. n.* 532. *Fl. dan. t.* 111. Woods in Norway.—(*L. suee. n.* 497, who quotes Tych. Holm, for its having been found in the mountains of Lapland, is probably K. platanifolius.)
R. montanus, acouiti folio, albus, florc minore, *Bocrh.* i. 31.
Aconitum batrachoides. *Lob. adv.* 300, in the mountains of Narbonne Auvergne and Savoy; *Sf repr. in ic.,i* 668.
R. inoriiairtis IV. *C/us. pann.* 370, on Schneeberg and other mountains of Austria; *repr. in Rati hist,* j. 2.-0,
R. ncoiiiti folio, *Ger. by Johns.* 954, # *cop. in*
R. flore albo, alpinus major. *Bauh. J.* iii. *b.* 860, v,ho do-'s not appear to have seen the plant.—*Rait hist.* 589; *eur.* 214, who marks it as not having fallen under his observation.
R. montanus albus. *Dalech.* 1031.
RANUNCULUS montanus. *Dale* 159.
8. RANUNCULUS *acris.* Leaves tripartite; segments multifid. Peduncles smooth. *Obs.* 3450. In meadows.—*L. suec. n.* 507; *sp.* 779. *Bot. arr.* 576. *Wale. t. Curt. lond.* i. 39. *t. Mart. rust. t.* 30. *Smith brir.* 593; *engl. t.* 652. *Woodv.* iv, 88. *t.* 246. R. napelifolius. *Cranls. austr.* i. 114. «. 10. /. 4.
R. pratensis erectus acris. *Boerh.* i. 30. *Vaill. pa' ris.* 169. *Raiisyn.* 248; «« «. 583. R. hortensis II. *Dod.* 422, repr. t'n R. pratensis, surrectis cauliculis. *Lob. obs.* 379; tic. i. 665, $ coi. t'n R. hortensis alter. *Dalech.* 1032, # R. pratensis acris. *Park. theatr.* 328, which air in Upright meadow Crowfoot.. *Pet. herb. t.* 38. *f.* 3. R. pratensis dulcis simplex. *Park, theatr.* 328.
(The name & descr. It. repens.) R. rectus non repens, flore simplici luteo. *Bauh. J.* iii. 416. RANUNCULUS acris. *Dale* 158. *Kroch. n.* 884. R. pratensis. *Murr.* iii.JT5. *Quar. febr.* 429. R. pratensis erectus acris. *Rutty* 421. *Fog.* 115.
9. RANUNCULUS repens. Leaves ternate. Pedun cles sulcate. Calyx patulous. Shoots creeping. *Obs.* 392. Near wet ditehes.—*L. suec. ».* 505; *sp.* 779. *Curt. lond.* iv. 38. *t.* 211. *Fl. dan. t.* 795. *Bot. arr.* 575. *Smith brit.* 592; engf. . 516. *Jfarf. r«sf. t.* 29.
R. pratensis repens. hirsutus. *Tourn. parts.* 32. *Vaill. parts.* 169. *Bonk.* i. 31. R. pratensis repens. *Rati hist.* 581; *syn.* 247.
Park theatr. 3i9. (The fig. R. polyanthemos.) R. hortensis I. *Dod.* 422, *repr. in* R. pratensis etiamque hortensis, reptante cauliculo *Lob. obs.* 379, *repr in ic.* i. 664, R. pratensis etiamque hortensis. *Ger. by Johns.* 951, *and cop. in* R. hortensis. *Dalech.* 1031, *and* Creeping Crowfoot. *Pet. herb. t.* 38. *f.* 7. Thames Crowfoot. *Pet. herb. t.* 38. /. 8. R. sylvestris. *Trag.* 98, *imit. in* "R. repens, flore luteo simplici. *Bauh. J.* iii, 6. 419. R. dulcis. *Tab. ic.* 51. *Native* of Europe from the south to Lapland. RANUNCULUS pratensis repens. *Mill. Jos,* 367.
R. pratensis repens hirsutus. *Chom.* 653.
R. pratensis. *Geoffr. suite* ii. 173.
Ranunculus. *Dale* 158.
10. RANUNCULUS *hirsutus.* Leaves ternate and tripartite; folioles tripartite and trifid. Peduncles sulcate. Calyx retroflex. Root fibrous. *Obs.* 7464. In a court.—*Curt. lond.* ii. 40. *t. Bot. arr.* 575. *Smith brit.* 592. R. Philonotis. *Rets. obs.* vi. 31. ». 53; *scand. n.* 693. R. rectus, foliis pallidioribus, hirsutus. *Rail syn.* 247. *Vaill. parts.* 169. *Bauh. J.* iii. 417, *cop, in* Pale upright Crowfoot. *Pet. herb. t.* 38. *f.* 5. *Leaves,* the lower with cuneiform seg nents *Pe tiils obovate*, bright yellow. *Vectarium* cuneiform, of the same text re and colour with the petals. *Obs.* .'464. RANUNCULUS Sardous. *Roth germ.* ii. *pars* ii. 592,— *Krock. n.* 878. 11. RANUNCULUS *bulbosus*. Leaves ternate and tripartite; folioles petiolate, tripartite and pinnatifid. Peduncles siiicate. Calyx retroflex. Stem erect, with several flowers. *Obs.* 382. In meadows.—*L. lapp. n.* 229; *suec. n.* 504; *sp.* 778. *Bot. arr.* 574. *Curt. lond.* i. 38. *t. Lightf.* 292. *Mill. J. ill. t. Krock. n.* 881. *t.* 21. *Wok. t. Raii hist.* 581; *syn.* 247. *Smith brit.* 591; engl. *t*, 515. *Fl. dan. t.* 551. *Mart. rust.*

t. 28, *Lob. obs.* 380, *repr. in ic.* i. 067, and *Ger. by Johns.* 953, *cop. in Park, theatr.* 329, *and,* R. tuberosus. *JJalech.* 1032, *Sf repr. in Dod.* 428. R. pratensis, radice verticilli modo rotunda. *Tourn. paris.* 33. *Vaill. paris.* 169. *Boerh.* i. *31.* In Holland. R. luteus. *Trag.* 94. R. minor. *Fuchs.* 166. c. 57, *cop. in* R. tuberosus major. *Bauh. J.* iii. 417. i?oo roundish, depressed, solid, whitish, acrid. *Stems* sometimes 3, inserted distinctly into the upper surface of the root. *Radical leaves,* segments in some plants lanceolato-linear, in others cuneiform. *Petals* subrotundo-obovate. *Nectarium* cuneiform, rctuse, *Obs.* 382. *Native of* Europe from the south to Lapland. RA-NUNCULUS bulbosus. *Bart.* 23. *Coxe* 376. *Dale* 158. *Geoffr. suite* ii. 266. *Mill. Jos.* 367. *Murr.* iii. 88. R. pratensis, radice verticilli modo rotunda. *Chom.* 652. *llutly&l.* Ranunculus. *Lew.* ii. 262. 594. FICARIA. *Calyx* triphyllous. *Corolla* polypetalous, longer than the calyx. *Nectaria* inserted into the petals. *Capsules* numerous, monospermous. *Obs.* 4501. DM. 1. FICARIA *verna.* Huds. 244. *Sot. arr.* 579. Ranunculus Ficaria. *L. suec. n.* 496; *sp.* 774. *Curl, lond.* ii. 39. *t. Mart. rust. t.* 21. *Bot. arr.* 573. *Fl. dan. t.* 499. *Wale. t.* Smith brit. 589; engl. t. 584. Ficaria. *Curt. mat. tned. I.* 6. R. praecox, rotuudifolius, granulata radice. *Tourn. paris. 33.* R. vernus rotundifolius minor. *Vaill. paris.* 170. Chelidonion minus. *Trag.* 113, *repr. in* Chelidonium minus. *Cord. fol.* HI, p. 2. Dalechi 1048. *Bod.* 49, *repr. in Lob. obs.* 323; *ic.* i. 593; *Ger.* 6y *Johns.* 816, c«rf cop. fn *Park, theatr.* 617. i?aji /'» 579; sy«. 246. *Boerh.i.* 29. J«cAs. 823. c. 333, *cop. in* Scrophularia minor, sive Chelidonium minus Tulgo dictum. *Bauh. J.* iii. 468. Potamogeton rotundiori folio. *Bauh. J.* iii. 776.. No fructifications. (Name and descr. belong to a species of Potamogeton.) R. latifolius. *Dalech.* 1036. *Calyx* sometimes tetraphyllous; phylla oval, the outer membrane forming a transverse duplicative at the base somewhat resembling a stipula. *Germina* microscopically pubescent below. *Obs.* 4501. CHELIDONIUM minus. *Berg.* 494. *Dale* 157. *Geoffr.* iii. 314. *Krock. n.* 873. *Lew.* i. *329; disp.* by

Rother. 137. *Linn.* 170. *Mill. Jos.* 133, *Murr.* iii. 90. *Schrod.* 563. *Spielm.* 558. *Vog.* 97. 234. R. Ficaria. *Bry.* 127. Chelidonia rotundifolia minor. *Ch$m.* 759. *695.* TROLLIUS. *Calyx* triphyllous, coloured. *Corolla* polypetalous, as long as the calyx. *Nectaria* obsubulate. *Capsules* numerous, polyspermous. *Obs.* 4896. *Scop. L. Roth germ.* i. *236.* Differs from Ficaria in the polyspermous capsules, the insertion of the nectaria, and the calyx being of the same size and texture with the corolla.
1. TROLLIUS *rotundiflorus.* Nectaria somewhat shorter than the stamina. *Obs.* 4896. In a gar. den. T. sphaericus. *Sal. R. in lin. tr.* viii. 302. T. europaeus. *L. sp.* 782; *suec. n.* 510; *mant.* 408. *Bot. arr.* 580. Smith brit. 597; *engl. t.* 28, from a cultivated specimen.—*Scop. earn. n.* 694. *Gou. monsp.* 321. *Light/.* 295. *Retz. scand. n.* 701. *Roth germ.* i. 236; ii. 608. 27. *dan. t.* Helleborus. *L. lapp. n.* 226.
Helleboro-Ranunculus, florc luteo globoso. *Boerh.* i. 297. Ranunculus flore globoso. *Hod.* 427, *abr. in* Globe Crowfoot. *Pet. herb. t.* 43. /. 2, *$ repr. in* Ranunculus glomerato florc. *Clus. hist.* i. 237, *Sr* Ranunculus globosus. *Ger. by Johns.* 955. *and cop. in Park, theatr.* 331. *Raii cat.* 258. On the side of Snowdon near Llanberis, on the sides of Cadec Idris, in the meadows between Settle and Hinkelhaugh in Yorkshire, and in many places of the mountains in Wales Yorkshire and Westmorland.— *Raii syn.* 272. *Park. par.* 218. /. 219. /. 11.
Ranunculus flore globoso, quibusdam T. flos. *Bauh. J.* iii. 419.
Native of the south of France, Carniola, Germany, Scandinavia, Lapland, Wales, Yorkshire, Durham, Westmorland, Cumberland, and the lowlands of Scotland.—Dr. Jonathan Rogers Stokes observed it in coppices about Ingleborough hill in Yorkshire, and frequent on the side of water throughout Westmorland and Cumberland. TROLLJUS europaeus. *Krock. n.* 888 596. HELLEBORUS. *Calyx* none. *Corolla* pentapetalous. *Nectaria* 5 and more, tubular, bilabiate. *Capsules* several. *Obs.* 2651. L. 1. HELLEBORUS involucratus.

Scapus with an involucrnm. *Obs.* 2652. In a garden. II. hyemalis, *L. sp. 783; want.* 408. ' *Hort. kew.* ii. 272. *Curt. mag. t.* 3. *Krocl: n.* 892. *Jacq. austr. t.* 202. Eranthis hyemalis. *Sah R. in tin. tr.* viii. 304. Bulbosus unifolius aut bifolius batrachoides. *Lob. adv.* 300, *cop. in* Bulbus parvus unifolius. *Dalech.* 1505, *and repr. m* Aconitum Iiyemale. *Best. hort. hyem. fol.* 5. *Cam. epit.* 828. *Lob. ic.* ii. 676. /. 2. *Rait hist.* 700; *eur.* 52, frequent about Bologna and throughout
Lombardy.—*Lob. obs.* 385, *repr. in ic.* ii. 676.
f. 1, *and Ger. by Johns.* 968; *cop. in Park. theatr.* 314, *and abr. in par.* 214. *t.* 219. /. 1; *repr. from* Aconitum luteum minus. *Dod.* 437, *$ cop. in* Acouitum Lycoctonum luteum minus. *Dalech.* 1742,
Ranunculus cum flore in raeJio flore, rndice tubcrosa.
Jiauh. J. iii. 414. In the Euganean mountains in the Vicentine territory between Mount Gemula and
Vida. Aconitum aliud. *Dalech.* 1712. *Petals* deciduous, 6, the 3 inner somewhat smaller, circumstances which seem *to* shew that this forms the link between the other species and Tfollius. *Obs.* 2652. *Teb.* 9. 1792. *Natite* of Italy, Carniola, Austria, and Silesia, ACONITUM hyemale. *Cam. hort.* 5. *I.* HELLEBORTJS *niger.* Leaves pedate. Stem almost leafless. *Obs.* 2651. In a garden.— *L. mant.iOS; a Murr.* 519; *sp.783. Hort. kew.* ii. 272. *Jacq. austr. t.* 201. *Curt. mag. t.* 8; *mat. tned, t.* 1.. *Host.* 315. *Scop. cam.* «. *696.* Wood i. 50. *t.* 18. *Raii eur.* 142. Near Pontieba in the
Venetian territory.—*Lob. obs.* 388, *repr. in ic.* i.
681. H. grandiflorus. *Sal. R. in lin. tr.* viti. 304. Elleborus niger legitimum. *Clus. hist.* i. 274, *repr. in* Veratrum nigrum I. *Dod.* 381, *cop. in* Elleborus niger flore albo, interdum etiam valde rubente. *Rauh. J.* iii. 635, in woods; *repr. in* H. niger verus. *Ger. by Johns.* 976, *and cop. in Park, theatr.* 212; *par.* 344. *t.* 343. /. 6. *Raii hist.* 697. H. niger, flore roseo. *Boerh.* i. 297. Elleborus niger II. *Dalech.* 1636. Elleborum nigrum Matthioli flore purpureo. *Dalech.* 1634.

Folioles serrate, entire towards the base. *Petals* incumbent, white, green at the base on the inside and brownish reddish on the outside. *Nectaria* 14, tubular, pedicellate, yellowish green. *Capsules* univalve, unilocular, polyspermous. *Seeds* in 2 rows, fixed to the inner suture. *Obs.* 2651. 12 Feb. *Native* of Italy, Carniola, Austria, and Silesia. HELLEBORUS niger. Root. *Pharm, lond. # noviss. edin.—Alst.* 1. 456. *Berg.* 496. *Carth.* ii. 414. *CosteSf Willem, account from in med. comment.* v. 298. *Cull.* ii. 538. *Dale* 176. *Heb.* 261. *Herrn.* 135. *Hill* 559. *Home, F. clin.* 386. 387. *Kroch,* я. 893. *Lew.* i. 489; *disp. by Dune.* 232. *Linn.* 170. *Mead mon.* i. 96. 142. *Mill. Jos.* 2?6. *Monro* iit. 132. *Murr.* iii. 43; *J.* i. 269.288; ii. 91. *Pears. R.* i. 200. 292. *Quar. anim.* 22. 26. 178. 189. 200. 244. *Richard, accuentfrom in med.* VOL. 3. *s . comment,* ii. 165. *Spielm.* 634. *Wintr. in Mead mon.* i. 204. 276. Elleborus *nigcr. Rutty* 176. *Vog.* 194. Hclleborum nigrum. *Geoffr.* ii. 67. H. nigcr, flore roseo. *Chom.* 32. *Sckrod.* 761. Helleborus. *Quar. anim.* 11. Black Hellebore. *Cull. pr. n.* 1567. *Nenm.* ii. 104. Melampodium. *Denm.* i. 169. *Attic.* 131. BACHERS TONIC PILLS. *Ferr.* i. 60; ii. 143. 3. HELLEBORUS *viridflorus.* Leaves pedate. Stem leafy. Floral leaves serrate. *Obs.* 6263. la a garden. H. viridis. *L. sp.* 784; *mant.* 408. *Bot. arr.* 581. *Smith engl. t.* 200; *brit.* 598, on chalk.—*Jacq. austr. t.* 106. *Curt. lond.* vi. If. 34. Found by
Mr. Rayer in a wood near Finchley. H. nigcr, hortensis, flore viridi. *Raii hist.* 697; *eur.* 142; on the mountain of San Marino;—*si/n.* 271. Bigwin closes near Cambridge. Elleborus niger adulterinus hortensis. *Fuchs.* 277.
c. 96, *cop. in* Elleborus niger III. *Dalech.* 1637, # Elleborus niger vulgaris, flore viridi vcl hcrbacco, radicc diutuma. *Bauh. J.* iii. 636. In the Eu ganean mountains in the Venetian territory. Elleborus niger III. *Datech.* 1635. Elleborus niger adulterinus. *Trag.* 405. Veratrum nigrum II. *Dod.* 381, *repr. in* Hellcborastrum. *Lpb. obs.* 387; *ic.* i. 680, *and Ger. by Johns.* 976, *and cop. in* Ilelleboraster minor, flare viridante. *Park, theatr* 212. H. niger, flore viridi. *Besl. Iwrt. hyem. fol.* 2.
Stem about 1 foot long. *Leaves* shining underneath. *Flowers* solitary, terminal, opposite to the leaves and axillary. *Petals* subrotundo-elliptic,.with a glaucous bloom on the inner side, the 3 outer incumbent. *Pistils* 3. *Obs.* 6263. *Native* of Italy, Germany, Kent, Sussex, Cambridgeshire, Worcestershire, and Yorkshire. HELLEBORUS viridis. *Coste and Willem. in med. comment,* v. 298. *Krock. n.* 894. *Murr.* iii. 68. *SchoepfM.* H. hortensis, flore viridi. *Herm.* 136. H. niger hortensis, flore viridi. *Geoffr.* ii. 71. *Schrod.* 761.. *A*
H. niger vulgaris, flore Yiridi. *Chom.* S3.
4. HELLEBORUS *orientalis.* Stem with many flow ers. Leaves pedate, hirsute underneath. *L. a Willd.* ii. 1337, from a dried specimen.—*Lam.* H. officinalis. *Sal. R. in lin. tr.* viii. 305. H. niger. *Bellen.* 196. On Mount Olympus in Anatolia. HELLEBORUS niger orientalis, amplissimo folio, caule praealto, flore purpurascente. *Tourn. cor.* 20.—*Geoffr.* ii. 71.76. Black Hellebore of the antients. *Tourn. voy.* ii.
358. 5. HELLEBORUS *foetidus.* Leaves pedate. Stem leafy. Floral leaves entire at the margin. *Obs.* 3436. *L. sp.* 784. *Huds.* 245. In woods between Gounsberry and Blackwcll in Somersetshire. —*Bot. arr.* 582. *Woodv.* i. 53. *t.* 19. *Smith brit.* 598, on chalk; *engl. t.* 613. *Gou. hort.* 268. Near Montpelier.— *Poll. n.* 540. *Roth germ.* i. 234. Near Frankfort on the Oder.
H. niger foetidus. *Tourn. parts.* 200. *Vaill. parts.* 97. *Boerh.* i. 296.
Elleborus niger adulterinus sylvestris. *Fuchs.* 277. c. 96, *cop. in Dalech.* 1637, #
Elleborus niger silvestris adulterinus, etiam hyeme virens. *Bauh. J.* iii. 880, in the neighbourhood of Lyons ⎯ *and abr. in*
Consiligo Ruellii. *Trag.* 251.
Veratrum nigrum III. (misprinted II.) *Dod.* 382, *repr. in*
Sesamoides magnum Cordi, et
Consiligo Ruellii. *Lob. obs.* 387; *ic.* i. 680, *repr. in*
Consiligo Ruellii, et Sesamoides magnum Cordi. *Ger. by Johns.* 976, in fruit.
Helleboraster maximus, flore et semine praegnans. *Lob. ic.* i. 679, *cop. in*
Helleboraster maximus, si?e Consiligo. *Park, theatr.* 212, *and*
Elleboraster maximo flore, et semine praegnans. *Dalech.* 1638, o *repr. in*
Helleboraster maximus. *Ger. by Johns.* 976. *Best. hort. hyem. fol.* 3. *Raii syn.* 271. In hedges about Cherry Hinton near Cambridge, and observed *by* James Sherard near Brundish in Suffolk, and by Dillenius on the downs near Chichester in Sussex.
H. maximus. *JRaii hist.* 698. On the sides of the mountains on each side of the Rhine between Cologne and jyienlz. *Native* of France, the Palatinate, Brandenburgh, Sussex, Somersetshire, Gloucestershire, Oxfordshire, Northamptonshire, Cambridgeshire, Suffolk, and Norfolk. HELLEBORUS foetidus. *Pkarm. loud, noviss.*
Leaves.—*edin.—Bart.* 41. *Berg.* 497. *Coste and Willem. in tned. comment,* v. 298. *Lew. by Dune.* 232. *Linn.* 171. *Pears. R.* i. 201. *Schoepf* 94. H. niger foetidus. *Chom.* 33. *Geoffr.* ii. 71. Helleborastrum. *Dale* 177. Helleboraster. *Pharm. lond.—Lew.* i. 485. *Monro* iii. 128. *Murr.* iii. 70. Veratrum. *Geoffr. "suite* iii. 274. Bearsfoot. *Bisset ess.* 195, 597. CALTHA.
Calyx none. *Petals* 5 to 7. *Nectaria* none. *Cap«/«* 4 to 17, polyspermous. *Obs.* 81. L. 1. CALTHA *palustris.* Leaves cordato-reniform.
Stem erect. *Obs.* 81. In wet ground.—*L. sp.* 784. *Bot. arr.* 583. *Curt. lond.* i. 40. *t. Forst. T. m tin. tr.* viii. 323. *Walc. t.* FL Va«. *t.* 668.
Smith brit. 599; *engl. t.* 506. Caltha. *L. lapp. n.* 227. *Gron. virg.* 87. C. palustris simplici flore. *Best. hort. hyem. fol.* 4. C. Populago. *Gou. hort.* 268. Near Montpelier. Populago flore majorc. *Tourn. paris.* 295. *VailU parts.* 163. *Boerh.* i. 298. In Holland. Populago. *Dill. ap. Raii syn.* 272.
C. Vergilii. *Trag.* 142, *repr. in*
Chelidonia palustris. *Cord. fol.* 122. *p.* 1, *and cop.* 600. Teuchium. 619. Marrubittm. 602. Hyssopus. *Corolla,* upper lip bipartite; segments distant. *Obs.* 4040.

Corolla, upper lip bifid. *Calyx* decemeostate, quinquedentate and decemdentate. *Obs.* 360. *Corolla,* upper lip straight, semibifid. *Stamina* distant. *Obs.* 5259. 615. Hyptis. *Corolla,* upper lip semibifid. *Antherae* pendent. 614. Bystropogok. *Corolla,* upper lip bifid. *Calyx,* mouth bearded with bristles. *Obs.* 3051. *Corolla,* upper lip semibifid. *Calyx,* throat closed by a circle of bristles. *Obs.* 3370. 616. Origanum. 607. Glecuoma. *Corolla,* upper lip erect, semi bifid. *Antherae* approaching in form of a cross. *Obs.* 5552. *Corolla,* upper lip erect, semibifid. *Stigmata,* the shorter sheathing the other. *Obs.* 5505. *Corolla,* upper lip emarginate; lower lip, middlemost segment crenate. *Obs,* 311. *Corolla,* upper lip shorter than the stamina, emarginate. *Obs.* 2816. *Corolla,* upper lip erect, emarginate. *Stamina* remote. *Obs.* 2983. *Corolla* quadrifid; segments nearly equal. *Stamina* distant. *Corolla,* upper lip entire, slightly vaulted. *Stamina* scarcely extending beyond the throat. *Obs.* 3986. *Corolla,upper* lip slightly vaulted, crenate. *Calyx* decemcostate. *Obs.* 4013. 608. Dracocephalum. *Corolla,* upper lip vault ed; throat inflated. *Obs.* 193. *Corolla,* upper lip vaulted; lower lip tripartite; segments acuminate. *Obs.* 5710. 605. Sideritis. 603. Nepeta. 601. Satukeia. 606. Mentha. 613. Ballota. 610. Galeobdolon. 612. Stachvs. 609. Labium. 620. Piii.omis. *Corolla,* upper lip vaulted; lower lip trifid; lateral segments deflex. *Stamina* after shedding their pollen bent sideways. *Obs.* 3876. *Corolla,* upper lip vaulted; lower lip tripartite; lateral segments very short, dentate; middlemost segment bifid. 06s. 5665. *Corolla,* upper lip vaulted; lower lip trifid; middlemost segment bilobate. *Obs.* 3871. 2. *Calyces bilabiate.* L. 629. Scutellaria. *Calyx,* lips entire, the upper calcarate. *Obs.* 562. Ocimdm. *Calyx,* upper lip orbicular.
Plectranthus. *Calyx,* upper lip ovate. *Co.*
rolla resupinate, calcarateand gibbous at the base. *Obs.*
2959.
Calyx, upper lip entire; lower lip semiquadrifid. *Obs.* 538.

Calyx, lips entire dentate and cloven. *Corolla,* upper lip longer than the lower, flat.
Filaments bifid at the end, one of the branches bearing an anthera. *Obs.* 5313. *Calyx,* upper lip trifid; lower lip bipartite. *Corollat* throat inflated. *Obs.* 509. 628. Scohodonia. 604. Lavandula. 630. Brcnella. 623. Moldavica. *Calyx,* upper lip semitrifid and semibifid; lower lip bifid. *Corolla,* lower lip trifid, middlemost segmentcrcaate. *Obs.* 6305.
Calyx, upper lip trifid; lower lip bifid; throat pilose. *Coroll a,* lower lip trifid; middlemost segment emarginate. *Obs.* 5860. *Calyx,* upper lip semitrifid; lower lip bifid; throat pilose. *Corolla,* lower lip trifid; segments entire. *Obs.* 4755. *Calyx,* upper lip semitrifid; lower lip bifid. *Corolla,* upper lip semibifid; lower lip trifid. *Obs.* 5131. *Calyx,* upper lip entire and emarginate; lower lip obsoletely bidentate. *Corolla,* upper lip emarginate; lower lip trifid. *Obs.* 7516. *Calyx,* upper lip quadrifid. *Filaments* united into a tube, sheathing the style. *From Lour.* 652. Baeleria. base of the germen. *Obs.* 4557. *Capsule* bilocular, opening elastically. *Corolla* infundibuliform; segments nearly equal. *Obs.* 5605. *Capsule* bilocular. *Corolla* ringent. *Antherae* cuspidate. *Obs.* 5150. 631. Rhinanthcs. *Capsule* bilocular, compressed. *Corolla* rimrent. *L.* 637. SCROPHULAAIA. 634. Pedicularis. 635. Antirrhinum. 657. COLUMNEA. 636. Maktyma. cordate. *Antherae* with divaricate lobes. *Lour. Capsule* bilocular. *Corolla* campanulate; segments unequal. *Stamina* 4, with the rudiment of a fifth. *L. Capsule* bilocular. *Corolla* subbilabiate. *Filaments* supporting 2 antherae. *Capsule* bilocular, fusiform. *Corolla* tubuloso-campanulate; segments unequal. *Seeds* bordered and woolly. *Capsule* bilocular. *Corolla* bilabiate; tube globular; upper lip erect, bipartite; lower lip tripartite. *Ob si* 4008. *Capsule* bilocular. *Corolla* bilabiate; upper lip vaulted, compressed. *Nectarium* at thebaseofthegermen. *Obs.* 4877. *Capsule* bilocular. *Corolla* bilabiate, calcarate and gibbous at the base; throat closed. *Obs.* 557. *Capsule* bilocular. *Corolla* rin»

gent, gibbose above the base. *Antherae* connected. L.
Capsule quadrilocular, lignose. *Corolla* campanulate. *From* 654. Clerodendrum. *Berry* tetraspermous. *Corolla* infundibulilbrm; upper segments more deeply separated. 655. Vitex. *Berry* quadrilocular; cells monospermous. *Corolla* bilabiate; lips trifid. 640. Citharexvlum. *Drupe* unilocular, dispermous. *Nuts* bilocular. *Corolla* infundibuiifoimj segments nearly equal. 658. Acanthus. *Capsule* bilocular. *Corolla* unilabiate, trifid. *Anlhcrae* villose. *L* 653. Volkameria. *Drupe* bilocular; cells monospermous. *Nuts* bilocular. *Corolla* hypocrateriform; segments nearly equal. *Obs.* 5134., .«..:,...
' ' v.....xr,:i.. 5. *Calyces tetraphyllous.* 659. Picria. *Berry* bilocular. *Corolla* bi labiate. *From Lour.* 6. *Calyces pentaphyllous.* 638. Digitalis. *Capsule* bilocular. *Corolla* tubuloso-campanulate; segments unequal. *Stamina* decimate. *Obs.* 4127. 7. *Homers superior.* 646. Linn Aba. *Berry* trilocular, dry. *Corolla* campanulate. *L.*
Consolida media. *Cam. epit.* 702. *Fuchs.* 387, *c.* 148, *imit. in* Prunella germanis. *Trag.* 311, *8f cop. in* Consolida media, quibusdam Bugula. *Bauh. J.* iii. 430. /. 1,—but the leaves more distinctly serrate than in my specimens;—/. 2 a good representation. of it. *Stem* villose. *Obs.* 2816. *Native* of Europe, from the south of France to Denmark and Scotland. BUGULA. *Chom.* 561. *Dale* 156. *Geoffr.* iii. 229. *Lew.* i. 242. *Mill. Jos.* 96. *Rutty* 75. *Spiclm.* 202. *Vog.* 95. *a*
A. rcptans. *Murr.* ii. 123.
Consolida media. *Schrod.* 570.
2. AJUGA. *irifidifolia.* Leaves trifid. *Obs.* 4649.
Specimen raised from seeds gathered by Mr. Or doyno on Lincoln heath. A. Chamaepitys. *L. a WiUd.* iii. 10. *Smith engl. t.* 77; *brit.* 605. *Roth germ.* i. 252. Bugula Chamaepitys. *Scop. earn. n.* 718. Teucrium Chamaepitys. *L. sp.* 787. *Bot. arr.* 590. *Fl. dan. t.* 733. *Gou. hort.* 270. Near Mont pelier. Chamaepithys lutea vulgaris. *Tourn. paris.* 326, *Vaill. paris.* 35.
Chamaepitys lutea vulgaris, sive folio trifido.

Boerh. i. 183.
Chamaepitys. *Riv. mon. t.* 14.
Chamaepitys prima. *Dod.* 46, *repr. in* Aiuga. *Lob. obs.* 207; *ic.* i. 382, *and* Chamaepitys mas. *Ger. by Johns.* 525.
Chamaepitys prior. *Dalech.* 1159.

Chamaepitys terlia. *Trag.* 80. *Fuchs.* 840. c. 340, *cop. in* Chamaepitys vulgaris odorata, florc luteo. *Bauh. J.* iii. 295. /. 1;—*f.* 2. Chamaepitys vulgaris. *Park, theatr.* 283.

Native of Europe from the south to Denmark, and of the eastern side of England from Kent to Lincolnshire. CHAMAEPITHYS. *Pharm. austriaco-prov.* 28. *suec.*— *Alst.* ii. 111. *Carth.* iv. 168. *Hcb.* 51. *Lew.* i. 326; *disp. by Pother.* 136; *by Dune.* 318. *Linn.* 172. *Monro* iii. 60. *Murr.* ii. 121. *Quar. anim.* 291. *Schoepf* 95. *Schrod.* 561. *Stoll med.* i. 140. *Fog.* 59. Chamaepitys. JSerg. 500. J)a/e 156. *Iterm.* 496. itftf/. *Jos.* 131. Sptefei. 209. Chamacpithus lutea vulgaris. *Geoffr.* iii. 306. Chamaepithys lutea vulgaris, sive folio trifido. *C/iom.* 688. *Rutty* 120. 1. AJUGA Ira. Leaves linear, dentate towards the end. Flowers axillary, solitary. *L. a Willd.* iii. 11. *Schrcb.* Teucriumlva. *L. sp.* 787. *Gou. hort,* 271. Near
Montpelier. Tcucrium moschatum. *Sal. R. hort.* 76. Chamaepitys moschata, foliis serratis. *Bocrh.* i.
183. Anthyllis altera. *Clus. hisp.* 482, *repr. in hist.* ii. 186,.. Iva moschata monspeliaca. *Ger. by Johns.* 525, *cop. in* Anthyllis altera herbariorum. *Park, theatr.* 281, *and*
VoL. 3. T *l*

Chamaepitys, sive Iva moschata monspeliensium.
Bauh. J. iii. b. 296, *andrepr. in* Anthyllis Chamaepityiiies minor. *Lob. obs.* 208, *Sf*
ÍC i. 584, inner fig.;—outer fig. *repr. from*
Iva moschàta mouspelii. *Lob. adv.* 164. Anthyllis li herbariorum. *Dahch.* 1149. CHAMA E PITH YS moschata. *Geoffr.* iii. 307.
Chamaepithys altera. *Dale* 156.
Chamaepithys moschata, foliis serratis. *Скот.* 688.
600. TEUCRIUR Calyx quinquefid. *Corolla,* upperlip bipartite; sfgments distant. *Obs.* 4040. *L. l.* TEUCRIUM creticum. Leaves lanceolato-Iinear, entire at the margin. Flowers racemose, in threes. *L. a Murr.* 526; *sp.* 788. *Gou. hort.* 272.
T. foliis lanceolato-linearibus integerrimis subsessili-
bus, floribus solitariis pcdunculatis. *L. ups.* 159. T. calice campanulato, stoechatlos facie. *Boerh.* i. 181. Rosmarinum stocchados facie. *Alp. exot.* 103. *t.* 102, *cop. in. Hist. ox. s.* 11. *t.* 16. row l.f. 3. Poliura angustifolium creticum. *Park, iheatr.* 26. FOLIUM creticum. *Berg.* 502. *Dale* 145. *Linn.* 173. *Mill. Jos.* 353. *Murr.* ii. 112. *Spielm.* 289. *Vog.* 135.
Polium angustifolium creticum. *Lew.* ii. 239. *Rutty*
402. 2. TEUCRIUM Marum. Leaves entire at the margin, ovato-deltoid, acute, tomentoso underneath. Flower» solitary. Calyces semiquinquefid, hirsute. *Obs.* 6071. In a garden.—*L. sp.* 788; *mant.* 409. *H, K.* ii. 276. *Woodv.* i. 153. *t.* 56. Marum syriacum, Tc! creticum. *Boerk.* i. 182. Tragoriganum alterum. *Lob. ic.* i. 493, *repr. in* Tragoriganum Lobelii. *Ger. by Johns.* 668, *and cop. in* Tragoriganum latifolium, sive Marum Cortusi Mat thioli. *Park, theatr.* 17. Marum Cortusi. *Bauh. J.* iii. 242. Marum Matthioli. *Dalech.* 884. MARUM. *Pharm. suec.*—*Chom.* 390. *Lew.* ii. *91.* Ploucq. bill. i. 202. *Schrod.* 621. T. Marum. *Cull.* ii. 154. *Pears. R.* i. 113. Marum verum. *Pharm. austriaco-prov.* 48.—*Berg.* 502. *Carth.* ii. 281. *Geoffr.* iii. 821. *Linn.* 173. *Murr.* ii. 107. *Vog.* 67. Marum Cortusi. *Rutty 311.* Marum syriacum. *Alst.* ii. 173. Z)afe 145. *Lew. disp. by Dune.* 317. *Mill. Jos.* 286. iIfo«ro iii. 166.
S. TEUCRIUM Then. Leaves ovato-lanccolate. Slem procumbent. Peduncles axillary, triflorous *Lour* ii 440
4. TEUCRIUM Scordium. Leaves oblong, sessile, crenato-serrate. Flowers axillary. *Obs.* 7567. In Mr. Knowlton's garden.—*L. a Murr.* 527 i *sp.* 790. *Fl. dan. t.* 593. Huds.9Al. *Bot. arr.* 591. *Sibth. ox.* 180. TFooxfo. i. 156. *t.* 57. Soti/a *engl. t.* 828. Chamaedrys palustris canescens, seu Scordium officinarum. *Tourn. paris.* 414. *Vaill. parts.* 33

Scordium. *Riv. mon. irr. t.* II. *Cam. epit.* 588.
l'uchs. 776. ed. fol. cop. *in 735, c.* 298, *and Bank. J.* iii. *b.* 292. *Rati syn.* 246. In marshes in the isle of Ely.—*Dod.* 126, *repr. in Get. by Johns.* 661, *and Lob. obs.* 261, *cop. in* Scordium legitimum. *Park, thcatr.* Ill, *and rcpr. in* Scordium, sive Trixago palustris. *Lob. ic.* i. 497. Scordion. *Trag.* 885.
Scent of the *plant* resembling that of hops. Branches terminated by leayies not leafy racemi as in T. Chamaedrys, quadrangular, hirsute. *Calyx* semiquinquefid, hiisitte; segments equal, triangular. *Corolla* twice as long as the calyx; segments of the upper lip erect, ensiformi-triangular; lower lip tripartite; lateral segments ensiformi-triangular, acute, pa-ulous, somewhat longer than the upper lip; middlemost segment oblong, thrice as long as the lateral ones. *Obs.* 7567..
SCORDIUM. Water Germander. Herb. *Pharm. lond.*—*Alst.* ii. 105. *Berg.* 504. *Carth.* ii. 535. *Chom.* 278; *suppl.* 91. *Cull.* ii. 82. *Dale 156. Gepffr.* suite ii. 422. *Herm.* 531. *IIill* 368. *Lezo.* ii. 355; *disp. by Rother.* 240; *by Dune.* 318. *Linn.* 173. *Mill. Jos.* 402. *Monro* iii. 256. *Murr.* ii. 114. JS'eum. ii. 220. *Quar. febr.* 146. 240. 308. *Rutty* 473. *Schrod.* 677. *Spielm.* 226. *Vog.* 82. Wintr. in Mead mon. i. 230. 5. TEUCRIUM Chamaedrys.' Leaves cuneiformicllip-tic, inciso-serrate, hirsute. Racemi leafy. *Obs.* 7565. In a garden.—*Smith brit.* 607; *engl. t.* 680. *L. sp.* 790; *a Murr.* 527. *Huds.* 247, who justly nutfks it as a dubious native.—*Bot. arr.* 592. *Woodv.* iv. 82. *t.* 243, from a cultivated plant. CHAMAEDRYS. *Pharm. austriaco-prov.* 28. *suec.*—*Aht.* ii. 105. *Berg.* 506. *Carth.* iv. 165. *lleb.* 51. //em. 509. *Lew. disp. by Dune.* 348. *Linn.* 174. il/o«ro iii. 57. *Quar anim* 277. 292. *Schrod.* 561. *S/»Wro.* 206. *Fog-.* 59. *majus.* Larger in all respects than 0. Corolla palish, purple. *From Clus.*—*L.* «.
Chamaedrys major. *Clus. pann.* 610; *hist.* i. 351. No *(is;.*—*Rati hist.* 527; *eur.* 92. In mountainous situations between Vienna and Venice.

Chamaedrys major repens. *Magn. hort.* 52. *Boerh.* i. 182. In Holland.—

Dod. 43, *repr. in*

Chamaedrys. *Lob. obs. 260; ic.i.* 491, 4'

Chamaedrys major latifolia. *Ger. by Johns.* 656, *Sf cop. in*

Chamaedrys vulgaris. *Parle, theatr.* 104, has scarcely any resemblance of the plant.—*Riv. mon. t.* 10. Stems slightly ascending, 14 inches long, obsoletely tetragonous. *Obs.* 4040. In the area of Caris brook castle in the isle of Wight. *minus*. Smaller in all respects than a;. Corolla deeper purple. *From Clus.*—*L. &*

Chamaedrys minor. *Clus. pann.* 610. No fig.— *hist.* i. 351. No fig.

Chamaedrys vulgaris. *Raii hist.* 527. Found more than once in England, but doubtful whether native; *eur.* 92. In Italy, Germany, and France.

Chamaedrys vulgaris seu sativa. *Raii syn.* 231. On the borders of fields, but though at a considerable distance from any house, I dare not assert that they grew there spontaneously.—Found by James Sherard on the ruins of Winchelsea castle.

T S

Chamaedrys minor repens. *Tourn. paris.* 69. *Vaill. parts.* 33. Chamaedrys vera mas. *Fuchs.* 825; *c.* 334. *cop. in* Chamaedrys vulgo vera existimafa. *Bauh. J.* iii. *b.* 288. *Magn. monsp.* 58. Sometimes glabrous. Chamaedrys repens minor. *Dod.* 43, *repr. in* Chamaedrys major. *Lob. ic.* i. 491, Chamaedrys vulgaris sive II. *Clus. hist.* i. 351, *and* Chamaedrys minor. *Ger. by Johns.* 656, *and abr. in* Chamaedrys. *Park. par.* 456. *t.* 457. /. 5, has still less resemblance to the plant.—*Cord. Jal.* 126. *p.* 1, *repr. from* Chamaedrys vera. *Trag.* 204.

Stems stightly ascending, obsoletely tetragonous, hirsute, 9 inches long. Leaves attenuate at the base; of a scent somewhat similar to that of T. Marum, the under surf.ice with numerous minute globules; margin revolute, the lower half entire. *Bracteae*, the lower cuneiformi-elliptic, the upper elliptic and enlire at the margin. Flowers 6 in a whirl. *Calyx* quinquefid; segments pubescent and white at the margin, the uppermost patulous, somewhat broader, the rest erect, the 2 lowermost narrower. *Obs.* 7565. CHAMAEDRYS. Dale 145. *Geoffr.* iii. 296. *Mill. Jos.* 129. *Murr.* ii. 119. *Rutty* 116. *Stoll med.* i. 140.

Chamaedrys minor repens. *Chom.* 462.
6. TEUCRIUM *fiavum*. Leaves cordato-ovate ovate and obovate, crenate and nearly entire at the margin, villose. Floral leaves ovate, mostly entire at the margin. Flowers in threes. Stem shrubby. *Obs.* 4041. Specimen gathered by M. Broussonett, probably at Montpelier. — *L. sp.* 791. *H. K.* ii. 280. *Gou. hort.* 273. Near Montpelier. T. calice lubulato, flore pallide lutcolo. *Boerh.* i. 181. Chamaedrys assurgens. *Dod.* 44, *repr. in* T. vulgare fruticans, sive I. *Clus. hist.* i. 348, *and* T. latifolium. *Ger. by Johns.* 658, *and cop. in* T. majus vulgare. *Park, theatr.* 109. Chamaedrys fruticosior, flore ochroleuco. *Hist. ox. s.* 11. Í. 22. /. 1. T. multis. *Bauh. J.* iii. *b.* 290. /. 2.—/ ". 1, *and* T. alterum. *Dalech.* 1166, *cop. from* TEUCRIUM. *Fuchs, fol ed.* 829, *cop. in* 787. *c.* 321.—*Dale* 145. *Schrod.* 691.
7. TEUCRIUM *revolutum*. Leaves lanceolate and lineari-lanceolate, tomcntose underneath; margin entire, revolute. *Obs.* 3456. Specimen gathered in France, very slightly aromatic. T. montanum. X. *sp.* 791. *Gou. hort.* 270. Near Montpelier.—*Hort. kew.* ii. 280. „ villosulum. Leaves villosulose on the upper surface.

Obs. 3456. Polium lavandulae folio. *Tourn. paris.* 518. *Vaill. paris.* 160. *Boerh.* i. 183. Symphytum pctraeum Matthioli. *Dalech.* 1174. Polium majus. *Cord. fol.* 125. *p.* 1. Polium lavandulae folio. *Lob. obs.* 258, *repr. in* Polium recentiorum femioa, lavendulae folio. *Lob. is.* i. 488,

Polium VII cum flore. *Clus. hist.* i. 363, *and*

Pol in m lavandulae folio, flore albo. *Ger. by Johns.* 655, *and cop. in* Polium montanum, lavendulae folio. *Park, theatr.* 25. Another fig. of the lavander leaved Poley. *Ger. by Johns.* G55. No fructifications.

POLIUM montanum. *Murr.* ii. 113.
Polium alterum. *Dale* 144.
Polium lavendulae folio. *Tourn.* ii. 222.
8. TEUCRIUM *Polium*. Spikes roundish and oblong.

Leaves oblong, obtuse, obtusely serrate, sessile, to mentose. *Obs.* 8256. Specimen gathered in the

Vienna garden.—*L. a Murr.* 528; *sp.* 792 *a. Gou. hort.* 271 *a*. Near Montpelier. T. aurenm *β. L. a Willd.* ii. 34. T. verum. *Besl. hort. aest. ord.* 7. *fol.* 11. Polium montanum luteum. *Raii hist.* 525. *Magn. monsp.* 207. *Boerh.* i. 183. *Ger. by Johns.* 653, *repr. from* Polium. *Dod.* 282, *which repr. in* Polium montanum III. *Clus. hist.* i. 361, *cop. in* Polium montanum luteum. *Hist. ox. s.* II. *t.* 2.

row 1. /. 1, *Barrel, t.* 1082, *Sf* Polium montanum vulgare. *Pari: theatr.* 24, *and repr. in* POLIUM luteum. *Lob. obs.* 257, *and ic.* i. 487.

—*Geojfr. suite* ii. 26. Polium montanum. *Dale* 144. *n.* 2. *Spielm.* 289. Polium. *Aht.* ii. 202. *Herrn.* 477. Polium montanum luteum. *Chom,* 367. *Tourn.* ii. 9. TEUCRIUM *Teuthrion*.—Heads roundish, on short peduncles. Leaves lanceolate, crenate, tomentose, hoary. Stem decumbent. *Willd.*—*Schreb.* T. Polium. *L. a tVilld.* iii. 36; *sp.792$. Hort. hew.* ii. 281 *a* Polium montanum album. *Raii hist.* 524. *Ger. by Johns.* 653, *repr. from* Polium tenuius. *Dod.* 282, *which repr. in* Polium montanum I. *Clus. hist.* i. 361, Polium montanum. *Lob. obs.* 257, & *ic. i.* 486, *and cop. in* Polium montanum minus. *Park, theatr.* 24. POLIUM album. *Geoffr. suite* ii. 28. Polium montanum album. *Chom.* 367. *Monro* iii.

224, *Tourn.* ii. 222. Polium montanum. *Dale* 144. *n. 1, Murr.* ii. 112. 10. TEUCRIUM *capilatum*. Heads pedunculate. Leaves lanceolate, crenate, tomentose. Stem erect.

L. sp. 792. *Hort. hew.* ii. 291, T. Polium 0. *Gou. hort.* 270. Near Montpelier, T. scu Polium maritimum erectum monspeliacum. *All. nic.* 42. Polium montanum album. *Raii eur.* 206. Polium monspessulanum. *Bauh. J.* iii. *b.* 299. On the seashore near Montpelier. POLIUM maritimum erectum mospeliacum. *Magn. tnonsp.* 207. *Raii hist.* 524. In Italy and the south of France, near the sea.—*Lew.* ii. 239. *Rutty* 402. *Tourn.* ii. 222. Polium montanum. *Dale* 144, *n.* 4. *Mill. Jos.* 352. *Murr.* ii. 113. 601. SA-

TUREIA. *Calyx* semiquinquefid. *Corolla*, upper lip erect, emarginate; lower lip tripartite; segments nearly equal. *Obs.* 2983. L.

Scarcely distinct from Thymus.

1. SATUREIA *capitata.* Flowers spicate. Leaves carinate, punctate, ciliate. *L. sp.* 795. *IJort. leers,* ii. 282. Thymus capitatus, qui Dioscoridis. *Boerh.* i. 155. *Rati hist.* 519; Cw r. 249. Near Syracuse. Thymum cephaloton. *Dod.* 275, *repr. in* Thymum legitimum. *Clus. hist.* i. 357, Thymum. *Lob. obs.* 231; *ic. i.* 424, # Thymum crcticum. *Ger. by Johns.* 574. Thymum legitimum capitatum. *Park, theatr.* 7. Thymum creticum incanum capitatum. *Barrel. t.* 897. Til YMUS creticus. *Berg.* 508. *Linn.* 175. Thymum creticum. *Geoffr. suite* iii. 185. Thymum verum. *Dale* 142. Thymus capitatus, qui Dioscoridis. *Chom.* 374. *Butly* 516. 5. SATUREIA *Thymbra.* Flowers verticillate, hispid.

Leaves oblong, acute. *L. a Murr.* 528; *sp.* 794.

Hort. 1cm. ii. 281. S. cretica, folio rigido brevi crasso. *Boerh.* i. 161. Thymum creticum Ponae verticillatum. *Barrel, t.* Thymbra legitima. *Clus, hist, i.* 358, *cop. in*

Tbymbra, sive S. cretica legitima. *Park, theatr.* 5, -and *repr. in* SATUREIA cretica. *Ger. by Johns.* 576.—*Chom.* 387. Thymbra vera. *Dale* 142.

3. SATUREIA. *virgata.* Panicles pedunculate, axillary, dicliotomous, fastigiate. Leaves lineari-Ianceolate, revolute at the margin. *Obs.* 3078. In Mr. Hunter's nursery. S. Juliana. *L. sp.* 793. *Mill. Ph. diet. n.* 6. *Horl. kew.* ii. 281. S. sive Thymbra vera Sancti Juliani. *Lob. adv.* 181, *repr. in* Thymbra Sancti Juliani, sive S. vera. *Lob. ic.* i. 425, *cop. in* S. spicata Sancti Juliani. *Park, theatr.* 5, S. foliis tenuibus, sive tenuifolia Sancti Juliani quo rundam. *Bauh. J. iii. b. 273,* Thymbra vera Penae. *Dalech.* 897, *8f* S. perennis, verticillis spicatim & densius dispositis. *Hist. ox.* iii. *s.* 11. *t.* 17. row 4. /. 4, *and repr. in* fi. Sancti Juliani. *Ger. by Johns.* 576. *Raii hist.* 518. On the hills about Messina, and on the walls of Florence. Stems ascending, 16 inches long, with a few short branches at the base; the flowering part 10 inches long, straight. *Panicles* opposite, about as long as the leaves. *Pedicles* short. *Calyx* cylindrical, with about 12ribs; segments subulate, erect. *Corolla* bilabiate; upper lip bifid; segments rounded; lower lip half as long again at the upper; lateral segments oblong, middlemost cuneiformi-subrotund. *Obs.* 3078. SATUREIA spicaia. *Dale* 142.

S. scu Tbymbra vera. *Gcoffr. suite* ii. 380.

4. SATUREIA *brachiata.* Panicles pedunculate, axf illary. Leaves lineari-lanceolate, ratber obtuse, punctate. Stem brachiate, fastigiate. *Obs.* 2983.

In a garden. S. hortensis. *L. sp.* 795. *Hort. hew.* ii. 282. *Gou. hort.* 273. About Montpelicr.—*Ra-i hist.* 518. *Ger. by Johns, 5i5, repr. from Lob. ic.* i. 426, *which repr. in* S itureia. *Lob. obs.* 232, *and Bod.* 288. *Trag.* 45, *repr. in Cord. fol.* 146. *p.* 1, *cop. from* S. sativa. *Fuchs.* 301, *which cop. in Bauh. J.* iii. *b.* 272. ' S. vulgaris bortensis Matthioli. *Dalech.* 898. S. altera. *Cam. epit.* 487. Cahjx with 10 costae; segments triangular, rather obtuse, witb hairs on the inner side and along the margin. *Obs.* 2983. SATUREIA. *Pharm. austriaco-prov.* 65. *suec.— Alst.* ii. 219. *Berg.* 507. *Carth.* iii. 135. *Dale* 142. *Geoffr. suite* ii. 376. *Herm.* 456. *Lew.* ii. 314; *disp. by Rother.* 237. *Zinn.* 174. *Mill. Jos.* ;,. 395. *Mart-,* ii. 145. i2«*My* 466. *ScArorf.* 674. *Spielm.* 296. *Fog.* 81. S. bortensis. *Bry.* 143. S. hortensis, sive Cunila sativa Plinii. *Chom.* 387; *suppl.* 121. 5. SATUREIA *mucronifolia.* Panicles pedunculate, axillary, dichotomous, fastigiate. Leaves lanceo late, mucronate, punctate. Segments of the calyx mucronate. *Obs.* 2982. In a garden. S. montana. *L. sp.* 794; *manl.* 410. *Hort lew.* ii. 282. *Scop. car»,* n. 738. *t.* 30. *Gou. hort.*273. About Montpelicr.

S. pedunculis dicholomis. *L. vps.* 161. *Roy.* 324. S. montana durior, flore in pediculis ramosis ex alis foliorum. *Hoerh.* i. 161. S. montana flosculis candidis. *Magn. monsp.* 230. S. bortensis. *Lob. obs.* 232, *repr. in* S. sive Thymbra altera. *Lob. ic.* i. 426, # S. hortensis acstiva. *Ger. by Johns.* 575. ' Si durior. *Banh. J.* iii. *b.* 272. (The fig. is that 1 of some other plant.)—*Raii hist.* 518, In the south of France and in the bed of a torrent near Radicofani in Tuscany.— *Dalcch.* 897.

Thymbra. *Dod.* 287, *cop. in* Thymbra'c effigies Dodonaci. *Dalech.* 898.

Saxífraga secunda. *Cam. epit.* 717. B. *Leaves* carinate, ciüate at tire base. *Panicles* disposed *in* terminal leafy racemi. *Calyx* slightly bit labiate, with 10 costae; upper lip trifid; lower lip bipartite; segments subulate, acute, with erect hairs at the base on the inner side and at the commissures,. in all which respects it accords with Thymus. *Seeds* sometimes 2. *Obs.* 2982. SATUREJA montana. *JTzy.* 143. S. hortensis. *Mill. Jos.* '296. Thymbra. *Dale* 112.

602. HYSSOPUS. *Calyx* quinquefid. *Corolla,* upper lip.straight, scmibifid; lower lip tripartite; middlemost segment with 2 patent lobes. *Stamina* distant. *Obs..* 5259. L. 1. HYSSOPUS *officinalis.* Racemi secundose. Leaves lanceolate. *Obs.* 5259. In a garden.—*L. a Murr.* 529; *sp.* 796. *Hort. hew.* ii. 283. *Woodv.* i. 181. /. 65. *Jacq. austr. t.* 254. *Host.* 320. In Car niola. Hyssopum goritienso, floribus verticillatim ambienti- bus. *Bauh. J.* iii. *b.* 276. A specimen gathered by Agerius near Gortz in Carniola. H. oflicinarum caerulea scu spicata. *Boerh.* i, 160. H. arabum Mesuae & oflicinarum. *Lob. obs.* 237', *fepr. in ic.* i. 433, *8f* II. arabum. *Ger. by Johns.* 579, *and cop. in* H. coronata sive comosa Clusii. *Park, theatr.* 2. H. hortensis. *Fuchs.* 798. c. 325, *cop. in* Hyssopus. *Trag.* 47. H. vulgaris. *Dod.* 286. (The fig. a different plant. *Calyx* slightly hirsute within, somewhat bilabiate, upper lip trifid; lower lip bipartite. *Obs.* 5259. HYSSOPUS. *Pharm. austriaco-prov.* 42. *suec.* —*Alst.* ii. 152. *Berg.* 509. *Carth.* iii. 124. *Cull.* ii. 147. Date 142. *Geoffr.* iii. 611. *Herm.* 475. .tft'tf 363. *Zea.* i. 503. Z/«h. 175. *Mill Jos.* 239. ATonro iii. 137. *Murr.* ii. 133. *Neum.* ii. 218. *P/ouca. WW.* i. 40. *Quar. febr.* 283. 287. 288. 334. 335; *anim.* 91. 110. *Rosenst.* 247. ' *Rutty* 245. ScAroa. 605. *Sjie/n.* 269. *Vog.* 64. II. officinalis. Herb. *Pharm. edin.—Bry.* 138.

X,ra. *disp. by Dune.* 238. il/«rr. *J.* i. 207. Hyssop. *Baylies in med. pap.* 44.

Chalm. ii. 165. Hysope. *Chom.* 386; *suppl.* 120.

603. NEPETA. *Calyx* semiquinquefid; segments equal. *Corolla,* middlemost segment of the lower lip crenate. *Stamina* approaching. *Obs.* 311. L. 1. NEPETA *Cataria.* Raccmus spikelike. Whirli on short peduncles. Leaves petiolate, cordate, crenato-serrate, *Obs.* 311. Among the ruins of Lilleshall abbey in Shropshire on limestone, on gravel near Worcester, and on gravel and red cos between Sutton and Birmingham.—*L. suec. n.* 514; *sp,* 796. *Huds.* 249. *Fl.dan. t.* 580. *Bot. arr.* 593. *Smith brit.* 608; *engl. t.* 137. *N.* major vulgaris. *Dill, ap Rail syn.* 237.

Cataria major vulgaris. *Tourn. parts.* 254. *Vaill. paris.* 31.

Cattaria herba. *Dod.* 99, repr. in

Cataria, sive Mentha catti. *Lob. ic. i.* 511,

Mentha felina, seu Cattaria. *Ger. by Johns.* 682, abr. in

Nep, or Cat Mint. *Pet. herb. t.* 32. /. 1, *and repr. in*

Mentha Cataria. *Lob. obs.* 276. *Raii syn. ed.* ii. 127; *hist.* 548. *Bauh. J.* iii. *b.* 225, *abr. from*

Calaminthae primum genus. *Furhs.* 426, c. *1G6,* who describes the corolla as purple.

Nepeta. *Trag.* 15. *Riv. mon. t.* 52. Ilcrba Cattaria. *Matth.* 719.

Calyx with 15 ribs, when in fruit ventricose underneath *i* segments subulate. *Obs.* 311. NEPETA. *Phartn. austriacoprov.* 52.—*Berg.* 510. *Dale* 150. *Geoffr. suite* i. 157. *Herm.* 470. *Lew.* ii. 130; disp. by *Roth.* 202. *Linn.* 175. *Mill. Jos.* 310. *Murr.* ii. 156. *Rutty* 345, *Schoepf* 95. *Schrod.* 631. *Vog.* 110.

N. vulgaris. CAom. 176;.w//;/)/. 62. Cataria. *Spielm.* 252.

Mentha Cataria. *Alst.* ii. 181.

604. LAVANDULA. *Calyx* tubular, bilabiate. *Corolla,* upper lip larger than the lower lip, flat, semibifid; lower lip trifid. *Stamina* not projecting. *Obs.* 3049. *L.*

Linnaeus calls the corolla resupinate, from the stamina being inserted into the lower side of the throat.

1. *Lower lip of the calyx quadridentate.*

1. LAVANDULA *Spica.* Leaves lanceolato-liuear and lanceolate, those of the branches revolute at the margin. Racemus spikelikc, interrupted. *Obs.* 199. In a garden.—*L. sp.* 800. *L.fil. ap. L. am. x. pars* ii. 52. *Hort. hew.* ii. 287. *Gou. /-ort.* 276; *monsp.* 86. LAVANDULA. *Pharm. land, iwciss.*—*Berg. n.* 322. Lavendula. *Pharm. lond.*—*Carth.* iii. 170. *Cull.* ii. 147. *Ileb.* 302. *Ilerm.* 571. .777/423. *Monro* iii. 155. *Quar. anim.* 10. *Spielm.* 274. *Vog.* L. Spica. Flowering spikes. *Pharm. edin.*—*Less. disp. by Dune.* 248. *Mutt. J.* i. 343. *Pears. It.* i. Ill; ii. 185. Lavendar. *Kirkl. apopl.* 143. a deltoidea. Bracteae ovato-deltoid. Corolla blue. *Obs.* 199. L. Spica. *L. a. Ehrk. quoted in L. a Willd.* iii. GD *a. Lin. jil. up. L. am. x. pars* ii. 58 «. *Woodv.* i. 150. *t.* 55. Lavandula angustlfolia. *Mill. Ph. diet. n.* 2. L. foliis lanceolatis integrLs, spicis nudis. *L. cliff.* 303; ups. 162, where it is said to be for the most part perennial. L. latifolia. *Bocrh, i.* 152. *Magn. monsp.* 151; *hort.* Ill Pseudonardus mas. *Fuchs.* 845. c. 303, *cop. in* Pseudo-uardus, quae vulgo Spica. *Bauh. J.* iii. *b.* 280, *and air. iii* Spica. *Trag.* 58. Lavendula major. *Park. par.* 447. No fig.

Lavendula. *Dod.* 273, repr. in Spica rircentiorum, sive Nardus italica. *Lob. obs.*

235, Nardus italica, sivc Spica recentiorum. *Lob. it.* i.

431, L. flore caeruleo. *Ger. by Johns.* 583, *Sf cop. in* Lavendula major, sive vulgaris. *Park, theatr.* 73. *Rail hist.* 512; *eur.* 161. In the south of France. L. foemiha. *Dalech.* 919. *Stem* fruticose, 3 feet long, erect. *Leaves* of the stem tapering downwards, scarcely revolute at the margin, green with a few stellate hairs, 2 inches 3 tenths to 2£ inches long, '2 to 4 tenths of an inch U broad; those of the branches very much revolute at the margin, whence appearing linear and obtuse, glaucous, hoary, tomentose with stellate hairs. *Bracteae* brown, those at the base of the verticilli ovatodeltoid, acuminate; those at the base of the pedicles subulate, unequally bifid; segments subulate. *Calyx* somewhat longer than the bracteae, 2 tenths of an inch long; tube with 13 costae; upper lip erect, roundish ovate, tapering at the base, with 3 costae, projecting beyond the lower lip; lower lip truncate, with 3 obsolete teeth. *Corolla* violet coloured; upper lip erect, bifid, just sensibly broader than the lower, half as long again, tomentose without, slightly so within; segments roundish oblong; lowerlipdeeply trifid; segments ovato-oblong, smaller than those of the upper lip. *Stamina* inserted on the lower side of the tube of the corolla, the 2 upper being opposite to the commissures of the upper and lower lips. *Obs.* 199. $ *linearis*—*Sal. W.* 52.— Bracteae linear. Leaves spa tulate. *From Ehrh. quoted in L; a Willd.* iii. 60. *Hort. hew.* ii. 287 y. *L.* (3? is described as annual.

—*L. jil. ap L. am. x. pars* ii. 58? is described as having oval leaves. L. latifolia. *Donn* 141. Lavendula Spica. *Mill. Ph. diet. n.* 1. Leaves of the shoots much shorter and broader than those of a, those of the stems somewhat broader than those of a. Stems taller. Panicles larger. Flowers smaller. Does not often flower. LA VEND ULA angustifolia. *Rutty* 276. ' L. major. *Geoffr.* iii. 683.

Lavendula. *Alst.* ii. 159. *Dale* 141. Lea', ii. 45.

Mill. Jos. 259. *Murr.* ii. 135.

L. latifolia. *Chom.* 382; *suppl.* 119. Spica mas. *Schrod.* 685.

Spica latifolia. *Mill. Jos.* 422. Leaves broader than those of *a,* not quite so hoary. Stems taller. Pa nicies larger. Flowers smaller. L. altera. *Dod.* 273, repr. in Spica Lavendula. *Lob. ic.* i. 431, # L. minor, sive Spica. *Ger. by Johns.* 584. *Park. theatr.* 73. No figure. Pseudo-nardus foemina. *Fucks.* 845. c. 303, cop. t« Pseudo-nardus, quae Lavendula vulgo. *Bauh. J.* iii. 6. 281. Lavendula. *Trag.* 57. Lavendula minor, seu Spica. *Park. par.* 447. *t. t.* 451./. 2.

L. mas. *Dalech.* 9W.

L. arigustifolia. *Magn. hort.* 113. *Boerh.* i. 152.

LAVENDULA latifolia. Lea;, ii. 47.

L. minor. *Geoffr.* iii. 684.

L. Spica latifolia. *Murr.* ii. 135.

L. angustifolia. ////. ii. 160. *Chom.* 382; 5«ppl 119.

Spica Lavendula vulgaris. *Da/e* 141.

Spica latifolia. Mi//. Jos. 422.
Spica. Linn. 176.
Spica foemina. Schrod. 685.
2. LAVANDULA Stoechas. Leaves linear, sessile, tomentose; margin revolute. Spike compact, comose. Bracteae with mostly 3 lobes. L. sp.SOO, H.K.u.288.
Stoechas. Dod. 274, repr. in Lob. obs. 234;
Stoechas, sive Stichas. Lob. ic. i. 429,
Stoechas, sive Spica hortulana. Ger. by Johns. 585, and
Storcbas brevioribus ligulis. Clus. hist. i. 344, and cop. in Hist. ox. s. 11. t. 1. row 3. f. 1, and
Stoechas vulgaris. Park, theatr. 67, and abr. in
Stoecbas. Park. par. 448. t. 451. /. 3.
Stoechas arabica vulgo dicta. Bauh. J. Hi. 277.
Stoeclns arabica. Barrel, I. 301.
Catyx with 12 ribs; upper lip reniformicordate, incumbent on and just longer than the lower lip; lower lip with 4 obsolete teeth. Obs. 5540. Specimen gathered in the garden of Fothergill. STOECHAS. Alst. ii. 231. Geoffr. ii. 280. Hcrm. 581. Lew. ii. 389; dUp. 232. Murr. ii. 138. Schrod. 687. Spielm. 300.
Stoechas arabica. Dale HI. Linn. 176. Mill. Jos. 425. Rutty 499. Fog. 155.
Stoechas purpurea. Chom. 385. Neum. ii. 217. 605. SIDERITIS. Stamina within the tube of the corolla. Stigma, the shorter half sheathing the other. Obs. 5505. L. . 1. Without bracteae. L. 1.
SIDERITIS montana. Calvx bilabiate; upper seg ment trifid. 06s. 7896. Specimen gathered in the Vienna garden.—L. sp. 802. Hort. keic. ii. 290. Jacq. austr. r. 16. t. 434.
Murrubiastrum sideritidis folio, caliculis aculeatis, flore flavo cum limbo atro-purpureo. Boerh. i. 171.
    S. hirsute, pallido flore. Jiaii hist. 564.
    S. montana, parvo flore nigro-purpureo, capite medio croceo. Col. ecphr. i. /. 196.
    S. (losculis vix ex vasculis prominentibus fuscis.
Bavh. J. iii. 427.
Leaves entire at the margin. Obs. 7S9G.

SIDEMT1S pannonica III. Clus. pann. 601, repr. in
    S. VI. pannonica. Clus. hist. ii. 41, and
    S. angustifolia. Ger. by Johns. 697. Corollae represented nearly twice as long as the calyces, though described as barely projecting beyond them.
2. SIDERITIS hirsuta. Calyx semiquinqucfid. Bracteae with spinose teeth. Flowers verticillate. Leaves spatulato-elliptic, serrate, hirsute. Stems, villose, decumbent. Upper lip of the corolla twice as long as the lower. Obs. 5510. Specimen gathered in FothergilPs garden.—L. sp. 803; mant. 410; a Mutt. 532. Hort. hew. ii. 293.
S. heraclea. Clus. hisp. 390, repr. in hist. ii. 38,
    Tetrahit herbariorum. Lob. ic. i. 523, /
    Herba judaica. Dod. 94,
    Herba judaica Lobelii. Ger. by Johns. 690, and cop. in
    Tetrahit, S. heraclea Dioscoridis. Dalech. 1119.
    S.Clusio hispanica hirsuta. Bauh. J. iii. 426. No flgS. sive Ferrnminatrix. Lob. adv. 223, repr. in Lob. ic. i. 523, was probably intended to represent if, though so ill agreeing with the descr. of the leaves.
Leaves similar to those of Teucrium Scordium. Calyx hirsute, with 10 ribs; segments triangular, terminated by a short spine; hairs acute, articulated. Corolla just longer than the calyx, hirsutulous above; upper lip oblong square, cmarginato-semibifid; lower lip twice as short as the upper, trilobate; lobes incumbent, the middlemost emarginate, the lateral ones twice as small, triangulari-ovate. Obs. 5510. SIDERITJS. Dale 153. Diosc. I. iv. c. 33. Schrod. 683.
S. hirsuta procumbens. Magn. hort. 184;
M. spicata, folio longiore acuto glabro nigriori.
Bank. J. iii. 230, and abr. in Nepeta aquatica. Trag. 20. (M. romana ofticinarum, sive praestantior angusti folia. Lob. obs. 271, repr.in ic. i. 507, M. tertia. Dod. 95. Sr M. romana. Ger. by Johns. 680, is a pretty good representa-

tion of it, but is M. sylvestris. M. quarta. Dod. 95, is M. gentilis.) Leaves when chewed not exciting a sense of warmth in the mouth as those of M. piperata. Corolla purplish white; segments with a purple bloteh, Stawina shorter than the corolla, Antherae without pollen. Obs. 5965.—Calyx, segments triangularisubulate, hirsute. Corolla, upper segment emarginate, microscopically hirsute on the outside, the rest retuse. Stamina extending beyond the corolla to a fifth of the length of the corolla. Obs. 5966. Specimen gathered in a garden in Worcestershire. MENTHA viridis. Pharm. lond. notiss.—Bry, 105. Murr. J. i. 206. Pears. R. ii. 188. Schoe'pf 96. M. romana. Geoffr. suite i. 32. M. sativa. Spear Mint. Herb. Pharm. lond.— Alst. ii. 180. Cull. i. 149. 153. Heb. 274. Hill 357. Lew. ii. 101; disp. by Dune. 254. Mill. Jos. 290. M. angustifolia spicata. Chom. 436. M. sativa acuta. Schrod. 624. Mentha. Dale 145. Monro iii. 170. Rutty 322. Mint. Blane 452. Chalm. i. 154. 186. 191. 193. 203; ii. 41. 116. Denm. i. 254. 194. Graing. 51, Rush i. 136. Und. i. 306.
Spear Mint. Lind hot clim. 314.
3. MENTHA tomentosa. Racemi terminal, oblong, composed of verticilli. Leaves cordato-lanceolate tomentose underneath. Stem tomentose. Calyces villose; segments subulate; hairs longer than the breadth of the segments. Obs. 6038. Specimen from Prof. Jos. F. Jacquin. M. candicans. Mill. Ph. diet. n. 3. M. villosa prima. Sole 3, t. 1. Me»thastrum sylvestre foliis latis. Besl. hort aest ord 7 t 3 f 2. Menthastrum, sive M. sylvestris. Cam. epit. 479. Menthastrum. Riv. mon. t. 51. f. 1, Dod. 9Q, repr. in Clus. hist. ii. 32, cop. in Mentastrum hortense, sive M. sylvestris. Park. theatr. 33, and repr. in Mentastrum. Lob. obs. 273; ic. i. 509, and Ger by Johns. 684. Trag. 20, repr in Cord, fat 157. p. 1. Fuchs. 289. c. Ill, cop. in Menthastrum spicatqm, folio longiore candicante. Bauh. J. iii. 221. Rati syn. 234. Found by Lister at Burvvelbeck in Lincolnshire, and by Dale in a meadow behind the alms houses at Great Yeldham in Essex. M. tertia. Dod. 95, repr. in M. romana officiuarum, sive praes-

tantior angustifolia. *Lob. obs.* 271; *ic.* i. 507; *Sr*

M. romana. *Qer. by Johns.* 680.

Stem tomentose, whitish. *Leaves* whitish underneath, the upper lanceolate. *Racemi* from to $ of an inch long. *Calyx* nearly membranaceous; hairs flexible, jointed, numerous, set close along the margin in a pectinate form, extending beyond the end of the segments, extremely fine, as narrow again at the ends as those of M. villosa. *Corolla,* uppermost segment emarginate, hirsute on the outside; 3 lower segments oblong. *Stamina* nearly as long again as the corolla. *Obs.* 6038.—*Calyx* as above described. *Corolla* not expanded. *Obs.* 6037. In a garden at Dolgethly in. Merionethshire, where used for the same purposes as M. vhidis.—*Stamina* longer than the corolla. *Obs.* 6794. Specimen from Dr. Boehmer. MENTHA sylvestris. *L. sp.* 804. Huds. 250. *Fl. dan. t.* 484. *Bot. arr.* 596. Smith in lin. tr. v. 179a; *brit.* 609 a; *engl. t.* 686.—*Linn.* 177. *Murr.* ii. 152. Mentastrum. *Alst.* ii. 181. *Dale* 146. Menthastrum. *Rutty* 324. *Herm.* 470. *Mill. Jos,* 293. M. longifolia. *Berg.* 515. 4. MENTHA *villosa.* Racemi terminal, composed of verticilli. Leaves ovato-elliptic and elliptic, rugose, acute, villose underneath. Calyces hirsutulous; hairs straight; segments triangulari-subulate. *Obs.* 6036. On the side of the road in Beightoa *in* Derbyshire, a village south of Rotherham. — Huds. 250. « *elliplicifolia.* (Variation.) Leaves elliptic. *Obs.* 6036; M. villosa secunda. *Sole* 5. *t.* 2. M. sylvestris £ *Smith brit.* 610. Menthastri aquatici genus hirsutum, spica latiore. *Bauh. J.* iii. 222. (The fig. seems a species of Nepeta.) *Raii sj/n.* 234. S(em purple at the base. *Leaves* sessile and on very short petioles, some cordato-elliptic, pubescent above, villose and pale green underneath. *Racemi* when in flower attenuate; lowermost verticillus someate, hirsute; hairs shorter than the breadth of the segments. *Stamina* extending nearly half as far again as the corolla. *Obs.* 3105.—*Leaves* when chewed at the end of 8 years slightly acrid but not diffusing the glowing warmth of M. piperata. Specimen. *Obs.* 3105.—*Stamina,* 2 extending just beyond the corolla, the other 2 somewhat shorter than the corolla. *Obs.* 6768. Specimen from Mr. Robson gathered by Mr. Flintoff near the sea at Saltburn. ,*6 variegata.* Leaves variegated with straw colour. *Obs.* 719. In a garden. M. rotundifolia *0 Smith in lin. tr.* v. 183 i *briL* 611. M. sylvestris $ *Sole* 7. Menthastrum niveum anglicum. *Besl. hort. aest. ord.* 7. *fol.* 3. *Ger. by Johns.* 684, *cop. in* Menthastrum spicatum, folio crispo rotundiore, colore partim albo partim cinereo vel virente. *Bauh. J,* iii. 219. *Racemi* numerous. *Calyx,* segments whitish at end; hairs shorter than the breadth of the segments. *Stamina* not extending so far as the end of the tube of the corolla, sometimes extending a little beyond. *Obs.* 719.—*Leaves* when chewed bitterish and slightly acrid, not diffusing the glowing warmth of M. piperata; their scent somewhat aromatic but not like that of the generality of mints. *Obs.* 6782. In a garden. ' MENTHA alba. *Geoffr. suite* i. 36. M. sylvestris. *Dale* 146. M. sylvestris, rotundiore folio. *Chom.* 177. 6. MENTHA *piperata.* Umbels in terminal racemi. Leaves lanceolate, serrate, petiolate. Stamina shorter than the corolla. *Obs.* 4089. On the eastern side of the old turnpike road between Whittington and Unston in Derbyshire, a little to the north of the bridge at a distance from any house, observed for two years successively.

M. piperita. Huds. 251. *Mitt. Ph. diet. n.* 6. On the side of the river between Mitcham and Croydon in Surry,—but he describes the stamina as longer than the corolla. Perhaps all the plants in which the stamina are shorter than the corolla may have become barren by having propagated themselves solely by the roots; but I am inclined to suspect that he mistook styles for stamina. The description of the stamina may possibly have been formed from Dillenius's fig. in Raii *syn.—Knigge t. at p.* 40. *Bot. arr.* 599. *var.* 2. Smith in tin. tr. v. 189; *engl. t.* 687; *brit.* 614 *a.* Zorn *t.* 156. *Regn.* —Wood-o. iii. 461. *t.* 169. (*L. sp.* 805, is M. glomerata iS)

M. piperita officinalis. *Sole* 15. *t.* 7.

M. piperis sapore. *Black-a. t.* 291.

Leaves when chewed exciting a glowing heat in

the tongue and palate continuing for a few minutes.

A specimen at least 50 years old excited the same sensation of heat. 20 Sep. .. *pubescem.* (Variation.) Leaves pubescent on the upper side. *Obs.* 4089.—*Obs.* 5260. In a wet diteh between Grenhill moor and Great Norton in Derbyshire; but the plants in both instances probably the refuse of gardens.— *Obs.* 6739. In a garden cultivated for distillation. 20-Atig.

M. spicis brevioribus & habitioribus, folks M. fuscae, sapore fervido piperis. *Raii syn. erf.* ii. 124. Found by Eales in Hertfordshire.—*Ditt. 'ap Raii syn.* 234. *t.* 10/. 2, may be the plant, but verticilli too distant, floral leaves too large and stamina re *Stem* slightly hirsute, branched above. *Leaves* undulate and curled at the margin, villose underneath, when chewed exciting some warmth but not equal to that of M. piperata. *Racemus,* the terminating one to 1 inch long; lowermost verticillus separate from those above. *Pedicles* glabrous. *Calyx* nearlyquinquefid, glabrous, hirsutulous above; hairs very short, scattered; segments subulate. *Corolla* purplish, one third longer than the calyx. *Stamina* extending as far as the middle of the limb. Probably a curled variety of a species whose usual form we are unacquainted with. The habit of its fructifications induces me to suspect it to be a variety of M. piperata. *Obs.* 6796. MENTHA crispa. *Pharm, avstriaco-prov.* 49.

suec.—*Berg.* 514. *Carlh.* iii. 127. *Herrn.* 467. *Lew. disp. by Dune.* 344. *Linn.* 177. *Murr.* iL 146. *Spiebn.* 280. *Vog.* 69. M. sativa crispa. *Schrod.* 624. Mentha. *Quar. febr.* 80. 82. *92.* 207. 375. 376. 382: *anim.* 167. 229. 235. 8. MENTHA *multifida.* Braclae multifid. *Obs.* 6771. Specimen gathered in the Paris garden. M. cervina. *L. sp.* 807; *mant.* 411. *Hort. kew.* ii. 295. Pulegium angustifolium, sive cervinum monspelien sium odoratius. *Lob. adv.* 214, *repr in ic.* i. 501, *cop.* with a separate branch *in* Pulegium angustifolium, sive cervinum. *Park. theatr.* 31, *and repr. in* Pulegium angustifolium. *Ger. by Johns.* 672. *Hist. ox.*

s. 11. *t. 7. row 3. f. 7.* Near Montpelier. Pulegium ccrYinura angustifolium. *Iiauh. J.* iii.

Stems slightly scabrous, with minute defies rigid hairs. *Leaves* linear, glabrous, dotted underneath. *Bracteae* nervose at the base, dotted above. *Flowers* sitting and on very short pedicles. *Pedicles* glabrous. *Calyx* glabrous, without any circle of hairs on the inside; the margin minutely ciliate; segments ending in short spines. *Corolla* as long again as the calyx. OAs.6771. *PULEGIUM* cervinum. *Mill. Ph. diet. n. 3. Dalech.* 892— *Alst.* ii. 181. *Dale* 147. *Lew.* ii. 250. *Mill. Jos.* 363. 9. MENTHA *Pulegium.* Leaves obovato-oblong. Calyx pubescent, with a circle of hairs on the inside. Pedicles pubescent. *Obs.* 6772. Specimen gathered by Mr. Hollefear, probably on the side of a pool at Roberts-end near Hanley castle in Worcestershire.— *Smith in lin. tr.* v. 217; *brit.* 624; *engl. t.* 1026. *L. sp.* 807. *Lour.* ii. 437. *Huds.* 254. *Lightf.* 306. 1135. *Bot. arr.* 602. *Sibth. ox.* 183. Wet moors and commons.

« *repens.* Stem creeping. *Obs.* 6772. M. Pulegium. *Sole* 51. *t,* 23. *Woodv.* iii. 466. *t.* 171

Pulegium vulgare. *Mill. Ph. diet. n.* 1. Pulegium latifolium. *Tourn. parts.* 224. Pulegium, quae M. aquatics, seu Pulegium vulgare.
Vaill. parts. 126.
Pulegium mas, sive sativum. *Fuchs.* 198, *ed. fol.*
cop. in 198. *c.* 73, *Sf* Pulegium. *Bauh. J.* iii. *b.* 256, *impr. in Trag.* 13. *tirunsf.* i. 227. *Cam. epit.* 471. *Rait syn.* 235. *Riv. mon. t.* 23. /. 1.

Pulegium regium. *Dalech.* 891. *Ger. by Johns.* 671, *cop. in* Pulegium vulgarc. *Park, theatr.* 29, and ill abr. in Pulegium *Pari· par t* 475. /. 5
Stem putescent, tetragonous, 4£ inches long. *Leaves* obovato-oblong; margin mostly entire, sometimes obsoletely serrate. *Pedicles* microscopically pubescent; h;drs horizontal. *Corolla,* upper segment mostly emarginate. *Stamina* longer than the corolla. *Obs.* 6772,— *Stem* curved, 9 inches long. *Leaves* ovali-oblong and ovali-elliptic, sometimes serrate. *Pedicles* as in Obs. 6772. —*Obs.* 6774. Specimen gathered in a garden. *PULEGIUM.* Pennyroyat. Herb and flowers. *Pharm. lond.—Alst.* ii. 181. *Berg.* 518. *Cull.* ii. 151. *Date* 147. *Geoffr. suite* i. 37. *llcrm.* 472. *Hill* 341. *Lew.* ii. 250. *Linn.* 178. *Monro* iii. 225. *Murr.* ii. 153. *Rutty* 416. *Schrod.* 657. *Spielm.* 289. *Vog.* 76. M. Pulegium. Herb. *Pharm. cdin.—Tordyce, G. fev.* iv. 140. *Leio. disp. by Dune.* 254.' *Murr. J.*
"i. 207. *Pears. R.* i. 146;' ii. 189. Pulegium latifolium. *Chom.*372; *suppl.* 115. Pulegium vulgare. *Mill. Jos.* 362. B *erecta.* Stem erect. *Obs.* 6773. Specimen in an old herbarium collected in Britain. Pulegium mas Plinii. *Lob. ic* i. 501, *cop. in Bauh. J.* iii. 257, *and repr. in* Pulegium mas. *Ger. by Johns.* 671, *Rati hist.* 534.
Stem a foot long. *Leaves* ovato-oval. *Pedicles* microscopically pubescent; hairs slightly deflex. *Calyx* pubescent on the outside, with a circle of hairs on the inside. *Obs.* 6773. *PULEGIUM* erectum. *Mill. Ph. ditt. n.* 2, from seeds sent to him from Gibraltar.—*Dale* 147. 10. MENTHA *arvensis.* Flowers verticillate. Cauline leaves ovate, floral leaves elliptic. Corolla villose within and without. *Obs.* 5006. On the brink of a canal near Aldercar in Derbyshire.—*L, suec. n.* 516; *sp.* 806. *Huds.* 253. *Bot. arr.* 601. *Sole* 29. *t.* 12. *Smith brit.* 623. *Fl. dan. t.* 512.
Pulegium quae M. arvensis verticillata hirsuta. *Vaill. parts.* 126.

M. arvensis verticillata hirsuta. *Tourri. parís.* 495. *Boerh.* i. 185. *n.* 9. *Bauh. J.* ii. *b.* 217, *cop. from* '

Caliminthae secundum genus. *Fuchs.* 426. *c.* 166, *which imit. i»* " '
Nepeta agrestis. *Trag.* 16, *which cop. in*
Nepeta IIII. *Daksh* 907
M. aquatica exigua. *Trag.* 24.
M. aquatica belgarum. *Lob. obs.* 270, *repr. in ic.* i. 505, ft
Calamintha aquatica. *Ger. by Johns.* 684, 8ç *cop. in*
Calamintha arvensis verticillata, sivë aquatica belgarum. *Park, thealr.* 37, # Polycnemum Lobellii. *Dalech.* 932. '

Villose, whitish green. *Branches* patent. *Corolla*
Villose within and without. *Stamina* abortive. *Obi;* 5006.
CALAMINTHA arvensis. -*Geoffr.* ili. 239. Calamintha aquatica. *Rutty* 80.
Calamintha palustris. *Dale* 147.
Calamentha aquatica. *Mill. Jos.* 103.
Calaraentha arvensis verticillata hirsuta, *thorn.* 373.
VOL, 3. X 11. MENTHA *rubra.* Flowers verticillate. Stem branched. Corolla nearly glabrous wiihin; upper lip villose on the ou'side. *Obs.* 5183. In a wet itteadow.—*tiuds.* 252
Af. gentilis. *L. sp.* 05. *Sole* 35. *t.* 15. *Bot. arr.* 600. jM. jncills. *Smith brit.* 622; *engl. t.* 449. M. fasca sive vulgaris. *Rati syn.* 232, where instead of 3 species, read 1 species, as evident from ed. i...
Menfa sativa quarfa. *Fuchs.* 288, c. 11-1, *cop. in*
M. vcrticillata minor acuta non crispa, odore ocymi.
Bauh.J. iii 6.216.....-",.
M quarla. *Dod* 95, *repr. in*
M-romana angustifolia sive cardiaca. *Lob. obs.*
271; *andic.* i. 508, *cop. in Park, theatr.* 31, *Sc repr. in..* M cardiaca. *Ger. by Johns.* 680.
Stems smoothish, shining, blackish purple. *Leaves* strongly tinged with blackish purple. *Stamina* as lon$ as the corolla, sometimes abortive when shorter than the corolla. *Obs.* 5183. MENTHA cardiaca. *Ceoffr.suitei.il,* M fusca. *Dale* 147. M. balsamina. *Berg.* 520. L
M. hortensis verticillata, ocimi odore. *Chotn.* 436.

12. MENTHA *stricta.* Leaves ovate, hirsutulous. Stem erect. Throat of the corolla glabrous. Pcdicles glabrous. Cajyx glabrous below. *Obs.* 6780. On the b inks of the liother below Chesterfield, some feet above the Wiiter. M rubra *Smith in tin. tr.* v. 205; *ettgL t.* 1413; *brit.* 619, but the leaves described as shining.
M. rivalis. *Sole* 45. *t.* 20, as it appears when first come into flower. Corolla described as very pale pink. Jvi. sativa. *Sole* 47. *t.* 21, as it appears in its more advanced state of flowering. Veins of the leaves described as red. M. sativa

prima. *Fuchs.* 267. *c.* Ill, *cop. in* M. crispa verficillata, folio rotundiore. *Bauh. id.* 215. *Raii syn. ed.* ii. 124. M. verticillata. *Dill. ap. Rait syn.* 232. (M. prima. *Dod.* 95, *repr. in* M. vnlgata serpens, rotundiore folio. *Lob. obs.* 271 j M. cruciata. *Lob. ic.* i. 507, *and* M. sativa rubra. *Ger. by Johns.* 680, *and cop. in* M. crispa. *Park, theatr.* 32, has leaves *too* oblong, and a stem too hairy, and described as decumbent at the base.), *Scent* very strong, similar to that of dried M. viridis. *Stem* glabrous, brownish purple. *Corolla* glabrous; uppermost segment slightly hirsute. *Stamina* extending beyond the corolla one third of its length. *Obs.* 6026. In water at Matlock on the side of the road to Tansley. —*Root* creeping. *Stem* branched, 4J feet long, erect, brownish purple below, hirsutulous, branched from about the middle. *Branches* patent, flexuose. *Leaves* ovate, lower ovalt-ovate, rather obtuse, recurvate, dull, hirsululous, dark green above, paler underneath, not hot in the mouth as those of M. piperata; *fioral leaves* subrotundoovatej acute. *Petioles* short. *Whirls* numerous, each consisting of 2 umbels. *Umbels* pedunculate. *Pkduncles* about as long as (he pedicles, sometimes shorter, glabrous. *Bracteae* ciliatej outer lanceolate, inner subulate. *Pedicles* brownish purple, some what shorter (han the calyces. *Calyx* glabrous below, hirsutulous above, brownish purple on one side,
glabrous within and with a few hairs on tho inner side of Ihe segments; segments subulato-triangular.-
Corolla one third longer than the calyx, rose coloured purple. *Stamina* shorter than the corolla, abortive,
in a few flowers a little longer than the corolla and containing perfect antherae. *Pollen* white. *Obs.* 6780.
MENTHA sativa. *Bry.* 104.
M. crispa. *Dale* 147. *Geoffr. suite* i. 29.
M. crispaverticillata. *Boecl.ap.Herm.* é68. *Chom.*
435; *suppl.* 136.
β *slerilis.* (Variation.) Antherae without pollen.
Obs. 4142. In a sandy road.
Stem slightly hirsute, erect, straight,

simple above, with barren branches below. *Stamina* as long as the corolla. Hence it appears probable that when plentifully supplied with water the stamina are fertile. This opinion may be ascertained by transplanting barren plants into a watery situation. *Obs.* 4142. 13. MENTHA glomerate. Verticilli terminal, rounded at the end. Lower leaves ovato-oval, upper ovate.
Obs. 5113. In water on the edge of a canal.
M. aquatica. *Httds.* 252. *Sibth. ox.* 182. *a glahriuscula.* (Variation.) Leaves nearly glabrous.
Stamina longer than the corolla. *Obs. 1160.* Ou
Ae banks of the Sow near Staflbrd. 16 Oct.
M. aquatica. *L. sp.* 805. Plant not hairy. Verticilli, the terminal ones crowded into a head or obtuse spike. Stamina longer than the corolla.—Dr.
Smith assures us that the specimen found in the
Ljnnacan herbarium under this name is a verticillate Mint.—*Bot. arr.* 598. M. aquatica minor. *Sole* 23. *t.* 10, in its smoother state as said to be found in Somersetshire Wiltshire and Wales. Stem and leaves represented as glabrous.
Stem tetragonous, rigid, pubescent, 2 feet long and upwards. *Leaves* ovate, acute, horizontal, somewhat recurvate, rather rigid, dotted; veins and costa underneath pubescent, above with distant very short hairs. *Petioles* pubescent, sulcate on the upper side. *Verticilli* crowded into a subrotundo-oblong head. Has the scent and taste of M. piperata. *Ob,s* 1160, but whether I attended only to the flavour apd pmitted to notice the warmth 1 know not. The leaves chewed at the end of 29 years excite no sense of heat. £ *piperata.* (Variation.) Leaves nearly glabrous. Stamina shorter than the corolla. *Obs.* 1222. Specimen gathered probably in the neighbourhood of Birmingham, by Withering, who informed me that it had the taste of M. piperata, but the leaves chewed at the end of 29 years excite no sense of warmth. M. piperita, *L, sp.* 805. *Huds.* 251 0. *Bot. arr.* 599. *tar.* 1.

M. piperita vulgaris. *Sole* 19. *t.* 8.
M. hirsuta y *Smith brit.* 617.
M. nigricans. *Mill. Ph. diet. n.* 12,
Stem pubescent above. *Leaves* ovali-elliptic; uppermost ovate; costa below on the upper side pubescent; costa and veins underneath pubescent. *Obs.* 1229. y *hirsutula.* (Variation.) Leaves pubescent. Stem hirsute; hairs deflex, adpressed. Stamina longer than the corolla. *Obs.* 5113. On the side of the Cromford canal.
M. hirsuta. *Smith engl. t.* 447.
M. aquatica major. *Sole* 25. *t.* 11. Hairs of the stem horizontal.
M. palustris. *Mill. Ph. diet. n.* 11.
Origanum vulgare. *Fl. dan. t.* 638.
M. rotundifoliapalustris, sive aquatica major. *Tourn. paris.* 212.
Pulegium, quae M. rotundifolia palustris, sive aquatica major. *Vaill. paris.* 125.
Sisymbrium. *Fuchs.* 684. c. 276, *cop. in*
M. aquatica, sive Sisymbrium. *Bauh. J.* iii. 6. 223. *Raii syn.* 233. *Ger. by Johns.* 684, *repr. from*
Sisymbrium. *Dod.* 97, which abr. in Common water Mint. *Pet. herb. t.* 31. /. 6, *cop. in*
Sisymbrium silvestre. *Dalcch.* 677, *Sʃ repr. in* 3V1. aquatica sive sisymbria rubro folio, & flore nir grae menthae. *Lob. obs.* 272, # *ic.* i. 509; *adv.* 218. No fig.
MENTHA aquatica. *Alst.* ii. 181. *Dale* 146. *Geoffr. suite* i. 34. *Herm.* 469. Jl«0. ii. 104. *Afttf. Jos.* 292. *Sjjie/m.* 280.
M. rubra. *Pharm. austriaco-prov.* 49.— *Lew. disp. by Dune.* 344.
b,t. rotundifolia palustris, seu aquatica major. *Chom.* 177. J *abortiva.* (Variation.) Leaves and stem as y. Stamina shorter than the corolla. *Obs.* 5184. In a dryish ditch. *Stem* Tillóse. *Leaves* pubescent above, villose underneath. *Corolla* 2£ tenths of nn inch lon, villose without, glabrous within. *Obs.* 51S4.
607. GLECHOMA. *Calyx* scraiquinquefid: segments nearly equal. *Corolla,* upper lip erect, semibifid; lower lip trifid. *Antherae,* each pair approaching in form of a cross. *Obs. 5592. L.* 1. GLECHOMA *hederaceum. L. suec.* 518: *sp.* 807. *Bot. arr.* 603. *Curt. load.* ii. 44.

l. 143; *mat. med. t. II. Fl. dan. t.* H-9 *Wood-o.* i. 84. *t.* 28. *Smith brit.* 625. *Huds.* 254. *Mart. rust. t.* 61, *Light/.* 307. *Gou. hört.* 280. Near Montpelier, Hederá minor. *Rh. mon. t.* 67. *Calyx* sublabiate; 3 upper segments equal, 2 , lowet shorter; hairs articulated. *Corolla,* middle» most segment emnrginate; lateral segments shorter than and thicc as narrow as the middlemost. *Obs.* 5536. Native of Europe, from the south to Sweden, and of Madeira. GLECHOMA hederacea. *Phys. journ,* xvii. 562. *Ploucq.* ЫЫ. i. 4)9. Hederá terrestris. *Pharm, austriaco-prov.* 41. *suec, -rAUt.* ii. 146. *Berg.* 521. *Carth.* iv. 16b *Culi.* ii-145. *Dale* 154. *Geoffr.* iii. 541. *Herrn* 1J4. *Hill* 361. *Lew.* i. 484; *disp. hy Rother.* 168; *by Dune.* 342. *Linn.* 178. *Mead mon.* ii. 59, *Mill. Jos.* 221. *Monro* iii. 127. *Murr,* ii, 174. *Rutty* 233. *Schoepf* 96. *Schrod.* 600. *Spielm.* 380. *Vog.* 64. *a rotundatum.* Leaves cordatoreniform; teeth rounded. *Obs.* 5532. Specimen gathered near Worcester.— *Wide. t.* Calamintha humilior, folio rotundiore. *Tourn. parts* 181. *Dill. ap. Raiisyn.* 243. Chamaeclema vulgare medium. *VailL parts.* S3, f. *6.f.* 6. Hedera terrestris major. *Bank. J.* iii. 855. Hedera humilis. *Lob. obs.* 336, *repr. in ic.* i. 613, IJedera terrestris. *Ger. by Johns.* 856, *and cop.* «» *Park, theatr.* 677. *Rail hist.* 567; *syn. ed.* ii. 131. *Sloane cat.* 65. In Madeira. Leaves to 7 tenths of an inch long. *Ohs.* 5532. *$ parcifolium.* Leaves cordate; teeth rounded. *Obs.* 394. Near Worcester.
Chamaeclema vulgare minus. *Vaill. paris. 33. l. 6. / 5.*
Calamintha humilior, folio rotundiore, cauliculis ercctioribus brevioribus, et foliis minoribus. *DHL ap. Raii syn.* 243.
Chamaecissos. *Fucks.* 831, e. 336.
Leaves to inch long. *Antherae* abortive. *Obs.* 394. *Obs.* 5536. Specimen gathered near Edinburgh. J *grandifolium.* Leaves cordato-reniform, from 1 to If inch long; teeth rounded. *Obs.* 5534. Specimens in two old herbals collected in England.
Chamaeclema vulgare majus. *Vaill. paris.* 33. *t.* 6.
Lamium III peregrinum. *Clus. pann.*

597, *repr.*
Lamium pannonicum III. *Clus. hist.* ii. 58, *and*
Ger. by Johns. 704.
Leaves, teeth transversely semi-oblong, sometimes
emarginate. *Obs.* 5534. *cordi folium.* (Variation.) Leaves cordate; teeth acute. *Obs,* 5531. Specimen gathered near Worcester.—*Buds. 0. Bot. arr.* 604 g
Chamaeclema majus hirsutius. *Vaill. parts.* 33.
Hedera terrestris montana. *Dill. ap. Raii syn.* 243.
Chamaecissos, seu Hedera terrestris. *Trag.* 799. *Stem* sometimes 2 feet long. Leaxts to If inch lpng. *Obs.* 5531, 608.
DRACOCEPHALUM.
Calyx semiquinquefid. *Corolla,* throat inflated. *Obs.* 193. L. *Tourn.* 1. DRACOCEPHALUM *ternatifolium.* Flowers spicate. Leaves ternate. *Obs.* 193. In a garden.
D. canariense. *L. sp.* 829. *Hort. kew.* ii. 317.
Dracocephalo affinis americana trifoliata, terebinthinac odore. *Folk.* 145. *t.* 145.
Cedronella canadensis viscosa, foliis ex eodem pedicel Io temis. *Commel. Casp. hort.* ii. 81. *t.* 41.
Camphorosma. *Hist. ox. s.* 11. *t.* 11. row. 3.*f.* the last.
Melissa forte canariana triphyllos, odorem camphorae spirans penctrantissirrfum. *Pluk. phyt. t.* 325. /. 5. No fructifications. *Calyx,* ribs 15; segments ovate. *Obs.* 193.
MELISSA canadensis. *Carth.* iii. 99, *Murr.* ii,
Moldavica. *Lew-*ii. 113.
Melissa canaria. *Linn.* 181.
609. LAMIUM.
Calyx quinquefid. *Corolla,* upper lip entire, vaulted; lower lip tripartite: lateral segments very short, dentate; middlemost segment bifid. *Obs.* 5665. X. 1.
LAMIUM *purpureum.* Leaves cordate, obtuse, obtusely crenate, petiolate. Lateral segments ot the lower lip of the corolla with 1 tooth on each side; margin of (he upper lip entire. *Obs.* 5665. On diteh banks.—*Hort. kew-*ii. 297. *L. suec.n.* 5il; *sp.* 809; *mant. t.* 534. *Bot. arr.* 605. *Curt. lond.* i. 42. *t. Wale. t.*

Mart. rust. t. 25. *Smith brit.* 627; *engl. t.* 769. *Fl. dan. t.* 523. L. purpureum foetidum, folio subrotundo, sive Galeopsis Dioscoridis. *Tourn. paris.* 206. *Bocrh.* i. 157. In Holland. Galeopsis minor. *Riv. man. t.* 62. Galiopsis, si ve Urtica tners folio et fiore minore. *Bauh, J.* iii. *b.* 323. No fig. L. rubrum. *Rati hist.* 559; *syn,* 240. *Ger. by Johns.* 703, *repr.ftora* Urtica iners altera. *Dod.* 153, *rrpr. in* "'*;.* Urtica non mordax vulgaris foetens purpurea. *Lob, ic.* i. 520, *& cop. in.* L. vulgarc, flore rubro. *ParIc. tfiratr.* 605, *and* Galeopsis purpurea. *Pafech.* 1248. *Corolla* i inch long; lateral segments with a short LAMIUM album. *Berg.* 523. *Dale* 153. *Geojr.* iii. 657. *Linn.* 179. *Mill. Jos.* 251. *Monro* iii..: 154. JHim-. ii. 178. Lamium. *Pharm. austriaco-prov.* 44.—*Alst.* ii. 158. *Zero.* ii. 40. *Rutly* 270. *Spte/m.* 652. *Vog.* 131. Urtica inere, sive Lamium I. *Ckom.* 596. 3.
LAMIUM *maculatum.* Leaves cordate, obtusely crenate, rugose, hirsute. Stems hirsute. Whirls multiflorous. Lateral segments of the lower lip of the corolla with a setaceous tooth about the middle. *Obs.* 7414. In Mr. Knowlton's garden. —*L. sp.* 809; *a Murr.* 534. *Roth germ.* i. 252. *Rati hist.* 561. *Host* 325. Do«n 143. L. inontanum campoclurensium. *Col. ecphr.* i. *t..* 192, *cop. in*
Lamium inontanum Columnae. *Park, theatr,* 605.
A
L. alba linea notatum. *Boerh.* i. 158. JfaV Ais.
560; *ear.* 159. In Italy, and the south of prance. L. montanum, flore ex albo purpurascente, foliis albis maculis nonnihil aspersis. *Tilli pis.* 93. Galeopsis folio maculato. *Bauh. J,* iii. 322. No *Stem* 9 inches long, ascending; hairs jointed, deflex. *Leaves* crenate; *petioles* as long as the laminae. *-Fiokcts* 10 in a whirl. *Corolla* white; upper lip concave, irregularly crenate, hirsute at the margin; lower lip, lateral segments with a setaceous tooth about the middle, and an obsolete tooth near the middlemost segment; middlemost segment obrenU . form, obsoletely crenate. *Antherae* hirsute, tawny. *Pollen* orangccoloured, *Seeds* 4, oblongo-cuuei Lamium flare luteo. *Riv. mon. t.* 20.

Lamium luteum. *Rati hist.* 560; -*syn.* 240. *Lob. ic.* i. 521, *repr. in Ger. by Johns.* 702, *cop. in Park, theatr.* 606, *abr. in*

Yellow Archangel. *Pet. herb. t.* 53. /. 6, # *repr. in*

Urtica iners tertia, sive Lamium luteo flore. *Dod.* 153.

GALEOPSTS, sive Urtica iners flore Iuteo. *Tourn. part's.* 450. *Vaill. parts.* 77. *Boerh. 'i.* 162. In Holland.—*Bauh. J.* iii. *b.* 323. (The fig. Lamium album.) *Geoffr.* iii. 513.

Lcucas montana. *Dale* 153.

. 611. BETONICA. . *Calyx* quinquefid; segments spinosc. *Corolla*, upper lip slightly bowed back; lower lip trifid. *Stamina* and *pistil* scarcely extending beyond the throat of the corolla. *Obs.* 3986. L 1. BETONICA *officinalis*. Upper lip of the corolla entire and emarginate; middlemost segment of the lower lip emarginate. Segments of the calyx subulate, somewhat shorter than the tube; tube glabrous, Spike mostly interrupted. Upper leaves lanceolato-oblong. *Obs.* 3986. On the side of a Toad.—*Hort. kew.* ii. 299. *L. sp,* 810. *Wale. t. Curt. lond.* iii. 33. *t.* 154. *Bot. art.* 611. *Smith cvgl. t.* 1142; *brit.* 632. *TVoodv.* iv. 78. *t.* 241. j*Ri dan. t.* 726. *Lour.* ii. 411.. B. purpurea. *Tourn, parts.* 320. *Vaill. parts.* 20. *Boerh.* i. 154, 612. STACHYS. *Calyx* quinquefid. *Corolla*, upper lip vaulted; lower lip trifid; lateral segments bent down. *Stamina* after shedding their pollen bent sideways. 06s. 3876. L. 1. *Leaves entire.* . STACHYS *sylvatica*. Leaves cordate, acute. Six flowers in a whirl. *Obs.* 3876. In hedges.—*L. suec. n.* 526; *sp.* 811. *Bot. arr.* 612. *Curt lond.* iii. 34. *t.* 183. *Smith engl.t.* 416; *brit.* 633. i?n.

«io». *t.* 26. Henclea. T*Vag.* 5. Galeopsis procerior foetida spic&ta. *Tourn. parts.* 196. *Vaill. paris.* 77. *Boerh. i.* 162. Galeopsis legitima, *Clus. hist.* ii. 36, repr. in Galeopsis vera. *Ger. by Johns.* 704, S*r cop. in* Galeopsis legitima Dioscoridis. *Park, theatr.* 608, does not well express the habit of the plant. Tour uefort thinks it is Lamium laevigatum. GALEOPSIS. *Dale* 150. *Geoffr.* iii. 510. Lihn. 180. Galiopsis. *Rutty* 213. Lamium maximum sylvaticum foetid ura.

Chom. 761.. '- 2. STACHYS *germanica*. Lower leaves ellipticocordate, woolly; serratures imbricate. Many flowers in a whirl: Calyces pungent. *Obs.* 8257. Specf men gathered in the Paris garden. —*L. sp.* 812. *Huds.* 259. Found by Richardson 4 miles to the south of Grantham.—*Sibth. ox. n.* 530. *Fl. dan. t.* 684. *Gou. hort.* 283. Near Montpelier *Bot. arr.* 613. *J acq. austr. t.* 319. *Smith brit.* 634. On calcareous soil; *engl. t.* 829.

S. alba Iatifolia major. *Barrel, t.* 297.

S. montana. *Itiv. mon. t.* 27.

Stacbys. *Fuchs.* 727. *c.* 293, *imit. in* Marrubium agreste, *Trag.* 9, 8*f cop. in*

S. Fuchsii. *Bauh. J.* iii. 6. SI9; near Basle; *and Dalech.* 963. *Raii hist.* 554; *syn.* 239. *Dod.* 91, *repr. in Ger. by Johns.* 530,

S. Dioscoridis. *Lob. obs.* 285; *ic.* i. 530, *ill cop. from*

Pscudostacbys. *Dalech.* 963, *and cop. in*

S. major germanica. *Park, theatr.* 48. *Tourn. paris.* 151. *Vaill. parts.* 189. *Boerh.* i. J53. *Native* of Germany, Switzerland, France, Oxford shire, and the south of Lincolnshire.

STACHYS. *Boerhi u* 217, *Geofr. suite* iiu 118 3» STACHYS *recta*. Leaves lanceolate and oblongoelliptic, crcnato-serrate, scabrous. Racemi verticillate. *Obs.* 5515. Specimens gathered in Champagne.—*L. mant.* 82. *Hort. kexe.* ii. 302. *Jacq. austr. t.* 359. *Roth germ.* i. 256; ii. *pars* ii. 31»

Sidcritis vulgaris hirsuta erecta. *Boerh.* i. 171.

Sideritis hirsuta procumbens. *Tourn. paris.* 534. *Vaill. paris.* 184.

Sideritis flore lateólo Rivini et officinarum. *Jiupp. ab Hall.* 231.

Syderitis parinonica spicato flore, *dits, pann.* 599. No fig.

Sideritis I. *Clus. hist.* ii. 39, *repr. in* Sideritis vulgaris. *Ger. by Johnst* 6У7. J*Raii hist.* 563.

Sideritis prima. *Fuchs;* 730, *c.* 296, *cop. in*

Sideritis vulgaris hirsuta. *Bauh. J.* iii. 425, *b*

Tetrahit. *Dalech.* 1119.

Leaves lanceolate. *Obs.* 5512. Specimen from

Prof. Jos. *P.* Jacquin.—Leaves oblongo-elliptic.

Corolla upper lip entire. *Obs.* 5515. *Native* of Italy, Hungary, Germany, and France. SIDERITIS. Date 154. *Geofir. suite* iii. 41.

Sideritis flore luteolo. *Dale* 154.

4. STACHYS *palustris*. Leaves cördato-lanceolate. Flowers from 6 to 10 in a whirl. *Obs.* 541. In moist ground.—*L. suec. n.* 528; *sp.* 81Í. *Curt, lond.* iii. 35. *t.* 208. *Light/.* 313. *Riv. mon. t.* 26. *Bot. arr.* 613. *Smith brit.* 633; *engl. t.* 1675. *Pari-, thealr.* 1231, *cop.* the separate flowers and tubera of the root omitted, *from* Panax coloni. *Get. by Johns.* 1005. Galeopsis palustris, betonicae folüs, flore taricgato, voi, *$. t Tourn. parts.* 196. *Vaill, parts,* 77. *Bberh'. 1,* 162.;"- Sideritis anglica, strumosa radicc. *Park, theatr.* 587. *Rati hist.* 563; *syn.* 242. Clymenum minus. *Dalech.* 1357 '' '".

S. aquatica. T*a&. c.* 377.

ieates, lower petielate, uppelr nearly sessile. 05. 541.;."'. '; ' "' STAC*ffy*S palustris. *L. am.* T.67.

S. palustris foetida. CAom. 761; s«pp/. 203.

Panax coloni.' *Dale* 150.

Panax coloni Gerardi. *Mill. Jos.* 327, ; '"'

Galcopsis angustifolia foetida. *Cfeoffr.* iii. 512.

5. STACHYS *annua*. Leaves trinervose, nearly gla brous, elliptic and lanceolate. Flowers 6 in a whirl, *Obs.* 5514. Specimen from M. Broussonett.—*L. sp.* 813; *moid.* 411. *Hort. hew.* ii. 303. *Jacq. austr. iv. t.* 360. '; N

S. Betonica. *Crantt. austr.* iv.264.

Betonica verticillata, calycibus spinosis. *L. ups*

165...-. Betonica arvensis, annua, flore ex albo flavescente.

Tourn. paris. 248. *Vaill. parts.* 31. Sideritis arvensis latifolia glabra. *Bauh. Casp. pin.* 233. *Vaill. paris.* 184. *Boerh.* i. 171. Sideritis glabra arvensis. *Bauh. J.* iii. 427. Sideritis arvensis glabra, flore pallido. *Bauh. Casp. phytop.* 441. V o' Alyssum majus. *Tab. ic.* 929, *cop. in . s.* Sideritis latifolia glabra. *Ger. by Johns.* 699; (Sideritis II. *Matth.* 1003, not the plant as J. Bau hine justly observed.)

SIDERITIS. *Fog.* 138.
Sideritis arvensis latifolia glabra. *Dale* 154.
Sideritis arvensis glabra, flore albo. *Bocc. piante* 37.
2. *Leaves divided.* 6. STACHYS *triloba.* Leaves trilobate, upper lanceolate. *Obs.* 1005. On a dunghill near Worcester. Leonurus Cardiaca. *L. suec. n.* 532 who marks it as biennial; on rubbish and only near houses and villages; *sp.* 817. *Fl. dan.t.* 727. *Bot. air.* 618. *Smith engl. t.* 286; *brit.* 637. In hedges on gravelly and calcareous soils in several parts of Norfolk and Suffolk;—apparently considering it as indigenous.— *Poll. n.* 571. *Abb.* 131. On the sides of roads.—*Huds.* 261. On rubbish and in hedges in the isle of Selfey near Chichester, and in Yorkshire between Tickhill and Worksop.—*Scop. earn. n.* 703. On rubbish and about gardens.—*Host.* 331. On rubbish, and in hedges in villages.—*Roth germ.* i. 246. On rubbish and in hedges in villages. Leonurus foliis caulinis lanceolatis trilobis. *Guelt.* ii. 237. Common in the woods of St. Lazurd, and on the warren of Villemartin near Estampes.
Cardiaca. *Riv. man. t.* 20. *Fuchs.* 390. c. 149. No fructifications.— *Vaill. paris.* 28. *Bauh. J.* iii. 320. No fig.—*Rati hist.* 571 (mispr. 563); *syn.* 239. On dunghills, and on the outside of gardens.— *Boerh.* i. ISO, who marks it as biennial.—*Dalech.* 1249. *Dod.* 94, *repr. in Lob. obs.* 278; ic. i. 516, *St Get. by Johns.* 705, # *cop. in Park. theatr.* 42; *Native* of Orleanois in France, and possibly of Norfolk Suffolk and Yorkshire. In general it appears to be the outeast of gardens. CARDIACA. *Berg.* 528. *Chom.* 325. *Dale 152., Geoffr.* iii. 256. *Lea.* i. 282. *Linn.* 180. *Mill. Jos.* 113. *Murr.* ii. 180. *Raii hist.* 572, *par.* 6 to the end of the chapter. *Rutty* 96. *Schrod.* 555. *Spielm.* 203. *Vog.* 126.
7. STACHYSrte»i/5Ja. Leaves pinnatifid. Whirls multiflorous. *From Lour.* ii. 443. . 613. BALLOTA. Calyx semiquinquefid, with 10 ribs. *Corolla,* upper lip slightly concave. *Obs.* 4013. Z.
Differs from Marrubium in the upper lip of the corolla being slightly concave and entire.

1. BALLOTA *nigra.* Leaves ovate. Segments of the calyx acuminate. O6s. 4013. In hedges in Worcestershire and Staffordshire, but rare in the gritstone and limestone districts of Derbyshire.— *L. suec. n.* 529, near villages; *sp.* 814, on rubbish.— *Bot. arr.* 615. *Smith engl. t.* 46; *brit.* 635.
Mentha aqnatica. *Fl. dan. t.* 673.
Ballote. *Matth.* 825. *Cam. epif.* 572. *Matth. a C B.*601. *Dalech.* 1253. *Tourn. paris.* 247. *Vaili. paris.* 20. *Boerh.* i. 175. In Holland.
Marrubiastrum. *Riv. man. t.* 65.
Ballotte. *Dill. ap. Raii sj/n.* 244.
Ballote, sive Marrubium foctidum. *Fuchs.* 134. «*f. fol. cop. in* 161. c. 56, *impr. in*
MarruWuin nigrum, sive Ballote, *Bavh. J.* iii. *b.*
Ballote, seu Marrubium nigrum. *Dod.* 90, *repr. in Lob. obs.* 279; *Sf ic.* i. 518, *cop. in* Marrubium nigrum foctidum, Ballote dictum. *Park. theatr.* 1230, *abr. in* Stinking Horehound. *Pet. herb. t.* 32. /. 4, *o repr.* 'i«.'' ' '
Marrubium nigrum. *Ger. by Johns.* 701. *Rati hist.* 571; *syn. ed.* ii. 132; *Corolla* pinkish purple; upper lip oval, slightly concave, unequally crenate, villosc; lower lip tripartite; lateral segments roundish, crenate, slightly villose; middlemost 4 times larger, transversely emarginale, glabrous. *Obs.* 4013. "I./ *MARRUBIUM* nigrum. *Dale* 155. *Geoffr.* iii.
818. *Mill. Jos.* 285. *Rutty* 310. *SchroWwl.* n'.'fa2:'": di:.H'.' '"-"; M. nigrum foetidum, Ballote Dioscoridis. *Chom.* n 614. BYSTROPOGON.;ri
Ca/y.r quinquedentate; mouth bearded with bristles inserted into the margin. *Corolla,* upper lip bifid; lower trifid. *Obs.* 3051. *Lherit.*
Differs from Origanum in the bristles of the calyx being inserted into the sinuses of the mouth, and not fajto'-the throat as in Origanum Thymus and Melissa.
1. BYSTROPOGON *suaveolens.* Flowers capitate.. Peduncles trichotomous. Leaves angular, crenate. *Obs.* 5528. Specimen gathered in the Vienna garden;—£. *a Willi,* iii.72. *Lherit.*

Ys
Origanum. *Cam. epit.* 466.
Majorana #yriaca vel cretica, varietas. *tfaii hist,* 538. Origanum ereticum. *Baich. J.* iii. *b.* 238. (Name and descr apparently belong to a drug.) Majorana sylvestris. *Trag.* 34. *Q.* heracleoticum Ruejiii» sive Majorana major, *Bauk. J.* iii. *b.* 237, is described as having flowers in heads.),i ORIGANUM heracleoticum. *Bry,* 139, *Dale* 2. ORIGANUM *creticum.* Spikes aggregate, long, prismatic, straight. Bracteae membranaceous, twice as long as the calyx. *L, sp.* 823. *Donn* 79.
Lour ii. 453.
O. foliis ovatis aculis glabris, venis scabrjs, spicis fetragonis. *L. mat. med. n.* 300. *Gron. orient.* 75. *n.* 186. O. foiio subrotundo, flore albo. *Burs. ap. L. am.* i. 320. *n.* 136.
0. mompeiiense pulchrura. *Cam. cpit,* 468. *cop. in*
Batth. J. in. 6. 238.
O. Onites dictum. *Best. aut. ord.* 2, *fol.* 5. Flowers in corymbose racemi.
ORIGANUM ereticum. *Pharm.succ.—Berg.*5S0. '
Vale 149. *Linn.* 181. *Mill. Jos.* 322. jl/*urr.* ii. 140.5/,. 286. *Fog.* 73. 3. ORIGANUM *vulgare.* Racemi aggregate, corym bose. Biacteae rhombeo-elliptic, longer than the calyx. *Obs.* 6013. On dry banks about Matlock bath in Derbyshire—*L. suec. tu* 534; *sp.* 824. *Curt. lond. y.* 39. / 338. *Bot. arr.* %2. *IVoodv.* 618. M4JORANA. *Calyx* with an oblique mouth; mouth obsolelely bilabiate. *Corolla* bilabiate; upper lip eraarginate; lower, lip trifid. *Obs.* 7516. *Tourti.* 1. MAJORANA *tomentosa.* Spikes solitary. 06 . 7516.--In Mr. Shore's garden. Origanum Dictamnus. 3//W. *Ph. diet. n.* 10. £,. «m 823, but as he characterises it as having only the lower leaves tomentose, Miller conjectures that the c plant from which he formed his specific character was Miller's Origanum bybridinum, which plant «f
Miller'sis probably OriganumTournefortji.—*Hort. fore,* if. 311. *Curt. mag. t.* 298. *Lour.* ii. 452.
Woodv. iv. 80. *t.* 242. Dictamnus creticus, *Boerh.* i. 178. Par/;. fAeafr. 27, *cop. from*' J"' /.:.! Dictamnum Yerum. Dorf.

280, which repr. in Dictamnum. *Lob. obs.* 267; *ic.* i. 502, *and*
Dictamnum creticum. *Otrhy Johns..* 795. Dictamnus crctica, seu vera. *Bauh. J. iti.* 253. Dictamnum cretense. *Cam. epit.* 472. Matth. 705.,': *Sfetn.* tomenlose. *Leaves,* ovato-subrotund, tomen-I *tasef* peiiolate, opposite.; margin entire. *Peduncles* hirsutulons below, rufous, with one spike, opposite. *Spikts* oblong, glabrous, slightly nodding, similar *to* the female spikes of Humulus Lupulus. *BracUae* ovali-subrotund, entire, disposed in 4 rows, concave, patulous, greenish, with reticular veins and scattered shining rufous hemispheric olearia, sometimes 2 a little below thespike and opposite. *Calyces* solitary, scarly sessile, nearly twice as short as the bracteae, tubular, sprinkled with honeycoloured olearia, below whitish with green lines; mouth oblique, obsoletely bilabiate; upper lip broader than and half as long again as the tube, oval, entire at the margin; lower lip very short, consisting of two rounded scarcely projecting teeth with an obtuse shallow sinus between them. *Corolla* flesh coloured, nearly thrice as long as the calyx; lube twice as long as the calyx, the lower part cylindric, the upper twice as broad, gibbous on the underside; upper lip oval, concave, not arched, straight; lower lip nearly as long as the upper, slightly trifid; segments oblongo-oval, the lateral ones somewhat shorter. *Stamina* fleshcoloured, extended one third beyond the corolla. *Pistil* somewhat shorter than, the stamina. *Obs.* 7516.
DICTAMNUS. *Aht.* ii. 129.
D. creticus. *Pharm. austriaco-prov.* 36. s«ec—
Berg. 529. *Chom.* 392. *Dale* 148. *Gebffr.* ji. 272. *Ilerm.* 477. *Lew.* i. 399; *disp.* by Rother. 154; by Dune. 345. *Linn.* i. 399. *Mill. Jos.* 177. Monro iii. 90. *Murr.* ii. 139. *Rutty* 167. *Schrod.* 583. Dittany of Crete. *Neum.* ii. 183. . MAJORANA *scutellifolia.* Leaves obovato-subrotund. *Obs.* 7595. In the garden of Saville, who assured me that the root is perennial.—*Obs.* 8771. Specimen in Mr. Knowlton's herbarium from the Lonsborough garden.
Origanum acgyptiacum. *L. sp.* 822.

Hort. kea. ii. 311. *JIasselq.* 251. *Mill. Ph, diet. n.* 8.
M. rotundifolia scutellata exotica. *Tourn, inst.* 199; *hort.* 53. *Batrh.* i. 178.
Amaracus fulgatior, siveVI. nostras. *Lobi ic. u* 498, # Marjorana major. *Ger. by Johns.* 664, *imit.* in "Majorana. *Park. par. t.* 451./. 7, *and cop. in* " M. Vulgaris. *Park, thealr.* 33. *Raii hist.* 538. *Boerh.* i. 178. M. tenuifolia. *Tab. ic* 340, *repr. in* Amaracus, sive M."tenaifolia. *Matth. a C. B.551.* M. vulgaris annua. *Hist. ox. s. 11. t.* 3. row 1. /. 1. Amaracus, sea Majorana. *Daleih.* 882. *Fuchs.* 635. c. 259, *cop. in* Amaracus Fuchsii. *Dalech.* 882, *Sir* " M..altera, majori folio, ex semine nafa. *Bauh. J.* iii. *b.* 240. *Stem* erect, stratght, 14 inches long, purplish, pubescent; hairs bowed in. *Branches* a few short ones at the base; flowering branches patulous, shorter than the stem. *Leaves* oval, decurvate, entire atthe margin, slightly pubescent; upper surface apparently glabrous. *Spikes* at the ends and sides of the branches. *Bracteae* roundish and oval, sometimes emarginate. *Calyx* bilabiate, as short again as the bracteae, obcorclate; mouth oblique, bilabiate; upper lip 4 times as long as the lower; lower lip with 2 obsolete teeth; teeth very near to the upper lip. £b *rolla* not expanded. *Obs.* 7596. MAJORANA. Sweet Marjoram. Herb. *Pharm, lond.*—*Alst.* ii. 166. *Berg.* 532. *Carth.* iii. 112. *Cull,* ii. 148. *Dale* 148. *Herm.* 451. Hill 374. *Lew.* ii. 82. *Linn.* 182. *Mill. Jos.* 280. Monro iii. 164. *Murr.* ii. 142. *Ploucq. bibl, L* 423. *Schrod.* 618. *Spielm.* 277. *Fog.* 65. Origanum Majorana. Herb. *Pharm. edin.*—*Bry.* ,'- 139. *Lfiw. dispi*by Dune. 268, Jf«rr, Jf.L,34. *Pears. R.* i. 112j ii. 192.
M. vulgaris. *Chan.* 388. 147. *Geoffr.* iii. 761. *Rutty* 299.
4. MAJORANA *ovatlfolia.* Bracteae acute. Leaves ovate, obsoletely serrate. *Obs.* 8772. Specimen from Dr. Heise. Origanum Majoranoides. *L. a Willi,* iii. 137. Origanum Majorana. *L. sp.* 825 в Origano congener Zatarendi. Дам *hist.* 1871, from Zaterhendi. *Vesl.* 189. /. *which abt. in* Amaracus, sive M. tenuifolia. *Matth* 727, *cop. in* Dalech. 882, *St imit. in* Amaracus tenuior. *Lob. obs.* 265, *which*

repr. in ic. i. 498, *abr. in* M. tenuifolia. *Hist. ox. s.* II. *t.* 3. roa» I, /. 3, # *repr. in* Marjorana tenuifolia. *Cer. by Johns.* 664. *Rait hist.* 538. M. tenuior et Jignosior. *Bauh. J.* iii. 6. 241? No fig. Epimajorana. *Tab. ic.* 340. (Origano cognata Zaterendi. *Hist. ox.* iii. 360. *s. 11. t.* 3. rozo 3. *f.* 17, has sessile leaves.) MAJORANA tenuifolia. *Dale* 148. *Herrn.* 451. M, nobilis. *Geoffr.* iii. 762. 619. MARRUBIUM. *Calyx* with 10 ribs, with 5 and 10 teeth. *Corolla,* upper lip bifid, linear, straight. *Obs.* 360. L. 1. Calyces quinqucdentate. L. *I.* MARRUBIUM *Alysson.* Leares wodgeshaped, .with 5 teeth, plaited. Bracteae none. *L. sp.* 815. *U.K.* ii. 304. M. verticillatum, foliis profunde incisis. *Bocrh.* i. 156. Alysson verticillatum, foliis profunde incisis. *Jiaii hist.* 557. Alysson Galeni. *Clus. hisp.* 387, *repr. in hist.* ii. 35, *Dod.* 89, *and Ger. by Johns.* 465, *cop. in* Alyssum Galeni Clusio. *Park, theatr.* 590, *Sf abr.*
M. album, foliis profunde incisis, flore cacrulco.
Hist. ox. s. 11. I. 10. *rozo l.f.* 12. AL YSS UM Galeni. *Dale* 152. 2. *Calyces decemdentatc.* 2. MARRUBIUM *uncinatum.* Calyx tubular; teeth
Looked, setaceous. *Obs.* 360. Near Worcester, in marie. M. vulgare. *L. succ. n.* 531; *sp.* 816. *I/uds.* 261. *Ughlf.* 315. i?of. art-. 617. H. *dan. t.* 1036. *Smith* eng7. *t.* 410; 6n't; 636. *Woodv.* ii. 265. £. 97. C/ws. *hist.* ii. 34, *cop. i/t* M. album vulgare. *Pari, theatr.* 44, !y *repr. in* M. album, ioft. *obs.* 278; tc. i. 517, *and Ger. by Johns.* 693. *Raii syn.* 239. *Dalech.* 961. 7ivj. мо«. /. 66. *Bauh. J.* iii. &. 316, *ctfji. from* Marrubium. *Fuchs.* 590. /о/. *cd. cop, in* 563; *c.* 225. (M. candidiim. *Trag.* 8, must surely have been intended for some other plant.) *Calyx* tubular, with 10 ribs; teeth whitish brown it the-ends. *Obs.* 360. MARRUBIUM. *Pharm. lond. ncxhs.*—*Alst.* ii. voc. 3. z
Verbascum IIH silvestre. *Dalech.* 1300, *which repr. in* Bouillon IIII sauvage de Matthiol. *Dalech. plantes* ii, 191. Verbascum silvestre Matthioli. *Clus. hist.* ii. 28, *repr. in* Verbascura sylvesfre alterum. *Dod.* 146, Verbascum salvifolium fruticosum luteo flore. *Lob. obs.* 302, Verbascum 4 Matthioli. *Lob. ic.*

i. 560; *and* Verbascum Matthioli. *Ger. by Johns.* 767, *Sf cop. in* Salvia fruticosa lutea latifolia, sive Verbascum sylvestre quartum Matthioli. *Park, iheatr.* 52.

Raii hist. 511. Near Taormiua in Sicily. (Verbasculum salvifolium. *Alp. exot. t.* 108, *cop. in* Salvia minor lutea cretica- *Park, theatr.* 52, must surely be a distinct species.) *Calyx,* angles 5; ribs 10; teeth 5, setaceous. *Obs.* 3871. PHLOMIS. *Dale HO.* 2. PHLOMIS *octodenlata.* Calyces obliquely truncate, octodentate. Leaves lineari-lanceolate, obsoletely serrate. *Obs.* 5488. Specimen gathered in tho
Vienna garden.

P. zeylanica. *L.* sp.820; *a Murr.* 539i *ntant.* 412.
J *acq. ic.* i. *t.* 111. *H. K.* ii. 308. Leonurus indicus. *L. sp.* 817.-Clinopodium hyssopi latioribus foliis, maderaspata, num. *Pluk.phyt. t.* 164. /. 2. (Cardiaca, sive Leonurus hyssopi hirsutis foliis, ma' deraspatana, floribus dilute rubris, unico tantura verticillo in ramulorum cymis. *Pluk. aim.* 81; *phyt. t.* 118. /. 4, is represented as haying the stem and leaves hairy.) Cardiaca minor annua amcricana, flore argenteo. *PluU. aim.* 81; *phyt. t.* 80. /. 7, has serrate leaves and is described as from America.) *Stem* and *leaves* microscopically pubescent. *Obs.* 5488. HERBA ADMIRATIONIS. *Rumph.* vi. *39. t.* 16. *f.l.* 621. THYMUS. *Calyx* bilabiate; upper lip semitrifid, lower bifid; throat with a circle of hairs. *Corolla* bilabiate; upper lip flat, semibifid, lower trifid; segments entire. *Obs.* 4755. L, 1. THYMUS *Serpyllum.* Flowers in heads. Stems creeping. Leaves flat, obtuse, ciliate at the base. *L. suec. n.* 535; *sp.* 825. *Bot. arr.* 623. *Curt.* ii. 47. . *Woodv.* ii. 301. *t.* 110. *Huds.* 262. *Lightf. SlS. Smith brit.* 639; *engl. t.* 1514. *Fl. dan. t.* 1165. Serpyllum flore minore. *Rh. mon. t.* 42. Serpillum vulgare minus. *Tourn. parts.* 148. *Vaill. parts.* 183. *t.* 32./. 7. Serpyllum. *Fuchs.* 251. *fol. ed. cop. in* 253. *c.* 94, *imit. in Trag.* 40, *and cop. in* Serpyllum vulgare. *Bauh. J.* iii. *b.* 268. *Rati syn.* 230. *Dod.* 277, *repr. in Ger. by Johns.* 570, Serpillum. *Lob. obs.* 230, *and* Serpyllum, et Saxifranga Dodtmaei. *Lob. ic,* i. 423, *and cop. in* ,3 *latifolius.* Leayes elliptico-ovate. *Obs.* 4755. *L. e. ii.K.t*
T. vulgaris. *Woodv.* ii. 299. *t.* 109.

Thymum durius Plinii. *Lob. ic.* i. 425, *repr. in*

Thymum durius. *Dod.* 275, *and Ger. by Johns.* 573, *and cop. in Park, theatr.* 7. THYMUS vulgaris folio latiore. *Boecl. ap. Hernu* 454. T. vulgaris latiore folio. *Carth.* in. 117. *Chom.* 147.374. Thymum vulgare. *Geoffr. suite* iii. 187.

3. THYMUS *Mastichina.* Whirls spicate. Segments of the calyx setaceo-subulate, villose, *Obs.* 6140. Specimen from Mr. Ballard's garden.—*L. sp.* 827 j *mant.* 413. *Hort. kezo.* ii. 315.
Mastichina. *Boerh.* i. 156.
Marum vulgare, Clinopodium. *Dod.* 271, *repr. in*
Tragoriganum I. *Clus. hist.* i. 355, Marum. *Lob. ic.* i. 499, *and Ger. by Johns.* 670, *Sf cop. in* Marum vulgare. *Park, theatr.* 12. Clinopodium quibusdam, Mastichina gallorum. *Bauh, J.* iii. 245.
Marum verum vulgo Mastic-*Dalech.* 885.
THYMUS Mastichina. *Bry.* 145.
Marum Mastich. *Geoffr.* iii. 824.
Marum. *Alst.* ii. 173. *Dale* 143. *Mill, Jos.* 286.
Rutty 310.
Marum vulgare. *Lew.* ii. 92.
THYMUS *Tragoriganum.* Flowers verticillate. Stem fruticose, erect. Leaves hispid, acuminate. *L.aMurr.* 542; *mant.* 81.

Tragoriganum II" altera species. *Clus. hist.* i. 555, *repr. in* ....

Tragoriganum cretense apud venelos. *Lob. ic.* i.
m, &
Tragoriganum cretense. *Ger. by Johns.* 668, *and pop. in* Traijoriganum creticum. *Park, theatr.* 17. TflJGORIG-ANUM. *4lp. exot.* 79. *t.* 78. *Dale* 144
5. THYMUS *bidentatus.* Flowers verticillate, nearly sessile. Leaves elliptic, acute, with few serratures, dotted. *Obs.* 5258. Specimen from Prof. Jos. F. Jacquin. Melissa floribus verticillatis subsessilibns secundum longitudinem cautis. *Gron. virg.* 90. Mentha exigua. *L. sp.* 806; *Smith if. t.* 38..

Leaves dotted. *Calyx* gibbous underneath. *Obs.* 5258. CUNILA pulegloides. *L. a Marr.* 67; *sp.* 30. *J fori. hew.* i. 35. *Smith in lin. tr.* iii. 22—Schoepf 6. 6.
THYMUS *gibbasus.* Flowers verticillate. Pedun cles with 1 flower. Leaves acute, serrate, without dots. Calyx gibbous underneath. *Obs.* 5257. 4 Oct, 1797. Specimen gathered in Surry, *on* chalk.—*Obs.* 8262. Specimen gathered in Dove dale in Derbyhire, on limestone. I have never seen it on the sand and grave! of Worcestershire, Warwickshire, Staffordshire, Derbyshire, and Nottinghamshire. T. Acinos. *L. suec. n. 536,* on dry gravelly hills; *sp.* 826, on dry gravel and chalk.—*Huds.* 263. On dry hills of gravel and chalk.—*Curt. lond.* i. 43. *t. Bot. arr.* 624. *Smith engl t.* 411, which I did not examine till Dec. 1797;. —6rtf. 641. *Fl. dan. t.* 814. Hairs not expressed. Cabmen! um montanum. *Trag.* 37Ocima.-trum. *Fucks.* 851. c. 343, Coji. *in* Acinos multis. *Bauh. J.* iii. *h.* 259. J?a» syn. 238. Ocimnm sylvestre Acinos. *Dod.* 279, *repr in* Clinopodium vulgare, odore pulegio jucundiore. *Lob. obs.* 270, Clinopodium vulgare. *Lob. ic.* i. 506, # Ocymum sylvestre. *Ger. by Johns.* 675, *and cop. in* Small wild Basil. *Pet. herb. t. 32. f.* 10, # Clinopodium minus, sive vulgare. *Park, theatr.* 21. ACINOS. *Riv. mon. t.* 43,— *Dale* 151. 7. THYMUS *alpimis.* Flowers verticillate, 6 in whirl. Leaves rather obtuse, concave, somewhat serrate. *L. sp.* 826. *Hort. lew.* ii. 314. *Jacq. austr.* i. 60. *t.* 97. *Curt, lorid.* under T. Acinos remarking that the flowers are larger than those of

T. Acinos. Clinopodium foliis ovatis acutis serratis, flore folio majori. *Hall. hist. n.* 238. Clinopodium montanum. *Bocc. plant, t.* 45. Leaves represented as acute and entire at the margin. Clinopodium austriacum. *Clus. pann.* 623, *repr in hist.* i. 353, *Ger. by Johns.* 676, *cop. in Park theatr.* 21, *Sf* a branch *cop. in* Acini pulchra species. *Bauh. J.* iii. *b.* 260, outer fig. Inner fig. with serrate leaves. CLINOPODIUM. *Yog.* 98, 62& MELISSA.

Calyx bilabiate; upper lip with 3 divisions, lowet with 2; throat pilose. *Corolla,* upper lip semibi fid, lower trifid; middlemost segment emarginate. *Obs.*

5860. L.
Differs from Thymus in the middle segment of the lower up.

1. MELISSA *Calamintha*. Panicles axillary, dichoto mous. Lower lip of the cilyx twice as long as the upper. *Obs.* 3459. Specimen galher.-d near Worcester, on marlc—*I/. sp.* 827. *Gou. hort.* 291. *Rot. arr.* 626. Thymus Calamintha. *Scop. earn. n.* 733. *Smith brit.* 641; *engl. t.* 1676. Calamcntha. *Rh. mon. t.* 46. Calamintha vulgaris, vel ofheinarum germaniac.
Tourn. paris. 405. *Vaill. paris.* 26. *Boerh.* i. 175. Calamintha flore magno vulgaris. *Bank. J.* iii. *b.* 228. Common Calamint. *Pet. herb. t.* 34./. 1. Calamintha montana vulgaris. *Besl. hort. acst. ord.* 7. *fol.* 7. *Lob. obs.* 274, *rcpr. in ic.* 513, *abr. from* Calamintha. *Matth.* 716, *repr. in* Calamintha montana. *Dod.* 98, *Sf* Calamintha vulgaris officinarum. *Get. by Johns.* 687, *St cop. i)i* Calamintha vulgaris. *Park, thealr.* 36. *Rati syn.* 243. CALAMINTHA. *Aht.* ii. 95. *Herrn.* 471. *Murr.* ii. 130. *Schrod.* 551. *Spielm.* 242. *Vog.* 57. Calamintha vulgaris. *Geoffr.* iii. 238. jLfzr. i. 250. *MШ. Jos.* 101. . Calamintha montana. *Pharm. austriaco-prov.* 25 Dale 154. *Linn.* 183. Calamintha vulgaris, Tel officinarum gcrmnnniac. *Chom.* 370; *suppl.* 114. 2. MELISSA *Nepela*. Panicles axillary, dichotpmous, longer than the leaves. Calyx scarcely bilabiate. *Obs.* 7597. In Savillc's garden.—*L. sp.* 828. *Bot. ar'r.* 626. *Curt, lorid.* vi. *t.* 40. Thymus Nepeta; *Smith br'tt.* 642; *engl. t.* 1414. Calamentha folio incano. *Riv. mon. t.* 47. Calamintha pulegii odore, sive Nepeta. *Vaill. paris.* 26. ' " i Calamintha flore minore, odore pulegii. *Bauk. J.* iii. *b.* 229. Caiauimtha odore pulegii. *Raii hist.* 569; *syn.* 243 *Ger. by Johns.* 087, *repr. from* Calamintha altera odore gravi pulegii foliis maculosis. *Lob. obs.* 275, which *repr. in ic.* i. 513, *abr. from* Calamintha montana. *Matth.* 617, *and repr. in* Pulegiuin sylvestre, sive Cahmintha altera. *Dod.* 98, a branch of which *cop. in* Calamintha minor incana. *Park, theatr.* 37. Stem 20 inches long, hirsute, branched from the base. *Branches* patent. *Leaves* ovate, acute and obtuse, distantly serrate, slightly hirsute. *Panteles* secundose. *Calyx* striate, scarcely bilabiate; throat closed by hairs; upper lip trifid, seg. menls triangular, patulous; lower lip bipartite, segments triangulari-subulate, patulous. *Corolla* whitish purple, pubescent, twice as long as the calyx; tube hairy within; upper lip oblongo-subrotund, straight, emarginate, keeled; segments rounded; lower lip somewhat longer, patent, trifid; segments roundish, middlemost twice as" large, with 3 purple streaks or spots at the base, erose and curled at the margin.
" *Stamina,* 2 upper twice as short as the lower. *Obs.* Native of Italy, France, Germany, Holland, Cambridgeshire, and Oxfordshire. MELISSA Nepeta. *Schoepf* 97. S/nVfot. 242. Calamiotha. Dale 154. *Monro* iii. 35. Calamintha officinalis. *Mill. Jos.* 102. Calamintha pulegii odore. *Geoffr.* iii. 239. *Lew.* i. 249. Calamintha pulegii odore, sive Nepeta. *Chom.* 370; *suppl.* 114.. 3- MELISSA *grandiflora*. Peduncles axillary, dichotomous, shorter than the leaves. Lips of the calyx nearly equal. *Obs.* 3461. *L. sp.* 827. *H. K.* ii. 316. *Curt. mag. t.* 208.
Thymus grandiflorus. *Scop. earn. n.* 732.
Calamintha magno flore. *Boerh.* i. 175.
Calamintha montana. *Cam. hort.* 32. In the mountains of the Veronese and Vicentine territories.
Calamintha monfana, flore magno ex calyce lon«o. *Bavh.J.* iii. *b.* 229, *cop. from*
Calamintha montaua pracstantior. *Lob. ols.* 274 *winch repr. in ic.* i. 512, *Ger. by Johns.* 687, *and abr. in Park, theatr.* 37. *Best. hort. aest. ord.* 7. *fol.* 7. *Raii hist.* 569. In mountainous woods of Tuscany, and on mountains near the Grande Chartreuse. „...... *Calyx*, ribs 11; upper lip trifid, recurrato-patent, lower bipartite, straight, slightly incurvate. *Corolla* inflated as in Dracocephalum and Moldavica, pur plish rosecoloured; upper lip straight, recurvate at the sides. *Obs.* 3461. 5860.
CALAMINTHA magno florc. *Dale* 154. *Geoffr.* iii. 239. *Lew.* i. 250. *Rutty* 78. 4. MELISSA *crelica*. Racemi terminal. Peduncles solitary, very short. *L. sp.* 828; *a Murr.* 543. *Sort. kew.* ii. 316. *Mill. Ph. did. n.* 6. Calamintha pulegti odore minor. *Barrel t.* 1166.
Leaves sessile. Peduncles aggregate. Calamintha clinopodii austriaci foliis, odore pulegii.
Pluk. aim. 75;*phyt. t.* 163./. 4. Peduncles aggregate. Calamintha secunda incana. *Lob. obs.* 275, *repr. in ic.* i. 514, *cop. in Dalech.* 906, *repr. in* Calamintha montana vulgaris. *Ger. by Johns.* 687, *8f cop. in* Calamintha minor incana. *Park, theatr.* 37, the entire plant. Calamintha montana incana minor. *Tub. ic.* 351. Calamintha cretica. *Cam. hort.* 33. MELISSA cretica. *Lour.* ii. 446. 5. MELISSA *officinalis*. Corymbi axillary, nearly sessile. *Obs.* 3458. In a garden.—*L. sp.* 827. *Scop. earn. n.* 739, who asserts that the throat is not closed by hairs. About Quelb and Trieste.— *Hort. lew.* ii. 315. *Woodv.* iii. 398. *t.* 147, not well done.
M. hortensis. *Boerh.* i. 167.
Mclissophyllum, sive Apiastrum adulterinum. *Fuchs,* 483. c. 191, *cop. in* M. vulgaris, odore citri. *Bauh. J.* iii. *b.* 232.
M. vulgaris. *Trag.* 13. No fructifications.—*Park, theatr.* 40, *cop, from* -Äpiastrnm, sive Melissophyllqrt. *Lob. obs.* 277, which *repr. in* Aniastium. *Lob. ic-*i. 514, *Sf* Melissa. *Dod.* 92, *Ger. by Johns.* 689, *abr. in Park. par. t.* 481. /. 3, and badly *imit.from* Melissophyllum Matthioli. *Dalech.* 957. *Calyx,* throat with hairs on the inside, *Obs.* 3458.'
MELISSA. Balm. Herb. *Pharm. lond.—Alst.* ii. 179. *Dale* 155. *Geoffr. suite i.* 2. *Heb.* 3. *Herrn.* 457. *Hill* 360. *Lew.* ii. 99. *Mill. Jos.* 290. *Monro* iii. 168. *Quar. febr.* 172. 207. 376.
382. 404; *anim.* 206. 207. *Rutty* 320. *Schrod.* 622. S/jie/m. 279. Fog-. 68. M. officinalis. Leaves. *Pharm. edin.'— Lew. disp. by Dune.* 252. *Pears. R.* ii. 187. M. citrata. *Linn.* 183. M. citrina. *Berg.* 537. *Carth.* iii. 95. *Murr.* ii. 127. *Baum. Rush.* i. 113. Balm. *Darw.* ii. 194. *Fordyce, G. fev.* iii. 215.
Jwí. Ä. ed. ii. 289. *Pringle* 132. ÄaiA iii.
285; v. 120. Melisse. *Chom.* 157 ;,*suppl.* 52. 6. MELISSA *glomerala*. Flowers in roundish heads and whirls. Bracteac

setaceous. *Obs. 361.* Near Worcester. Clinopodium vulgare. *L. suec. n.* 533; *sp.* 821.
Fl. dan. t. 930. *Bot. arr.* 620. *Smilh. Irit.* 638; eng/, f. 1401. Clinopodium. *Rh. mon. t.* 43. *Cam. epit.* 503. Clinopodium origano simile. *Raii syn.* 239. *Magn. mensp.* 71.
Acinos. *Ldb. obs.* 269, *repr.inic.* i. 504, 8?

Acynos. *Ger. by Johns.* 675; *and cop. in*
Acinos, sive Clinopodium majus. *Pari, theatr.* 22.

Origanum minus. *Trag.* 36.
Clinopodium majus. *.Rati hist.* 558.
Clinopodium quorundam, origani 'facie. *Bauh. J.* iii. 6. 250. No fig. Near MoriDbeliard, Geneva, Lyons, Montpelier, and Padua.
Acinus, sive Clinopodium silvtfstre. *Dakch.* -919 *repr. in.*
Clinopodium prius. *Dalech.* 931.
Calyx tubular, bilabiate, with 13 ribs, pubescent.within, below the base of the upper lip and at the base of the lower lip pilose; throat closed by hairs; upper lip trifid; segments subulato-triangular; lower lip bipartite; segments subulate. *Corolla* purplish pink; upper lip roundish, emarginate, flattish reflexo-erect, lower lip trifid; lateral segments roundish, the intermediate one emarginate. *Obs. 361.* CLINOPODIUM vulgare. *Linn.* 183. note. 623. MOLDAVICA. *Calyx,* upper lip semitrifid, ldWer bipartite. *Co Tolla* upper lip vaulted; throat inflated. *Obs.* 509. *Tourn. Boerh.* i. 168. 1. MOLDAVICA setosa. Plowers verticillate. Leaves, ovato-oblong, crenate. Bracteae with setaceous serratures. *Obs.* 509. In a garden. Dracocephalum Moklavica. *L. sp.* 830. *Hart, hew. U.* 318.
Moldavica betonicae folio, flore caerulco. *Boerh.* i. / 168.

Melissophyllon turcicuin. *Lob. adv.* 220, *repr. in ic.* i. 515.
Melissa moldavica. *Dalech.* 960. *Cam. epit.* 576.
Melissa turcica alia. *Dalech.* 960.
Melissa turcica raultis dicta. *Bauh. J.* iii. b. 231,
cop. in
MELISSA turcica. *Park, theatr.* 40. *Ger.*

Ay
Johns. 689.—*Berg.* 559. *Linn.* 1S4. *Murr.* ii. 157.
Melissa peregrina folio oblongo. *Carth.* iii. 99.
624. MELITTIS. *Calyx* bilabiate; upper lip semitrifid and semibifid, lower bifid, crenate. *Corolla,* upper lip flat, entire and bifid, lower trifid; middlemost segment crenate. *Obs.* 6305. *L.* 1. MELITTIS Melissophyllum. *L. sp.* 832". *Huds.* 264. In the New forest in Hampshire.—*Bot. arr.* 627. *Scop. earn. n.* 726. *Host* 336. *Mill. J. ill. t. J acq. austr. t.* 26. *Smith engl. t-*577, from a plant in Chelsea garden, the root of which was brought by Hudson from Devonshire; *brit.* 643. *Gou. hort.* 293. Near Montpelicr. — *Roth germ.* i. 261. Near Jena.
Melissophyllum. *Riv. mon. t.* 21.
Melissophyllum verum. *Vaill. parts.* 125.
Melissa humilis latifolia, maximo flore purpurascente.
Tourn. parts. 493. *Hoerh.* i. Ib7.
Lamium montanum, mcllissae folio. *Rati hist.* 56L
in woods in the western parts of England as about Totnes in Devonshire, and Haverfordwest in Pembrokeshire; and in mountainous woods near Geneva;— *cat. ed.* i. 186; *syn. ed.* ii. 129. *Magn. monsp.* 149, With purple, with flesh coloured, and with white corollae.,
Melissa Fuchsii. *Dill. ap. Raii syn.* 242. *Lob. ic.* i. 515, *repr.from*
Mclissophyllon. *Lob. obs.* 277, *which repr. in*
Melissa Fuchsii, flore purpurco. *Ger. by Johns.* 690, *and cop. in*
Melissophyllum Fuchsii. *Park, thealr.* 41.
Melissophyllum, sive Apiastrum verum. *Fuchs.* 483. c. 191, *cop. in*
Mclissophyllum Fuchsii et Dodonaci. *Dalech.* 958.
Melissa. *Trag.* 12, Sf
Melissa adulterina quorundam, amplis foliis, et floribus non grati odoris. *Bank. J.* iii. b. 232. /. 2. In fruit.—/. 1 in flower.
Melissa Tragi. *Magn. hort.* 133.
Herba sacra quorundam. *Dalech.* 1336.

Lamium pannonicum I. *Clus. pann.* 592, *repr. in*
Lamium pannonicum I, versicolore flore. *Clus. hist.* ii. 37. *Calyx* wider than the tube of the corolla, very uncertain in its divisions; lower lip obsolctcly bifid; segments obtuse, acutely crcnate. *Corolla,* upper lip mostly entire, roundish; lower lip and lower side of the throat dullish purple. *Obs.* 6305. In Mr. Watson's garden.
Native of Cumióla, Austria, Switzerland, France,
Franconia, Cornwall, Devonshire, Pembrokeshire,
Hampshire, and Sussex.
MELISSOPHYLLUM. *Murr.* ii. 131.

Vol. 3. A a

Melissa sylvestrjs. *Geoffr. suite* i. 8.
Melissa Tragi. *Chom.* 692.
Pseudo-Melissa. *Dale* 155.
Lamium Plinii. *Spielm.* 653.
Lamium Plinii oflicinarum. *Vog.* 132.
625. OCIMUM.
Calyx, upper lip orbicular, lower quadrificl. *Corolla* resupinate, one lip quadrifid, the other undivided. *Filaments,* outer with a process from the base. *L.* 1. OCIMUM *gratissimum.* Stem suffruticose. Leaves lanccolato-ovate. Rucemi terminal. *L. a Murr.* 545; *sp.* 832; *mant.* 414. *Jacq. coll.* iv. 208; *ic.* iii. *t.* 495. Ocyraum zeylanicum perenne odoralissimum latifo lium. *Burnt. J. zeyl.* 174. *t.* 80./. 1. OCYMUM gratissimum. *Lour.* ii. 448. 2. OCIMUM *Basilicum.* Leaves ovate, glabrous. Calvces ciliate. *L. sp.* 833. *Hort. kezo.* ii. 320. Ocymum caryophyllatum majus. *Bocrh.* i. 170. Ocymum. *Browne* 260. *Cam. epit.* 308. Basilicum medium. *Besl. horl. aest. ord.* 7. *M.* 9. Basilica major. *Trag.* 31, which repr. in O. nigrum. *Cord. fol.* 114. *p.* 2, who describes the leaves as If inch long, *imit. from* O. magnum. *Fuchs.* 848. c. 343, Idaica *cop. in Bnuh. J.* iii. b. 246. /?ai'i Ate.' 541. *Ger. by Johns.* 673, rrpr. /row O. tertium maximum. *Dod.* 279, *vhich repr. in* 3. OCIMUM *minimum.* Leaves ovate, entire at the margin. *L. sp.* 833. *Hort. kew.* ii. 321. *Gou. hort.*293. *Magn. hort.* 146. *Boerh.* i. 170. *Rati hist.* 541. *Bauh.* ,7. Hi. 6. 247. (The fig. which *cop. from* O. exiguum. *Fuchs.* 847. c.

343, has serrate leaves.) O. caryophyllatum. *Dalech. 68, cop. from O. minus. Dod.* 278, a branch of which' *cop. in Park, theatr.* 19, *and* the whole rr/ir. *in* O. minus gariophyllatum. (C?er. *by Johns.* 673. O. minimum, sive gafiophyllatura. *Park. par.* 450. *t.* 451.'/. 5. Leaves lanceolate. O. parvum. *JDalech.* 681. O. minimum cariophyllatum..Bes/. Ae.rf. *aest. ord, 7. fol.* 10, *cop. in* OCIMUM minimum. //»«. *ox.* iii. 407. «. 17. J.
20. *row* 2. /. *n.—Chom.* 368. O. caryophyllatum. Da/e 149. *Lew.* ii. 156. O. seu Basilicum minimum. *Geoffr. suite i.* 213. 4. OCIMUM *tenuiflorum.* Leaves ovato-oblong, ser rate. Bracteae cordate, reflex, concave. Spikes filiform. *L. sp.* 833. *Hcrt. kew.* ii. SSL *Sal. R. hort.* 88. Mentha zeylanica spicata pusilla, angustissimo folio dentato. *Burm. J. zeyl.* 158.*t*.10. *f.* 2. Leaves oblong. Ocymum maderaspatanum frutescens, gretissimi odo ris, flore parvo, caulibus villosis. *Pluk. aim.* 268; *phyt. t.* 208. /. 4. Leaves ovali-elliptice. BASILICUM agreste. *Rumph.* v. 265. *t.* 92. /. 2. 5. OCIMUM *scutellarioides.* Corollae falcate. PedU cles branched. *L. tnant.* 84; *sp.* 834. MA J ANA rubra. *Rumph.* v. 291. . 101. 626. COLEUS. *Filaments* united into a tube, sheathing the style.
Lour. ii. 451.
1. COLEUS *amboinicus. Lour.* ii. 452. Upper lip of the corolla quadriiid, lower entire. Monarda zeylanica. *Burm. Lour. ind.* 12. Monarda floribus verticillatis, foliis subcordatis, caly cibus pilosis involucro longioribus. *L. zeyi. n.* 24. Jakwanassa. *Herrn, zeyl.* 30. (Marr ubi um album amboinicum. *Rumph.* v. 294. /. 102, seems a different plant. Spikes naked.
The description of the corolla docs not accord with that of Lour.) MARRUBIUM odoratissimum, betonicae folio.
Burm. J. zeyi. 153. *t.* 71. /. J. Spikes leafy.
Upper lip of the corolla linear, bipartite. Iribeli. *Rhccde* ix. 145. *t.* 74. Root and radical leaves.
627. PLECTRANTHUS. *Calyx,* upper segment larger. *Corolla* resupinatcj tube gibbous and calcaratc. *Obs.* 2959, # front *L. a Willd.* ft *Lhetit.* 1, PLECTRANTHUS *crassifolius.* Nectari urn gibbous. Racemi bracteate. Leaves ovate, fleshy. *Fahl, symb.* i. 44. & Leaves cuneato-oblong, with mostly 4 teeth on each side. From OCYMUM Zatarrhendi *d Forsk.* 110. 628. SCORODONIA. *Calyx* bilabiate; upper lip orate,lower semiquadrifid. *Corolla* ringent; upper lip bipartite; segments distant; lower lip tripartite. *Stamina* longer than the upper lip of the corolla. *Obs.* 538. *Riv.* 1. SCORODONIA *solitaria. Obs.* 538. On banks. Scorodonia. *Riv. mon. t.* 12. (*Cord. fol.* 91, *repr. from* Salvia sylvestris. *Trag.* 15, has a galeate upper lip.) Teucrium Scorodonia. *L. sp.* 789; *mant.* 409. *Curt. loud.* v. 40. *t.* 295. *Gou. hort.* 270. Near Mont pelier.— *Bot. art:* 591. *Light/.* 303. *Ft. dan. t.* 485. *Smith, engl. t.* 1543. Chamaeclrys fruticosa sylvestris melissac folio. *Toum. paris.* 70. Scordium alterum, sive Salvia agrestis. *Boerh.* i. 183. In Holland. S. seu Salvia agrestis. *Raii hist.* 576; *syn.* 245; *Vaill. paris.* 180. *Ger. by Johns.* 662, *rcpr. from* Scordion alteram Plinii. *Lob. obs.* 262; *zchich repr. in ic.* i. 497, *Sf* Salvia agrestis, sive Sphacelus. *Dod.* 289, *and cop. in*
S. sive Scordium alterum quibusdam, et Salvia agrestis. *Park, theatr.* 111.
Scordotis, sive Scordium folio salviac. *Sauk. J.* iii.
b. 293. SCORODON1A. Dale 156. *Geoffr. suite* ii. 429. Salvia agrestis. *Mill. Jos.* 387. *Rutty* 456. Scordium alteram, sive Salvia agrestis. *Cham.* 279. 629. SCUTELLARIA. *Calyx* bilabiate; lips entire, the upper with a spur rising from the upper side, *Obs.* 562. *L.* 1. SCUTELLARIA *galcriculata.* Leaves cordatd lanceolate, distantly crenate; florat leaves crenate. *Obs.* 562. On the side of a ditch.—*L. sp.* 835. *Jiot. arr.* 629. *Curt. land.* iii. 36. *t.* 155. *Wale. t. Fl. dan. t.* 637. *Smith engl. t.* 523; *brit.* 615. S. foliis cordato-lanccolatis, crenatis. *L. lapp. n.* 239. Scutellaria. *Riv. mon. t.* 77. Cassida palustris vulgatior, flore caerulco. *Tourn. paris.* 244. *Vaill. paris.* SI. *Raii syn.* 244. Tertianaria, aliis Lysimachia galericulata. *Bank. J.* iii. 435. Lysimachia galericulata. *Lob. obs.* 186, *repr. in ic.* i. 344, *and cop. in* Dalech. 1060, *Ger. by Johns.* 477, co;i. *in* Gratiola caerulea, sive latifolia major. *Pari;, theatr.* 821,4 a6r. m Hood Mint..Per. Aer6. r. 31. /. 10. *Leaves,* lower remotely crenate, those above sparingly crenate, glabrous above; veins underneath slighth pubescent. *FTbwers* solitary, axillary. *Pe fancies* as short again as the calyx. *Bractcae* 2 at the base of each peduncle, setaceous, half as long as the peduncle. *Calyx* lubular, gradually widening; mouth circular with a slight emarginaturc on each side with an elevated line extending from each emargiitature to the base, and at which lines it is easily separable into 2 parts; the upper half with a spur rising perpendicularly and transversely from the upper side about midwny between the mouth and the base; spur square, slightly emarginate; becoming larger as the seed advances to maturity, closing when the corolla falls, and containing the seeds as in a capsule, the upper half at length separating and falling oft. *Seeds* roundish, scabrous, fulvous. *Obs.* 562. SCUTELLARIA. Date 155. Tertianaria. *Geojfr. suite* iii, 166. 71/«rr. ii. 182. *Schoepf* 98. Lysimachia caenilea galericulata, vel Gratiola caeru lea. *Chom,* 468. 2. SCUTELLARIA *allissima.* Leaves cordato-oblong, acuminate, serrate. Spikes nearly without bracteal,. *L. sp.* 836.—*Lour.* ii. 445. 630. BRUNELLA. *Calyx,* upper lip tridentate and trifid, lower bifid. . *Corolla,* upper lip entire and with 2 lobes, lower trifid. *Filaments* bifid at the end; one of the brunches with an anthera. *Stigma* bifid at the end. *Obs.* 5313. *Juss. Tourn. L. gen. ed.* ii; *phil.* 34.
Prunella. *1-.* 1. BRUNELLA *vulgaris.* Leaves pctiolate, oblongo ovate. Upper lip of the calyx with 3 teeth; lateral teeth as narrow again as the middlemost, laterally patent. *Obs.* 5313.
Prunella vulgaris, *L. sp.* 837; *suec. n.* 540. *Lightf.* 321. *Bot. arr.* 631. *Curt. fond.* iv. 42. *t.* 229.
Wale. t. Fl. dan. t. 910. *Smith brit.* 646; *engl. t.* 961. *Park, theatr.* 526. No fig.— *Trag.* S10, *and*
Prunella flore minore, vulgaris. *Bauh. J.* iii. 428, cop. *from* Prunella. *Fucks.* 621. *erf. fol. cop. in* 594. c. 238. *Haii hist.* 551; *sy».* 238. *Ger. by Johns.* 632, *repr.*

from Brunella. *l)od.* 136. *Riv. mon. t.* 29. B. major, foliis non dissectis. *Mill. Ph. ic.* 47.

70. /. 2. Consolida minor. *Cam. epit.* 703. BRUNELLA. *Geoffr.* iii. 218. *Vog.* 115. Prunella. *Pharm. austriaco-prov.* 58.—Berg'. 541. *Dale* 151. Z.em. ii. 245; d«p. ty *Rother.* 221. ii«n. 185. il/ i7/. Jo. 358. 3/urr. ii. 181. *Rutty* 411. *Schoepf* 98. ScArorf. 655. SpiWm. 390. Brunelle. *Chom.* 561; *suppl.* 160. . ANGIOSPERMIA, 631. RHINANTHUS. Cafyjr: bifid; segments lateral, bifid. *Corolla* bilabiate; upper lip vaulted, compressed, emarginate, lower trifid. A *gland* at the base of the germen. *Capsule* compressed. *Obs.* 4876. X.

1. RHINANTHUS *cristalua.* Leaves obtusely serrate.

Lower lip of the corolla shorter than the upper.

Calyx pubescent at the margin and keels. *Obs.* 4876. In meadows. It. Crista galli. *L. saec. n.* 542 *a* ; *sp.* S10 *a. Bot. arr.* 634. *Poll. n.* 579. *Curt. lond.* v. 43. *t*-320.

Smith brit. 649; *engl. t.* 657. *Fl. dan. t.* 981. *Gou. kort.* 296. Near Montpelier. Ithinanthus. *L. lapp. n.* 248 *a* Pedicular is pratensis lutea, vel Crista galli. *Tourn. paris.* 294. *Vaiu. parts.* 157. Crista galli foemhia. *Bauh. J.* iii. *b.* 436. Crista galli. *Riv. mon. U* 92. *Dod.* 546, *tepr. in Ger by Johns.* 1071, Crista galli herbariorum. *Lob. obs.* 285, *Sc ic.* i. 529, *&r cop. in* Yellow Rattle. *Pet. herb. t.* 36./. 3, # Pedicularis, sive Crista galli lutea. *Park, thealr.* 713. *Raii. hist.* 769; *syn.* 284. *Corolla* from 4 to G tenths of an inch long; tube cut round at the base, the upper half falling off, the lower permanent, forming a circular border surrounding the base of the germen; lower lip one third shorter than the upper; upper mostly with a purple spot on each margin just below the emarginature*Obs.* 4876. *Native* of Europe from the south to Lapland. ALECTOROLOPUUS. *Dale* 195. 632. EUPHRASIA. *Calyx* qumlrificl; segments equal. *Corolla* bilabiate¡ upper lip cmarginatc, lower trifid. *Antherae* cus 1. LATHRAEA *Squamaria.* Lower lip of the corolla scmitrifid. *Obs.* 7012. At the foot of a cluster of sycamores at Fullwood near Sheffield, where it was found by Mr. Salt.—*L. suec. n.* 550; *sp.* 844. *Bot. arr.* 642. *Smith engl. t.* 50; *brit.* 654. *Fl. dan. t.* 136. Squamaric Orobanche. *Scop. cam.* 438. Anblatum. *Cord. fol.* 89. *p.* 2. Tonrn. parts. 387. Found by Chomel. Squamaria. *liiv. mon. t.* 89. Anblatum Cordi, sive Aphyllon. *Bauh. J.* ii. 783.

Raii syn. 288. Orobanche radice dentata, sive Dentaria Matthioli major. *Park, theatr.* 1363. Dentaria major Matthioli. *Daleck.* 1296, *imit. in Gcr. by Johns.* 1585. Aphyllon. *Watson in ph. tr. abr. by Hutt.* x. 250.

Near Hareficld in Middlesex.

Roots fibrous from the sides of the stems. *Stem* subterranean, branched, succulent, whitish. *Branches* terete, horizontal, erect, patent, deflex, imbricate. *Leaves* succulent, greyish white, opposite, subrotnnd, sometimes ovato-subrotund, amplexicaul, disposed in 4 rows, glabrous, J . tenth of aa inch thick. *Scapi* above ground, solitary, terminating the branches, erect, slightly curved, from 3 to 6 inches long, whitish, tinged with pink, pubescent here and there. *Floral leaves* opposite, obovate, thin, yellowish white. *Racemi* terminal, from 2 to 4 inches long, sccundosc, with from 1 to 4 rows of flowers. *Braeteae* lanceolato-rhomboidal, whitish erect. *Pedicles* erect, pubescent. *Flowers* deflex at an acute angle. *Calyx* flesheoloured white, slightly Til lose, quadrifid; segments triangular, acute, con, nivent. *Corolla* pale brownish flesheoloured, tnbnlar, slightly compressed, somewhat longer than the calyx, separating from the receptacle as soon as the germen begins to enlarge, and projecting beyond the calyx so as to appear half as long again as the calyx and changing to yellowish brown; tube whitish; limb as long as the tube, bilabiate, slightly pubescent; lips erect; upper acutely emarginate; lower semitrifld; segments refuse; throat pubescent on the lower side. *Stamina* 4, inserted into the throat of the corolla, the 2 lower inserted into the base of the lower lip, as long again as the 2 upper, ascending and at length projecting beyond the corolla. *Filaments* thick. *Antherae* oblong, pubescent. *Germen* ovate, glabrous, soon becoming nearly as large as the calyx, yellowish white. *Nectarium.* transversely semioval, at the base of the germen, fleshy. *Style* projecting beyoud the stamina, pressing against the emarginature of the upper lip. *Stigma* roundish, emarginate. *Capsule* not yet ripe. *Seeds* numerous, attached to 2 receptacles on tfie sides of the valves. *Obs.* 7042.— *Stem* 10 inches long. *Flowers* larger than those of Obs. 7042, which grew in a very shady place and covered with the foliage of other plants. *Corolla* half as long again as the calyx. *Obs.* 4557. Specimen gathered by Broughton. SQUAMARIA, *Dale* 197, 634. PEDICULARIS. *Calyx* qninquefid and bifid. *Corolla* bilabiate; upper ljp vaulted, compressed, lower trilobate. A Alccforolophus III. *Clus. pann.* 709, $ Alectorolophi III genus alterum. *Clus. hist.* ii. 211. *Stems* with short branches at the base. *Calyx* sexangular, glabrous on the outside; margin and inside of the mouth pubescent. *Obs.* 4877. PEDICULARJS. *Dale* 196, 635. ANTIRRHINUM. *Calyx* quinquepartite. *Corolla* ringent, calcarate and gibbous at the base; throat closed; upper lip bifid, lower trifid. *Capsule* with 2 cells. *Obs.* 3990. *L.* 1. *Corolla without a spur.* L.

A. repens...

1. ANTIRRHINUM *craniolare.* Calyx longer the corolla. Stem and peduncles slightly hirsute. *Obs.* 1524. In a corn field near Worcester, on gravel. A. Orontium. *L. suec. n.* 559; *sp.* 860. *Bot. art.* 650. *Curt. loud,* iv! 45. *t.* 234. *Fl. dan. t.* 941. *Smith engl. t.* 1155; *brit.* 662, who says it grows on calcareous as well as sandy soils. A. arvense.' *Jliv. mon. irr. t.* 82. A. arvense majus. *Tourn. paris.* 246. 388. *Vaill. parts.* 13. A. arvense majus, flore rubro. *Boerh.* i. 233. A. angustifolium sylvestre. *Bauh. J.* iii. 464. *Rati syn.* 283. In sandy soil. A. sylvestre, Phyteuma. *Dod.* 182, *repr in* A-minimum. *Lob. ic.* i. 405, $ A. minus. *Ger. by Johns.* 549, # *cop. in* A. sylvestre medium. *Park, theatr.* 1SS4 *Peduncles* mostly very short, sometimes f inch long, axillary, solitary. *Calyx, phylla* linear. *Corolla* with a slight prominence at the base. *Capsule* ovate, oblique, obliquely truncate at the end, bilocular, the upper cell ending in 1

rounded prominence, the lower larger, ending above in 2 rounded prominences. *Seeds* oval, whitish brown, convex on one side with a ridge along the middle, concave on the opposite side with an elevated fungose margin; margin inflex, dentate, whitish, the surface composed of minute microscopic scales pointing to the center of the side of the seed. *Nucleus* oval, strawcoloured. *Obs.* 1524. ANTIRRHINUM Orontium. *Schreb. ap. Linn.* 86. Antirrhinum. *Dale* 193. *Vog.* 124.

2. ANTIRRHINUM *grandijlorum.* Flowers racemose.
Leaves lanceolate. Calyx shorter than the corolla.
Obs. 3838. In a garden. A. majus. *L. sp.* 859. *Hort. ke&.* ii. 338. *Jluds.* 2/74, who justly considers it as a naturalised plant. *Bot. arr.* 650. *Smith, engl. t.* 129; 6ri7. 661. *Park. par. t.* 267. /. 5. Antirrhinum. *Riv. mon. t.* 82. *Cam. epit.* 924. *Tiod.* 182, *repr. in Lob. obs.* 221; *ic.* i. 404, & A. purpureum sive album. *Ger.' by Johns.* 549. A. majus alterum, folio Iongiore. *Mill. Ph. ic.* 28 . *t*-42.
A.vulgare. *Bauh. J.* iii. 462. *Yaill. paris.* 14.
　On the walls of gardens.—*Raii. hist.* 760. A. latifolium. *Boerh.* i. 233. n. 1—8.
　A. purpureum. *Rail ear.* 65. On banks and in hedges near Montpelier.
　A. majus flore rosep. *Cam. hort.* 18. About Montpelier Nismes and Salernum.—*Magn. monsp.23; hort.* 18.
　Cynocephalus Plinii. *Dalech.* 830. Segments of (lie upper lip of the corolla acute.
　A. II Matthioli. *Dalech.* 1340.
　A. magnum. *Dalech.* 1341.
　Antirruini vulgaris icon 3. *Bauh. J. Hi. b.* 463.
　A. purpureum sive roseum. *Park. par.* 269. No (A. latifolium, pnllido amplo flore. *Bocc. pianti* 19.
t. 41, is A. molle.) *Calyx,* phylla ovate. *Corolla* pink, with a slight prominence at the base. *Obs.* 3838. *Native* of Italy and the south of France, but in the north of France, Germany and England it seems to be only naturalised. ANTIRRHINUM. *Linn.* 186. *Schrod,* 536. 2. *Corolla* calcaratc; *spur longer than the calyx. Leaves angular, mostly alternate.*
S. ANTIRRHINUM *quinquelobum.* Leaves cordate, with 5 lobes. *Obs.* 4022. On gifirden walls on each side of the road at Plaisley in Derbyshire) where it was sown by a botanist 40 years ago. A Cyrabalaria. *L. sp.* 851. *Bot. arr.* 645. *Scop. cam. n.* 770. On the walls of Vipach, Trieste, and Gortz.—*Curl. loud.* i. 45. *t.* Huds. 271. On old walls about London.—*Gou. hort.* 299. On moist walls about Montpelier.—*Sibth. ox. n.* 550. Walls in Oxford.—*Host* 311. In Frhili and Litorali
Vol. 3. *B* b on old walls, rubbish, and rocks.—*Schreb. lips.* 14. On the walls of a garden.— *Reich, franc. n.* 425. On old walk.—*Poll. n.* 589. On walls about Heidelberg. A. foliis allernis cordatis quinquelobis. *Gutlt.* ii. 209. On walls and about the mouths of wells and fountains, in Estampes and Orleans. Linaria folio glabro subrotundo, hederae folio clematitis. *Hist. ox. s.* 5. *t.* 14. /. 30. Boerh. i. 232. In Holland. Linaria hederaceo folio glabro, seu Cymbalaria vulgaris. *Dill. ap. Raii syn.* »282. On the walls of Chelsea garden and its vicinity. Found by Richardson in the quarries about Darford in Yorkshire (a misprint, as Mr. Knowlton suggests, for Bradford, where Mr. K. says Richardson was reported to have sown it.) Cymbalaria foliis hederaceis, flore caeruleo. *Besl. hort. nest. ord. G.Jol.* 5, Cymbalaria italica, hederaceo folio. *Lob. adv.* 269. On the walls of houses in Venice Padua and the neighbouring villages; *ohs.* 337, *repr. in* Cymbalaria italica, folio hederaceo. *Lob. ic.* i. 615, *and* Cymbalaria italica. *Ger. by Johns.* 530. Cymbalaria hederacea. *Parle, theatr.* 681. About Hatfield in Hertfordshire, in gardens and other places. Cymbalaria. *Matth.* 1124. *Cam. epit.* 860. *Datech.* 1322. *Riv. mon. irr. t.* 86. *Raii Hist.* 759. In Italy, on moist walls rubbish and rocks. Cymbalaria flosculis purpurascentibus. *Bauh. J.* iii. 685. On moist old walls, rubbish, and rocks. —*Rupp. ab Hail.* 24?. On walls about Jena, whither brought by Rolfino from Italy.—*Zannich.* 77. Í. 252.
Native of Italy, and domesticated from the south of France to Estampes, Orleans, Gottingen, Holland, Derbyshire and Yorkshire. CIMBALARIA. *Bale* 193. *Fog.* 124. 4. ANTIRRHINUM *Elatine.* Leaves hastate. Stems procumbent. Peduncles glabrous. *Obs.* 6395.
In corn fields near Chesterfield.—*L. sp.* 851. *Curt. land.* i. 46. *t; mat. med. t.* 7. *Bot. arr.* 646. *Fl. dan. t.* 426. Smith engl. *t.* 692; *brit.* 658. (*Gou. hört.* 299, observed near Montpelier is a variety with a blue corolla noticed by Magn. and observed on the continent by Ray, Tourn. and Vaill.) Linaria Elatine dicta, folio acuminato. *Raii hist.* 759; *syn.* »282. Linaria segctum, nummulariae folio aurito & villoso, flore luteo. *Tourn. paris.* 111. Elatine folio acuminato in basi auriculato, flore lúteo.
Vaill. paris. 48. Elatincs altera. *Dod.* 42, *repr. in* Elatine altera. *Lob. ic.* i. 470, *Ger. by Johns.* 625. Elatine foemina, folio anguloso. *B auk, J.* iii. *b.* 372. Elatine folio acuminato. *Park, theair.* 553. *Stem* beginning to flower when only an inch long, and continuing till sometimes 33 inches long. *Leaves,* the lowermost pair ovate, entire at the margin, the 2nd pair ovali-ovate, dentate, those above hastate. *Peduncles* capillary, hirsutulous at the base. *Calyx* quinqnepartite; segments ovato-lanccolate, acute, membranaceous at the margin below and at the com« missures. *Corolla* somewhat longer than the calyx; throat just open so as to expose the stamina to view; upper lip erect, purple; lower patulous, brimstone coloured, with 2 oblong prominencies on the upper side; spur yellowish, attenuate, once and a half as long as the calyx. *Obs.* 6395.—*Capsules* bilocular; cells obliquely circumscinded,a circular portion separating from the upper part of the paries of each cell. *Seeds* roundish, rugose; ridges and cavities acute. *Obs.* 7650. Near Chesterfield. *Native* of Kent, Middlesex, Suffolk, Cambridgeshire, Bedfordshire, Oxfordshire, Worcestershire, and the north of Derbyshire. ELATINE. *Monro* iii. 105. *Vbg.* 125, (but what he relates from Lobel belongs to A. spurium.) Elatines. *Diosc. I.* 4, *c.* 40. *fol.* 206. *p.* 2. A. Elatine. *Schoepf* 98. 3. *Corolla* calcarate; *spur longer than the calyx. Leaves entire at the margin, mostly alternate or*

crowded. 5. ANTIRRHINUM *spurium.* Leares alternate, ovate, villose. Stems procumbent. Peduncles villose. *Obs.* 7648. Specimen gathered in Champagne.— *L. a Gmel.ii.930; sp.* 851. *Curt. lond.* iii. *51.t.* 205. *Bot. arr.* 646. *Fl. dan. t.* 913. *Host* 345. *Smith engl. t.* 691; *brit.* 657. *Gou. hort.* 300. Near Montpelier.

Elatine. *R'm. mon. t.* 86.

Linaria Elatine dicta, folio subrotundo. *Raii hist.* 759; *syn.* »282.

Linaria segetum, nummulariae folio villoso. *Tourn. paris.* 110.

Elatine folio subrotundo. *Vaill. paris.* 48. *Park, theatr.* 553.

Veronica foemina. *Fuchs.* 171. c. 59, *cop. in* Elatme mas folio subrotundo. *Bauh. J.* iii. *b.* 372, *Sf4»* V. foemina Fuchsii, sive Elatine. *Dod.* 44, *which repr. in Ger. by Johns.* 625. Ela-ine Uioscoridis. *.Lob. adv.* 197, *repr. in ic. i.* 470.

Leaves ovate, acute, entire at the margin. *Peduncles* vitlose. *Qbs.* 7650. Specimen gathered in the valley of the Danube between Stra&burgh and Lintz. — *Leavts* ovate, dentate, the upper hastate and triangular. *Peduncles* villose. *06s.* 7649. Specimen from M. Geltibrand. *Native* of France, Germany, Kent, Middlesex, Suffolk, Norfolk, Cambridgeshire, Bedfordshire, and Oxfordshire. ELATINE, *Alst.* ii. 131. *Dale* 193. *Geoff.* iii. 419. *Eea.* i. 409. *Mill. Jos.* 184. *Putty* 173. *Vog.* 1'25, the observation from Lob. adv. Elatine folio subrotundo. *Chom.* 681. 6. ANTIRRHINUM *Linaria.* Leaveslineari-lanceolatc, sparsc, crowdcd. Stem crcct. Racemi terminal, sssije. Flowers imbricate. *Obs.* 557. In hedges, —*L. sp.* 858. *Bot. arr.* 648. *Curt. lond.* i. 47. *t. Smith irit.* 660; *gngl. t.* 658. *Woodv.* iv. 24. *t.* £21. *Mart. rust. t.* 93. *Fl. dan. t.* 982.

Eiiaria. *Piv. mon. t.* 83. v Li iaria vulgaris lutea, flore majore. *Tourn. paris. .* g3. *Vajll. paris.* 117. *Boerh.* i. 231. In flol. land.

Osyris, Unaria. *Dalech.* 1332. Tragi 357.

Linaria prima. *Dod.* 183, *repr. in*

Osyris. *Lob. obs.* 222, *Sf ic.* i. 406, *cop. is*

Linaria vulgaris nostras. *Park, theatr.* 458, *and repr. in* Linaria vulgaris lutea. *Ger. by Johns,* 550. *Raii hist.* 752; *syn.* 281. Osyris, sive Linaria. *Fucks* 532. c. 210, *cop. in* Linaria lutea vulgaris. *Bauk. J.* iii. *4:56.* Capsules oblongooval, emarginate; cells cracking at the end. Seeds orbicular, with a crena in the margin on one side, brownish black. *Obs.* 557. LINARIA. *Pharm. austriaco-prov.* 46. *saec.— Berg.* 545. *Dale* 193. *Geofr.* iii. 730. *Lew. iu* 69; *disp.by* Dune. 329; *by Rother.* 189. *Linn.* 186. *Mill. Jos.* 270. *Murr.* ii. 183. *Quar. anim.* 263. *Rutty* 289. *SchoepJ99.Schrod. 6YJ. Spielm.* 459. Linaire. *Chonu* 727. 636. MARTYNIA. *Calyx* quinquefid. *Corolla* ringent. *Capsule* lignose, covered with a rind, with a hooked beak, quadrilocular, bivalve. L. 1. MARTYNIA *Cranio!aria.* Stem branched. Leaves opposite, quinquelqbate, dentate. *L. a WUld.* iii. 264. *Swartx. obs.* 230. *Glox.* Martynia annua villosa et viscosa, aceris folio, flore albo tubo loqgissimo. *Ehr. t. l.f.* 2. 2. 2. CRANIOLARIA annua. *L, sp.* 862; *mant.* 417; *a Murr.* 558.—*J acq. amer. t.* 110; 8t», 222. 637. SCROPHULARIA. *Calyx* quinquefid. *Corolla* bilabiate; tube globular; upper lip erect, bipartite; lower tripartite; lateral segments patulous, the middlemost reflex. *Capsule* of 2 cells. *Obs.* 4008. L. 1. SCROPHULARIA *marilandica.* Leaves cordate, serrate, rounded at the base. Angles of the stem obtuse. *L. sp.* 863. *Ilort. kew.* ii. 340. S. foliis cordatis serratis acutis bast rotundatis, caule obtuse tetragono. *L. ups.* 177. *Gron. virg.* 95. *Cutl.* 464.

SCROPHULARIA. Schoepf 99.

2. SCROPHULARIA *nodosa.* Leavestriangulo-cordate, acute. *Obs.* 4008. In hedges.—*L. suec. n.* 560; *sp.* 863. *Bol. arr.* 651. *Smith brit.* 663; *engl. t.* 1544. S. aquatica. *Fl. dan. t.* 507. S. nodosa foetida. *Boerh.* i. 234. In Holland. Scrophularia. *Riv. mon. t.* 107. *Cam. epit.* 866. *Dod.* 764, *cop. in* S. major vulgaris. *Park, theatr.* 610, *abr. in* Brown Figwort. *Pet. herb. t.* 35. *f.* 9, *and repr. in* S. major. *Lob. ic.* i. 533, *and Ger. by Johns.* 716. Ra-i *hist.* 764; *sy«.* «283. DafecA. 1085. Common Eye-bright. *Pet. herb. t.* 36. /". 5. (The name is Euphrasia officinalis.) SCROPHULARIA. *Pharm. austriaco-pror.* 66.
—. i. 517. *Carth.* ii. 333. *Dale* 194. *Gcoffr. suite* ii. 438. *Zea. disp. by Dune-* 347. *Aft//. Jos.* 404. A/arr. ii. 188. *Neum.* ii. 138. *Spic/m.* 579.

Sdirod. 679. S. nodosa. /,«. ii. 358. *Rutty* 476. *Fog;.* 118. 211.

S. foetida. *Berg.* 547. *Linn.* 186.

S. nodosa foetida. *Chom.* 755.

S. tertia. *Boerh.* 316.

9. SCROPHULARIA *aquaiica.* Leaves oblongo-cor date. Stem bordered. *Obs.* 2880. Specimen gathered on the side of a diteb,—*L. sp.* 864 *Curt. lond.* v. 44. *t.* 291. *Bot. arr.* 652. *Smith brit.* 663; *engl. t.* 854. (*Fl.* Лги. *t.* 507, is S. nodosa.) S. foliis cordatis petiolatis decurrentibus, caule aculan guio, racemis terrninalibus. *L. ups.* 177. S. foliis cordatis, pcdiculorum alis in caulem decurrentibus. *Guett.* ii. 201. S. radice fibrosa. *Boerh.* i. 234. In Holland. S. foemina. *Cam. epit.* 867. S. aquatica maJQr. *Raii hist.* 764; *syn,* 2S3. Betónica aquatilis. *Dod.* 50, *repr. in* Betónica aquatica. *Get. by Johns.* 715, *вор. in Parlctheatr.* 613, *andubr. in* Water Figvort. *Pet. herb. t.* 35. *f.* 10. S. maxima, radice fibrosa. *Bauh. J.* iii. *b.* 421.

(The fig. a different plant.) SCROPHULARIA aqHatica. *Akt.* i. 518. *Lac.* ii. 358. *Linn.* 187. *Mill. Jos.* 404. *Murr.* ii. 190. *Nevm.* ii. 121. *Rutty il5. Vog.* 118. S. aquatica rnajpr. *Chom.* 756. *Marchand, account from in ph. tr. abr. by Butt,* iv. 655. *Marchant in ac. sc. abr. by Southw.* iii. 205. S. quarta. *Boerh.* 316.

Betónica aquatics. *Dale* 194. Geofr. $ие ii. 444. P brasifiensis. So far like a, except what difference culture and climate might make. *From Yquetaya. Marchand in ac. sc. abr. by Southw.* iii.

Iquetaia. *Mnrchand, account from in ph. tr. air. by Jones* iv. S21.

638. DIGITALIS. *Calyt* pentaphyllons. *Corolla* ventricose, unequally quiuquefid and quadrifkl. *Capsule* ovate, of 2 cells, with many seeds. *Obs.* 4127. L. 1. DIGITALIS *purpurea.* Pbylla ovate, acute. Segments of the corolla obtuse, uppermost entire and slightly emarginate. *Obs.* 4127. On dry banks. —*L. sp.* 866; *mant.* 418. *Bot. arr.* 654. *Curt, lond.* i. 11. *t. cop,* under his inspection *in With, foxgl. t. Fl. dan. t.* 74. *Woodv.*

i. 71. . 24. *Huds. 976. Lightf.* 330. *Raii hist.* 767; *syn,* 283. *Tourn. paris.* 432. *Vaill. paris.* 47. *Smith engl. t.* 1297. *Fuchs.* 893. *fol. ed. cop. in* 239. *c.* 88, *Bauh. J.* ii. 812, *and Dalech.* 831. *Dod.* 168, repr. m io6. *obs.* 308; 'c. i. 572, *and Ger. by Johns.* 790, *St* cop. rn

D. purpurea vulgaris. *Parle, theatr.* 653.

D. flore rubro. *Besl. hprt. aest. ord.* 1. *fol. 3.*

Digitalis. *Curt. mat. med. t. 3. Riv. mon. t.* 104. *Thornt.* 590.

DIGITALIS. Herb. *Pharm. lond. 8f noviss.* — *Allen in phys. journ.* ix. 263. *Bailey, J. ib.* iii. 127. *Reddoes in med. facts* v. 17, *3c account front in ann. med. lustr. II.* i. 201; *in contrib* 521,$ *account from in phys-journ.* i. *29L2.*384; *chir. rev.* vi. S54; viii. 133, *Se med. rev.* vii. 68. Bree248; *in phys. journ.* ii. 314. 430. *Chir. rev.* vii. 588. *Chom.* 75. *Coley in phys, journ.* vii. 407. *Cox, account from in chir. rev.* xi. 299. *Cuming ib.* xii. 113. *Custance in phys. journ.* iv. 20. 420. *Dale* 195. *Drake in contrib.* 473, *8c account of in ann. med.* iv. 123, *and phys. journ.* i. 289; ii. 267. 417; iv. 521. *Darn,* ii. 105. III. 117. 291. 489. 503. 742. 745. *Douglas in mid. rev.* vi. 154. *Dunn in phys. journ*-x. 551. *Earn-st ib*-554. *Ferriar* i.-. 23. 83. 91. 176. 190; ii. 18. 139. 163. 161. *Field, ing in phys-journ.* v. 141. *Fogo ib.* xi. 147. *Fowler, R. in contrib.* 501; *8c account of in ann. med.* iv. 147; v. 146, *and phys. journ.* i. 291. *Friese, account ftom ib.* xi. 86 *Gapper ib.* vii. 155. *Gilb-rt. ib.* ix. 353. *Halesworth ib.* xvi. 229. *Harrington, T. ib.* iii. 202. *Heb.* 8. *Hufeland, account from in phys. journ.* xi. 192. *Hull phi.* 217. 219. *200. Hunt, account from in chir. rev*x, 272. *Kinglake in phys. journ.* iii. 120; v. 437; vii. 523; xi. 59, *and account from in chir. rev.* viii. 142, *and med. rev.* vii. 74. *Ki'lcr in phys. journ.* vi. 312. *Magennis ib.* iii. 129. *Low ib.* ix. 418, *Mill. Jos.* 178. *Mossman in phys. journ.* ii. 36. 238; iv. 309, *St med. rev.* iii. 2S3; vi. 161, *and account from in chir. rev.* vii. 523. 524. 525. *Murr. J.* i. 329. *Palmer in phys. journ.* xiv. 237. *Patterson ib.* v. 441. *Rogers, W. ib.* viii. 82. *Rolfe ib.* v. 406. *Rutty* 168. *Sherwen in phys. journ.* ii. 175. *Simmons, W. ib.* vi. 134. *Sugrue ib.* iv. 329.

S&*ift ib. v.* 35b. *WhUet account from in chir. rev.* viii. 60. D. purpurea. Leaves. *Pharm. edin.—Bartley in phys. journ.* v. 259. *Beddoes, account from in ann. med.* iv. 91. *Braestrup in act. med. hafn.* ii. 438. *Brera, account from in phys. journ.* i. 71. *Carson ib.* iii. 513. *Cox in med. comment, dec. JI.* iii. 425. *Cull,* ii, 555. *Currie m med. soc.* iv. 10. *Ferriar, digitalis, $ account of in ann. med.* iv-505. *Geoffr.* iii. 402. *Henry in phys. journ.* ii. 102. *Howard ib.* vi. 418. *Hufeland, account from in med. rev.* ii. 454. *Kohthaas, account from ib.* iv. 191. *Lentin, account from in Quar. anim.* 118, *and phys. journ.* ix. 94. *Letts, in med. soc.* ii. 145. *Lew.* i. 401; *disp. by Dune.* 218. *Maclean in phys. journ.* ii. *113;* iii. 150. 237. *Magennis ib.* v. 201. *May in new med. journ.* ii. 1. *Measet account from in phys. journ.* i. 56. *Monro* iii. 91; *Alex, account from in ckir. rev.* iv. 361. *Moore, J. account from ib.* xviii. 5. *Murr.* i. 490; *J.* i. 130. 300; ii. 30. 75. *Musheau, account from in med. comment, dec. II.* x. 44. *Pears. R.* i. 145. 224; ii. 236. *Ploucq. bibl.* i. 130. *Quar. anim.* 117 *to* 121. *Rush* ii. 226. *Simmons in med. journ.* ii. 414; vi. 55. *Stevenson in med. comment, dec. 11. x.*356. *Und.* i. 281. *Vog.* 128. *Warren, J. in med. journ.* vi. 145. *Wright, J. in med. soc.* iii. 563.

D. purpurea, folio aspcro. *Cliom.* 395; *suppl.* 128. Foxglove. *Baker in med. trans,* iii. 287. 448. *Beddoes, account from in med. rev.* ii. 156. *Darw.* ii. 718; *in med. trans,* iii. 255; *C.* 65. 103, *repr. in phys. journ.* iii. 202. *Dune, in med. comment. x.* 357. *Hull phi.* 333. *Jones in med. comment.* xi. 302. 380. *Kinglake in phys. journ.* iv. 63.

Maclean ib. ii. 177; iv. 127. *Mossman ib.* v. 133. *Quin dropsy brain* 189 *to* 227. *Rush* ii. 174;' iv. 99. *Salmon, account from in med. rev.* v. 303. *With, foxgl. and account from in med. comment. x. 133.*

'. DIGITALIS lutea. PIrylla lanceolate. Segment of the corolla acute; upper lip bifid, *L. sp.* 867. *Jacq. hört,* ii. *t.* 105. *Hort. kew.* ii. 345. *Gou. Kort.* 305. Near Montpelier.—*Scop. earn. n.* 779.

Roth. germ. ii. *pars* ii. 60. *Kroch, n.* 998. *Ger. by Johns.* 790, *repr.from* D. lutea parva. *Lob. ic.* i. 573. 1). foliolis calycinis subulatis. *Roy.* 293. D. folüs calycinis lanceolatis, corollis acutis, labiosa. periore bifido. *L. ups.* 178. D. major lutea vel pallida, parvo flore. *Тоыся. paris.* 433. *Vaül. paris.* 47. *Magn. monsp.* 86. *fiaii eur.* 116. About Saleruum and Naples; *hist.* 768.:

D. lutea, minore flore. *Boerh.* i. 229.

D. flore minore subluteo, angustiore folio. *Bauk. J.* ii. 814. In the Grisons and Switzerland.

D. minor lutea sive pallida. *Park. par.* 382. No fig. D. lutea, parvo flore. *Hist. ox. s.* 5. *t.* 8. /. 5. DIO ITA LI S lutea. *Careno, account from in chir. rep.*'vii. 390. 639.

BIGNONIA. Catyx quinquefid, cuplike. *Corolla* campanula?, quiaquefid; throat ventricose underneath. *CqsuU* of 2 cells, cylindric. *Seeds* with membrana« ceuus borders and woolly. From L. .' ' i.... ; 1. *Leaves simple.* L. 1. BIGNONIA Catalpa. Leaves cordate. Stem erect. Seeds with membranaceous borders. *H. K.n.* 346. *L. sp.* 868. *Thunb.jap.* 251. B. urucu foliis, flore sordide albo intus maculis par purois et luteis adsperso, siliqua longissima et angastissima. *Cat.* i. *t.* 49.

(Cumbulu. *Rheede* i. 75. *t.* 41, has a drupe.)

BIG NO NJA CAT ALP A. *Sckoepf*99.

Kakusju. *Kaempf. am.* 841. *t.* 842.

2. BIGNONIA *tomentosa.* Leaves cordate, tomentose.

Flowers axillary, paniculate. *L. a IVilld.* iii. 290.

Thunb. jap. 252.

Too. *Kaempf. am.* 859. *t.* 860.

BIGNONIA tomentosa. *Thunb. trav.* iv. 38.

2. *Leaves conjugate.* L. 3. BIGNONTA oplithalmica. Leaves cirrhose. Foli oles ovato-cordate, glabrous, entire at the margin, dotted underneath. From *Anders, in med. comment, dec. II.* ix. 373. AKUSERUNEE. *Chish. in med. comment, dec. II.* ix. 368. 4. BIGNONIA *capreolata.* Leaves cirrhose, lower simple; folioles cordato-lanceolate. *L. sp.* 870. *Hort. hew.* ii. 347. *Bot. mag. t.* 864. Clematis tetraphylla americana. *Bocc. sic.* 31.1. 15. *f.* 3. *Raii hist.* 1329. Clematide tetraphylla americana. *Zanon. ist.* 74. *t.* 28,

repr. in B. americana caprcolis donata, siliqua brcviori. *Za non. hist.* 49. *t.* 33. *Cat.* ii. *t.* 82. *Breyn.it.* S3, *t.* 25. No fructifications. BIGNONIA capreolata. *Chish.* 24.

3. Leaves digitate. L3. BIGNONIA *Leuioxjjlon.* Leaves digitate; folioles lanceolate, entire at the margin, glabrous. Flowers terminal. *From L. a Willd.* iii. 300, *Swaris. obs.* 233, *and Andr. rep. t.* 43. *L. sp.* 870. B. pentaphylla arborea, flore subrubcllo. *Browne* 263. Leucoxylon, arbor siliquosa, quinis foliis, floribus ncrii, alato semine. *Pluk. aim.* 215; *phyt, t.* 200./. 4. Nerio affinis arbor siliquosa, folio palmato seu digitato, flore albo. *Sloane cat.* 154. Nerio similis arbor. *Raii-hist.* 1768. Nerii facie arbor. *Lob. adv,* 455, *repr. in it.* ii. 239, *and cop. in Bauh, J.* ii. 142, Nerii facie arbor indica. *Park, theatr.* 1471, *and* Falmacea pinnata spinosa. *Dalech.* 1851. WHITE CEDAR. *Chish.* 26. Cedar. *Graing.* 49. *t* 4. Leaves pinnate. L. 6. BIGNONIA *chelonoides.* Leaves pinnate with an odd one; folioles ovate, entire at the margin, pubescent. Corolla barbate. Stamina with the rudiment of a fifth. *L.JU. suppl.* 282? PADRI. *Raii hist.* 1750. Rheede vi. 47. *t.* 26, has leaves abruptly pinnate. 7. BIGNONIA *indica.* Leaves bipinnate; foliolei subrotundo-ovate, cordate, acuminate. Stamina5. Calyx tubular. Corolla quiaquefid. *L. a Willd.* iii. 306; *a Murr.* 564; *sp.* 871 *a. Ilort. kcw.* ii. 348. PALEGA-PAJANELI. *Rheede* i. 77. (where for 44 read 43,) *t.* 43. *Raii hist.* 1741. 8. BIGNONIA *longifolia.* Leaves bipinnate; folioles oblongo-lanceolate, subcordate, acuminate. Calyx hemispheric. Corolla quadrihd. *L. a Willi,* iii. 306, from authors., B. indica *S. L.sp.SH.* PAJANELI. *Rheede* i. 79, (where for 45 read 44,) *t.* 44. *Raii hist.* 1741. 9. BIGNONIA *brasiliana.* Leaves bipinnate; folioles oblong, acute. Panicle axillary. Siliquae repandose. *L. a Willd.* iii. 307, from authors.—Lam. Jacamnda. *Marcgr.* 136. No fig. *JACARANDA* II. *Pis. ind.* 165. Jacaranda brasiliensibus. *Raii hist.* 1648.

640. CITHAREXYLUM. Calyx quinquedentate. *Corolla* infundibuliform; segments nearly equal. *Drupe* dispermous. *Nuts* bilocular. *Obs.* 8428. *L. Sf L. a Willd.* 1. CITHAREXYLUM *melanocardium.* Branches tetragonous. Flowers paniculate. Stamina 4. Leaves subrugose, veined and slightly scabrous underneath. *Swart, ind. occid.* 1046. C. paniculatura. *Gaertn.* i. 270. *t.* 56. Petioles with an articulation near the end. Leaves elliptic, acuminate, dotted above, pubescenti-tomentose underneath. *Obs.* 8369. Specimen gathered by Dr. Wright in Jamaica.

CITIIAREXYLON foltis rugosis ovatis oppositis, petiolis geniculars, raccmis termiaalibus, calicibns quadrifidis. *Browne* 265. 641. CRESCENTIA. *Calyx* bipartite; segments equal. *Corolla* gibbous. *Berry* pedicellate, unilocular, potyspermous. *Seed* bilocular. *L.* 1. CRESCENTIA *Cujete.* Leaves cuneato-lanceolate and lanceolate, crowded. *Swarlz. obs.* 234, *L. sp.* 872. *Mill. Ph. diet. n.* 1. *J acq. amer.* 175. *t.* Ill; *ed.* 8co, 223. C. arborescens, foliis confertis obovato-obloDgis basi angustioribus, fructu sphaerico maximo. *Browne* 265. C. arborescens, foliis confertis, fructu sphaerico mi nori. *Browne* 266. C. arborescens, foliis confertis, fructu oblongo-ovato minori. *Browne* 266. Cujete foliis oblongis et angustis, raagno fructu orato. *Plum. ic. t.* 109. Arbor araericana cucurbitifera, folio longo mucronato, fructu oblongo. *Commel. J. hort.* i. 137. *t.* 71. Macocquer virginiensium. *Bauh. J.* i. *a.* 254. Folium dictum Higuero. *Dalech.* 1843, *cop. in* Higuero Oviedi. *Bauh. J.* i. *a.* Ill, the upper leaf. Arbor cucurbitifera americana. folio subrotundo, *Raii hist.* 1667. *Sloane cat.* 206. Cohyne. *Dalech.* 1845, *cop. in Park.* 1666. Higuero. *Clus. exot.* 23. Nojfig.—232. Outer%, *cop. in* Fructus Higuero. *Dalech.* 1844, # Higuero fructus Clusii. *Park, theatr.* 1633. Seeds. CRESCENTIA Cujete. *Wright in med. journ.* viii. 249. 642. TANAECIUM. *Calyx* cylindric, truncate. *Corolla* tubular, quin, quefid; segments nearly equal. Rudiment of a 5th *stamen. Berry* corticose. *From Swarlz. ind. occid.* ii. 1049. 1. TANAECIUM *Jaroba.* Lower leaves ternate, upper geminate. Cirrhi between the petiolules, terminal Stem climbing. *Swartz. ind. occid.* ii. 1050. Crescentia scandens, foliis inferioribus pinnato-ter natis, superioribus geminatis clavicula interpositis. *Brovne* 267. Cucurbitifera fruticosa trifolia scandens. *Sloane cat.* 207; *hist.* ii. 173. JAROBA. *Marcgr.* 25, *repr. in Pis. ind.* 173. *Rati hist.* iii. *dendr.* 82; Phaseolus brasilianus, Jaroba indigenis dictus. *Raihist.* 889. 643. GMELINA. *Calyx* mostly quadridenlate. *Corolla* quadrifid, cam' panulate. *Antherae,* 2 bipartite, 2 undivided. *Drupe. Nut* trilocular. *From L. and L. a Schreb.* ' L GMELINA asiatica. *Ia a Mutr.* 565; *p.*'873. *Iour.* ii. 456.

Vol. 3. c c

Lvcium maderaspatanum, indici Alpino putati acraulum, foliis minoribus et majoribus bijugie et grandioribus, aculeis horridum. *Pluk. aim.* 234; *phj/t. t.* 305. /. 3; . 97./. 2.

JAMBOSA eilvestris parvifelia. *Rumph.* i. 129. *t.* 40. 644. PREMNA. *Calyx* bilobate. *Corolla* quadrifid. *Drupe. Nut* quadrilocular. *From L. a Schreb. n.* 1025. 1. PREMNA *inlegrifolia.* Leaves entire at the margin, glabrous. *From L. a Willd.* iii. 314, *and mant.* 252. Cornutia corymbosa. *Burm. N. ind.* 133. f. 41. /. 1.

FOLIUM JIIRCINUM. Rumph. iii. 208. *t.* 134 rugoso majore, flore purpureo, fructu esculento purpureo. *Shane cat.* 164 ;-*hist.* ii. 82. *t.* 195. 2. LANTANA *Cámara.* Spikes hemispheric. Leave» elliptico-ovate, scabrous above. Bracteae subulate, mostly shorter than the flowers. *Obs.* 6848. *In* Sir Sitwell Sitwell's garden —*I. sp.* 874. *Hort. lew.* ii. 351. *Swartz. obs.* 238. L. frutescens, foliis cordato-ovatis, floralibus lineari« bus, floribus croceis, pedunculis longis. *Browne* 268. 269. *par.* 5. Cámara melissae folio, flore variabili. *Dill. hort.* 64. *t.* 56./.65. Cámara alia, flore varicgato, non spinosa. *Plum. ic.* 50. *t.* 71./. 1. Viburnum amcricanum, urticae foliis, laraii odore, floribus miniatis. *Commet. J. hort.* i. 151. *t.* 78. Viburnum amcricanum non spinosum, melissae foliis, floribus coccineis. *Plvk. aim.* 385; *phyl. t.* 114. f.4. Cámara Juba. *Pis. bras.* 86, *repr. in* Cámara flore rubro. *Marcgr.* 5.

Stem whitish brown, with a few small prickles here and there. *Leaves* hirsute, scabious above with prominences ending in hairs, serrate; teeth of the serratures rather obtuse, sometimes deflex. *Bracteae* with acute hairs, two thirds as long as the tube of the corolla. *Receptacle* oblongo-oval, pubescent. *Calyx* tubular, very short, membranaceous; margin repandodentate, obspletely bidentate, ciliate. *Corolla* hypocrateriform¿ yellowish orangccoloured becoming purplish rosecoloured; tube as long again as the pistil, glabrous at the base, pubescent upwards, as long again as the limb; mouth with hairs; limb unequally
c c S semiquadrifid. *Obs.* 6848.— Branches with a few short prickles. *Bracteae* with acute hairs. *Calyx* obsoletely quadridentate. *Pistil* as short again as the tube of the corolla. *Obs.* 0849. Specimen from Leske.
LANTANA Camara. Schoepf 100. Wright in wed. journ. viii. 265. 3. LANTANA odorata. Flowers capitate. Leaves rugose, elliptic, longer than the peduncles. Bracteae nearly as long as the flowers, lanceolate. *Obs.* 7113. Specimen from Mr. Hunter's nursery.— *Ilort. hew.* ii. 351. L. a. Murr. 566. S&artz. obs. 239. Camara arborescens, salviae folio. Plum. ic. 60. f. 71./. 2. *Leaves* rhombeo-elliptic, half as long again as the peduncles. *Obs.* 7143.
LANTANA involucrata. Wright in med. journ. viii. 265.
Wild Sage. Graing. 24. 32. 35. 58.
2. Stem prickly. i. LANTANA aculcata. Spikes hemispheric. Leaves ovate, villosc underneath, shorter than the peduncles. Bracteae shorter than the flowers. *Obs.* 34b9. Specimen gathered in the garden of Fothergill—// K. ii. 352. L. sp. 874; mant. 419.
L. frutescens spinosa, foliis amplioribus suhrotundoovatis, pedunculis longissimis, floribus kermesinis. Broicne 269.
Viburnum americanum odoratum, urticae foliis latioribus, spinosum, fiorilius miniatis. Pluh. aim. 385; phyt. t. 233. /. 5.
Stem, prickles numerous, decurvate, thrice as short as the breadth of the stem. *Leaves* ovate, acute, whitish underneath, not scabrous with prominences. *Peduncles* axillary, opposite, patent, half as long again as the leaves. *Bractcae* hirsute, the lower subulate, more than half as long as the tube of the corolla, with hairs some acute others shorter and glandular at the ends; the upper ovate, thrice as short as the tube of the corolla, with acute hairs. *Calyx* tubular, very short, membranaceous; margin erect, obsoletely dentate, ciliate. *Corolla* hypocratcriform; tube glabrous at the base, pubescent upwards, thrice as long as the pistil, thrice and four tims as long as the limb. *Obs.* 3469. LANTANA aculeata. *lFrighl in med. journ.* vii. 265.

646. CAPRARIA. *Calyx* quinquepartite. *Corolla* campanulate, qninquefid; segments acute. *Capsule* bivalve, bilocular, polyspermous. L. 1. CAPRARIA bijlora. Leaves alternate. Flowers in pairs. L. sp. 875. Ilort. kew. ii 353. Swartz. obs. 239. Jacq.amer. 182. r. 115; Svo, 233. Capraria. Browne 268. C. corassavica. Herm.par. 110.?. 110. Gratiolae affinis frut scens americana, foliis agerati sive verouicae erectae majoris. Commel. J. hart. i, 79. (.. 40. lysimachiae peruvianae affinis americana procumbens ononidis vernae frutescentis folio singular! glabro. Pluk. L 98./. 4.
I. STEMODIA maritima. Leaves opposite, semiamplexicaul. Flowers sessile, solitary. Sisartz. obs. 242. L. am. v. 399; sp. 881. J acq.amer. 181. t. 174. /. 66. A leaf. Scordium maritimum fruticosum procumbens, (lore caeruleo. Sloane cat. 66; hist. i. 175. I. 110./. 2. No fructifications. STEMODIACRA. Browne 261. . 22./. 2.
649. OROBANCHE. *Calyx* bifid quadrifid and quinquefid. *Corolla* rlngent; upper lip emarginate and bifid, lower trifid. *Nectarium* glandular, surrounding the base of the germen. *Capsule* unilocular, bivalve, with many seeds. *Obs.* 2561, and fiora L. a Willd. iii. 347. L. 1. *Bracteae solitary. Stamina shorter than the corolla.* 1. OROBANCHE genistae. Stem pubescent, simple. Upper lip of the corolla entire; segments of the lower lip entire. Style pubescent Filaments pubescent upwards. *Obs.* 2561. On a common near Kidderminster.

O. major. L. suae. n. 561; sp. 882. Bot. arr. 657. Curt. land. iv. 44. t. 232. Smith engl. t. 421; brit. 669. Reth. ed. i. n. 452. Clus. pann. 242. No fig.
Orobanche. Jliv. mon. t. 89.
O. major, garyophyllum olens. Rati syn. 288. On the roots of Genista.
O. sive Rapum genistae. Rati hist, 1227; cart, 110. In broom fields at Gamlingay.
O. major foctidissima sylvae bononiensis. VaiU. paris. 154. O. I. Tab. ic. 684. Clus. hist. i. 270, repr. in Rapum genistae, sive Orobanche. Ger. by Johns. 1311, and Hypog-enista. Lob. ic. ii. 268, outer fig.—Inner fig. repr. from Genista scoparia vulgi. Lob. ic. ii. 89, *which repr. in*
Genista cum rapo. Dod. 749, inner plant, *and*
Genista. Ger. by Johns. 1311, and cop. *in*
Rapum genistae. Park, theatr. 229, *and* Genista cum rapo. Bauh. J. i. b. 390, inner fig.
O. flore minore. Bauh. J. ii. 781.
Stems from 10 to 19 inches long. *Calyx* bracteifonn, dimidiate, semicampanulate, quadrifid. *Filaments* glabrous below. *Nectarium* orbicular, dentate. *Obs.* 2561. OROBANCHE. Dale 197. 2. *Bracteae in threes.* Smith. 2. OROBANCHE virginiana. Stem branched. Corolla quaJridenlate. L. sp. 882. Walt. 167.
O. canle ramoso, corollis quadridentatis. Gron. virg. 96. '"''.
O. minor virginiana lignosior, per totum caulem floribus minoribus onusta. Hist. ox. s. 12. t. 16. row I. /. 9.
OROBANCHE virginiana. Coxe 374. Schoepf 101. 650. DIGERQS. Catyx quinqucpartite.. *Corolla* campanulate, quadrifid; segments obcordate, one larger. *Anther ac* divaricate. *Capsule* bilocular. Lour. 1. DICERGS cochinchinensis. Lour. ii. 463. 651. SESAMUM. *Calyx* quinqucpartite. *Corolla* campanulate, quinqueful; lower lobe largest. Rudiment of a 5th *filament. Stigma* lanceolate. *Capsule* quadrilocu lar. L. J. SESAMUM orientate. Leaves entire, ovato-oblong.
L. sp. 883. Hort. hew. ii. SCO. Lour. ii. 464. S. foliis omnibus oblongis serratis.

Browne 370. Digitalis orientalis, S. dicta. *Burnt. J. zeyl.* 87. *t..* 38./. 1. A leaf. Schit elu. *Rkeede* ix. 105. *t.* 54. S. veterum. *Sloane cat.* 59. Sesamum. *Boerh.* i. 318. *Raii hist.* 1327. *Dod.* 522, *repr. in Lob. obs.* 514; *ic.* ii. *68, Sf '* S. sive Sisamum. *Ger. by Johns.* 1232, *and cop. from* S. vernm. *Dalech.* 483. *Cam. hort. t.* 44, *cop. in SESAMUM. Park, theatr.* 254, *andabr. in Bauh. J.* ii. *S9G.* —*Carth.* i. 336. *Dale* 267. *Linn.* 188. *Murr.* i. 493. *Rutty* 483. *Schrod.* 682. *Vog.* 180.

S. orientale. *Bry.* 345.

3. SESAMUM indicum. Lower leaves trifid. *L. sp.* 884. *Hort. kew.* ii. 360. *Rumph.* v. 201. *t.* 76. *f.* lj lowermost leaves represented as tcniate.

S. foliis inferioribus trifidis dentatis, superioribus ob longis serratis. *Browne* 270. S. alteram, folits trifidis, orientale, scmine obscuro.

Boerh. i. 318. *Pluh. dm.* 344; *phyt. t.* 109. *f.* 4.

Leaws trilobate. SESAMUM indicum. *Bry.* 346. *Wright in mtd. journ.* viii. 282.

Zezegery. *Spence in phys. journ.* viii. 553.

652. RUELLIA.

Calyx quinquepartite. *Corolla* irregular. *Capsule* bilocular; dissepiment contrary; cells polyspermous. *Obs.* 5606. L. 1. RUELLIA tuberosa. Peduncles unifloroas. Leavo ovate, crenate. *From L. sp.* 885. *Stoartz. obs.* 245. Gentianella utriusque indiae, impatiens, foliis agerati.

JPluk. aim. 167; *phyt. t.* 186. /. 2. Gcntianella flore caeruleo integro, vasculo seminali ex humtdi contactu impatiente. *Sloane cat.* 52; *hist.* i. 149. *t.* 95. /. 1. A leaf and fruit. *RUELLIA* erecta asphodeli mdice, pedunculis Ui partitis alaribus. *Browne* 268. 2. RUELLIA repanda. Leaves lanceolate, obtusely dentate, petiolate. Stem creeping. *L. sp.* 886; *meant.* 422; *a Murr.* 575. *Burm. N. ind. t. 00.* /.2. P/StTVZXdomesticaangustifolia. *Rumph.* vi. 30. *t.* 13. *A. B.* 653. BARLERIA. *Calyx* tetraphyllous; 2 outer phylla larger. *Corolla* infundibuliforra. *Capsule* bilocular; dissepiment contrary; cells monospermous and dispermous. *Obs.* 5605. *L.* 1. BARLERIA *quadrispinosa.* Spines axillary, compound, with mostly 4 branches. Leaves elliptic. *Obs.* 5605. Specimen 'gathered in the Vienna garden.

B. Prionitis. *L. a Murr.* 576; *sp.* 887. *Dorm,* 152.

Barlcria. *Roy.* 291. *L. zeyl. n.* 233; *cliff.* 487.

(Lycium indicum, spinis quaternis ad foliorum singulorum exortum. *Seb.* i. 21. *t, 13. f.* I, is B. Hystrix.) *HYSTRIX FRUTEX. Rumpk.* vii. 22. *t.* 13.

Coletta-vectla. *Rheede* ix. 77. *t,* 41. *Boerh.* ii. 263.

g. BARLERIA *buxifolia.* Spines axillary, opposite, solitary. Leaves, roundish; margin entire. *L. sp.* 887. *CARASCHULLI. Rheede* ii. 91. *t.* 47. *Rati hist.* 1755. 654. VOLKAMERIA. *Calyx* campanulate, quinqvrefid and quinquedentate. *Corolla* hypocrateriform; limbquinqnepartite; segments nearly equal. *Stamina* longer than the corolla. *Stigma* bifid. *Berry* dispermous. *Seeds* bilocular. *Obs.* 5134. *L.* 1. VOLKAMERIA *inermis.* Branches unarmed. Peduncles pubescent; hairs adpressed. *Obs.* 5134.

In Mr. Sitwcll's garden. — *L. sp* 889; *mant.* 423.

Hort. kew. ii. 364 0. *J acq. coll. suppl. 117. t.* 4./.I.

Periclyraeni similis myrtifolia arbor maderaspatensis.

Pluk. aim. 287; *phyt. t.* 211. *f.* 4. Jasmini flore frutex philippinensis, foliis floribusque

fere ternis. *Pit. gaz t* 42. *f.* 7.

Nir-notsijl. *Rheede* v. 97. *t.* 49.

Leaves elliptic, glabrous, opposite, *Peduncles* axillary, triflorous. *Calyx* quiixluedcntate. *CoroUa* white; tube many times longer than the calyx, the inside below the middle villose and containing nectar; limb more than twice as long as the tube ;egments oval, oblique, one truncate with a very short mucro. *Obs.* 5134. *JASMINUM* litoreum. *Rumph,* v. 86. *t.* 46. 655. CLERODENDRUM. *Calyx* quingucfld, campanulate. *Corolla,* tube filiform; limbquinqueparite; segments equal. *Slamina* very long, between the gaping segments of the corolla. *Drupe* tetraspcrmous. *Nuts* unilocular. *L. Vent. tabl. t.* 9. *f.* 2. h CLERODENDRUM *mfotunatum.* Leaves cordate, tomentosc. *L. sp.* 889; *mant.* 423. C. folulato et acuminato. *Barm. J. ze,/l.* 66. *I.*

Peragu. *Rheede* ii. 41. *t.* 25. *Raii hist.* 1571.

PETASITES agrestis. *Rumph.* iv. 108. . 49.

656. VITEX.

Calyx quinquedenlate. *Coro//a* bilabiate; lipstriful. *Stigmata* 2. *Berry* quadrilocular; cells monosperraous. *From L. a Schreb. L.* 1. VITEX *Agnus.* Leaves digitate. Spikes verticillate. *Obs.* 5242. Specimen in an herbal collected in England.—*Gou. hort.* 309. V. Agnus castus. *L. sp.* 890. *Hort. Icezo.* ii. 365. *Woedt.* iv. 20. . 222. *Thornt.* 589. *Gaertn.* i. *f.* 50. *Sfo/i. rar«. «.* 783. About Trieste, and in Istria. *a inlegerrima.* Margin of the folioles entire. *Obs.* 5242. *L. sp. a* V. Agnus castus angustifolia. *Hort. kczo.* ii. 365. V. foliis angustioribus cannabis modo dispositis. *Boerh.* ii. 222. Agnus castus. *Magn. hort.* 7. *Raii cur.* 53. In

Sicily, and the kingdom of Naples. Viticis ramulus cum flore. *Dod.* 762, *repr. in* Eleagnon Theophrasti. *Lob. ic.* ii. 138, $ V. sive Agnus castus. *Ger. by Johns.* 1387, $ *cop. from* V. Matthioli. *Dalech.* 281. Vitex. *Lod.* 762. *Cam. cpit.* 105, *cop. in* Agnus folio non scrrato. *Bauh. J.* i. *b.* 805, $ V. sive Agnus castus folio angusto. *Park, theatr.* 1437. EAaixyvov Theophrasti. *Lob. adv.* 423. No fig. *AGNUS* castus. *Bag.* 550. *Chom.* 177. Do/ 297. *Linn.* 188. *Mitt, Jos.* 19. *Mnrr.* ii. 195. *Schoepf* 101. *Schrod.* 538. *Spielm.* 373. *Fog.* 173. Agnus. *Alst.* ii. 321. *Geoffr.* iii. 44. *Zero.* i. 41.

2. VITEX *trifolia.* Leaves ternatc and quinate; foli oles ovate, acute, slightly hoary underneath; margin entire. Rachis of the panicle straight Pedicles dichotomous. *L. JU. suppl.* 293. //. *K.* ii. 365. *Lour.* ii. 472.

V. trifolia, ftoribus per ramus sparsis. *Burnt. J. zeyl.* 229. *f.* 109.

Frutex indicus baccifer, fructu calyculato monopyreno, Negundo dicta. *Raii hist.* 1575.

(V. trifolia minor indica. *Pluk. phyt. t.* 206. /. 5, has alternate leaves, as Mr. Knowlton observed. No fructifications. *LAGONDIUM* vulgare. *Itumph.* iv. 48. *t.*

18.
Caranosi. *Rhecde* ii. 13. *t.* 10.
Threeleaved Vitex. *Jones in as. res.* iv. 301.
3. VITEX *Negundo*. Leaves quinate and ternate; folioles sometimes serrate. Flowers paniculato racemose. *From L. sp.* 890, and Rumph.— *Hort. kew.* ii. 365. *Curt. mag. t.* 364, is V. incisa.) V. orientalis, angustis foliis semper tripartito divisis. *Pluk. aim.* 590; *phyt. t. 321. f.* 2. Negundo foemina Acostae. *Dalech.* 1867, *cop. in* Negundo arbor mas. *Bauh. J.* ii. 189. /. 2. (*f,* 1, *cop. from* Negundo mas. *Dalech.* 1866, *which cop. in Pari, theatr.* 1650, has flowers in interrupted spikes.) LAGONDIUM litoreum. *Rumph.* iv. 50. /. 19. Bera-npsi. *Rheede* ii. 15. *t.* 11. *Rati hist,* 1575, 4. VITEX *spicata*. Leaves quinate and ternate; folioles crenate. Spikes linear, terminal. *From Lour.* ii. 475. 657. AVICENNIA. *Calyx* quinquepartite. *Corolla* bilabiate; upper lip square. *Capsule* coriaceous, rhomboidal, monospermous. *L.* 1. AVICENNIA *tomentosa*. Leaves oblong, tomen tose underneath. *From L. a Murr.* 579; *gen.* 579, *Jacq. amer.* 178. /. 112. /. 2, a leaf; 8ro. 227, # *Smarts, obs.* 248. Bontia gcrminans. *L. sp.* 891. Bontia. *Browne* 263. Mangle laurocerasi foliis, flore albo tetrapetalo. *Sloane cat.* 156. OEPATA. *Rheede* iv. 95. *t.* 45. *Rati hist.* 1566.
2. AVICENNIA *resinifera,* Leaves elliplico-lanceo late, tomentose underneath. *Font. G. austr. n.* 246;—*esc.* 72. 658. COLUMNEA. *Calyx* quinquepartite. *Corolla* ringent, gibbous above the base; upper lip vaulted. *Antfierae* connected. *Capsule* bilocular. *From L. and Lour.* k COLUMNEA *stellata*. Leaves stellate. Flowers solitary. Stem creeping. *Lour.* ii. 467. 659. ACANTHUS. *Calyx* tetraphyllous. *Corolla* unilabiafe; lip trifiil, bent dovfl. *Capsule* bilocular. *Obs.* 8263. *L.* 1. ACANTHUS *mollis*. Leaves pinnate below, pinnatifid above. Spines very short. *Obs.* 826S. Specimen gathered in Lady Clifford's garden.—*L. sp.* 891. *Hort. kew.* ii. 366. *Gou. hort.* 309. Near Montpelier.—*Host* 350. In Littoral!.
Acanthus. *L. tips.* 181.
A. sativus, vel mollis Virgilii. *Boerh.* i. 238.

A. vera. *Fuchs.* 52. *c.* 15, *cop. in* Carduus A. sive Branca ursina. *Bauh. J.* iii. *a.* 75.
A. sativus. *Dalech.* 1443. JRaii hist: *1326; eur.* 49. In Sicily, and about Naples and Baia.—*Dod.* 707, *repr. in Lob. obs.* 477i *ic.* ii. 2, & *Ger. by Johns.* 1147, *cop. in Park, theatr.* 992, # *abr. in par. t.* 331. /. I.
ACANTHUS mollis. *Quar. febr.* 232. *Spielm.* 450.
Acanthus. *Dale* 197. *Geoffr.* iii. 20. *Lett.* i. 15.
A. Branca ursina. *Mill. Jos.* 9.
Branca ursi. *Linn.* 188.
Branca ursina. *Murr.* ii. 204. *Rutty* 70. *Vog.* 94 *a*
Branca ursi italica. *Carth.* iv-207.
Branca ursi vera. *Pharm. attstriacoprov.* 24.
Acanthe. *Chom.* 719.
2. ACANTHUS *spinosus*. Leaves pinnate below, piniKif itid above. Spines as long as the breadth of the segments of the leaves. *Obs.* 8264. Specimen gathered in the Edinburgh garden.—*L. sp.* 891. *Hort. Icew.* ii. 367. A. aculeatus. *Boerh.* i. 339. *Rait hist.* 1326. A. sylvestris. *Dod.* 707, *repr. in Lob. obs.* 477, *cop. in Park, theatr.* 992, *abr. in par. t.* 331. /. 2, *repr. in* Chamaeleonta monspelliensium. *Lob. ic.* ii. 2, *Sf* A. sylvestris aculeatus. *Ger. by Johns.* 1147, *and cop. in* Branca ursina aculeata. *Dalech.* 1445, *Sf* Carduus A. sive Branca ursina spinosa. *Bauh. J.* iii. *a.* 77.
ACANTHUS spinosus. *Spielm.* 450.
A. sylvestris. *Dale* 197.
Branca ursi. *Berg.* 551.
3. ACANTHUS *ebracteatus*. Leaves lanceolato-elliptic, dentate. Spike terminal. Stem fruticose, unarmed.
Calyx tetraphyllous. *Vahl. symb.* ii. 75. *t.* 40. ACANTHUS ilicifolius. *Lour.* ii. 455. Aquifolium indicum. *Rumph.* vi. 163. *t.* 71. *f.* 1. 4. ACANTHUS *edulis*. Leaves in fours, lineari-lanceo late, dentate, spinose. Stem fruticose. *Vahl. symb.* i. 48.
Ruellia ciliaris. *L. mant.* 89.
Ruellia persica. *Burtn. N. ind.* 135. *t.* 42. *f.* 1.
ACANTHUS edulis. *Forsk.* 114.
661. CttAMBE.
662. Isatis. 668. Coronopus. 663. Draba. 669. Lunaria., 665. Mtagrcm. 1. *Fruit entire. Capsule* not opening, unilocular. *Obs.* 2568. *Siliqua* not opening, unilocular, bivalve, monospermous, apatulate. *Obs.* 8206. *Capsule* not opening, bilocular; cells monospermous. *Ob:.* 7905. *Silicula* oval oblong and ovate; valves parallel to the dissepiment. *Obs.* 4717. *Silicula* pedicellate, flat; Valves parallel to the dissepiment. *Obs.* 5688. *Silicula* obovate; valves parallel to the dissepiment, carinte. *Qbs.* 7907. 667. COCHLEARiA. *Silicula* oval; valves globose; cells polyspermous. *Obs.* 4226. 2. *Silicula* mostly emarginate at the end. Order 2. SILIQUOSAE.
1. *Phylla longitudinally connhent.* From L. 680. Cakile. *Siliqua* not opening, tetrago nous; internodia dropping off. *Obs.* 5146. *Siliqua* not opening, terete, attenuate. *Obs.* 5178. *Siliq ua* angular. *Petals* erect. *Obs.* 2837.
Siliqua tetragonous. *L.*
674. Cheibanthus. *Siliqua* with a tooth on eacв side. 675. Hespebis. *Nectaria* 2, at the base of Ö 679. Raphanus. 676. Tunnms. 673. Erysimum. 2 shorter stamina. *Obs.* 908. 677. Brassica. *Nectario* 4, 2 between the shorter stamina and the pis« til, 2 between the longer stamina and the calyx, *Obs.* 2841. 670. Dentaria. *Siliqua* bursting elastically; valves revolute. *L.* 2. *Ends of the phylla distant.* From L. 681. Oleome. *Siliqua* unilocular. 671. Card Amine. *Siliqua* bursting elastically; valves revolute. *L.* 672. Sisymbrium. *Siliqua,* valvesstraightish. Ca« *lyx* patulous.
C78. Sinapis. *Nectario* 4,2 between the shorter stamina and the pistil; 2 between the longer stamina, and the calyx. *Calyx* patent. *Obs.* 3835. SILICULOSAE, 661. CRAMBE.
filaments, the 4 longer furcate at the end, one of the brandies supporting an anthera. *Capsule* not opening, unilocular, globular. *Obs.* 2568. *L.* 1.. CRAMBE *maritime.* Leaves glabrous, sinuate. *Obs.* 2568. In a garden.—*L. sp.* 937. *Bot. arr.* 718. ITuds. 299. S/«M Arft. 695; *engl. t.* 924. *Ft. dan. t.* 316. Gaertn. ii. 293. C. maritiraa, brassicae folio. JDt/i. ap. i?fl» yn. 307. doerh. ii. 1. Brassica marina anglica. *Ger. by Johns.* sI5. Brassica marina sylvestris multiflora

monosperraos. *Lob. adv.* 92, *repr. in ic.* i. 245, *and cop. in* Brnssica mon'ospermos anglica. *Bauh. J.* ii. 830, 4" Brassica marina moriospermos. *Park, thedtr.* 9.10, with a portion of a racerrius in fruit added.—*Rati ' syn. ed.* ii. 176. Brassica maritiraa. *liaii hist.* 838. CRAMBE maritiraa. *Bry.* 124. Brassica sylvestris. *Dale* 208. 662. ISATIS. *Siliqua* spatulate, unilocular, monospermous, bivalve, not opening; valves carinate. *Obs.* 8206. L. 1. ISATIS *linctoria*. Radical leaves crenate, cauline leaves sagittate. Racemi and siliculae glabrous. *Obs.* 8206. Specimen gathered by my servant in fields, cultivated, 2 miles west of Boston in Lincolnshire.— *L. sp.* 936. *Host* 353. *Mart. rust. t.* 41. *a angustifolia*. Siliculae much smaller than those of 0. *From .*

I. sylvestris, sive angustifolia. *Vaill. parts.* 109. *Tourn. par is.* 342. *Boerh.* ii. 3.

I. linctoria. Po//. «. 645. *Roth germ.* i. 274. X. *suec. n.* 614. On the sea shore.

I. dalmatiea. *Mill. Ph. diet. n.* 2?
Glastum sylvestrc. *Raii eur.* 134. Along the Rhine. —*Ger. by Johns.* 491, 8f

I. agria. Zo». *ic.* i. 352, repr. /ro/«

I. sylvestris. *Lob. obs.* 190, which *repr. in Dod.* 79. *Tab.ic.*737. *Cam. epit.* 4JO. *Dalech.*499. *Fuchs,* 326. c. 126, cop. fa

I. sive Glastum spontanea. *Bauh. J.* ii. 909. /. 2, who found it in Switzerland Wirtemberg and Alsace.

Native of Switzerland, France, Germany, and the sea shores of Sweden.

ISATIS sylvestris, vel angustifolia. *Chom.* 765. *& latifolia.* Siliculae 5 tenths of an inch long, If broad. *Obs.* 8206. *L. sp.* 0 I. tinctoria. *Muds.* 299, who marks it as a naturalised plant, found rarely in corn fields and on the borders of ploughed fields.—*Bot. arr.* 717. *Reth, n.* 496. New Barns near Ely.—*Mill. Ph. diet. n.* 1. *Smith engl. t.* 97, in flower, from a cultivated . plant; *hrit.* 693.

I. sativa, sive latifolia. *Boerh.* ii. 3.

I. domestica. *Cam. epit.* 409.

Glastum sativum. *Raii hist.* 842; *syn.*

307. Cultivated in. the midland counties; *cant.* 62. Planted about Liltleport in the isle of Ely.—*Lob. obs.* 189, *repr. in ic.* i. 351, *Sf Ger. by Johns.* 491, *cop. in Park, theatr.* 600, *and repr. in I.* sfttlva. *Dpd.* 79. *Dalech.* 499. *Fucfis.* 326. c, 126, cop. in

I. sive Glastum sativa. *Bauh. J.* ii. 909, *St abr. in* JSATIS. *Trag.* 256.—*Berg.* 583. *Dale* 208.

Vog. 105.

Glastum. *Mitt. Jos.* 215. *Rutty* 219. Woad. *Lew. in Neum.* iii 240.

663. DRABA. *Silicula* oval oblong and ovate; dissepiment parallel to the valves. *Style* short. *Obs.* 4717. L. 1. DRABA *verna*. Flowers on scapi. Petals bifid. *Obs.* 4717. On walls.—*Bot. arr.* 668. *L. sp.* 896. *Curt. lond.* i. 49, *t. Wale. t. Smith bril.* 677; *engl. t.* 586. *Fl. dan. t.* 983. PARONYCHIA. *Dale* 460. « *integrifolia*. (Variation.) Leaves entire at the margin. *Obs.* 269. Specimen gathered near Worcester.

Alvsson vulgare, polygoni folio, caule nudo. *Tourn. parts.* 53. *Vaill. parts.* 11. *Boerh.* ii. 4. In Holland.

Paronychia vulgaris. *Raii syn. 'SS. Dod.* 112, *repr. in Ger. by Johns.* 624, and

Paronychia alsincfolia. *Lob. ic. i.* 469, *and cop. in Dalech.* 1214.

Pilosella siliquata minima. *Thai.* 84. *t. 7. E. 8 serratifolia.* (Variation.) Leaves sparingly dentatoserrate. *Obs.* 4717.

Alysson vulgare, foliis incisis. *Vaill. parts.* 11.

Alysson vulgare, polygoni folio, caule nudo. *Seg. £.* 375, *t* 4./. 3.

Paronychia vulgaris, foliis dentatis. *Dill, ap. Ran syn.* 292. Bursa pastoria minima, oblongis siliquis, verna,loculo oblongo. *Bauh. J.* ii. 937. Myosotis parva. *Dalech.* 1318.

Glands 4, 1 between the shorter and each adjoining long stamen. *Obs.* 4717. 664. LEPIDIUM. *Silicula,* compressed, emarginate and entire; valw carinate; cells monospermous and dispermoui. *Obs.* 4647. 1370. 7077.4644. *L.* 1. Siliculae entire.

I. LEPIDIUM *latifolium*. Leaves ovatolanceolate and lanceolate, serrate. *Obs.* 4646. In a garden.

—*L. sp.* 899. *Fl. dan. t.* 557. *Bot. arr.* 671.

Smith evgl. t. 182. *brit.* 682. *Jtuds.* 279. *Gou. hoTt.* 315. Near Montpelier.— *Roth germ.* i. 278.

In Holstein and near Tubingen.—*Tourn. parts.* 343.

VaiU. paris. 115. *Raii hist.* 828, on the sides of rivers; *syn.* 304. L. sativum. *L. suec. n.* 571. Found by Leche about thewalls of Landskron and Hederstrom, and on rubbish near the castle of Westervic. L. foliis ovato-lanceolatis integris serratis. *Guett.* ii. 144.

Lepidium. *FucTis.* 471. c. 185, *abr. in Trag.* 88, *which repr. in h.* majus. *Cordfol.* 124. p. 2, # *cop. in* L. Pauli. *Bauh. J.iimO.f.* 1.—/. 2. Onthcside pf the river at Montpelier.

L. Plinii. *Dod.* 704, *repr. in*

Raphanus sylvestris officinarum. *Ger. by Johns.* 241, *Sf cop. in* Piperitis, sive L. vulgare, *Park, theatr.* 855.

Siliculae oval, entire. *Obs.* 4646. Native of France, Germany, Denmark, Essex, Norfolk, and ossibly Sweden, on the sides of riv rs. LEPIDIUMlatifolium. *Chom.*5A3; *su,,pl.* 159. *Lah* ii. 53. Lepidium. *Date* ..06. *Lew. disp.* 165. *Mill. Jos.* 2G5. *Rutty* 282. *Spielm.* 58. L. vulgare. *GeoJV.* iii. 709. 2. LEPIDIUM *triandrum*. Leaves pinnate; segments linear, acute, serrate; serratures rare. Cells of the siliculae monospermous. Stamina mostly 3. *Obs.* 4648. *In* a garden from seeds gathered by

Dr. Cutler in New England, and specimen from

Dr. Cutler. Lepidium. *Browne* 216. Thlaspi. *Cutl.* 466. Thlaspi virginianum, foliis ibcridis araplioribus ct serratis. *Boerh.* ii. 8. Iberis humilior annua virginiana ramosior. *Shane cat.* fcO; *hist.* i. 195. /. 123./. 3. *Rati hist.* 827. Iberis ramosior virginiana annua. *Hist. ox. s. 3. t.* 21. *row I. f.* 2. LEPIDIUM virginicum. *Swarlz. ohs.* 251. *L. sp.* 900. *Hort. km.* ii. 375.—*Bry.* 104. Nasturtium sylvestre. *Schocpf* 102.

2. Siliculae emarginate. 3. LEPIDIUM *Iberis*. SWiWaai. Petals!. Lower leaves lanceolate, serrate; nppor linear, entire at the margin. *L. sp.* 900; *mant.* 425. *Jlort. keto.* ii. 375. L. gramíneo folio, sive Iberis. *Boerh.* ii. 9. *Vaill. paria.*

115. Iberis. *Bauh. J.* ii. 918. *Dod.* 703, rcpr. m Iberis cardarhantica. *Ger. by Johns.* 253, Sjr *cop. in* Iberis cardamantice latiore folio. *Park, thealr.* 851. Style permanent, as short again as the emarginature of the silicula. *Silicula* emarginate, orbicularioval; dissepiment lanceolate, straight, contrary to the plane of the silicula; cells monospermous. *Obs.* 7077. Specimen from Dr. Heise. *JBERJS. Dale* 206. *Lew.* ii. 53. *Linn.* 189. *Mill. Jos.* 243. *Rati hist.* 827. *par. the 2 last.* —*Rutty* 247.

L. hortense. *Geogr.* iii. 711.

L. gramineo folio, sive Iberis. *Chom.* 544.

4. LEPIDIUM *Piscidium*. Leaves cllipticoblong, acute, entire at the margin. Stamina tctradynamotts. *Forst. G. austral, n.* 249;—«c. 70. 5. LEPIDIUM *sativum.* Stamina 6. Leaves pinnato« pihnatifid. *Obs.* 4647. In a garden.—*L. sp.* 899, where erase Fl. suee. 2. n. 571.— *Hort. hew.* ii.

S73. Nasturtium hortense vulgatnm. *Boerh.* i. 8. Nasturtium hortense. *Dod.* 699, *repr. in ed.* ii. 711, ..Y *Ger. by Johns.* 250. *Rati hist.* 825. *Fuchs.* 356. c. 137, *cop. in Tras;*. 82, y Nnsturtium vulgare. *Bauh. J.* ii. 912. Nasturtium sativum. *JPark. par. t.* 501. /. 4.

Siliculáe emarginate. Ois. 4647. *JLEPIDIUM s&tirum. Bry.* 103. J5Troci. it. If 19, (the officinal name erroneously inserted under n. 1018.) *Pears. R.* i. 51. Nasturtium hortense. *Berg.* 552. *Carth.* ii. 266. 296. *Chom.* 434; *suppl.* 156. *Dale* 206. *Lew.* ii. 128. X,«Vm. 189. Afttf. *Jos.* 310. JHfarr. ii. 352. *Rutty* 313. *Schoepf* 109. *Spielm.* 59.

Nasturtium. &f. ii. 187. *Herm.* 305. 520. Cardamum, sive Nasturtium hortense. *Geoffr. suite* i. 136.

Nasturtium hortense Iatifolium. *Schrod.* 633.

Cresses. *Darte.* ii. 40.

0 *crispum.* Leaves pinnatifid; segments cuneiform,
curled at the margin. *Obs.* 3829. In a garden.— *Hort. kew.* ii. 373 8. *L. sp.* 0 Nasturtium crispum. *Bauh. J.* ii. 913. Nasturtium hortense crispum Iatifolium et augustifo-
Hum. *Park, theatr.* 825.

Nasturtium hortense crispum angustifoUum. *Bauh.*
Casp. prodr. 44. *t.* 43.
NASTURTIUM crispum. *Berg.* 553.
Nasturtium hortense crispum vulgatura. *Schrod.* 633.

6. LEPIDIUM *ruderale.* Stamina mostly 2. Petals mostly wanting. Lower leaves pinnate, with dentate segments; the upper linear, entire at the margin; terminating segments rounded at the end. Cells of the siliculae monospermous. *Obs.* 1370.

At the edge of a wharf above the end of Pitchcroft near Worcester, where the salt made at Droitwich used to be discharged into barges in the Severn previous to the making of the Droitwich canal. *L. suec. n.* 572; *sp.* 900. *Bot. an.* 672. *Fl. dan. t.* 184. *Relh. n.* 471. On the bank of the rivet at Wisbeach.—*Smith engl. t.* 1595; *brit.* 682, who supposes Withering to have found petals and 4 stamina, but I apprehend the observation at p. 557.1.6 in Bot. arr. ed. iv. is only a condensation of the remarks which I inserted from Haller, &c. at the end of the specific character.—*Huds.* 280. At Yarmouth and at Clay in Norfolk.—*Ligktf.* 340. In waste places near wharfs on the sea coast. *p0U, n.* 606. On the sides of roads in several places, and plentifully about the salt springs of Creuzenach.—*Kroch.* ii. *n.* 1020. *t.* 29. 30.

Thlaspidii genus. *Trag.* 83.

Thlaspi angustifolium. *Fuchs.* 303, *cop. in Bauh. J.* ii. 914, *St Dalech.* 662, which repr. *in* 1181.

Thlaspi minimum. *Dod.* 701, *repr. in*

Thlaspi minus hortense vulgare, osyridis folio, acerrimum luteum et album. *Lob. ic.* i. 214, *and*

Thlaspi minus. *Ger. by Johns.* 262, *Sf cop. in*

Nasturtium sylvestre, osyridis folio. *Park, theatr.* 829. *Raii syn.* 303. Near the sea in many places, as at Maldon in Essex, Lynn in Norfolk, and Truro in Cornwall.

Nasturtium sylvestre. *Raii hist.* 825. Petals none. Siliculae oval, emarginate. Stamina 2. *Obs.* 1370. THLASPI angustifolium. *Bauh. J. ib.* 7. LEPIDIUM chinense. Leaves pinnate; folioles entire at the margin. Petals emarginate, smaller than the calyx. From LEPIDIUM p«traeum. *Lour.* ii. 479. 3. *Silkula anarginate or entire uncertain.* 8. LEPIDHJM *oteraceum,* Leaves ellipico-oblong, acute, serrate. Stamina 4. *Hort. has.* ii. 374. *Forst. G. austral, n.* 248;— *esc. n.* 38. 665. MYAGRUM. *Stiicula* obovate and roundish; valves concave, parallel to the dissepiment, carinate at the margiu. *Style* permanent. *Obs.* 7907. £, 1. MYAGRUM *sativum.* Siliculae obovaie; cells polyspermous. Leaves amplexicaul. *Qbs.* 7P07. Specimen from J'rof. Jos. F. Jacquin.—*L. syec. n.* 564, who considers it as imported along with flax seed; *sp.* 894. *Huds.* 277, who found it near Bridport and Lime in Dorsetshire, and who considers it sis imported.—*Bot. arr.* 665. *Reth. n.* 1071, in Chippenham gravel pits.—*Poll. n.* 602. *Fl. dan. t. 1038.* Amongst flax.— *Gqu. hort.* .311. Near Montpelier.— *Mill. Ph. diet.* «. *1.* Amongst corn in Easthamsted park.—*Magn. monsp.* 180. *Jfcrock. n.* 1008. *Matth. a C. B.* 815, *repr. from*
M.I. *Tab. ic.* 865.

Alyssum sativum. *Scop. n.* 794. *Smith brit. 6J9; engl.t.1254.*

Camelina sativa. *Crantz. austr.* 18.

Moenchia sativa. *Roth germ.* i. 274; ii. *pars* ii. 75. ∴

Alyssum foliis sagittatis, siliquis cordiformibus. *Hall. hist. n.* 489. 4 Alyssori segetum, foliis auriculatis acutis. *Tourn. parts.* 315. 385. *Bocrh.* i. 4. *Rupp. ab Hall.* 85.

Dill. giss. 107. Alysson, M. sylvestre. *Vaill. parts.* 11. MYAGRUM. *Dak* 205. *Gecffr. suite* i. 05. *a integrifolium.* Margin of the leaves entire and obso letely dentate. *Obs.* 7907. *L. a Sesama. Trag.* 655. Pseudomyagrum *Matth.* 1172, *cop. in Matth. a C. B.* 815. *Dalech.* 1137. M. dictum Camelina. *Batth. J.* ii. 894, *cop. in* M. sativum. *Hist. ox. s. 3. t.* 21. *row* 2./. 1. Pseudomyagrum aiter ura. *Cam. epit.* 902. /. 1, *cop. in* M. turcicum. *Bank. J.* ii. 893. *Leaves* hirsute and hirsutulous. *Seeds* oval, glabrous, rufous, somewhat more than f tenth of an inch long. *Obs.* 7907. *0 dentatum.* Leaves dentate, *Obs.* 7908. Specimen from Leske, 10 inches long, the upper part of a stem. Pseudomyagrum. *Cam. epit.* 901. Camelinn, sive Myagrion. *Dod.* 523, *repr.in* Cameline Myagrum. *Lob. ic.* i. 224, *cop. in* M. sylvestre, scu Pseudomyagrum. *Pari;, theatr.* 868,. Myagrum. *Dalech.* 1136, *8f repr. in Lob. obs.* Ill, *and Ger. by Johns.* 273. In fruit.—*Rail hist.* 820; *syn.* 302. Amongst flax. Gold of pleasure. *Pet. herb. L* 48./. II. *Leaves* hirsutulous, teeth to *2* tenths of an inch long. *Obs.* 7908. —*Sil/quae* obovato-obcordate. *Seeds i* of the tenth of an inch long. *Obi.* 7909. Specimen from Dr. Boehmer. 666. THLA5PI. *Silicula* obcordate; valves mostly bordered; cells poly spermous dispermousand monospermous. *Obs.* 2773. *L.* 1. THLASPI *campestre.* Siliculae ovato-obcordate, glabrous; cells monospermous and dispermous. Caaline leaves sagittate, pubescent. *Obs.* 7080.

On shale out of ironstone pits.—*L. sp.* 902. *Bot. arr.* 674-. *Curt. fond. v.* 45. *t. 303. Smith brit.* 684; *engl. t.* 1385. *Krock. n.* 1026. Thlaspidii genus aliad. *Trag.* 85. descr. Thlaspi. *Trag.* 87, *cop. from* T. latifolium. *Fucks.* 303. *c.* 116, which *cop. in* T. vulgatius. *Bauh. J.* ii. 921. /. 1. *Rati syn.* 305. *Tourn. paris. 233. Vaill. par is.* 191. T. vulgatissimum. *Ger. by Johns.* 262, *cop. in.* T. vaccariae folio. *Park, theatr.* 836.

Root fusiform. *Stems* leafy, pubescent, corymbose at the end; sometimes single, erect, branching from the base, sometimes as many as 10, ascending and oblique. *Leaves,* radical ones oblong, sometimes pinnatifid at the base; cauline leaves sagittate, attenuate; margin dentate, entire above. *Calyx* glabrous, brownish white; phylla ovato-oval. *Petals* erect, white, one fourth longer than the calyx; laminae obovate, veined; ungues linear, very narrow, nearly twice as long as the laminae. *Siliculae* ripe, 2§ tenths of an inch long, microscopically tuberculate at the sides; margin glabrous, bordered above; border one sixth as long as the silicula; dissepiment falciform, ascending, at right angle? with the plane of the silicula. *Style* scarcely projecting beyond the silicula. *Seeds* ovate, blackish rufous, microscopically tuberculate, inserted by pedicles into the upper end of the dissepiment. *Obs.* 7080. In flower.—*Obs.* 7082. Specimen in fruit. *THLASPI* vulgatius. *Alst.* ii. 377.;Thlaspi. *Dale* 207. «. 2. *Geoffr. suite* iii. 175. *Herm.* 304. T. vulgatissimum. *Mill. Jos.* 436. T. arvense, vaccariae incano folio, majus. *Lew.* ii.. 429. *Rutty* 515. T. vaccariae incano folio, mnjus. *Chom.* 148. 326. 2. THLASPI *alliaceum.* Siliculae subovate, ventri cose. Leaves oblong, obtuse, dentate, glabrous. *Jacq. misc.* ii. 330; *ic.* i. *t.* 12J. *L. sp.* 90I, *from* .....,"" i- n T. siliculis 6ubovatis ventricosis, foliis oblongis ob tusis dentat is glabris. *Itoi/. 33i.* . Scorodothlaspi Ulyssis Aldrovandi, *Bauh. J.* ii. 932, from seeds sent by Aldrovandus from Italy; *impr.ty* , T. allium redolcns. *Hist. ox. s.* 3. *t.* 18. row 3. *f.* 28. SCORODOTHLASPI. *Geoffr. suite* iii. 178.

3. THLASPI *arvense.* Siliculae orbiculari-obcordate; cells polyspermous. Leaves oblong, glabrous. *Obs.* 216. On afield of turncps near Worcester.—*L' sp.* 901. *.Curt. land.* vi. . *Bot. arr.* 673. *Smith englt.* 1659; *brit.* 683. *Fl. dan. t.* 793. *Krock. n.* 1025.

T. arvense, siliquis latis, *Tourn. paris.* 233. *Vaffl, paris.* 191.

VoL. 3. E e

T. Dioscoridis. *Raii st/n.* 305. *Ger. by John. 26t, repr.from*

T. latins. *Dod.* 700, *8f cdp. in*

T. drabae folk). *Park, thtatr.* 836.

T. cmn siliquis la(is. *Bauh. J.* ii. *923.* Thlaspidium rolgarc. *Trag.* 85. No fig.

Leaves, radical ones entire and obsoletely dentate; cauline leaves oblong, sagittate at the base, obsoletely dentate, uppermost and tbose of the branches lanceolato-oblong, dentate. *Siliculae* flat, at first ovali-obcordate, when fully grown orbiculari-obcordate. *Style* very short. *Obs.* 216. *Native* of Staffordshire, Worcestershire, Oxfordshire, Berkshire, Cambridgeshire, Norfolk, Suffolk, and Essex, and mentioned in Lightf. *to* have been observed by Dr. Burgess in Tweedale. *THLASPI* latius. *Geoffr. suite* iii. 177. T. verum. *Alst.* ii. 376. Thlaspi. Pharfn. austriaco-prov. 71.—-Berg. 554.

Dale 207. *n.. Linn.* 190. *Mill. Jos.* 436. *Monro* iii. 581, *Murr.* ii. 354. *Schrod.* 691. *Fog.* 182. J. arvense siliquis latis. *Chom.* 326. 148. *Les.* ii. 429. *Rutty* 515. 4. THLASPI *cuueatutn.* SrJliculae not bordered, obcuneiform; cells polyspermous. *Obs.* 2773.

Nasturtium Bursa pastoris. *Roth germ.* i. 28l; ii. 96.

T. Bursa pastoris, *I. sp. 003. Pi. dan. t.* 729. *Bot. an:* 616. *Curt. land.* i. 50. f. *Wah. U Lightf.* 342. *Smith engl, t.* 1485. *Krock. n. 1032. Lour.* ii. 480.

Bursa pastoris major, folio sinuate *Tourn. parts. 11. Vaill. parts.* 24. *Boerh.* ii. 9. In Holland.

Pastoria bursa. *Rod.* 103, *rcpr. in*

Bursa pastoris. *Gtr. hy Johns.* 276. *Fucks.* 583. *c.* 233, *cop. in* Bursa pastoria. *Bank. J.* ii. 936. *Raii sy«.* 306. Bursa pastoris major vulgaris. *Park, theatr.* 866.

Nectdrta 2, bilobate, surrounding the base of the shorter stamina, extending each way till they almost meet. *Obs.* 2773. *BURSA PASTORlS..* *Alst.* ii. 93. *Berg.* 555. *Dale* 207. *Gcoff.* iii. 233. //era. 557. *Lew.* i. 243; dwp. 110. *Linn.* 190. Jiff//. *Jos.* 99. *Murr.* ii. 355. *Ploncq.bibl.* i-579. *Schoepf* 103. *Scl-rod.* 550. *Fog.* 56. Boursette. *Chom.* 466; *suppl.* 142. 667. COCHLEARIA. *Silicula* oval; valves gibbosc; cells polyspermous. 06. 4226. 6621. *Smith brit.* 687. *L. 1.* CQCHLEARIA *renifolia.* Radical leaves reniform; cauline leaves oblong, angular. *Obs.* 8006. On a wall in Riber near Matlock in Derbyshire.—On limestone rocks at the mouth of the cavern at Castlcton, and between Castlcton and Pinder mine. June. C. officinalis. *L.* sure. *n.* 577; *a Murr*; 588; *sp.* 903. *Bot. arr.* 677. *Fl. dan. t.* 135. On the shores of Norway and Denmark.—*Huds.* 283. In Cornwall.—*Light/.* 342. On rocks on the sea coast and on the Highland mountains.— *Wood's,* i. 86. *t.* 29. No radical leaves.— *Smith brit.* 688 j *engl. t.* 551. *Krock. n.* 1033.

C. folio subrotundo. *Boerk.* ii. 10. Id Holland.

Cochlearia. *L. lapp. n.* 256. On the shores of the

North Sea near the base of the Alps of Lapland.—

Bauh. J. ii. 942. *Rati hist.* 822; *syn.* 302. On the sea shore, especially in Cumberland and Lancashire, and near rills running down the sides of hills as at Castleton in Derbyshire, and on Penigent Jngleborough and Stanemore in Yorkshire.—
Cam. epit. 271. *Dod.* 583,*repr.in*
C. batava. *Lob. obs. 156; ic.* i. 293, #
C. rotundifolia. *Ger. by Johns.* 401, *and cop. in*
C. major rotundifolia, sive batavorum. *Park, theatr.* 285.
Stamina ascending, nearly equal. *Glands* 4, minute, green, 1 between the 2 shorter and longer stamina. *Obs.* 8606. COCHLEARIA. *Bang in act. haun.* i. 11. *Berg.*
556. *LinA.* 190. *Mead mon.* ii. 121. Mertens in
ph. tr. abr. by Hutl. xiv. 404. *Sckrod.* 569.
Schorpf 102. *Spielm.* 532. *Stoll med.* iii. 82. *Vog.* 60.
C. officinalis. Herb. *Pharm. edin.—Bry.* 96. *Ltic.*
disp. by Duuc. 201. *Pears. R.* ii. 175.
C. hortensis. *Pharm. lond.—Alst.* ii. 114. *Blanc*
501. *Carth.* ii. 263.296. *Cull.* ii. 164. *Geoffr.* iii.
343. *Herm.* 5)8. *Hill* 384. *Lew.* i. 351. *Murr.*
ii. 341. *Pugh in med. obs.* ii. 243. *Rutty* 133.
Rogai in act. haun. i. 189. *Syd.* 278.
C. batava. *Dale* 2Q6. *Mill. Jos.* 142.
C. folio subrotundo. *Chom.* 532.
Scurvygrass. *Baylies in med. pap.* 47. Monro-Don.
soid. ii. 185.
o 2. COCHLEARIA *otaHfoliq.* Radical leaves oval, entire at the margin obsoletely dentate. *Ohs.* 4228.
Specimen gathered on the sea shore near King's
Weston in the neighbourhood of Bristol. C. anglica. *Huds.* 284. *L. sp.* 903. *Mill. Ph. diet. n.* 2. *Bot. arr.* 679. *Ft. dan. t.* 329. *Smith brit.* 688; *engl. t.* 552. C. folio sinuato. *Rati hist.* 823, (mispr. 833) leaves sometimes entire at the margin sometimes slightly sinuate;

syn. 303-*Boer/i.* ii. 10. C Dodonaei. *Dalech.* 1320. C. britannica. *Lob. ohs.* 157, *repr. in Dod.* 583, *and Ger. by Johns.* 401, *cop. in Dalech.* 1320, *repr. in* C. britannica, sive anglica. *Lob. ic.* i. 294, *and cop. in* C. vulgaris. *Park, theatr.* 285, has inclso-scrrafe leaves. C. anglica, atriplicis folio. *Lob. adv.* 123. No COCHLEARIA britannica. *Dale* 206. *Mitl. Jos.* 143. C. marina; *Lew.* i. 351; *disp. by Rather.* 145.
3. COCHLEARIA land folia. Radical leaves oblongolanceolate, crenate. *Obs.* 4229. In a garden,
C. Armofacia. *L. suec. n.* 580, in fields and near fishponds near Lund; *sp.* 904. *Huds.* 234. *Lightf.* 1136, on the authority of Sibbald.—*Bot. arr.* 681. *Smith brit.* 690. *Gou. hort.* 318. In water below the citadel.—*Host* 360. Near villages.— *Woodv.* iii. 406; *t.* 150. *Reich, franc. n.* 441. On the sides of ditehes.
C. folio cubitali. *Magn. hort.* 60. *Kroch. n.* 1034. *Boerh.* ii. 10. In Holland.
RaphanuE sylvestris. *Fuchs.* 660. *fol. td. cop. in* 629. c. 236, ft Raphanns sylvestris, sive Armoracia multis. *Bauh. J.* ii. 851, near Lure on the borders of fields, aud *imit.* with an addition *in* Raphanus major, seu Armoracia radix. *Trog* 734. Raphanis magna. *Dod.* 667, *repr. in* Raphanus rusticanus. *Lob. obs.* 173, *and Ger. by Johns.* 241, *cop. in Park, theatr.* 860, the whole plant, *and repr. in Lob. ic.* i. 320, outer fig.—the 3 inner figures *abr. in Park, theatr.* 860, 2 inner figures.—*Raii hist.* 818; *syn.* 301, in ditehes and by the side of water about Alnwick and elsewhere in Northumberland, and found by Lister on the banks of Skipton beck and elsewhere in Bolland ia
Craveu Yorkshire.
Native of Europe, but in the greater number of instances the outeast of gardens. ARMORACIA. *Berg.* 558. *Herm.* 62. *Linn.* 191. *Schoepf* 103. *Spielm.* 42. *Vog.* 187. C. Armoracia. *Pharm. edin.—Bry.* 28. *Lew. disp. by Dune.* 202. *Murr. J.* i. 323. *Pears. R.* i. 54. 92.222; ii. 175.: j: J(y,
Ruphanus rusticanus. Horse Radish. Root. *Pharm. lond.—Alst.* i. 499. *Callisen in act. haun.* i. 74.

Carth. ii. 257. *Chom.* 545. *Clegh.* 228. *Cult.* ii. 168. *Geoffr. suite* ii. 192. *Lew.* ii. 263. *Monro Hi.* 228. *Murr.* ii, S48. JVc«m. ii. 169. *Rogcrt in act. haun.* i. 188. *Rutty* 424. Raphanus sylvestris. *Dale* 205. A/t7/. Jo. 369. Raphanus marinus, scu rusticanus. *Schrod.* 660. Horse Raddish. *Brieude, account from in chir, rev.* xi. 394. *Chalm.* ii. 18. 15. *Clegh,* £38. *Cull. clin.* 199. 250. *Pott* ii. 218. *Dane.* ii. 710. *Fordt/ce, G. fere,* iv. 115. *Guthrie in ph. tr. ahr. by HutU* xiv. 399. *Lind hot clim.* 514. *Monro, Don. sold.* i. 287; ii. 186. 187. 4. COCHLEARIA Draba. Leaves lanceolate, am plexicaul, dentate. *L. sp.* 904. *Donn* 85. *J acq. austr.* iv-*t.* 315.. *Host* 360. *Gou. hort.* 318. Near Montpelier.
Lepidium Draba. *Roth gprm.* i. 278; ii. *pars* ii.
Lepidium humile incanum arvensc. *JUagn. hort.* 115. Draba umbellata, vel Draba major, capitulis donata. *Magn. monsp.* 86. Draba Dioscoridis. *Ger. by Johns.* 274*j*. Draba umbellata major. *Hist. ox. s.* 3. *t.* 21. /. 1. Draba vulgaris I. *Clus. pann.* 461, *rcpr.* in Draba I vulgaris. *Clus. hist.* ii. 461, *and cop. in* Draba vulgaris. *Park, thcalr.* 819. Leaves represented as entire at the margin.—*Raii hist.* 821; *eux.* 118. Io Italy France and Germany, and within the walls of Antwerp. Draba multis, flore albo. *Bauh. J.* ii. 939, upper fig. (The lower fig. is a siliquosc plant.) Arabis, seu Draba Matthioli. *Dalech.* .664. Native of Italy, the south of France, Germany, and Hungary. DRAU4. ZWe205. *uf«ßn. Disse. L* 2. *c.* 187. 668. CORONOPUS. *Silicula* not opening, bilocular; cells monospermous. *Obs.* 7905. *Gaertn.*
I. COHONOPUS *coadunatus.* Siliculao cordate, acute.
Obs, 7906. On a dunghill near Worcester, C. Iiuellii. *Gaertn.* ii. 293. *t.* 142. *Smith brit.* 691. *Blackw. t.* 120. *Dalech.* 670, as it appears on first coining into flower.—*Park, theatr.* 502, *abr. from Ger. by Johns.* 427, *which repr. from* Cornu cervi alterum repens. *Dod.* 110, *which repr. in* C. repens Ruellii, et Cornu cervi alterum vulgi. *Lob. ic.* i. 438, $ *cop. in* C. repens. *Dalech.* 671. Cochlearia Coronopus. *L. suec.* ». 579;

sp. 904. *Bot. arr.* 680. *Ii. dan. t.* 202. *MarU rust. t.* 92. C. Ruellii, sive Nasturtium verrucosum. *Bauh. J.* ii. 919. Ambrosia prima. *Dalech.* 1148, *cop. in*

C. Ruellii recta, vel repens. *Park, theatr.* 502.

Nasturtium supinum, capsulis verrucosis. *Raiisyn.* 304:,

Nasturtium syl;estre, capsulis cristatis. *Boerh.* ii.

8. To«m. pim. 26.' *Vaill. paris.* 144. Pseudambrosia. '*Cam. epit.* 596. Leaves pinnatifid. *liacemi* supra-axillary. *Fruit* reniformi-cordate, rugose with some prominent points, compressed, indurated, each half divisible by some force into 2 valves. *Obs.* 7906. Native of Europe, and according to Gronoyius of North America. 669. LUNARIA,. . .. S *Hicu la* pedunculate, flat, entire; valves parallel to and as large as the dissepiment. *Obs.* 5688. *L,.* 1. LUNARIA *ovalis.* Siliculae oval. *Obs.* 5688. In a garden..
,,..,

L. annua. *L. sp. ed.* i. 653; *succ. n.* 583, retaining the trivial name though describing it as biennial; the plant found near Kinnekulle in West Gothland, (that found between Horva and Horby L. lanccolata, as also probably the rest;) *sp.* 911. quoting 11. succ. though giving only Germany as its place of growth; *a If'illd.* iii. 477. *Retz. obs. i. n.* 69, not a native of Scania; *scand. n.* 801, in formed by Linnaeus by letter that he had raised it from seeds gathered in West Gothland.—*Hort. kew.* ii. 385. *Roth germ.* i. 274. Near Rubeland and Tubingen in Germany; ii. *pars* ii. 77,,

L. rediviva. *Mill. Ph. did. n. 1. Gaerln.* ii. 288. *t.* 142.

L. foliis cordatis. *L. succ. ed.* i. 193.

L. graeca annua. *Best. hort. vern. fol.* 7.. '. Viola L. major, siliqua rotunda. *Jtaii hist.* 787.

L. major, Bolbonac aliis-. *Cam hort* 92...',,' 1.1... '. ......' !
Viola latifolia. *Dalech.* 805. *Clus. hist.* i. 297, *repr. in Dod.* 161, dr

Viola lunaris, sive Bolbonac. *Ger. by Johns.* 464, who says it had been found about Pinner and Harrow on the hill; *andabr. in*

Viola lunaris, sive Bulbonach. *Park, theatr.* 1366, *and par. t.* 263. /. 7.

L. major, siliqua rotundiore. *Boerh.* ii. 5. *Bank.*
J. ii. 881. Siliquae ill done.
Root biennial, dying as soon as the seeds are ripe.
Calyx reddish purple. *Petals* reddish purple, rather smaller than those of L. lanccolata. *Nectaria 2,* one at the base of each of the shorter stamina, sagittate; the upper end patulous between the base of the filament and the germen, 2 lower lobes deflex *Obs.* 5688.
BULBONACH. *Dale* 200.
Viola Lunaria. *Geoffr. suite* iii. 324.
2. LUNARIA *laneeolata.* Siliculae lanceolate. *Obs.* 7016. In a garden. L. rediviva. *Retz. obs.* i. *n.* 68. Between Hurfwa and Horby in Scania; *scand. n.* 800. £. *Sp. ed.* i. 653; *sp.* 911; *a Willd.* iii. 476. *Krock. n.* 1043. *Scop. earn. n.* 786. Host 365. *Hort. kew.* ii. 385. *Roth germ.* i. 274, on rocks in the forests of the Hartz and Thuringia, near Giessen, Herbora, Ilefeld, &c. ii. *pars* ii. 77. L. graeca perennis. *Besl. hort. vern. fol.* 7. Viola lunaris Iongibribus siliquis. *Rati hist.* 788; *eur.* 263. On Mount Salce and Mount Jura.-l *Ger. by Johns.* 464, who says k grew wild about

Watford, *cop. in* L. major, siliqua longiore. *Bauh. J.* ii. 882. On Mount Saleve near Geneva, and near Lake Scbcn.
—Boer A. ii. 5.
Viola lunaris altera, sen peregrjlia. *Park. par.* 265.
No fig.
Calyx white below and at the margin, green above.
Corolla white. *Nectaria* similar to those of L. ovalis-
Obs. 7016.
LUNARIA major alia, flore albicantc odorato,
perennis. *Cam. hort.* 92. In Switzerland. Viola Lunaria. *Dale* 200. SILIQUOSAE. 670. DENTARIA. *Siliqua* bursting elastically, the valves becoming revolute. *Stigma* emarginate. *Calyx* longitudinally connivent. L. 1. DENTARIA *bifolia.* Leaves tcrnate. Stems with 2 leaves. From DENTARIA *diphylla. Michaux* ii. 30. 2. DENTARIA *butbifera.* Lower leaves pinnate, up permost simple. *L. sp.* 912. *Bat. arr.* 683. *Smith*

engl. t. 309, from a garden where it propagates itself.—*Huds.* 286. In woods in Buckinghamshire.
—*Fl. dan. t.* S61. *Ger. by Johns.* 984, *repr.fror*n
D. IIII baccifera. *Clus. hist.* ii. 191.
DENTARIA bulbifera. *Krock.* n. 1047. *r* 3
DENTARIA *pinnata.* Leaves pinnate: folioles lanceolate, serrate. *Obs.* 8265. Specimen gathered in Fothergill's garden. *Hort. kew.* iii. 336, *L. a Willd.* iii. 480.
D. pentaphyllos *a L. sp.* 912;
D. heptaphyllos V. *Clus. pann.* 453 *repr. in*
D. VIII heptaphyllos. *Clus. hist.* ii. 123, *Sf*
Viola D. altera. *Dod.* 162, *cop. in*
Coralloides altera, sive septifolia. *Bauh. J.* ii. 901, (mispr. 899) *8f.*

D. heptaphyllos. *Park, theatr.* 620, *Sr repr. in Ger. by Johns.* 985. *Raii hist.* 785. On Mount Jura and Saleve.—*Watson in ph. tr. abr. by Hvtt.* x. 250. Found by Blackstone near Harefield in Middlesex.
DENTAlllA. *Cod. med. p. xlv.*—*Dale* 200. 671. CARDAMINE. Siliqua bursting elastically, the valves becoming re volute. *Stigma* entire. *Calyx* somewhat gaping. L. 1. Leaves pinnate. L.
I. CARDAMINE *hirsuta.* Folioles angular. Petals twice as long as the calyx. Stem mostly hirsuta lous. *Obs.* 4720. In marshy ground *Huds.* 295. *Sibth. ox.* 205. *Bot. arr.* 688. *Curt. land. iv.* 48. *t.* 277. *Wale. t. Scop. cam.* ii. 21. *t.* 38. *Smith engl. t.* 492; *brit.* 698.

C. impatiens. *Fl. dan. t.* 735.

C. impatieDs altera hirsutior *Raii syn.* 200.

C. IIII Dalechampii. *Dalech.* 659. Boerh. ii. 17. In Holland.
. Stamina 4, 5, and 6 in the same plant. *Glands* 4, 1 at the base of each pair of longer stamina, 1 embracing the base of each shorter stamen, and where those wanting between the sides of the germen and. the calyx. *Obs.* 4708. At the foot of a wall near Chesterfield. 20 May.—*Root* annual.. Cultivated jn a garden. SIS YMBRIUM C. hirsutum minus, flore parvo. (mispr. purpureo, as Haller observes.) *Bank. J.* ii. 888.. C. puraila, bellidis folio, alpina. *Rutty* 94? *a hexa-*

ndra. (Variation.) Stamina generally 6. *Obs.* 4709. Between Worcester and Ombersley. C. parviflora. *Huds. ed. 'i. Lightf..* 1105. *Bot. arr.* 686.!.-. '. 0 tetrandra. (Variation.) Stamina generally 4. *Obs.* 840. On a bank of marie on the side of the Severn at the Ridd between Worcester and Upton. C. hirsuta. *L,. sp.* 915. *Iluds. ed.* i. *Lightf* S48. *Bot. arr.* 688. *Siliquae,* valves rolling back so rapidly that the eye can scarcely discern the motion. *Obs.* 6327. 2. CAKDAMINE *mdajithera.* Folioles angular. Petals twice as long as the calyx. Stem glabrous. *Obs.* 7068. On the side of a wet ditch. ('. amara. *L. sp.* 915. *Bot. arr.* 689. *Curt. lond.* iii. 39. *t.* 158. *Smith brit.* 699; *engl. t.* 1000. *(Fl. dan. t.* 148 has paniculate flowers.) C. pratensis, flore majore, elatior. *Vaill. parts.* 28. *Dill. ap. Rati syn.* 299. *Boerh.* ii. 17. In Holland.
Sisymbrium C. sivc Nastnrlium aquaticum, flore majore, elatius. *Bauh. J.* ii. 885. Nasturtium aquaticum amarum. *Park, theatr.* 12S1, *Raii syn. ed.* ii. 171. Bitter Cress. *Pet. herb. t.* 47. /. I. (Nasturtium pyrenaicuin aquaticuin Iatifolium, purpurasceutc flore. *HcГm. par.* 223. *t.* 203, is C. latifolia.) Stem 2 feet long, throwing out roots at the lowe joints. *Leaves* warm, but as Vaillant observes not bitter. *Anthetae* blackish purple. *Nectario* 4, glandular, green, 1 surrounding the outer base of the shorter stamina, 1 at the base of each pair of longer stamina. *Style* short. *Obs.* 7068. CARD AMINE amara. *Caley in bol. arr. ed. IV.* iii. 169. Kroch, n. 1053. *Light/.* 350.
3. CARDAMINE *pratensis.* Folioles of the upper leaves mostly entire at the margin. Petals thrice as long as the calyx. Stem glabrous. *Obs.* 4711.
In a wet meadow.—*Huas.* 294. *L. sp.* 915. *Bot.* err. 688. *Curt. lond.* iii. 40. *t.* 175. *Wale. t. Smith brit* 699; *engl. t.* 776. *Fl. dun. t.* 1039. *Jf'ooà..* i. 89. *t.* 30. *Huds.* 294. *Mart. rust. t.* 95. *ö.* pratensis, magno flore purpurascente. *Boerh.* ii. 16. In Holland.. ::

Flos cueuli. *Dod.* 582, *repr. in* C. altera. *Lob. obs.* 106; *ic.* i. 210, % *Ger. hy*

Johns. 259, *St cop. in*

C. altera minor. *Park, theatr.* 826, which

repr.

in Cerdamine. *Park, theatr.* 1239. *Raii hist.* SU; *syn.* 299. *Ger. by Johns.* 259, *repr. from.*

C sive Sisymbrium alarum Dioscoridis. *Lob. obs.* 106, which *repr. in ic.* i. 210. Nasturtium agreste. *Fuchs.* 320. *c.* 123, *cop. in* Iberis Fuchsii, give Nasturtium pratense silvestre.

Bauh. J. ii. 889. Nasturtium pretense majus, sive C. latifolia. *Park. theatr.* 825. No fig. Nasturtium pretense. *Trag.* 8S.S *Leaves* glabrous; folioles of the radical leaves roundish, those of the cauline leaves lanceolate, mostly entire at the margin. *Glands* 4, 1 between each pair of longer stamina and the calyx, 1 almost encompassing each shorter stamen. *Obs.* 4711. CARDAMINE. Ladyssmock. Flowers. *Pharm. loud.* $ *noviss.—Baker in med. tr.* i. 442. *Boerh.* 434. *Bree* 251. *Cull.* ii. 166. *Dale* 204. *Dawson, Ambr. in leU.* 292. *£rock. n.* 1052. *Lew.* i. 279. *Linn.* 191. *Mill. Jos.* 111. *Monro* iii. 46. *Murr.* ii. 319. ifcrfty 94. «. L C pratensis. Petals. Leaves. *Pharm. edin.— Home, F. clin.* 199. *Lew. disp. by Dune.* 179. *Pears. It.* ii. 213. *Ploucq. bibl.* i. 411. *With, in bot. arr. ed. IV.* iii. 568. Nasturtium aquaticum. *Berg.* 560. 672. SISYMBRIUM. *Siliqua* opening with straightish valves. *Calyx & corolla* patent. *Obs.* 6698. L. 1. *Calyx* longer than the corolla. 1. SISYMBRIUM *terrestre.* Leaves pinnatifid. *Obs.* 6698. In dry ground on the side of a brick pit. ... 23 July, lately come into flower.—*Curt. land.* v.

49. *t.* 289. *Smith brit.* 701; *engl. t.* 1747. *Bot.*

arr, 692.;.,.r,..
.S. amphibium. *17. dan. t.93. Iluds.296. Light/.*
352 a, on the authority of Sibbald.
S. palustre repens, parvo (lore. *Vaill. paris.* 186,
accords in the admeasurements of the petals and calyx, but the root described as perennial.
S. palustre.. *Poll..* 625. *IVilld. ber.* 219. Rolh
germ. i. 290.-..'...,. . Radicola sylvestris, sive palustris. *Bauh. J.* ii. 866.
Flowers very small. Raphanus aquaticusi foliis in profundas lacinias divi.n.

sis. *Dill. ap. Rail syn.* 301....The paragraph which follows belongs to the preceding species n. I. i ±—*Bauh. Casp. prodr.* 38, *cop. in*

Raphanus aquaticus Buuhini. *PaJk. thcatr.* 1228, *Sf abr. in..* '.....'. 'A'..'.

Smnll jagged water Radish... *Pet. herb. t.* 49. /. 9.--*Stem* ascending, 6 inches long. *Leaves* pinnatind and lvrato-pinnatifid; segments inciso-serrate; teeth ' obtuse. *Calyx* yellow, tinged at the end with reddish brown, tenth of an inch long; phylla oblong. *Petals* somewhat more than half as long as the calyx. *Style* very short. *Siliquae* slightly incurvate, terete; valves opening from the base, straight. *Obs.* 5873. In gravelly soil near Stafford in dry situations, and near a wet diteh at the Broad-eye bridge in Stafford.—-*Stem* 2 to 22 inches long, branched from the base, striate. *Calyx* yellow, nearly 1 tenth of an inch long; phylla patent and patulous. *Petals,* patent, cunciformiobovate, about as long as the calyx, yellow. *JVec/a.ria* 4, green, roundish, 1 between the 2 shorter stamina. and the 2 pairs of longer stamina. *Siliquae* green,

SitiQuosAE. 672. Sisymbrium. 449 1 tenth of an inch long, terete. *Obs.* 6G98. RADÍCULA palustris. *Geoffr. suite* iii, 57. 2. SISYMBRIUM *Sophia,.* Leaves bipinnate. *Obs.* 2830. On rubbish.—*L. suec. n.* 595; *sp.* 920. *Bot. arr.* 693. *Smith brit.* 704; *engl, t.* 963. *Fl. dan. t.* 528. *Mart. rust. t.* 57. S. corolla calice minor, foliis multifidis linearibus. *L. lapp.* ». 261. S. annuum, absinthii folio. *Tourn. paris.* 231. S. annuum, absinthii minoris folio. *Vaill. paris.* 186. *Boerh.* ii. 16. Erysimum Sophia dictum. *Raii hist.* 812; *syn.* 298. Nasturtium sylvestre aliud. *Fuchs.* 321. *c.* 123, *cop. . in* Seriphium germanicum, sive Sophia quibusdam. *Bauh. J.* ii. 886, Sç Thalietrum. *Dalech.* 1146, 6 abr. *in* Seriphium germanicum. *Trag.* 338. Thalietrum. Ile.ba Sophia latifolia. *Tab. ic.* 6. Thalietrum. Herba Sophia angustifolia. *Tab. ic.* 7. Sophia. *Dod.* 133, *repr. in* Sophia chirurgorum. *Lob. obs.* 426; *ic.* i. 738 8¡ *Ger. by Johns.* 1068, *and cop. in Park, theatr.* 830. *Stem* corymbose. *Branches* patent. *Leaves* sessile, bipinnate. *Petiolules* slightly villose; hairs stellate and forked. *Calyx* greenish yellow; phylla patent. *Petals* yellow, erect, twice as short as the calyx. *Obs.* 2830. SOPHIA. *Berg.* 561. *Geoffr. suite* iii. 64. VQL. 3. F f *JJerm.* S03. *Krock. n.* 1064. *Linn.* 192. *Schoepf* 104. *Vog.* 139. 181. Sophia chirurgorum. *Dale* 204. *Mill. Jos.* 418. *Mutt.* ii. 313. *Pet. in ph. tr. air. by Loath,* iu 705; *by Hutt.* iv. 418. Talitron. *Chom.* 587; *suppl.* 167. 2. *Calyx shorter than the corolla.* 3. SISYMBRIUM *diversifolium.* Leaves lanceolate, lanceolato-oblong, inclso-serrate and pinnatifid with patulous lanceolate segments. *Obs.* 7481. On the banks of the Trent at King's Bromley in Staffordshire. S. amphibium. *L. sp.* 917, so called on the supposition that a variety of it grew in dry situations.— —*fFilld. her.* 219. *Roth germ.* i. 290. *Smith brit.* 702. *Krock. n.* 1059. S. amphibium aquaticum. *Lighlf.* 352, but whether he had found it in Scotland uncertain. *serratum.* Leaves inciso-serrate. *Obs.* 7481. S. amphibium aquaticum. *L. sp.* 917. *Huds.* 296. S. amphibium. *Bot. atr.* 691. *xar.* 1. *Fl.dan.t.* 984. *Smith engl. t.* 1840. S. aquaticum, raphani foiio siliqua breviori. *Tourn. paris.*230. *Vaill. paris.* 185. Raphanus aquations alter. *Bauh. Casp. prodr.* OS, *cop. in* Raphanus palustris alter. *Park, theatr.* 1229, *8f* Broad water Radish. *Pet. herb. t.* 49. /. 8,. *Stem* 4 feet long. *Calyx* yellow. *Petals* yellow, obovate. *Neetaria* 6, coalescing so as to form a tuberculated ring round the outer margin of the receptacle, 2 tubercles at the base of each of the shorter stamina between the stamina and the calyx, almost surrounding the base of the filament, and 1 at the base of each pair of longer stamina, between the stamina and calyx, smaller. *Germen* ovali-oblong. *Style* nearly half as long as the germen. *Obs.* 7481. *& incisum.* Leaves incise, serrate. *Obs.* 425. On the side of the Severn at the brick kilns under Bunds bill near Worcester. S. amphibium terrestre. *L. sp.* 917? *Huds.* 297 S. aquaticum foliis variis. *Vaill. par-s.* 185? Raphanus silvestris. *Daleck.* 635, *repr. in* Raphanns palustris. *Dalech.* 1090. *y pinnatifidum.* Leaves piiuiati/id. *Obs.* 4110. On the side of the Severn at the brick kilns under Bund's hill near Worcester.

S. amphibium palustre. *L. sp.* 917.
S. amphibium. *Bot. arr.* 692. *tar.* 2.
S. aquaticum, foliis in profundas lacinias divisis,
siliqua breviore. *Tourn. parts.* 230. *Vaill. paris.* 185. Radicula sylvestris seu palustris. *jRaii syn. 301.* Raphanus aquaticus Tabernaemontani. *Bauh. J.* ii. 867, *cop. in* Great jagged water Radish. *Pet. herb. t.* 49. /. s. Kaphanus aquaticus Lobelii. *Park, theatr.* 1228, *cop. from* RAPHANUS aquaticus. *Ger. by Johns.* 240.—. *Dale* 205. *Geoffr. suite* iii. 58. 4. SISYMBRIUM *tenuifolium.* Siliquae erect. Leaves pinnatifid; segments linear, distant, sometimes dentate; margin entire. Stem perennial, hirsululous below. Style of the fruit ensifonn. *Obs.* 758?.
In the garden of Mr. Knowlton, who gathered the seed from plants growing on the walls of Old Malton in Yorkshire.—*Gou. monsp.* 164. About MontpeHer, on old walls and barren places. —*Smith hrit.* 703. On old walls about Windsor ;—*engl. ti* 525. *Gort. belg. foed. n.* 555. *Poll. n.* 627. On walls, sides of roads, and grassy hills.— *L. sp.* 917, who adopted it from
S. foliis Inflmis bis terve pinnati6dis, supremis integris, omnibus non dentatis. *Guett.* ii. 150. Near Orleans, and naturalised at Estampes.
Brassica muralis. *Huds.* 291. On old walls about London, Exeter, Bristol, and elsewhere.-*Curt, land.* iii. 38. . 158. *Bot. arr.* 709.
Eruca sativa. *Fuchs.* 264. *c.* 100, *cop. in*
Eruca tenuifolia, perennis, flore luteo. *Bauh. J.* ii. 861. On old walk. *Tburn. parts.* 18. *Vaill. parts.* 50. Eruca sylvestris. *Ra-i syn.* 296. On the walls of Chester, Taunton castle, Yarmouth, Lichfield close,
Berwick, &c. Eruca sylvesiris. *Bod.* 696, *repr. in Lob. obs.* 102; *ic.* i. 204, *Ger. by Johns.* 246, *cop. in* Eruca sativa alba. *Park, theatr.* 817. Erysimum verum. *Dalech.* 653.
Style of the fruit twice as long as the stigma. *Obs.* 7672. Specimen gathered by Mr. Salt on a wall of the Green Park near Hyde Park corner Westminster. *Native* possibly of Germany, and naturalised ia France, England, and Wales,

possibly introduced by the Romans. ERUCA sylvestris. *Dale* 203. *Gcoffr.* iii. 437. *Lcis.i.* 416. MM. *Jos.* 188.
Eroca sylvestris major lulea, caule aspero. *Rutty* 182. Eruca tenuifolia perennis, florc luteo. *Chom.* 541.
5. SISYMBRIUM *sykestre.* Siliquae declinate. Leaves pinnate and pinnatifiJ; folioles and segments lanceolate, serrate. *O's.* 8135. In Mr. Knowlton's garden from a plant I gathered on the banks of the Severn at Upton in Worcestershire. July *Obs.* 8I3C. Specimen gathered by Mr.
Salt near Sheffield.—*L. suec. n.* 594; *sp.* 489. *Huds.* 2f 6. On the banks of the Thames.—*Curt, fond.* iii. 41. *t.* 153. *Bot. arr.* 691. *Smith brit.* 701. *Gou. hort.* 325. At Montpelier. *(Scop, earn. n.* 822 is described as having emarginate petals.)
S. palustre repens nasturtii folio. *Tourn. parts.* 37. *Vaill. parts.* 185.
Sium tenuifolium montanum hiteum. *Col. ecphr.* i. *t.* 269.
Sium alterum aquaticum luteum, vel Cardamine tenuifolium montanum. *Col. ecphr.* i. 266.
Eruca palustris minor. *Tab. ic.* 447, *cop. in*
Eruca aquatica. *Ger. by Johns.* 248, *and Park, theatr.* 1242. *Iioii hist.* 808; *syn.* 297.
Eruca quibnsdam silvestris repens flosculo purpnrco a misprint for parvo luteo. *Bauh. J.* ii. 866.
Sinapi tertium. *Cam. epit.* 334.
(Eruca sylvestris. *Fuchs.* 264, c. 100, *repr. in*
Sinapi alterum genus. *Fuchs.* 523, c, 205, is Brassica Eruca.) *Stem* flexuose, 14 inches long, angular, slightly compressed, brownish purple here and there, scabrous wiih very short microscopic points, below perceptibly to the lips. *Leaves* pinnate, towards the end pinnafifid. *Cetyx* yellow; phylla oblong, microscopicaily and obsoletely dentate at the end. *Petals yellow,* twice as long as the calyx, obovafe. *Ncctaria* 4, glandular, green, confluent, forming a ring round thf base of the germen, the 2 larger encompassiug the base of the 2 shorter stamina. *Obs.* 8135.
Natibe of Europe from Italy to Sweden,

of Middlesex, Oxfordshire, Worcestershire, Bedfordshire, Cambridgeshire, Suffolk, and Yorkshire. .*ERUCA* palustris. *Geoffr. suite* iii. 60. 6. SISYMBRIUM *Irio.* Leaves pinnate and pinnatifid, nearly glabrous. Stem nearly glabrous. Siliquae erect. Petals twice as long as the calyx. *Obs.* 7910. Specimen gathered in the Oxford garden.

—*Obs.7911.* Specimen gathered in the Edinburgh garden.—*L. suec. n.* 596, in gardens, into which-possibly introduced with other seeds; *sp.* 921.

Huds. 297. Common about Lonllon.—*Jacq. an sir.* iv. *t.* 322. *Bot. arr.* 694. *Curt. lond.* v. 48. *t.* 311. *Smith brit.* 705; *engl.t.* 1631. *Sibth. ox.* £07.

Under Merton wall and in Rose lane. Erysimum loins lyrato-pinnatis, extimo hastato. *L. ups.* 201. Irio laevis apulus, erucae folio. *Col. ecphr.* i. 264. Irio apulus alter, levi folio erucae. *Col. ecphr.* i. *t.* 265, *cop. in* Broad hedge Mustard. *Pet. herb. t.* 46. /. 4, # Erysimum latifolium neapolitanum. *Park, theatr,* 834. *liaii st/n.* 298. About London, at Faulk bourn in Ess x, and on the walls of Berwick. Erysimum latifolium majus glabrum. *Magn. monsp.* 93. *Tourn. pans.* 20. *Vaill. parfs.* 51.

Sinapi sylvestre morispessulanum, lato folio, flosculo luteo minimo, siliqua longissima. *Bank. J.* ii. 858.

Erysimon II. *Tab. ic.* 449.

Native of Europe from Italy *to* Sweden, and of

Essex; and found near London, Oxford, Wisbeacb, and Berwick on rubbish and buildings.

ER YSIMUM latifolium. *Dale* 204. v , Erysimum latifolium majus glabrum. *Chom.* 105. 7. SISYMBRIUM *Nasturtium.* Leaves pinnate.' Si liquae declinate. Folioles entire, roundish and ovate. *Obs.* 4108. In wet ditehes.—*L. a Murr.* 594. *Bot. arr.* 690. *JIuds.* 296. *Light/.* 350. *KrocL n.* 1055. *Ft."dm. t.* 690. *Woodv.* i. 134. *t.* 48. *Thornt.* 617. *Smilk brit.* 700; *engl. t.* 855. *Curt. lond.* vi. *t.*

S. Nasturtium aquaticum. *L. suec. n.* 592; *sp.*

916. *Poll. n.* 623.

S, aquaticum. *Tourn. part's.* 231. *Vaill. paris.lS5.*

Boerh.i. 15. In Holland.

S. Cardamine, sive Nasturtium aquaticum. *Rati syn.* 300. *Bauh. J.* ii. 884, *cop. from* S. Cardamine. *Fuchs.* 684. c. 276, *which cop. in* Nasturtium aquaticum. *Trag.* 82. *Dod.* 581 *r repr. .* in Sion erucaefolium Cratevae. *Lob. obs.* 105; *ic.* i. 209, # Nasturtium aquaticum, sive Cratevae Sium. *Ger. by Johns.* 257, *abr. in* Water Cress. *Pet. herb. t.* 42. /. 2, *and cop. in*

Nasturtium aquaticum vulgare. *Park, theatr.* 1239.

Raii hist. 816.

S. Cardamine I. *Dalech.* 658.

Early water Cress. *Pet. kerb. t.* 47. /. 3, is probably only a younger plant.

Si/iqitae, valves revolut", but not opening with the rapidity with whioh the valves of Cardamine hirsuta curl up. *Obs.* 6326. In Monsal dale in Derbyshire. SISYMBRIUM Nasturtium. *Pharm. edin.*— *Bry.* 114. *Lett. disp. by Dune.* 305. *Pears. R* i. 52. Nasturtium aquaticum. Water Cresses. Fresh herb. *Pharm. lond.*—*Aht.* ii. 187. *Bang in act. haun.* i. 11. *Carth.* ii. 266. *Chom.* 534; *suppl.* 155. *Cull.* ii. 165. *Dale* 204. *Geoffr. suite* i. 142. *Hill* 386. *Lew.* ii. 126. *Linn.* 191. *Mertensinph.tr. abr. by Hutt.* xiv. 404. *Mill. Jos.* 309, *Monro* iii. 183. *Murr.* ii. 309. *Pouteau in med. journ.* iv. 352. *Quar. anim.* 274. *Butty* 343. *Schocpf"* 101. *Schrod.633. Spielm.* 60. *Stollmed.* iii. 83. 88. *Vog.* 71. Nasturtium. *Mead. mon.* ii. 121. *Quar. anim.* 66. Wafer Cress. *Darw.* ii. 139. 710. 720. *Lindseam.* 20. *Monro, Don. sold.* ii. 185. *Rush* ii. 186. 673. ERYSIMUM. $ Hi qua columnar, square. *Calyx* closed. L. 1. ERYSIMUM *cheiranthoides.* Leaves lanceolate; margin obsoletely dentate. Siliquae erect. Pedicles of the fruit divaricate. Stigma as broad as the style. *Obs.* 7400. Specimen gathered in Sole's garden.—*Smith brit.* 708; *engl, t,* 942. *L. sp.* 923; *suec n.* 601. *Huds.* 287. *Poll. n.* 634. *Light/.* 357. Observed by Sibbald ¡n corn fields. — *Bot. nrr.* 697. *Jacq. austr.* i. *t.* 23. *Fl. dan. t.* 731. Siliquae represented as attenuate; *t.* 923. leaves serrate. Cheiranihus erysimoides. *Huds.* 287, the plant growing in osier holts about Godstow near Oxford, having been found by Sibthorp to be E. cheiran« thoides. Chdranthus scapigerus. *Willd. ber. n.* 663. *t.* 5. /. 10. E. foliis integris Ianccolatis. *L. lapp. n.* 263; *suec. ed.* i. *n* 5. Turritis leucoii folio. *Tourn. paris.* 369. *Vaïll. paris.* 197. *Boerh.* ii. 15. Annual. Myagro nffinis planta, siliquis longis. *Bauh. J.* ii. 894. *Rait syn.* 298. In willow holts near Ely, and near Ashburn in Derbyshire, and observed by

Newton in corn fields near Eiden in Suffolk. Myagrum alteram, thlaspi effigie. *Lob. obs.* 112, *repr. in* Caracline, Myagrura alteram thlaspi effigie. *Lob. ic.* i. 225, *8ç* Camelina. *Ger. by Johns.* 273, $ *cop. in* Myagrum aliud, thlaspi effigie. *Dalech.* 1137, Camelina, sive Myagrum altcrum amarum. *Park. ihcatr.* 868, *Se* Treacle Wormseed. *Pet. herb. t.* 45./. 2. E. Galeno et Theophrasto. *Raii hist.* 811.

Leaves microscopically pubescent; hairs stellate, sessile, with 3 and sometimes 4 branches. *Petals* If of the tenth of an inch long; laminae cuneiform, ungues attenuate downwards, as long as the limb.

£. vulgare." *Boerh.* ii. 14. *Tourn. parts.* 19. *Vaill. paris.* 51. Eruca hirsuta, siliqua cauli appressa, E. dicta. *Rai syn.* 29?. Eruca siliqua cauli appressa, E. dicta. *Rail hist.* 810. E. Irio I. *Tab. ic* 448. Verbenaca recta, sive mas. *Fuchs.* 566. c. *228, cop, in* Dalech. 1335, # E. Tragi, fiosculis luteis, juxta nuiros proveniens.

Ban I-. J. ii. 863, *abr. in* Verbena foemina. *Trag.* 102, *Sf cop. in* E. Dioscoridis, Lobelii. *Ger. by Johns.* 254, *which reprfrom* Irio, sive Erysimum. *Dod.* 702. *Lob. obs.* 103. No

Irio sive E. Dioscoridis. *Lob. adv.* 69, *repr. in ic.* i. 206, # *cop. in* Irio sive E. vulgare. *Pari, theatr.* 833. ERYSIMUM. *Alst.* ii. 135. *Berg.* 562. *Dale* 203..*fferw.* 521. *Kroch. n.* 1072. ic®. i. 418; *disp. by Dune.* 341. Li'/m. 192. *Mill. Jbs.*190. JW«rr. ii; 315.-R«/ty 185. *Schoepf* 104. *Spt'eAn.* 534. *Fog.* 62. E. vulgare. *Boulduc in ac. sc. abr. by Southw.* iii. 287. *Carth.* ii. 266. 296. *Geoffr.* iii. 444. E. Lobelii. *Jsnardin ac. sc. abr. by Southw.* iii. 287. 4. ERYSIMUM *lyrifolium.* Leaves lyrato-pinnate and lyrate.' Siliquac obsoletely tetragonous. *Obs.* 4784. In moist ground. E. Barbarea. *L. sp.* 922. *Bot. arr.* 696. *Wale. t. Smith brit.* 706. Sisymbrium erucae folio glabra, flore luteo. *Touru. parts.* 364. *Vaill. paris.* 185. Eruca lutea, sen Barbirea. *Raii syn.* 297. Hcrba Sanctae Barbarae. *Fuchs.* 705. *c.* 285, *abr. in Trag.* 101, *Sr cop. in* Barbarea. *Bauh. J.* ii. 869. *Rati hht.* 809. *Dod.* 700, *repr. in Ger. by Johns.* 243, *Sf cop. in* Barbarea simplex. *Park, theatr.* 820.

Nectaria 4, 1 between each pair of longer stamina and the calyx, 1 between each shorter stamen and the germen, embracing the base of the filaments. *Obs.* 4784. BARBAREA. *Berg.* 563. *Dak* 204. *Geoffr. suite* iii. 63. *Krock. n.* 1073. *Murr.* ii. 318. E. Barbarea. *Bry.* 99. *g temiifolium*. Leaves thinner. *Obs.* 4898. In a garden. E. praecox. *Smith brit.* 707; *engl.t.* 1129. E. Barbarea &. *L. sp.* 922; *suec.* 599. *Bot. arr.* 696. Barbarea foliis minoribus ct frequentius sinuatis. 'DHL *ap. Raii syn.* 297.

Barbarcae species alia. *Raii hist.* 809. Early winter Cress. *Pet. herb. t.* 46. /. 2. BELLE ISLE CRESS.

674. CHEIRANTHUS. *Calyx* closed; 2 of the phylla gibbons at the base. *Nectaria* 4 and 2. *Obs.* 7406. *L.* 1. CHEIRANTHUS *muralis*. Leaves lanceolate, acute; margin entire; strigae simple. Petals several times broader than the calyx. *Obs.* 97. In a garden.— *Salisb. R. hort.* 271. C. Cheiri. *L. sp.* 921. *Hort. hevo.* ii. 395. CHE1RI. *Pharm, austriaco-prov.* 29.— *Berg.* 565. *Dale* 200. *Herrn.* 599. *Kro-clc n.* 1080. *Lew.* i. 327. *Linn.* 193. *Murr.* ii. 339. *Sckrod.* 564. *Spie/m.* 556. *Vog.* 145. Leucoium. Л/sf. ii. 163. *Carth.* iii. 176. *Rutty* 283. Keiri. *Geojr.* iii. 640. *Mill. Jos.* 251. Giroflier jaune. *Cham.* 166; ыр/?/. 56. я *canescens*. Leaves hoary underneath. *Obs.* 7405. In an herbal collected at Stourbridge.—On the rock on which Nottingham Castle stands. A domesticated plant. C. Cheiri. *Wale. t. Bot. arr.* 699. C. fruticulosus. *Smith brit.* 709. (*L. mant.* 94 is described as having flowers 8 times smaller than those of C. Cheiri.) Leucoium luteum vulgare. *Tourn. paris.* 4S0. On the walls and ramparts of Paris. Leucoium petracum lignosius, folio rigido canescentc, vulgatissimum. *Pluk. aim.*

214. *Vaill. paris.* 115. Leucoium luteum, vulgo Cheiri, flore simplici. *Rati hist.* 782; *syn.* 291. On old walls and roofs.— *Bauh. J.* ii, 872, *cop. from* Viola lutea. *Fuchs.* 449. *c.* 175, which *abr. in Trag.* 560. Viola petraea lutea. *Tab. ic.* 305. B *herfensis*. Leaves green to the naked eye. *Obs.* 7406. In a garden where it has grown 3 years.— *Hort. kew.* β

Leucoion luteum. *Dod.* 160, *repr. in* Viola lutea. *Ger. by Johns.* 456, *Sf cop. in*

Keiri, sive Leucoium vulgare luteum. *Park, theatr.* 625. Keiri, sive Leucoium luteum vulgare. *Park. par. t.* 259. /. I. 2. CHEIRANTHUS *incanus*. Leaves lancolato oblong and lanceolate, entire, tomentose and gla brous. Siliquae truncate, compressed. Stem suf fruticose. *Obs.* 7407. In a garden.—*L. sp.* 924. *Hort. kcw.* ii. 395. *lateriflorus. Hort.* /. etc. ii. 396. C. incanus. *Mill. Ph. diet. n.* 6. Leucoion candid um majus. *Dod.* 159, *repr. in* Leucoium purpureum et album. *Lob. obs.* 179, Viola alba et purpurea. *Lob. ic.* i. 529, $ Leucoium album, sive purpureum, sive violaceum. *Ger. by Johns.* 458, S-*cop. in* Leucoium album vel purpureum. *Park, theatr.* 622. Leucoium' simplex sativum, diversorum colorum. *Park. par.* 258. *t.* 259. /. 5, 6. Viola matronalis. *Fuchs.* 310. *c.* 119, the 3rd of the 3 figures *cop. in* Leucoium hyemalc et diu durans, purpureum et roscum ac etiam album. *Bank. J.* ii. 74, *Sf* Viola purpurea, cacrulea, rosea, candida. *Trag.* 561, perhaps ought to be referred to *y*. Stew rather woody, termina;ed by leaves. *Flomering* branches lateral, from near the stem. *Nectaria* 2, green, glandular, pentagonal, almost surrounding the base of the shorter stamina. *Obs.* 7107. LEUCOIUM album. *Dak* 199. MM. *Jos.* 265. 675. HESPERIS. *Calyx* closed; 2 of the phylla gibbous at the base. *Nectaria* 2, at the base of the shorter filaments. Siliqua compresso-plane. Seeds compressed. *Obs.* 908, and the account of the fruit from *L.* 1. HESPERIS *matronalis*. Leaves ovato-lanceolate; margin dentate; hairs dichotomous. Petals mostly with a short mucro at the end. *Obs.* 7. In a garden.—*L. sp.* 927. *Hort. hew.* i.

398. *Krock. n.* 1082. II. hortensis. *Rati hist.* 790. In meadows between Salernum and Naples.

Viola matronalis. *Dod. Jlor.* 24, *repr. in pempt.* 161,

H. II. *Clus. pann.* 336, (the descr. belonging to H. inodora,)

H. III. *Clus. kist.* i. 297,

V. matronalis, flore purpureo sive albo. *Ger. by Johns.* 462, *Sf cop. in* II. pannonica inodora. *Park, theatr.* 1682, (the name and descr. at 628 belonging to II. inodora).

H. vulgaris. *Park. par. t.* 263. /. 5. *Slem* with flowering branches above. Leaves finely acuminate; hairs forked with simple ones interspersed. *Obs.* 7. 4823. HESPERIS. *Dale* 200.

Viola matronalis. *Geoffr. suite* iii. 322. « *purpurea*. Corolla whitish purple. *Obs.* 4823. Specimen from a garden.

H. hortensis. *Vaill. paris.* 101. In the park of Saint Maur.

Viola purpurea. *Fuchs.* 450. *c,* 175. II. flore purpureo. *Bauh. J.* ii. 877. No fig. *t alba*. Corolla white. *Obs.* 7. II. hortensis florc candido. *Vaill. paris.* 101.

Leucoion Dioscoridis. *Fuchs* 4+8. *r.* 175, *cop. in*

H. flore albo. *Bauh. J.* ii. 878. Under hedges in the vallie8 of those parts of Franche Compte and the southern parts of Alsace which are in the vicinity of the Rhine. Petals, ungues half as long again as the calyx; laminae obovate. *Obs.* 7.

....,, A-, .:!!. 676. TURRITIS! *Siliqua* angular. *Calyx* erect, connivcnt. *Petals* erect. *Obs.* 2837. *L.*

I. TURRITIS *glabra*. Radical leaves hirsute, cauline leaves glabrous. *Obs.* 2837. In sandy lanes near Kidderminster.—*L. suec. n.* 606; *sp.* 930. *Bot. arr.* 701. *Curt. land.* iv. 47. *t.* 253. *Krock. n* 1091. *Ft. dan.* f. 809. *Smith engl.t.* 777. T. foliis inferioribus cichoraceis, cacteris perfoliatae. *Tourn. paris.* 160. *Vaill. paris.* 197. *Bocrh.* ii. u. (;i

Turritis. *Rai-syn.* 293; *hist.* 799. *Lob. ic.i.* 220, *repr. in Ger. by Johns.* 272, # Turrita vulgatior. *Clus. hist.* ii. 126, *Sr£op.§f&* T. vulgatior. *Park, theatr.* 852, *if* Tower Mustard. *Pet. herb. t.* 47.

/. 10. Glastifolia cichoroides *Bauh. J.* ii. 836. §*SM* Sinapi album. *Dalech.* 1168. *Nectarium* surrounding the base of (he germen and filaments. *Siliajiae* compressed, tetragonous, to 2 inches long. *Obs.* 2837.. *TUmiTlS. DaleSOl.* 1 J.,.,,". *Nectaria* 4, glandular, 2 between the shorter filaments and the germen, 2 between the longer filaments and the calyx. *Calyx* erect, connivent. *Obs.* 2841. L. : ' '. '. .'. " '. i. " 1. *Style* rather obtuse. L.
.. . '. i..

1. BRASSICA *campestris* Leaves amplexicaul, lower lyrate, hispidulous; upper cordate. *From Roth germ.* i. 285; ii. *pars* ii. 113, *Smith brit.* 718, *and L. sp.* 931; *suec. n.* 608. *Fl. dan. t.* 550. Leaves sagittate, entire; margin entire.
Brassica. *L. lapp. n.* 265.
BRASSICA campestris. *Kroch. n.* 1094. 2.
BRASSICA *Napus.* Leaves amplexicaul, glabrous, dentate at the margin, lowermost lyrate..Style longer than the breadth of fhe siliqua. ' *Qbs.* 7085. In a garden into which transplanted the preceding autumn from a field where cultivated for spring fodder.—*Smith brit.* 719. *L. sp. 931; suec. n.* 547. *Mart. rust. t.* 103. *Bot. arr.* 707. (*Wale. t.* is Sinapis Rapa.)
B. gongylodes. *Mill. Ph. diet. n.* 8..
Napus sylvestris. *Raii syn.* 295. *Vaill. parts.* 144.
VoL. S. og *Boerh'. &* 13. In Holland. —.Ffccto. 180, c. 63, cop. fa *Dalech.* 645, *Bttth.J.* ii. 843, $
Napus. *TVag.* 730.
Bunias sylvestris Lobelii ref. &y *Johiis. &$5T top. in* Bunias, sive Napus sylvestris. *Park, theatr.* 865.
Stem glaucous. *Leates* glaucous, uppermost dentate at the margin. *Calyx* green and greenish yellow, some patulous, others arect with the ends horizontal. *Pctdlt* similar: to those of S-hapis Rapa, judt sensibly larger, bright yellow incumUent, slightly rugose and undulate. *Filaments,* the 4 longer one third tenger than the ungues of the petals. *Germen* and *siliquae* sessile. *Obs,* 708a NAPUS sylvestris. *Dak* 209. *Mill. Jos.* 307. Bunias. *Lew.* ii. 124. *Mittf.* ii 356. Buniuffl. *Geoffr. suite i.* 12&. £ *satka.* (Variation.) ftoot broader. *PfOftt tAefgures of au-*thors: Rapa Napus. *Mitt. Ph. Aid. h.* 3. Napus sativa. *Magn. monsp.* 181; *hort. lil.* B. radice caulescenfe fusiformi. *L. vps.* ltto. Napus sativus. *Dalech.* 644. *Park. par. t.* 507. /., 5. *Fttchs.* 180. c. 63, *cop. in* Napus. JBa«A. *J.* ii. 842. Dorf. 663, *repf. in Lob. obs.* 09, Bunias, site Napus. *Lob. ic.* i. 200, $ Bunias. *Get. by Johns. &S5.* Leavei purplish glaucous, upper amplcxicaul. *Style* enslfotm, longer thdn the breadth of he *geiinen,* thrice as long as the breadth of the siliqua. *Obs.* 2539. In a garden front seeds Sent die rty Br. Lcttsom under the titltf of Mowing Cabbage' «f the Abbe Commerell. -1 Z..-. j. *by Johns.* 316,-*md cop. in Park, theatr.* 269. *Raii cat. ed.* i. 46; *ed.* ii. 43. On Dover cliffs and divers other the like places.—*Mill. Ph. diet. n.* 4, where in the 2nd line from the bottom of column the 2nd, for second read fourth. B. arborea, scu procerior ramosa maritima. *liaii hist.* 796; *syn.* 293. *Leaves* iyrato-pinnate, slightly curled, glabrous; terminal foliole oval, pinnatifid below; lower folioles small, alternate, some *very* small. *Ractmi* erect. *Pedicles* divaricate. *Sitiquae* erect, slightly incurvafe,tetragonous, slightly compressed. *Style* subulatotriangular, truncate, shorter than the breadth of the siliqua. *Seeds* globular, blackish fuscous, glabrous. *Obs.* 7626, In the garden of Mr. Knowlton who informed me that the plant or seeds whence it was produced came from the sea coast of Yorkshire. BRASSICA sectilis. *Berg.* 576. B. oleracea, vel sylvestris. *Bry.* 76. 85. " (3 *viridis.* Leaves white with a tinge of glaucous. *From J. Bauhine.*—*L. P.*
B. vulgaris sativa. *Dod.* 610, *repr. in Lob, obs,* 122; *ic.* i. 243, *and Ger. by Johns.* S12, *and f.iv C0P-m* .,,!.1
B. sativa. *Pari: theatr.* 2CS.
BRASSICA alba vulgaris. *Bauk. J.* ii. 829. — *Geoffr.* in. 212...
B. non capitata. *Rutty* 71...-.- *y* subrubens. Leaves red. *From J. Bauhine.*
Brassicae primum genus. *Fuchs.* 406. *c. 15% cop in..* ..,i
Brassica. *Trag.* 720,
B. sylvestris, Crambe dicta. *Dod.* 612, *and* BRASSICA rubra vulgaris. *Bauk. J.* ii. 831.
Rati hist. 796.—*Geoffr.* iii. 212.

B. rubra. *Lew. i.* Я3в. ' Caulis rubra. *Dale* 201. ¡*t rubra.* Leaves red, before flowering forming a round-' ish head. From memory.—*L. sp. y. Hort. hew. ß.* Red Cabbage. *Park. par.* 504. No fig. BRASSICA capitata rubra. *Boerh.* н; 11. *Rati hist.* 795. *Batth. J.* ii. 831— *ПалеШ. Geoffr.* iii. 212. *Lew.* i. 236. *Spielm.* 46. B. rubra.. *Berg.* 571. *Linn.* 194. *Murr.* ii. 329.
Rutty 73. (*capitata.* Leaves before flowering forming a roundish head, smooth. *Obs.* 2812. In a garden.—*L. sp.* 932. Î. *Hort. hew. л:*
Brassicae quart um genus. *Fuchs.* 407. c. 159, шЛ/cA

ш2. in
Caulis capitatus. 2Veg. 717, ¿ cop. in B. capitata rubra..Dorf. 611, (the name and descr.
belonging to *y*) which repr. in *Ger. by Johns.* 313, the name and descr. belonging to *y*) $ *cop. again in* B. capitata alba. *Bauh. J.* ii. 826. *Rati hist.* 794.
Ger. by Johns. 312, *repr. from* B. capitata ajbicla. *Dod.* 612, which repr. in B. alba sessilis glomerosa. *Lob. ic.* i. 243, # B. capitata. *Lob. obs.* 123, and *cop. in Park. theatr.* 268. *Cam. epit.* 250.. *Leaves,* upper amplexicaul, 06i. 5177. —*Leaves,* upper sessile. Germina uadsiliquaesiipitate; stipites as long as the breadth of the receptacle. *Obs.* 7086. r-*Calyx* sometimes patulous. *Obs.* 2812. BRASSICA capitata alba. *Geoffr.* iii. 211. *Lew,* i. 236. *Murr.* Ц, 329. *Rutty* 71. B. alba. *Herg.* 568. Brassica. *Alst.* ii. 332.. 'Л.»
GgS

B. florida. *Ger. by Johns.* 314, *cop. in* B. porupeiana. *Dalech.* 522, 8*f imit. in* B. florida botrytis. *Lob. obs.* 123, which *repr. in*
ic. i. 245, & B. sabauda crispa. *Ger. by Johns.* 315, (name and descr. belonging to «) *imit. in* Caulis florida. *Patk. par. t.* 505 /. 4, *Sf cop. in* B. florida. *Park. Iheatr.* 269. *Raii hist.* 795. BRASS JCA Botrytis. *Mill. Ph. diet. n.* 3.—*Bry.* 76. 83. *Spielm.* 46. B. caulillora. *Berg.* 572. *Geoffr.* iii. 213. *Ltw.* i.
236. B. florida. *Dale* 201. Colleyflower. *Fordycc, W. fev.* 206. *H* Broccoli. Stem before flowering forming a roundish whitish head surrounded by oval leaves.

From memory.—Hort. hew. £ B. botrytis italica alba, Brocoli dicta. *Mill. Ph. diet. n.* 3. 2. BRASSICA Broccoli. *Berg.* 574. Broccoli: *Fordyce, W. fev.* 206. *Spielm.* 46. B. botrytis alba. *Bry.* 76. v purpurea. (Variation.) Head purplish. *From . memory.* B. botrytis italica purpurea, Broccoli dicta. *Mill. Ph. diet. n. 3.1.* BRASSICA botrytis nigra. *Bry.* 76. 0 Napobrassica. Stem globular at the base. *Obs.* 7235. In a garden, not yet in flower.—*L. sp. . Hort. kerf.* » B. radice napiformi. *Boerh.* ii. 12. NAPOBRASSICA. *Berg.* 577. B. Napobrassica. *Hermbstaedi, account from in 'fhys. journ.* iv. 348-, *m gongylodes.* Stem before flowering cylindrical, with shoots from the end and sides. *Plants* raised from seed bought in Germany. *Frommemory.—L. sp.* 9S2 .".'. i.
B. caulorapa. *Bauh. J.* ii. 820. Stem and leaves.
B. caule rapum gerens. *Dod.* 614, *repr. in* erf. ii. 625,:.
Rapa, B. peregrina, caule rapum gerens. *Lob. ie. .* i. 246, #
Caulorapum rotundum. *Ger. by Johns.* 318.
B. raposa. *Dalech.* 522.
Caulorapa. *Lob. adv.* 92. No fig..
Caulorapum. *Cam. epit.* 251......
Leaves, cauline ones amplexicaul; margin entire and dentate. *Obs.* 7085. Specimen from Prof. Jos.
F. Jacquin.
BRASSICA gongylodes. *Boerh.* ii. 11.— *Berg.*
"579. *Spielm.* 46. .... i : ; 9. Style ensiform. L. '
B. oleracea styligera......, 4. BRASSICA Eruca. Leaves lyrate. Stem hirsute.
. Siliquae glabrous. *L. sp.* 932. *Gou. hort.* 333.
In corn fields near Montpelier.—*Donn* 87.
Eruca sylvestris. *Fuchs.* 264. c. 100, *repr. in* '
Sinapi alterum genus. *Fuchs.* 523. c. 205, *Sr cop. in*
Eruca, sive Rucula marina. *Trag.* 102, hairs omitted
and
Eruca major sativa annua, flore albo. *Bauh. J.* ii,
859. Cultivated in gardens.—Boer A. ii.

15. *Rati hist.* 806. '"''
Eruca saliva. *Dalech.* 619. *Dod. 696, repr. in Lob,* subhirtose. *Obs.* 8777. Specimen gathered in the Paris garden, $ *from L. mant.* 95, # Lour.
Hort. hew. ii. 403. *Lour.* ii. 485. S. siliquis glabris subarticulatis divaricatis, foliis in ferioribus lyrato-pinnatis auriculatis, superioribus lineari-lanceolatis integcrrimis. *Aid.* i. 23. t. 10.
Siliqua thrice as long as the style. *a lyrifolia.* Leaves lyrato-pinnate. *Obs.* 8777. *fi integrifolia.* Leaves entire. *From Lour.* S. indicum maximum, lactucac folio. *Tourn. hort.* 81. *Herrn, par. t.* 230, has siliquae 5 times as long as the style.
S. SINAPIS cernua. Siliquae glabrous, patulous. Radical leaf lvrate; terminal lobe very large, ovate, inciso-dentate. *Tkunb.jap.* 261;—*trav.* iii. 138.
679. RAPHANUS. Calyx closed. *Siliqua* not opening, terete, attenuate. *Obs.* 5178. L.
I. RAPHANUS salhus. Seeds in 2 rows. *Obs.* 5178.
In a garden.— *L. sp. 935. H. K.* ii. 405.
Gaertn. ii. 299. *t.* 143. *Lour. t.* 481. *Kroch.* ». 1103.
Leaves lyrato-pinnate, glabrous. Siliquae ventricose below. *Obs.* 5178.
RAPHANUS. *Pharm, suec.—Boecl. ap. Herrn.* 310. *Ploucq. bibl.* i. 194. 360. *Schoepf* 105.
Spielm. 67.
R. sativus. *Bry.* 40. 128. *Pears. R.* i. 57.
VOL. S. H h
Radish. *Mertens in ph. tr. ebr. by Hutt.* xiv.
404. *m fusiformis.* Root fusiform. *Obs.* 5178. RAPHANUS. *Berg.9S2. Chom.16.* R. minor oblongus. *Chom.* 227; *ruppl.* 75. *Schrod.* 660. R. hortensis. *Dale* 203. *Mill. Jos.* 368. *Rutty* 422. R. minor. *Geoffr. suite* ii. 187. Radiculac. *Murr.* ii. 321. iS *rotunda.* Root roundish. From *memory.* Turnep Radish. J/. X. ii. 405 H RAPHANUS. *Herm.* 309.-c&m. 195. *Schrod.* 660. » mot«. Root black. From memory.—*H. K.* ii. 405 *y* RAPHANUS niger. *Pharm. austriaco-prov.* 60. — *Berg.* 582. *Murr.* ii. 321. ScArod. 660. *Vog.* 206. J *oleiferus.* R. satmis y. Z- . *sp.* 935. RAPHANUS chinensis annuus oliferus. *Phys. journ.* xii. 93. 2.

RAPHANUS caudatus. Siliquae longer the stem. *From L. mant.* 95, *Sr—L. fd. fasc.* 19. *t.* 10. 3. RAPHANUS artkulatus. Siliquae articulated. *Obs.* 3822. In a corn field. R. Raphanistrum. *L. suec. n.* 612; *sp.935; am.* vi. 448. *t.* 5. at *p.* 450. *Bot. arr.* 715. *Krock. n.* 1104. *Smith brit.* 723. *Cow. hort.33i.* Near Montpelier. Raphanistrum Lampsana. *Gaertn.* ii. 30. f. 143. Raphanistrum siliqua articulate glabra majore et mi norc. *Tourn. part's.* 34. *Leaves* lyrato-pinnate and lyrate, hispid. *Siliquae* terete, glabrous, unilocular. *Obs.* 3822. ARMORACIA. *Dale* 203. *Schrod.* 538. *m Jlava.* Corolla yellow. *Obs.* 1544. L. & K. Raphanistrum. *Smith engl. t.* 856. *Mart. rust. t.7l.* Sinapis arvensis. *Fl. dan. t.* 678. Raphanistrum arvense, flore luteo. *Tourn. parts,* 35. Rapistrum flore luteo, siliqua glabra atticulata. *Rait hist.* 805; *syn.* 296. Raphanistrum segetum flore luteo vel pallido. *Vaill. parts.* 171. *Boerh.* ii. 21. Rapistrum alterum arvorum. *Park, theatr.* 863. /8 *tenosus.* Corolla yellow, with blackish veins.— *L. a.* R. Raphanistrum. *Curt. lond.* iv. 46. *t. 261. y ochroleucus.* Corolla straw-coloured, with blackish veins. *Obs.* 1544. Lampsana. *Cam. epit.* 233, *cop. in* Rapistrum album articulatum. *Park, theatr.* 863. «" albus. Petals white, with black veins. *Obs.* 1544. Raphanistrum siliqua articulata glabra majore et mi nore. *Rati syn.* 296. Raphanistrum arvense, flore albo. *Tourn. parts.* 35. *Vaill. paris.* 171. *Boerh.* ii. 21. Lampsana Plinii apula. *Col. ecphr.* i. *t.* 263. Rapistrum flore albo striate. *Bauh. J.* ii. 851. Lampsana flore melino. *Tab. ic.* 408. Rapistrum flore albo, erucae foliis. *Lob. ic.* i. 199, iiuuer fig. *repr. in* R. sylvestris. *Ger. by Johns.* 240.
Rapistrum album articulatum. *Raii hist.* 805.
680. CAKILE.
Sitiqua articulated, tetragonous; internodia not open ing, mono8permous and dispermous. *Obs.* 6146, *Gaerln.* ii. 287. *Tourn. cor.* 49. *t.* 483.
I. CAKILE pinnatifida. Leaves pinnatifid and linear.
Obs. 5146. Gathered by Mrs. S. Shore on the seashore near Bridlington in Yorkshire.—*Obs,* 7971. Specimen from

Leskc. C. maritima. *Scop. earn. n.* 844. *Roth germ. i.* 287; ii. *pars* ii. 117. *L. a Willd.* iii. 416. C. Serapionis. *Gaerln.* ii. 287. *t.* 141. *Lob. adv.* 77. No fig. *obs.* 110, *repr. in ic.* i. 223, cop. *in Dalech.* 1395, Eruca marina anglica. *Pari: theatr.* 821, Eruca, siliqua torosa nobis, C. Serapionis. *Hist, ox.* ii. *s.* 3. *t.* 6, *Sr* Sea Rocket. *Pet. herb. t.* 46. /. 6, # *repr. in* Eruca marina. *Ger. by Johns.* 248. *Raii hist.* 840; *s/n. ed.* ii. 176. Bunias Cakile. *L. suec. n.* 613; *sp.* 936; *mant.* 430. *Light f.* 363. *Bot. arr.* 716. *Smith engl. t.* 231; frit. 694. *FL dan. t.* 1168. C. maritima, angustiori folio. *Tourn. cor.* 49. *Boerk.* ii. 21. *Zannich.* 45. . 13. 177. 193. C. quibusdam, aliis Eruca marina, et Raphanus marinus. *Bat-h. J.* ii. 867. *Dill. ap. Raii syn.* 176. Crambe maritima foliis erucae latioribus, fructu has tiformi. *Tourn. inst.* 212.

Erucago maritima. *Magn. hort.* 74. Eruca maritima. *Dalech.* IS93, but the leaves represented as decompound like those of Selinum palustre. Eruca maritima italica, siliqua hastae cuspidi simili. *Magn. monsp.* 92. *Bauh. Casp. prodr.* 40, but the segments of the leaves attenuate, acute, *cop. in Hist. ox.* ii. 891. . 3. /. 6, *Sc* Eruca maritima italica. *Park, theatr.* 821.

Ideates, augles rounded. *Si/iquac,* 7 tenths of an inch long; infernodia 2, lower from 2 to 3 tenths of inch lung; obdeltoid, monospermous, upper inch long,rhombeo- ovate,tetragonous,slightly compressed, monospermous and dispermous. Seeds oblong, rufous *O's.* 7972. Specimen gathered at Ostend. CAKILE Serapionis. *Cam. hort.* 32. Eruca maritima. *Rutty* 182. 9. CAKILE sinuatifolia. Leaves crenafo-sinuate. *From Bunias Cakile. Vahl symb.* ii. 78. *L. tnant.* 430. e

C. aegyptiaca, I/, a WiUd. iii. 417, from authors.

Isatis aegyptia. *Forsk. aegyptiacoarab.* 121.

C. maritima ampliore folio. *Tourn. cor.* 49.

C. live Eruca marina latifolia. *Bauh. J.* ii. 868. Specimen gathered by Agerius on the shore of the Adriatic, growing with C. pinnatifida.— *Boerh.* ii. 21, (but the mark denoting it a native of Holland, seems to have been placed through inadvertence under n. 1 instead of n. 2.)

Raphanus siliquis ovatis angulatis raonospcrmis. *Gron. virg.* 98.
CAKILE. *Schotp/105.* 681. CLEOME. *Nectaria* 3, 1 at the 3 upper divisions of the calyx. *Petals* ascending. *Siliqua* unilocular, bivalve. *L. Vent. tabl.* iv. *t.* 15. *f.* 3. 1. CLEOME dodecandra. Stamina 12. Leaves ter nae. *L. sp.* 939 ? C. foribus octandris, foliis (ernatis. X. *zeyl. n.* 242? SiimpUtrum triphyllum pumilum glabrum, flosculo purpureo, siliqua membranacea. *Burm. J. zcyl.* 216. *t.* 100. / 1 *i* Flowers axillary, solitary. Sinapistrum indicum triphyllum, flore cameo, non spinosuiu. *Sloane cat.* 80; *hist. i.* 191. *t. l£l, f. 1.* Racem us terminal. Sinapistrum indicum triphyllum, siliqua maxima, flore albo. *Boerk.* i. 3071 *Flowers* axillary. *Calyx* tetraphyllous, pubescent; hairs globifcrous. *Petals* obovate, as long as the calvx, while. *Stamina* 12, as long as the catyx. *Filaments* filiform. *Pistil* sessile, a$ long as the stamina. *Germen* pubescent. *Style* ftmr times shorter than the germen. *Obs.* 8776? Specimen gathered in the Vienna garden. CLEOME dodecandra. *Coxe* 370. *Sckoepf 106.*

Calyx quadrifid. Stamina longer than the corolla.

2. CLEOME peniapkylta. Stamina inserted into the stipes of the germen. Leaves 'quinate. Stem unarmed. 06s. 7633. Specimen gathered by Broughton in Jamaica.i. *sp.* 938; *mant.%30. J acq. hort.* i. 9. *t.* 24. *Hort. Icew.* ii. 408. *Vent. tabl.* iv. 113. *t.* 15. /. 3. *A.* Flower. Capaveela. *Rheede* ix. 43. *t.* 24. CLEOME procumbens pentaphyllum, spica Ion giori terminal!. *Browne* 273. 488 Class 16. MONADELPHIA. *Order* 1. TRIANDRIA. 682. Aphyteia. *Style* 1. *Petals* 3. *Calyxiru-* fid. *Berry* poljspcrmous.
Tamarindus. 33.
Order 9.
TETRANDRIA.
683. Stemona. *Style I. Pttalsi.* Anther at lateral. *Berry* polyspennous. *from Lour, Order S.* PENTANDRIA.
Celosia. 208. Gomphrena. 209. Acbyranthes lappaca, 207, *i.* 686. Erodium. 684. Passiflora. 685. Melochia. *Style* 1. *Petals* 5. *Capsule* pentecoccous, rostrate. *Calyx* pentaphyllous. *Obs,* 6935.
Styles % *Petals* 5, inserted into the calyx. *Nectar ¡um* inserted into the calyx. *Berry* unilocular, polyspermous. *Obs.* 8182. *Styles* 5. *Petals* 5. *Calyx* single and double. *Capsule* quinquelocular. *From L. a Order* 4. HEXANDRIA. 687. Pimela. *Style* 1. *Petals* 3. *Drupe. From Lour. Order* 5. HEPTANDRIA. 686. Pelargonium. *Style* 1. *Petals* 5. *Capsule* pentecoccous, rostrate. *Co» lyx* quiuqucpartite; upper segment terminating below in a tube running down the peduncle. *Obs.* 5138. *Order* 6. OCTANDRIA. 689. PoLydALa. 690. Pistia. *Style* I. *Petals* 3, unequal, connected by the intervention of the filament *Calyx* pentahyllous. *Capsule* bilocular. *Obs.* £337. S/y/e 1. *Corolla* none. Ccpsa/e unilocular.

Order 7. DECANDRIA.
Cytisus nitidifolius.
1. *Style 1.* 693. Eryyhmna. ' *VexVlum* many times longer than the alae and carina. *Obs.* 8780. 691. Derri. *Legumen* membranaceum. Pe fob falcate at the base. *Lour.* 692. Abrus. 694. Spartium. 695. Genista 699. Lupinos. 698. Anthyllis. 700. Aracuis. 696. Ononis. 697. Cbotalaria. *Legumen* rhombic. *Stamina* 9. *Filament* cloven along the upper side. *Calyx* quadridentate. *Obs.* 8272. *Calyx* bifid above; lower lip quinquedentate at the end. *Stigma* villose. *Obs.* 3372. *Calyx* bilabiate; upper lip bifid, lower trifid. *Stigma* glabrous. *Obs.* 3705. *Legumen* coriaceous. *Antherae,* 5 oblong, 5 sound. *Legumen* roundish. *Calyx* turgid. *Legumen* not opening, disper mous. *Corolla* resupinate. *Legumen* turgid. *Filament* entire below. *Obs.* 4976. *Legumen* turgid. *Filament* cloven along the upper side. *Obs.* 0869. 2. *Styles* 5. 701. HxiGonia. *Drupe* monospermous. *Calyx* quinquepartite; segments unequal. *Petals* 5. *From £» a Willd.*

. *Order* 8. DODECANDRIA. 702. Sterculia. *Style* 1. *Corolla* none. *Calyx* single. *Capsules* 5, unilocular. *Order* 9. POLYANDRIA. 1. *Flowers complete. Getmen superior. Style 1. Petals* 4. *Calyx*

te-traphyllous. iVu/.
Style 1. *Corolla* quinquefid, *Legumen. From L. a Willi,*
Style I. *Petals* 5. *Calyx* single, truncate. *Capsule* unilocular, polyspermous. S/yfe 1. Pefflfe 5 and 7. Ca/j/jr poly phyllous. *Capsule, Style* 1. Prfak 1 and 5. Co /yx single, quinquefid and trifid. *Capsule* quiuquelocular.
705. Adahsonia. *Style I. Calyx* single. *Cap 7 It.* Mesua. 703. Inga. 704. Cako-likea. 715. Camellia. 706. Bombas. *sule* decemlocular, polyspermous, with a farinaceous pulp. *L. a mild. Style* multipartite and seTeral. *Calyx* single. *Capsules* several, unilocular; cells monospermous dispermous and trispermous. *Obs.* 7195. *Style* 1. *Petals* 5. *Calyx* double; outer trifid. *Capsule* trilocular and quadrilocular. *Style* 1. *Petals* 5. *Calyx* double; outer trifid. *Capsules* unilocular, monospermous. *Obs.* 6088. *Style* 1. *Petals* 5. *Calyx* double; outersexfidandseptemfid. *Capsules* unilocular, monospermous. *Obs.* 6043. *Style* 1. *Petals* 5. *Calyx* double; outer partite; segments 9 to 12. *Capsules* unilocular, monospermous. *Obs.* 5059. *Style* 1. *Petals* 5. *Calyx* double; outer mostly triphyllous. *Capsules* unilocular and bilocular. *Obs.* 4039. *Style* 1. *Petals* 5. *Calyx* double: outer with from 3 to many phylla and multipartite. *Capsule* quinquelocular, quinquevalve. ; f. *Flowers complete. Germen inferior.* 7IS. MeteoBus. *Style I. CoroUa* monopctalous. *Calyx* quadrifid. *Drupe* raonospermous. *From Lour.* 717. Bariungtonia. *Style* 1. *Calyx* diphyllous. *fetals.* 718. Gpstavia. *Style* I. *Calyx* quadrifid and sexfid. *Petals* 4 and 6. *Berry* dry, quadrilocular and quiiiquelocular, polyspermy ous. *L. a Willd.* 8. *Floxeers calycine.* 719. Cobdyla. *Style* 1. *Calyx* quadrifid. *Berry* unilocular, stipitate.
From Lour.
TRIANDRIA. 682. APHYTEIA. *Calyx* infundibuliform, trifid. *Petals* 3, inserted into the calyx, shorter than the calyx. *Germen* nearly inferior. *Berry* unilocular, polyspermoas. *Prom L.fil. suppl.* 48. I. APHYTEIA *Hydnora. L. Jil. suppl.* 301, TETRANDRIA.
683. STEMONA. *Calyx* none. *Petals* 4, erect. *Antherae* lateral. *Berry* unilocular, polyspermous. *Lour.* 1. STEMONA *ti &erosa. Lour.* ii. 490. UBIZJM polypoides. *Rumph.* v. 364. *t.* 129. PENTANDRI A. 684. PASSIFLORA. *Petals* 5. *Nectarium* annular, on the inside of th« calyx. *Germen* stipitate. *Berry* unilocular, polyBpermoui. *Obs.* 8182. From P. caeruka.— *L.* 1. *Leaves undivided.* L. 1. PASSIFLORA *maliformis.* Involucrum triphyl lous, larger than the flower. Leaves cordato-ovate, triplinervose; margin entire. *Obs.* 3505. In Lady Clifford's garden.—*L. a Willd.* iii. 608; *sp.* 1355. *Hort. hew.* iii. 806. *Andr. rep.* if. r. 217., P. foltis indivisis cordato-oblongis integerrimis, pe tiolis biglandulosis, involucris integerrimis. *L. am.* i. 254. *n.* 5. *t. f.* 5. P. foliis cordatis productis, petiolis biglandulis, frusta sphaerico, pericarpio dure. *Browne* 329. Granadilla, quae Clematitis indica latifolia, flore cla vato, fructu maliformi. *Boerk.* ii. 82. Clematis indica latifolia, flore clavato, fructu maliformi. *Plum. amer.* 67. *t.* 82. PASSIFLORA *maliformis. Bry.* 208. *Wright in med. journ.* viii. 274.
2. PASSIFLORA *quadrangularis.* Leaves entire at the margin. Calyx triphyllous, shorter than the corolla. Peduncle triquetrous. *From Sow. in tin. tr.* ii. *t.* 3. /. *a. L. sp.* 1356. *H. K.* iii. 506. *Jacq. amer.* 231. *t.* 143; 8w, 296.
P. foliis i'mplioribus cordatis, petiolis glandulis sex notatis, caulc quadrigono alato. *Browne* 327.
PASSIFLORA *hexangularis. Wright in med. journ.* viii. 274. 3. PASSIFLORA *laurifolia.* Leaves entire at the mar gin. Calyx triphyllous, as long as the corolla. *From Sow. in lin. tr.* ii. 24. *t.* 4./. *c. L. sp. 1356. Hort. hew.* iii. 307. *Jacq. amer. Svo,* 297; *hort.* ii. 76. r. 162. P. foliis indivisis integerrimis, involucris dentatu. *L. am.* i. 255. ». 6. /. *at p.* 278. /. 6.
P. foliis ovatis, petiolis biglandulis, bacca molli ovata. *Browne* 327. P. arbórea, laurinis foliis, americana. *Pltik. aim.* 282; *phyt. t.* 211./. 3. No fructifications. Clematis indica, l'indu citriformi, foliis oblongis.
Plum. amer. 64. *t.* 80. PASSIFLORA laurifolia. *Bry.* 209. *Wright in meajourn.* vi-ii. 274. 2. *Leaves hilobate.* L. 4. PASSIFLORA *Murucuja.* Leaves bilobate, with a muero in the middle of the sinus. Petioles without glands. Nectarium campanulate, truncate, entire at the margin. *Obs.* 8764. Specimen gathered by Dr. Wright in Jamaica, and from *L. a TVilld.* iii. 612; *sp.* 1357; *mant.* 492, *Sf Swarlz. obs.* 336. *Sal. W.* 66.
P. foliis bilobis obtusis basi indivisis, nectariis monophyllis. *L. am.* i. 257. *t. at p.* 278. /. *We*
P. foliis tenuioribus trinerviis bicornibus lunatis, sinu anteriori obtuso. *Browne* 328.
Clematis indica, flore puniceo, folio lunato. *Plum. amer.* 72. *t.* 87.
PASSIFLORA rubra. *Wright in med. journ.* viii. 275. 3. *Leaves trilobate.* L¡ 5. PASSIFLORA *nörmalis.* Leaves emarginate at *the* base; lobes linear, obtuse, divaricate; middlemost obsolete, mucronale. *L. sp.* 1357; *mant.* 492; *am.* v. 408. *Sal. R. hort.* 155. YOL. 3. I i
P. foliis trilobis, cruribus angustis oblongis, intermedia fere obsoleta *Browne* 328. COANENEPILL1S. *Hern.* 301. *t.* 6.
PASSIFLORA *lutea.* Leaves cordate, glabrous; lobes ovate,; petioles without glands. *L. sp.* 1358; *ma/it.* 492. IJort. *kew.* iii. 308. *J acq. coll.* ii. 282; *ic.* iii. *t.* 607. P. foliis trilobis cordatis aequalibus obtusis glabris integerrimis. *L. am.* i. 259. *n.* 13. *t. f.* 13. Clematis passionalis triphyllos, flore luteo. *Hist. ox. s.* 1. *t.* 2./. 3. Clematis, seu Flos passionb americana, lufeo flore. *Raii hist.* 651.
PASSIFLORA *lutea. Schoepf* ISO.
7. PASSIFLORA *incarnata.* Lobes of the leaves ser rate, equal. Petioles with 2 glands *H K* iii. 310. *L sp.* 1360; *mant.* 293. *Jacq. coll.* i. 107; *ic.* i. *t.* 167. P. foliis trilobis serratis. *L. am.* i. 264. «. 19. *t. f.* 19. *A. to E. Gron. virg.* HO. Granadilla hispanis, Flos passionis italis. *Col. op. Hern. t.* 889. *Boerh.* ii. 81. *Raii hist.* 649. Maraooc, sive Clematis virginiana. *Park. par.* 393. *t.* 395./. 7, *unit, in* Clematis trifolia, sive Flos passiouis. *Ger. by Johns.* 1592. Granadilla hederae similis. *Bank. J.* ii. 114. No fig. Granadilla. *Dalech.* 1918. No fig. PASSIFLORA incarnala. *Schoepf* 131.
Passiflora. *Vog.* 266.
685. MELOCHIA. *Calyx* single and double. *Petals* 5, patent. *Filaments* subu-

late. *Styles* 5. *Capsule* quinquelocular; cells monospermous and dispermous. *From L. a Willd. and a Schreb. L. m '* .

MELOCHIA *corchorifolia.* Flowers capitate. Heads
Sessile. Capsules roundish. Leaves snbeordate, sublobate. *L. 6 Murr.* 611; *sp.* 944. *Hort. hew.* ii. 413.

M. corchori folio. *Dill. horl.* 221. *t.* 176. /. 217.

MELOCHIA corchorifolia. *Lour.* ii. 494.
686. ERODIUM. *Calyx* pentaphyllous. *Petals* 5. *Nectaria* 10, 5 lanceolate alterating with the stamina; 5 glandular, at the base of the stamina. *Fruit* pentecoccous, rostrate; beaks of the seeds spiral, bearded on the inner side. *Obs.* 6935. 5007. *Lherit.* Filaments in some species distinct; 1. ERODIUM *moschalum.* Leaves pinnate; folioles incise, unequally serrate, mostly on short petioles. *Obs.* 7588. Specimen gathered near Stourbridge
'in Worcestershire.—*Hort. hew.* ii. 414. *Smith brit.* 728. *Lherit.*

Geranium moschalum. *L. sp.* 951. *Bot. arr.* 725.

Jaeq. bort. i. *t.* 55. *Smith engl. t.* 902. *Ger. by Johns.* 94J, cop. *in Park, thealr.* 709, *and repr. from*
Myrrhida Plinii. *Lob. obs.* 376, *which repr. in ic.* i.

658, Geranium supinum. *Dod.* 63. Geranium I. *Fuchs.* 208, *cop. in* Geranium moschatum minus. *Bauh. J.* iii. *b.* 479. Geranium moschatum, folio ad myrrhidem accedente, majus. *Bauh. J.* iii. *b.* 479. Geranium III Plinii. *Dalech.* 1277. *Pedicles,* hairs fusiform. *Obs.* 7588. GERANIUM moschatum. *Dale* 236. *Lew.* i. 465. *Linn.* 196. *Mill. Jos.* 213. *Rutty* 219. *Sckrod. app.* 8. *Vog.* 63.
HEXANDRIA. 687. PIMELA. *Calyx* trifid. *Petats* 3. *Drupe. Nut* unilocular bilocular and trilocular. *Lour.* 1. PIMELA *oleosa.* Nut unilocular. Leaves glabrous.

Peduncles lateral. *From Lour.* Canarium microcarpum. *L. a lFilld.* iv. 760, *from* Nanarium minimum, sive oleosum. *Rumph.* ii. 162.

/. 54. PIMELA oleosa. *Lour.* ii. 496. 2. PIMELA *nigra.* Nut mostly bilocular. Leaves glabrous, ttacemi lateral. *From Lour.* ii. 495. Canarium sylvestre. *L. a Willd.* iv. 760, *from* CANARIUM sylvestre alteram, sive Nanarium
Nanery. *Rumph.* ii. 155. /. 49.
3. PIMELA *alba.* Nut trilocular. Leaves scabrous.

Racemi mostly terminal, crowded. *From Lour.*
Canarium sinense, seu Cana. *Rumph.* ii. 154.

Arbor excelsa e China heic introducta. *Thanh, jap.*
368.

PIMELA alba. *Lour.* ii. 495.
HEPTANDRIA. 688. PELARGONIUM. *Calyx* quinquepartite; upper segment ending below in. a tube running down the peduncle. *Corolla* pentapetalous, irregular. *Filaments* 10, unequal, 3 and 5 without anthc-rae. *Fruit* pcntecoccous, beaked; beaks of the seeds spiral, bearded on the inner side. *Lkerit. 1. Leaves* entire. 1. PELARGONIUM *acetosum.* Leaves cuneato-obovatc, crcnate, glabrous. Petals linear. Umbels with few flowers. Stem woody. *H. K.* ii. 430. *Curt. mag. t.* 103. *Lherit..*

Geranium acetosum. *L. sp.* 947.
GERANIUM africanum frutescens, folio crasso et glauco acetosae sapore. *Commet. Casp. prael.* 54. *t.* 4.—*Carta,* i. 411. # 2. PELARGONIUM *peltatum.* Leaves quinquelobafe, peltate, glabrous, fleshy; margin entire. Branches angular. Umbels with few flowers. Stem fleshy. *Obs.* 5138. In a garden.—*//. K.* ii. 428. *Lherit.*
Geranium peltatum. *L. sp.* 947. *Curt. mag. t.* 20.

Geranium calycibus monophyllis, foliis quinquclobis integerrirais glabris peltatis. *Mill. Ph. ic.* 94. *t.* 140. *Leaves* opposite, with a brownish purple zone towards the base. *Umbels with 3 flowers. Obs.* 5138.

GERANIUM africanum, foliis inferioribus asari, supcrioribus staphidis agriac maculatis splendentibus et aceiosae sapore. *Commel. Casp. prael.* 52. *t.2.—Carth.* i. 411. OCTANDRIA, 689. POLYGALA. *Calyx* pentaphyllous and triphyllous. *Petals 3,* connected by the intervention of the filament; middlemost variously divided. *Capsule* bilocular; ' cells monospermous. *Obs.* 2337. 5438. *L. 1. Calyx* pentaphyllous, 3 of the phylla larger. Middlemost segments of the corolla laciniate. 1. POLYGALA *amara.* Flowers racemose. Stems nearly erect. Radical leaves obovate, larger than those above. *L. sp.* 987.

P. buxi minoris folio, florc caeruleo. *Vaill. paris.* 161. *t. 32. f.* 2. POLYGALA amara. *Collin ols.* ii. 152. *Coste # Willem. in med. comment,* v. 298. *Krock. n.* 1142.

Lew. disp. by Dune. 345. *Murr.* ii. 445. *Quar. anim.* 80. 86. 87. 131. *Slollmed.* ii. 27. 181; *aph.*

». 192. Polygala. *Pharm. austriacoprov.* 55.—*Stoll med.* i. 136; ii. 96.98. 301. 324.- 369; iii. 78. 84. 94. Senega nostras. *Carth.* ii. 438. *Schreb. ap. Linn.* 200.

. POLYGALA *vulgaris.* Middlemost lobe of the corolla laciniate. Flowers racemose. Stems herbaceous, simple, ascending. Leaves lineari-lanceolate. *Obs.* 2337. In pastures.—*//, suec. n.* 632; *sp.* 986 (3. *Ft. dan. t.* 516. *Bot. arr.* 754. *Wale. t. Smith engl. t.* 76; *brit.* 752.
Polygalon. *Trag.* 571.

Polygalon multis. *Bauh. J.* iii. 386.
Flos ambarvalis. *Dod.* 253, *repr in*
P. rccentiorum. *Lob. obs.* 228; ic. i. 416, *8r*

P. purpurea. *Ger. by Johns.* 564, # *cop. in*

P. minor. *Par, theatr.* 1332.

Alsine major repens perennis. *Bauh. J.* iii. 362, the name and descr. belonging to a different plant.)

Polygala. *Raii syn.* 287; *hist.* 1335.
Flowers 3 tenths of an inch long. *Obs.* 2337.— *Corolla* monopetalous, not annular at the base, *Obs.* 7066. In sand, between Stafford and Weston. POLYGALA vulgaris. *Duham. in ac. sc. abr. by Southw.* iii. 297, *and account from in med. ess.* vi. 377. *Krock. n.* 1141. *Lew.* ii. 242. *Jtfurr.* ii. 444.

Polygala. *Dale* 196. *Geoffr. suite* ii. 31. *Lew. disp. by Dune.* 346.
3. POLYGALA *panieulata.* Racemi naked. Stems herbaceous, erect, branched above. Leaves linear. *L. sp.* 987. *Swartz. obs.* 272.*t.* 7.*f.* 2. POLYGALA herbacea minor erecta, foliis linearibus, spica multiplici terminali foliosa. *Browne* 287. 2. *Calyx triphyllous* 4. POLYGALA *dixersijolia. Swarlz. O's.*

273. *L, sp.* 988. Genistae affinis anonyma arbor, florc coluteae, buxi folio. *Sloane cat.* 141; *hist.* ii. 32. *t*, 170. /. 2. In fruit. POLYGALA fruticosa, foliis glabris ovatis, cap sulis subrotundis compressis emarginatis, racemis minoribus laxis axillaribus. *Browne* 287. *t*. 5. *f.* 3. 4.

3. *Cayx not examined.* 5. POLYGALA *Senega.* Flowers beardless, spicafe. Stems herbaceous, erect. Leaves lanceolate. *Obs.* 2336. Specimen gathered by Bartram in North America, without fructifications.—*L. sp.* 990. *Bot. mag. t.* 1051. *Mill. Ph. diet. ed.* vii. *t.* 5,*repr. in ed.* viii. *at art.* Polygala; $ *abr. by Trew qp. commerc. norimb pro ann.* 1741. *p.* 369.1. 4. *f.* 1. 2. *Ilort. lew:* Hi. 6. *Walt.* 178. *Woodv.* ii. 253. *t.* 93. *Thornt.* 629. P. floribus iinberbibus spicatis, caule erecto herbaceo simplicissimo, foliis lato-lanceolatis. *Gron. virg.* 103.

P. caule simplici erecto, foliis ovato-lanceolatis allernis integerrimis, racemoterminatrice erecto. *Gron. virg. ed.* i. SO.

Senega. *L. am.* ii. 139. *t.* 2. *at* p. 141./. I. 2.

SENEKA. Root. *Pharm. lond.*—*Archer, account from in phys.journ.* i. 83. 106, *chir. rev.* vi. 194, *Sf Und.* i. 336. *Bree* 258. *Cull.* ii. 532. *Darw.* ii. 19s. *Geoffr.* ii. 137. *Haen* i. 357. *Hill* 630.

Lew. ii-240. *Mackensie in vied. obs.* ii. 288.

Monro iii. 257. *Perch. T. in med. journ.* iv. 67, *repr. in Perciv. T.* ii. 395. *Und.* i. 338. Seneca. *Bang in act. haun,* i. 20. 111. 112.257.

Callisen ib. 73. *Chalm.* ii. U5. *Dara.* ii. 392.

Lem. Duham. 8f Juss. account from in med. ess, vi. 377.

Senecka. *Spielm.* 581.

Senega. *Pharm. lond. noviss.*—Bang in *act. haun.*

i. 239. 254. 255; ii. 41. 51. *Berg.* 595. *Carth.* ii. 435. *Linn.* 200. *Murr.* ii. 436. *Ploucq. bibl.* i.

661. *Schoepf* 110. Fog. 226.

P. Senega. *Pharm. edin.*— *Bart.* 25. 33. 35. 48.

Cappel, account from in med. rev. iv. 44. *Lew.*

disp. by Dune. 284. *Massie, account from in chir. rev.* xiv. 63. *Murr. J.* i. 331; ii. 46. *Pears. R.* i. 152. 230. 256.

P. Seneca. *Archer, account from in ann. med.* iv.

511, *and med. rev.* iii. 426. *Scott. J. ib.* 313.

P. virginiana, *Lem. Juss. and Bouxart in ac. sc.*

abr. by Southw. iii. 297.

Rattlesnake root. *Tcnnent dis. of Virginia, and*

account from in med. ess. vi. 376.

Senega Rattlesnake root. *Graing.* 66.

Seneka Snakeroot. *Rush* v. 176.

6. POLYGALA *theczans.* Flowers beardless. PeduiK cles uniflorous. Stem fruticose. Leaves alternate,

lanceolate. *L. mant.* 260.

P. frutescens, lavandulae folio viridi, flore caeruleo.

Burm. J. zeyl. 195. *t.* 85.

POLYGALA theczans. *Burm. N. ind.* 154.

690. PISTIA. *Calyx* tubuloso-cucullate, lingulnte. *Corolla* none. *Filament* inserted into the side of the calyx. *Antherne* 3 to 8. *Style* I. *Capsule* unilocutar, polyspermous. *From Swartz. L.* 1. PISTIA *Stratioles. L. sp.* 1S65; *mant.* 495. Plantago aquatica. *Rumph.* vi. 177. *t.* 74. /. 2. STRATIOTES. *Dalc* 267. *m obovatifo lia.* (Variation.) Leaves obovate. From P. Stratiotcs. *J acq. amer.* 234. *t.* 148; 8ro 303, Zala asiatica. *Lour.* ii. 492, $ Prstia. *Browne* 329. Zoe/7. 281. Lenticula palustris sexta vel aegyptiaca, sive Stratioles aquatica foliis sedo majore latioribus. *Sloane cat.* 11; *Aw,* i. 15. /. 2. /. 2. 0 ellipticifolia. (Variation.) Leaves elliptic. From

P. Stratiotes. *Swartz. obii* 343, # Hayhalem elmaovi. /p. aeg. /o/. 41. *p.* 2, *cop.* iVi y//p. « Fs/. ii. 51. *t.* 36, Stratiotes aquatica vera Dioscoridis, et aegyptiaca.

Park, theatr. 1249, lower fig. Sr Stratiotes aegyptia. *Bauh. J.* iii. 787, lower fig,— *Raii hist.* 1324. *Bank. J.* iii. 787, upper fig. *cop. from* Stratiotes aversis foliis. *Alp. aeg. fol.* 42. p. I, which *cop. in Alp. a Vesl.* ii. *t.* 37. DECANDRIA. 691. DERRIS. *Calyx* quinquecrenate, coloured. *Petals* ungues filiform. *Legumen* oblong, membranaceous. *Lour.* 1. DERRIS *pinnata.* Leaves pinnate. *From Lour.* ii. 526. 692. ABRUS. *Calyx* quadridentate; uppermost tooth broadest. *Filaments* 9. *Stigma* obtuse. *Obs.* 8272. i. 1. ABRUS *precatorius. L. a Murr.* 641. *Hort. Iceu.* iii. 7.

Glycine Abrus. *L. sp.* 1025; *mant.* 442.

Glycine scandens, foliolis pinnatis, spicis nodosii axillaribus. *Broome* 297.

Phascolus arborescens alatus et volubilis major orientals, fructu coccineo hilo nigro notato. *Pluk. aim.* 294; *phyt. t.* 214. /. 5. In fruit.

Fbaseolus glycyrrhizites, folio alato, piso coccineo atra macula notato. *Sloane cat.* 70; *hist.* i. 180. *t.* 112 *f.* 4. 5. 6. A. frutex. *Rumph.* v. 57. /. 32. Abrus. *Alp. aeg. fol.* 32, *cop. in* Phaseolus ruber, Abrus. *Alp. a Vest.* ii. 40. *t.* 22.

No fructifications. Konni. *Jiheede* vi- ii. 71. *t.* 39. Vicia africana. *Ctus. exot.* 87, *cop. in* Arachus indicus, sive africanus. *Park, tkeatr.* 1071, Anastatica. *Gent. mag. for* 1791; lxi. 25. *t.* 3. *f.* 1, Pisum americanum coccineum, aliis A. et idem nigrum. *Bauh. J.* ii. 263. /. 2. In fruit.—/. 1.

legumen and smls con. *from* Pisum coccineum amcricum. *Lob. obs.* 516, which *tepr. in ic.* ii. 67, *Sf cop. in* Pisum americum. *Dalech.* 451, Aracbi indici rubri siliqua cum semine. *Parle. tkeatr.* 1072, *Sf* Arachus indicus. *Gent. mag.* Ixi. 25. *t.* 3. *f.* 2. Guiney Peas. *Grew. mm.* 233. *Leaves* pinnate; folioles elliptico-oblong, mucronate. *Spikes,* lower axillary, upper terminating lateral branches. *Calyx* pubescent; uppermost tooth the shortest, obscurely emarginate; lowermost somewhat longer the rest. *Obs.* 8272. Specimen gathered by Brougbton in Jamaica. ABRUS. *Dale217. SchoepflU.* A. pfecatprius. *Wright in med. journ.* viii. 257. Wild Liquorice. *Graing.* 24. 69S. ERYTHRINA. *Vexillum* several times longer than the alae and carina. *Obs.* 8780, from E. herbacea.—*L*.

1. ERYTHRINA *orienlalis.*—Leaves ternate, unarmed.
Stem arboreous, aculeate. Calyces spathaccous.
WiUd.—Murr.
E. indica *L. a. Willd.* iii. 913.
Kuara. *Bruce* v. 65. *t.* Petioles aculeate.
ERYTHRINA Corallodendron. £. q. 995 A—
Lout. ii. 519.

. 694. SPARTIUM. *Calyx* bifid with obliquely rounded segments; lower lip quinquedentate at the end. *Stigma* longitudinal, villose. *Obs.* 3372, *L.* . i 1.
SPARTIUM *junceum.* Branches terete, opposite, with flowers at the end. Leaves lanceolate. *L. sp.* 995. *Hort. hew.* iii. *10. Curt. mag. l.* 85. *Host* 388. Near Trieste.—Co«. *hort. 355.* Near Montpelier. S. dioscorideum hispanicum ct norbonense vimineum majus. *Lob. adv.* 408. No fig. S. dioscorideum narbonense et hispanicum. *Lob. obs. 532, repr. in ic.* ii. 91, j.

Genista italica. *Dod.* 749, *Sr*
Genista hispanica. *Ger. by Johns.* 1313, *cop. in*
Spartum hispanicum frutex vulgare. *Park, theatr.*
231, *Sf abr. in*
Spartum hispanicum. *Park. par. t.* 443. /. 4.
Flowers represented as lateral. *Maxpoto&ov. Ren.* 34. *t. S3.* Middlemost flowering branch flexuose. S. Dioscoridis. *Dalech.* 168. GENISTA juncea. *Scop. earn. n.* 870. *Bauh. J.* i. b. 395. (The fig. a different species.)—*Chom.* 248. Genista hispanica. *Dale* 341. *Geoffr.* iii. 519. Genista. *Pharm. austriaco-prov.* 40.
695. GENISTA. *Calyx* bilabiate; upper lip with 2 divisions, lower with 3. *Corolla* papilionaceous; petals patent, leaving the stamina and pistil uncovered. *Stigma* glabrous. *Obs.* 3705. *L.* 1, *Unarmed. Leaves simple, I.* GENISTA *tinctoria.* Leaves lanceolate; margin pubescent. Branches terete, striate, erect. *Obs.* 4571. Near Chesterfield.—*L. sp. suec. n.* 634 *sp.* 998. *Huds.* 311. *Smith brit.* 754; *engl. t.* 44. *Bot. arr.* 758. *Dod.* 750, *cop. in ed.* ii. 763, # cop. /toot Tinctorius flos. *Fuchs.* 768. c. 312, *which cop. in Bauh. J.* i. 6. 391, *Sf Dalech.* 175, 4-impr. in Ferula. *Trag.* 604. Genistella tinctoria. *Rail syn.* 474. Genista tinctoria germanica. *Tourn. parts.* 270. *Vaill. paris.* 78. (Genistella infectoria vulgi. *Lob. obs.* 531, repr. *in tc.* ii. 89, G, tinctoria vulgaris. *Clus. hist.* i. 101, *Sf* Genistella tinctoria. *Ger. by Johns.* 1316, is G. germanica.) *Leaves* 2 tenths of an inch broad. *Calyx* obsoletely bilabiate, the fissure between the 2 upper and 3 lower segments being scarcely deeper than the fissure between the 2 upper segments; segments triangularisubuiate, straight; upper lip bipartite; lower lip tripartite; segments narrower than those of (he upper lip, lowermost subulate and narrower than the intermediate ones. *Legumen* linear, compressed, with a short mucro at the end, with protuberances from th» seeds. *Ols.* 4571. GENISTELLA. *Dale* 341. Genista. *Berg.* 598. *Krock. n.* 1148. *Linn.* 202. Fog. & Genet. *Odhelius, account from in med. comment.* i. 373. 2. *Unarmed. Leaves simple and ternate. .*
GENISTA *scoparia.* Branches with acute angles.
Leaves ternate aud simple. Flowers lateral. Three minute bracteae on the peduncles. Style spiral.
Obs. 3705. Near Chesterfield. Spartium scoparium. *L. succ. n.* 633; *sp.* 996. *Bot. arr.* 756. *Curt. lond. y.* 52. *t. Smith brit.* 753. *Hort. hew.* iii. 12. *Fl. dan. t.* 313. *Huds.* 310. *Lightf.* 382. *Woodv.* ii. 243. /. 89. *Thornt.* 651. Cytiso-Genista scoparia vulgaris, flore luteo. *Vaill. paris.* 45. Cytisus scoparius vulgaris,flore luteo. *Tourn. paris.* 429. G. angulosa trifolia. *Rati hist.* 1723; *syn.* 474. *Bauh. J.* i. 6. 388, *cop. from* Genista. *Fuchs.* 219. *fol. ed. which cop. m* 218. *c* 79, *8t abr. in Trag.* 961. *Riv. tetr. t.* 65. /. 1. *Ger. by Johns.* 1311, *repr. from* G. cum rapo *Dod.* 749, *which repr. in* G. scoparia vulgi. *Lob. ic.* ii. 89, *cop. in* G. vulgaris. *Park, iheatr.* 229, $ *repr. in* Spartium. *Lob. obs.* 531; *adv.* 407. Peduncles solitary, axillary, glabrous, as long as the leaves. Bracteae 3, ovato-lanceolate, 2 on one side of the peduncle, about the middle, the 3rd underneath and below. *Calyx* bilabiate; lips ovate; upper slightly bifid at the end; lower slightly trifid; middlemost segment projecting. *Petals* of the carina distinct and slightly coherent by a villose margin. *Stamina* monadelphous. *Style* thrice as long as the germen, at first ascending, afterwards recur jate, sometimes spiral, villose and filiform below, towards the end lanceolate canaliculate, and glabrous. *Stigma* simple. *Legumina* flat, oblongo-lunate, decurvate, villose at the margin. *Obs.* S705. GENISTA. Top. Seed. *Pharm. lond.* —*Chom.* 75. *Cull.* ii. 534. *Dale* 342. *Ilerm.* 320. *Hill* S96. *Lew.* i. 458. *Meadmon.* ii. 18. 19. *Mill. Jos.* 210. *Monro* iii. 115. *Murr.* ii. 360. *Jlutty* 216. *Schrod.* 595. *Spielm.* 652. *Swict.* iv. 257.
Vog. 62. Spartium. Tops. *Pharm. lond. no-ciss.* Spartium scopariuin. Tops. *Pharm. edin.*—*Krock. n.* 1146. *Lew. disp. by Dune.* 307. *Murr. J.* i. 304. *Pears. It.* i. 210. G. vulgaris. *Geoffr.* iii. 516. G. angulosa et scoparia. *Chom.* 248; *suppl.* 84. 3. *Unarmed. Leaves ternate.* 3. GENISTA *canariensis.* Folioles obovate, pubescent underneath; hairs patulous. Branches angular. Peduncles terminal,multiflorous. *Obs.* 8273. Specimen gathered in FothergilFs garden.— *L. sp.* 997. *Ilort. Jcew.* iii. 13. ' Cytisus canadensis sempervirens et incanu»-*Commel. Casp. horl.* ii. 103. f.1 52. From the Canaries.

Cytisus canariensis, flore candido et citrino. *Seb.* ii. 6. i. 4./.6. 6.

Cylisus canariensis microphallus angustifolius prorsus incanus. *Pluk, aim.* 128; *phyt. t.* 277. /. 6.

Cytisus I. *Otts. hisp.* 191, *repr. in hist.* i. 94. Habit well expressed, but the shape of the leaves corresponds better with G. candicans.

RHODIUM. *Pharm, austriaco-prov.* CO. *suec.* —*Berg.* 597. *Linn.* 201. *Monro* iii. 233.

Lignum Rhodium. *Carth.* iii. 200. *Geoffr.* ii. 218. *Herrn.* 231. *Lew.* ii. 62; *disp. by Rather.* 185. *Murr.* ii. 363. *Rutty* 285. *Schrod.* 661. *Spielm.* 347.

Lignum Aspalathi. *Dale* 345. *Mill. Jos.* 58. (mispr. Asphaltum Lignum.)

Âspalathus roseus. *Alst.* ii. *36.*

Rosewood. *Neum.* ii. 212.

696. ONONIS. *Filament* without any fissure at the base. *Calyx* quinquciid. *Legumen* tuTgid, unilocular. *Obs.* 4976.

4977. 5249. *L.* In O. Natrix, rotundilolia, arvensis, and probably all the species, uppermost filament readily separable from the rest. 1. *Peduncles cbracteale. t.* ONONIS *arvensis.* Flowers solitary. Leaves ter nate, upper simple; folioles oblong and oval.
Branches unarmed. Corolla one third longer than the calyx. *Obs.* 4976. Near Chesterfield on gritstone.—*L. nat.* ii. 478; *a Murr.* 651; *a Reich,* iii. 424 *a. Smith brit.* 758 *a. Bot. arr.* 763. *Gou. hort.* 359. Near Montpelier. O. inermis arvensis. *Ihids.* 312. O. mitis. *Mill. Ph. diet. n.* 2, who cultivated it bj seeds, and never observed it io have any spines. O. florihus fere sessilibus solitariis lateralibus, rami iuermibus. *Gudt.* i. 237. (The descr. belongs to n. 2, and that of n. 2 to n. 1.) Anonis spinis carens purpurea. *Itupp. ab Hall.* 265. *Boerh.* ii. 33. In Holland. O. purpurea, sine spinis. *Bauh. J.* ii. 394, Gain.
ered by Agerius in Sclavonia. No fig. Anonis spinosa, flore purpureo, denuc d' epines. *Vaill. par is.* 13. Anonis n«n spinosa purpurea. *Rait syn.* 332. ,AnonTs nostras vulgaris non spinosa purpurea. *Rail hist.* 957, under n. 2.
Branches villose. Folioles mostly retuse, hirsute With globiferous hairs. *Calyx* semiquinquepartite; hairs with oval heads; segments lanceolato-ensiform, With 5 and C ribs. *Filaments* monadelphous, without any fissure below, uppermost separable without laceration from the rest. *Style* attenuate, glabrous, permanent, that of the legumen deflex, adpressed. *Stigma* simple. *Legumen* oval, with from 1 to 3 seeds. *Obs.* 4976. *t Native* of Sclavonia, France, and Britain, on gravel marie gritstone and limestone. ANONIS spin is carens purpurea. *Rutty* 30. . ONONIS *spinosa.* Flowers mostly solitary. Leaves feniate, upper simple. Branches spinose. Corolla twice as long as the calyx. *Obs-*4977. Specimen gathered at Winkburn in Nottinghamshire, on red clay.—*Uvds.* 312. *hot. on.* 7(W. Stouton com. toon, 4 miles south of Worcester, on red clay. —*£. nunc. n.* 637(3; *sp.* 1006/3. *Murr. op. L a Jfurr.* 651, from Retz. scand. but the reference omitted.—*Willd, ber.* 233. *Krock. n.* 1151. *Fl. dan. t.* 783.

O. arrensis. *L. a Reich,* iii. 424 iS. *Smith engl. t.* 682; *brit.* 758 £. *Reich, franc. n.* 502.
A. spinosa, (lore purpureo et albo. *Rupp. ab Hall.* 265.
Anonis spinosa fruticosa erecta, flore purpureo. *Vaill. paris.* 13,
Anonis spinosa, flore purpureo. *Tourn. parts.* 53. *Raiisyn.* 332; *hist.* 957. Resta bovis. *Trag:* 869, *imit. from* Anonis. *Fuchs.* 60. *fol. ed. cop. in* 60. *c.* 18. *Dod.* 731, *repr. in*
Anonis, sive Resta bovis. *Ger. by Johns.* 1322, # *cop. in*
Anonis aut O. spinosa, flore purpureo. *Park, thcatr.* 994.
Anonis, sive Resta bovis vulgaris purpurea spinosa. *Bauh. J.* ii, 391. (The fig. Epimedium alpinum.)
Epimedium quorundam. *Bauh. J.* ii. 391. (The name and descr. Epimedium alpinum.)
Anonis spinosa. *Besl. aest. ord.* 10. *foL* 2. *f.* 8.
Branches villose. Folioles oval, often refuse, nearly glabrous; hairg few, globiferous. *Flowers* solitary, rarely geminate. *Calyx* deeply quinquefid; hairs with oval heads; segments ensiform, nearly equal, with 5 and 6 ribs. *Filaments* monadelphous, without any fissure below. *Style* attenuate, glabrous. *Stigma* simple. *Obs.* 4977. ONONIS spinosa. *Monro* iii. 188. Ononis. *Pharm. suec.*—*Berg.* 599. *Herm.* 92. *Lew.* ii. 160; *disp. by Dune,* 344. *Linn.* 202. *Murr.* ii. 365. *Schrod.* 639. *Spielm.* 566. *Fog.* 110. 220. Anonis. *Alst.* i. 368. *Dale* 227. *Geoffr.* iii. 98. *Mill. Jos.* 41. % Anonis spinosa, flore purpureo. *Chotn.* 220; *suppl.* 70. *Rutty* 30. , ",'..-.. ',' ip"' '.igkf. i-wi;A; 697. CROTALARIA. *Legumen* inflated. *Filaments* connate, with a fissure on the upper side. *Obs.* 6869. *L.* 1. CROTALARIA *retusifolia.*— Leaves oblong, cuneiform, retuse. Racemi terminal. *L.*
C. retusa. *L. a Willd.* iii. 976 ; *sp.* 1004. *Hort. l.v:.* iii. 18.
C. asiatica, floribus luteis, folio singulari cordiformi. *Herm. hort,* 200. *t.* 201.
Tandale-Cotti. *Itheede* ix. 45. . 25. CROTALARIA major. i?«n/pA. v. 278. f. 96. 698. ANTHYLLIS. Filament clavate,

cuspidate. *Calyx* slightly bilabiate. *Legnmen* covered by the calyx. *Obs.* 3331. 7434. *L.* 1. Herbaceous, *L. 1.* ANTHYLLIS *pubescent.* Leaves pinnate; terminal foliole generally larger. Heads 2 and 3together.
Stem and petioles pubescent; hairs adpressed.
Obs. 3831. Pastures about Chesterfield. A. Vulneraria. *L. suec. n.* 638; *sp.* 1012. *Asson.* (577. *Roth. germ.* i. 303. *Smith brit.* 759; *engl. t.* 104. *Bot. arr.* 765. *Krock. n.* 1154. *Gou.hort.* 361. Near Montpelier...:i..1
Vulneraria Anthyliis. *Scop. earn.* «. 779.., Vulneraria rustica. *Bauh. J.* ii. 362. *Rai-syn.* 325. *Tourn. paris* 174. *Vaill.paris.* 205. A. lenti similic. *Dod* 542, *repr. in* A. leguminosa. *Ger. by Johns.* 1240, (mispr. 1204.) *Calj/x* slightly bilabiate; upper lip semibifid, lower trifid. *Stamina* monadelphous. *Filaments* clavate and inflated at the end. *Germen* stipitate, dispermous. *Style* thrice as long as the germen. *Stigma* simple, obtuse. *Obs.* 3831.. ,-., '. '.
Native qf Europe rom Spain tq Sweden, nnd of Britain in pastures on chalk limestone gritstone and basaltes....,,;..-.....
VULNERARIA. *Dale* 221. *Geoffr. suite in.* 417..-.-.. 2. Calyces bract cate. 2. LUPINUS *varius.* Flowers in half whirls. Upper lip of the calyx bifid, lower mostly tridentate. *L. sp.* 1015. *Hort. kev.* iiu 28, *Gou. hort.* 362.
Near Montpelier. L. sylvestris, florc oaerulea. *Boerh.* ii. 48. *Rail eur.* 172. About Messina, L. caeruleus minor. *Ran hist.* 907. *Park. par.* 335. No fig. L. silvestris, purpureo flore, semine rotundo yario.
Bauh. J. ii. 290. *Magn. monsp.* 167. L. segetum silvestris, flore purpureo. *Lob, adv.* 396, *cop. in ic.* ii. 64, *which repr. in* L. flore caeruleo. *Get. by Johns.* 1217, *Sf cop. in jL* minimus caeruleus. *Park, theatr.* 1074. LUPINUS sylvestris. £a/ e219. L. sylrestris, flore caeruleo. *Rutty* 295. L. s.ylrestiis, purpureo flore, semine rotundo yario majore. *Boecl. ap. llerm.* 424. 700. ARACHIS, Calyx bilabiate. Corolla resupinate. *Lcgumen* torose. *Obs.* 8370, *Sr from L.* 1. ARACHIS *hypogaea. L. sp.* 1040; monf. 443. /Tort, *kew.* iii. 27. Arachidna

quadrifolia villosa, flore luteo. *Ehret t.* 5./. 3, in flower; *t.b.f. the last.* Fruit. Cbamaebalanus japonica. *Rumph.* y. 426. f. 156. /.2.
Arachidna indhe utriusque, tetraphylla. *Herm. prodr.* 314. *Sloane cat.* 72. Senna fetraphylla, sive Absi congener hirsuta mader aspatensis, folliculos sab terra condens. *Pluh. aim.* 341; *phyt.* r.60,/. 2. Mundubi. *Marcgr. bras.* 37, repr. in *Worm.* 207, and *Pis. ind.* 256, the 2 inner of the 3 lower figures *cop. from* Manobi. *Worm.* 208. Arachus upogaios americanus. *Park, theatr.* 1069.
t. 1070, the separate lcgumina. *Legumina* dispermous. *Obs.* 8370. From Jamaica. ARACHIS. *Broicne* 295, occasionally cultivated in Jamaica and the seeds frequently imported thither from Affica. —*Brozonrigg.in ph. tr. abr. by Butt.* xii. 665. *Schoepf* 113. A. hypogaea. *Bry.* 298. *Wright in med. journ.* vjji. 225, Pindals. *Long* iii. 788. 701. HUGQNIA. *Calyx* quinquepartite; segments unequal. *Petals* 5. *Styles* 5. *Drupe* monospermous. *JYut* striate, mostly decemlocular. *L. a Willd. L.* 1. HUGONIA *inlegerrima.* Leaves entire at the margin. *From* ,..'./.
H. Mystax. *L. sp.* 044; *a Willd.* iii. 694.
Frutex baccifer malabaricus, fructu caly culato rotundo monopyreno. *Raii hist.* 1570.
MODERA-CANNJ. *Rheede* ii. 29. *t.* 19. ' DODEC ANDRI A. 702. STERCULIA. *Calyx* with 5 divisions. *Corolla* none. *Stamina* and pistils stipitate. *Style* 1. *Stigma* bifid and quinquelobate., *Capsules* 5, unilocular, opening on the inn side. *From Roxb. and from Aubl. Sf Cav. in Juss. Sf L. a Schreb. L.* Some flowers with only the.rudiment of a gerraen. *From Roxb.* 1. STERCULIA *Balqngjias. r* Leaves ovato-lanceo late. Capsules obova'te.' '£ a WUld.ii.B72; sp. USO.—Forst.G. esc.* 55. Clompanus minor. *Rumph.* Hi. 169. . 107. Cavalam. *ttheede.* i. 89. (where for fig. 50 read 49) r. 49, /
Arbor siliquosa malabarica, pluribus ad singulos flores lobis. *Rati hist.* 1754.
2. STERCULIA urens. , Leaves cordate, quinquelo bate. Calyces semiquinqaefid. *From Roxb.* i. 25. /. 24. 3. STERCULIA digitifolia.—Leaves digitate. *L.* Nux

wylanica, folio multifido digitato. *Pluk. aim.* 266; *phyt. t.* 208. /. 3. Folioles sessile. No fructifications excepting a nut. Clompanus major. *Rumph.* iii. 168. *t.* 107. Folioles sessile. STERCULIA foetida. Z. j. 1431. J?. JT. iu. 377.—fori/. *G. esc.* 55. Karil. *Rheede* iv. 73. /. 36. Folioles pctiolate, 3
&5. Prunus pentaphyllos malabarica, fructu calyci insU clcnte. *Rati hist.* t564. j,l: . '..: POLYANDRIA.
705. INGA.
Ca/y.r quinquefid. *Corolla* tubular, quinquefid. *Lcgumen. Obs.* 8781. *L. a Willd.*
Male flowers intermixed.
.
1. *Leaves bigeminate. L. a Willd.*
1. INGA *felina.* Folioles oval. Sfem spinose. *Obs.* 8781. Specimen from Dr. Wright. Mimosa Unguis cati. *L. sp.* 1499. *Swartz. obs.* 389. *H. K.* iii. 439. Mimosa fruticosa, foliis ovatis binatobinatis, semini bus compressis atro-nitentibns, flosculis rubellu adnatis. *Browne* 252. Acacia quadrifolia, siliquis circinatis. *Plum, ic,* 2. «. 4. Acacia arborea major spinosa, pmnis quatuor majori bus subrotundis, siliquis varie intortis. *Sloane cat.* 152. Brasiliensis siliqnosa, siliquis varie intortis. *Rai hist.* 1761. (Acaciae quodarnraodo accedens, si ve ceratiae et aca« ciae media jamaicensis spinosa, bigeminatis foliis. *Pluk. phyt. t.* 1. /. 6, is referred to I. micro. ABAREMO TEMO. *Pis. bras.* 77, *cop. in* Avaramo-temo, Pis. ММ?. 168. In fruit. Foliolee acute.,..-.;-..', i $. INGA rfufcfe. Folioles oblong. Stemspinose. Leguroina pulpy. *From L. a Willd.* iv. 1005, # MIMOSA dulcis.' Лодгъ; Í. 67. f. 99. 2. *Leaves pinnate. Petiole bordered.* L. a Willd. 3. INGA *marginata.* Unarmed. Leaves bijugate; fix lióles oblongo-lanceolate, acuminate, glabrous, with. a gland between each pair. Petiole bordered at the end. Spikes axillary, mostly in fours. Co rollae glabrous. *L. a Willd.* iv. 1015. (Mimosa Bourgoni. *Aubl.* ii. 94), r. 358, is described as having petioles not bordered. Mimosa fagifolia. *L. sp.* 1498; *a Murr.* 913, ¿ir *Jubf.* ii. 943, is described by Linnaeus as having no glands between the folioles.) 3. *Leaves pinnate. Petiole not bordered.* L.

a Willd.
4. INGA *punctata.* Unarmed. Leaves bijugate and trijugate; folioles oblong, acuminate, shining, with with a gland between each pair. Petiole terete» etrigose. Spikes paniculate, axillary. Corollae eericeo-villose. *L. a Willd.* iv. 1016? MIMOSA fagifolia. *Jacq. amer.* 8w, *339.* ?*J* 794..CAROLINEA. ; *Calyx* entire. *Petals* ensiform. *Stigmata* 5 and 6. *Capsule* unilocular, raultivalve, polyspermous. *From L. fii. Sf Swartz. ind. occid.* 1202.
f. J J.
1. CAROLINEA *princeps.* Leaves mostly quinate;, folioles ovato-lanceolate. *Swartz. prodr.* 101. L,. *Jil. suppl.* 314. PACS IRA aquatica. *Aubl.* 725. f. 291. 292.
" L 705. ADANSONIA.
Calyx deciduons. *Style* very long. *Stigmata* many. *Capsule* lignosc, deccmlocular, polyspermous, with a farinaceous pulp. *L. 1.* ADANSONIA digitata. *L. a Murr.* 620. *Hort. l«:ZD.* ii. 439.
A.-Bahobab. *h. sp.* 960.
Baobab, sive Abavi. *Clus. exot.* 21, *cop. in Bauft. J.ua.UO.,* Abavus aethiopicus fructus Bello. *Bauh. J.* i. a. 109. *Raiihist.* 1371. Guanabanus Scaligeri. *Rati hist.* 1371. *Bauh. J.* i. a. 109. No fig. B A HO BAB. *Alp. aeg. fol.* 27. p. 1; *fol.* 28, frait, *cop. in Alp. a Vest.* ii. 37. f. 17. 18. Leaves represented as ternute and simple.
.
; v:.Vtt. r.;V..-..V
. 706, BOMBAX. t l...ij'..v.
Catyx quinquefid. *Qapsttti* lignose, quinquelocular.mrna many. *From L. sp.* 960. J *acq. amer.* 8, 246. Gossypium, seu Xylon arbor orientale, digitatia foliis laevibus, fructu quinquecapsulari alba et nitente lanugine farcto. *Pluk. aim.* 172; *phyt. t.* 188. *f.* 4. Petals oblong. MOUL-ELAVOU. *Rheede* iii. 61. *t.* 52. Petals acute. Moul Elavou, give arbor lanigera spinosa. *Rati hist.* 1899. *i* 707. SIDA. *Calyx* quinquefid. *Style* multipartite and several. *Capsules* unilocular, monospermous dispermous and trispermous. *Obu* 7195. *L. a Gruel. £.* 1. *Capsules* monospermous, 5. L. a Gmel. 1. SIDA *acuta.* Leaves lineari-lanceolate,

dentate.
Peduncles solitary, axillary. Capsules bicuspidate.

Stipulae lanceolate. *L. a Willd.* iii. 735. *Bum. N. S.* scoparia. *Lour.* ii. 504. Althaea coromandeliana, angastis praelongis foliis, semine bicorni. *Pluk. mant.* 10; *phyt. t.* ss4.
fol. 10. *pi.* 2. Tjeru parua. *Rheede* x. 105. *t.* 53. SILAGURIUMlongifoUnm. *Rumph.* vi. 45. *f.* 18./. 2. *S.* SIDA *jamaicensis.* Leaves ovate, serrate, tomento«e. Flowers axillary, subpedunculate. Capsules 5, with 2 horns. *L. sp.* 962; *am.* v. 401. *Swartz. obs.* SIDA humilior, foliis ovatis serratis altcrnis distiche sitis, petiolis et peduncuhs brcvibus, ramulis flori feris foliolatis alaribus. *Browne* 260. 3. SIDA *a hi i folia.* Leaves subrotundo-ovate, dentate; margin entire at the base. Peduncles several, axillary, shorter than the leaves. Capsules with 2
horns. *L. a Willd.* iii. 741; *sp.* 981. Malvinda stellata alnifoKa. *Burtn. Jl zei/l.* 150.
SIDA alnifolia. *Lour.* ii. 502.
4. SIDA *capitata.* Leaves obsoletely lobate. Capi tula pedunculate, invohicratCi with mostly 7 flowers.

Involucrum trifoliate. Stem hirsute. *Obs.* 8779.

Specimen from Prof. Jos. F. Jacquin. —L, *sp.* 965.
Loef.. 225. Malachra capitata. *L. a Murr.* 624. *Hart. kew.* iu 445. *Srcart2. obs.* 262. Malva frutescens hirsuta, (loribus Iuteis in capitulum congestis. *Plum. ic. t.* 169. /. 1. (Malva aspera major aquatica, ex hortensium seu rosearum genere, flore minore luteo, seminc acule ato. *Sloave cat.* 96; *hist.* i. 217. . 137./. 1, Las sessile verticillate flowers.) *Involucrum*, leaves stipulate. *Stipulae* setaceous, 1 on each side at the base. *Obs.* 8779. SIDA hirta assurgens, foliis angulato-cordatis obtuse lobatis atque dentatis, floribus conglobatis, capitulis foliolatis, pedunculis validis alaribus. *Browno* 281..
2. *Capsules motiospermous*, 9. *L. a* Gmel. 5. SIDA *r-etusifolia.*—leaves cuneiform, retuse, serrate, toraeatose un,deraet!u *L..:."....*
S. retusa. *L. sp.* 961.

Althaea indica, latiori folio cordiformi ad sumtnum sinuato. *Pluk. aim.* 26; *phyt. t.* 9./. 2. SJLAGURIUM rotundum, seu vulgare. *Rumph.* vi. 44. *t.* 19. Leaves pale green underneath.
6. SIDA *althaeifolia.* Leaves cordate, subangular, obtuse, serratO'crenate, tomentose on both sides.
Capsules shorter than the calyx. *Swartx. prodr.* 101; *ind.occid.* 1207. Althaea flore luteo. *Sloane cat.* 96; *hist.* i. 218. *I.* 136./. 2. SIDA erecta subincana villosa, ramulis brevioribus, foliis oblongo-cordatis serratis, floribus confertis ad alas superiores. *Browne* 279.
3. *Capsules trispermous, more than* II, L. a Gmel, 7. SIDA *indica.* Leaves cordate, acute, crenate, veI- vety. Stipulac reflex. Upper peduncles longer than the petioles, velvety, pilose at the end. Capsules longer than the calyx, scabrous with stellate hairs. *Obs.* 6493? In Mr. S. Shore's garden from seeds from the Calcutta garden.—L. *sp.* 964? H. K. ii. 444? (Abutilon indicum. *Cam. hort.* 3. *t.* 1, *cop, in Bank. J.* ii. 959, is represented with hirsute petioles and peduncles.) SIDA indica. *Lour.* ii. 503. Glabrous.
8. SlDA.*populifolia.* Leaves subrotundo-cordate, acu minate, unequally repandodentate. Peduncles solitary, longer than the petioles. Capsules acute, truncate, longer than the calyx. *L. a lViltd.* iii. 751. *a Gmel.* 1048. *Sal. R. hort.* 382. BELOERE. *Rheede* vi. 77. *t.* 45.
Abulilo indico Camerarii simile si non idem, Beloere.
Raiihht. 1880;
9. SIDA *Abutilon.* Leaves subrotundo-cordatc, undividcd, longcr than thc pcduncles. Capsules bifid at the end. *L. a GmeL* ii. 1048; *sp.* 963. H. K. ii. 443.
S. foliis subrotundo'cordatis acuminatis. *L. ups.* 198. *Gron. virg.* 101; *ed. i.* 78.
Althaca altera, sive Abutilon. *Cam. epit.* 668.
Althaea Theophrasti, flore luteo, quibusdam Abutilon. *Bauh. J.* ii. 958.
Althaea lutea. *Rati hist.* 699. *Ger. by Johns.* 935, *repr. from*
Althaea Iutuis floribus. *Lob. obs.* 374, *thick repr. in ic.* i. 655, *cop. in*
Althaea Theophrasti. *Dahch.* 594, $.
Althaea lutea, sive Abutilon Avicen-

nae putatum. *Park, theatr.* 304 *Sf repr. in* ABUTILON. *Bod.* 645. *Boerh.* i. 274.— Dale 192-Schoepf 107.
i0. SIDA *hirta.* Leaves reniformi-cordate, tridentate, tomentoso-pubescent. Petioles and peduncles pilose arid pubescent. Capsutes longer than the calyx, hirsute with stellate hairs. *Obs.* 7195. In Mr.
Shore's garden from seeds from the Calcutta garden.
—*L. a Gm-l.* ii. 1048; *a Willd.* iii. 751. *Car.* Stem erect, 1 foot long. *Leaves* subrotundo-cor datei obsolete!/ tiidentate, with 11 ribs underneath, 3 inches long, 4 broad, villoso-pnbescent above with 2 & more hairs from the same point, underneath with

VoL. 3.J L 1 stellate hairs, with yellow shining globules interspersed; teeth acute, middlemost rather more projecting; margin dentate with acute teeth. *Petioles* as long again as the laminae. *Peduncles* solitary, patent, hirsute, pubescent, with a knot near the end. *Calyx* quinquefid, half as long again as the upper internodium of the peduncle, hirsute and pubescent with shining yellow globules interspersed; segments ovato-triangular, acuminate, carinate below. *Corolla* rotate, longer than the calyx, buffcoloored yellow; segments purplish brown at the base. *Style* very short. *Stigmata* several. *Fruit* stil green, ovate, truncate, umbilicate at the end. *Capsules* trispermous, 22, adhering laterally, hirsute with short stellate hairs. 06s. 7195.

ABUTILON hirsutum. *Rumph.* iv. 29. *t.* 10. Leaves ovato cordate. 708. AL THAEA. *Calyx* double; outer partite; segments 9 to 12. *Capsules* unilocular, monospermous. *Obs.* 5059. L. 1. ALTHAEA *sublobata.* Leaves obsoletely Iobate, tomentose. *Obs.* 5060. Specimen gathered for me in a lane near Freistoneshore in Lincolnshire.
A. officinalis. *L. sp.* 966. *Bot. arr.* 735. *Smith engl. t.* 147; *brit.* 739. *Fl. dan. t.* 530. *Wbodv.* i. J46. *t.* 53. Leaves too green.—*Thornt.* 625. *Huds.*306. *Light/.* 373. *X.* vulgaris. *Cam. hort.* 12. *Raii hist.* 602; *syru* 252. *Park, theatr.* 304. 710. LAVATERA. *Calyx* double; outer trifid. *Capsules* monospermous. 06s.

6088. *L.* 1. LAVATERA *arborea.* Stem ligneous. Leaves septangular, tomentose, plicate. Peduncles crowded, uniflorous, axillary. Outer calyx longer than the inner; segments obtuse. *Obs.* 564. Jn a garden. —*L. sp.* 972. *Bot. arr.* 743; iii. exxvi. *Smith brit.* 742; *engl. t.* 1841. *Lightf.* 374. Found by Sibbald on islands in the firth of Forth.—*Ifuds.* 306. In Cornwall and Devonshire.—*Gou. hort.* 349. L. caule arboriformi, foliis septemangularibus tomentosis plicatis, pedunculis coufertis unifloris axillaribus. *L. ups.* 202. *All. nic.* 27.
Malva arborea marina nostras. *Pari: theatr.* 301. JVo fig-—*Rati* syn. 252. On the sea side at Hurst Castle opposite to the isle of Wight, and on Portland Caldey and Basse islands.

Malva arborescens. *Best. hort. aest. ord,* 6. *fol.* 6. *Cam. hort.* 95. On the road from Pisa to, Leghorn, and elsewhere in Italy.

Malva arborea, *Bauh. J.* ii. 952. In gardens.

Native of Italy and Britain on the sea shore.

LAVATERA arborea. *Spielm.* 461,

Malva arborea. *Rutty* 301.

Malva arborea maritima. *Dale* 191.

Malva arborea marina nostras. *Cod. med. p.* lxxi.

2. LAVATERA *thuringiaca.* Stem herbaceous. Lower leaves cordate, lobate; upper deltoid, trilobate. Outer calyx nearly as long as the inner. Corolla twice and a half as long as the calyx. *Obs.* 6591. Specimen from Prof. Jos. F. Jacquin. —*L. sp.* 973. *Hort. kew.* ii. 451. *Roth germ.* i. 295, in Saxony in mountainous forests; ii. 146. *Schreb. lij)s.* 8 *Host* 385, *J acq. austr. 1.311.*

Ll.S *Calyx* double; outer triphyllous monophyllous diphyllous & tetraphyllous. *Capsules* unilocular & bilocular; cells mostly monosperraous. *Obs.* 4039. *L.*

I. *Capsules monospermous. L.* a Gmel.

1. MALVA *sylrestris.* Stem rough. Leaves cordate; lobes 3 to 7, acute. *Obs.* 4039. In a churchyard.
—*L. suec. n.* 627; *sp.* 969. *Smith engl. t.* 671.
Curt. land. ii. 15. *t. Bot. arr.* 738. *Light*

f 375. *Huds.* 307. *Woods, i.* 148. /. 54. CoroUae too red.—*Ger. by Johns.* 930, *repr. from* M. sylvestris procerior. *Dod.* 642, *which repr. in ed.* ii. 653, M. vulgaris procerior. *Lob. obs.* 371, *Sr* M. silvestris procerior vulgaris. *Lob. ic.* i. 650. M. major I. *Daltch.* 585. M. vulgaris. *Raii syn.* 251. *Curt. mat. med. t.* 5. M. sylvestris elatior. *Fuchs.* 509. *fol. ed. ill cop. in Ger. by Johns.* 951, *abr. in Park. par. t.* 497, has racemose flowers.) *Fuchs.* 80. *fol. erf. cop. in in* 493. c. 194, *well cop. in* M. sylmtris recta. *Cord. fol.* 114 p. 1, M. sylvestris major. *Dalech.* 587, *Sr* M. vulgaris, florc majore, folio sinuato. *Bauk. J.* ii. 949. *Tourn. paris.* 212. *Vaill. paris.* 124. Malva vulgaris, flore purpureo. *Park, theatr.* 299. (The fig. M. rotundifolia.) MALVA. Mallow. Leaves. Flowers. *Pharm. lond. Sf noviss.*—*Alst.* ii. 169, *Dale* 191. *Leva.* it. 85. *Monro* iii. 165. *Plovcq. bibl.* i, 696. *Vog.* 66. M. sylvestris. Herb. Flowers. *Pharm. edin. Krock. n.* 1129. *Lew. disp. by Dune.* 250. *Murr. J.* i. 386. *Pears. JR. ed.* ii. 299. *Quar,febr.* 150. 230. *Butly* SOI. *Spielm.* 461. M. vulgaris. Flowers. *Pharm. austriacoprov.* 47. —*Geoffr.* iii. 766. jtfi'tf. *Jo.* 280. Jtf«rr. iii. 364. M. folio sinuato. *Ilerm.* 418. 549. M. vulgaris, florc majore, folio sinuato. *Chom.* 700; *suppl.* 190. Mallow. JBm. ess. 162. Blizard, account from in vied. rev. i. 331. *Fordyce, G. fev.* iii. 230. . MALVA *rotundifolia.* Stem prostrate. Leaves subrotundo-cordate, quinquclobate. Peduncles of the fruit declinate. *Obs.* 2615. On banks.—*L suec. n.* 627, who remarks that about Upsal the flowers were smaller and the corolla white, at Stockholm the corolla larger and purplish; *sp.* 969. *Curtu lond.* iii. 4S. *t.* 157. *Fl. dan. t.* 721. *Huds.* 307. *Lightf.* 374. *Bot. arr.* 737. *Smith brit.* 741; *engU t.* 1092. *Krock. n.* 1128. *f.* 1, *Sr repr. in* M. cristatis oris. *Lpb. obs.* 372, *and ic.* ii. 651.

M. hortensis crispa. *Cprd. fol.* 1J4. *p.* 1. M. foliis crispis. *Boerh.* i. 268.
Stem nearly glabrous, pbspletely striate here and there. *Leaves* alternate; laminae glabrous; teeth terminated by 2 and 1 shprt hairs. *Petioles* longer than the internodia, pubescent above, glabrous underneath. *Peduncles* very short. *Ca-*

lyx triphyllous; phylla ensiform, ciliate, inserted into the base of the inner calyx; inner calyx quinquefid. *Petals* cuneiform, deeply retuse, one third longer than the calyx, whitish, purplish at the end; sinuses semicircular,

slightly erose. *Capsules* monospermous. *Seeds* not yet ripe, containing a green plumule. *Obs.* 856S.
MALVA crispa. *Dale* 191.
M. foliis crispis. *Cod. med. p.* lxxi.

4. AJALVA *Alcea.* Stem erect. Leaves multipartite, somewhat scabrous. Catyces tomentose; phylla of the outer lanceolato-elliptic. *Obs.* 8803. Specimen gathered by liroughton in a garden in Britain.— *Curt. lond.* under M. moschata.—*L. suec. n.* 628; *sp.* 971; *matd.* 436. *Krock. n.* 1130. *Bot, arr.* 742. *note.*—*Host* 384. *Scop. earn. n.* 86Q. *Poll,* «. 660.

Alcea vulgaris major, flore ex rubrq rosep. *Boerh.* i. 270.

Alcea vulgaris major. *Tqurn. paris.* 241. *VailL paris.* 3.

Alcaca. *Cam. epit.* 669.

Alcea. *Tab. ic.* 771. *Matth.* 927. (*Dalech.* 593, 83, *Sr cop. in Trag.* 365. c. 27, *abr. in* Alcea vulgaris. *Bauh. J.* ii. 953. *Park, theatr.* 302. (*Besl. hort. aest. ord.* 6. *fol.* 3. *n.* I, is M. moscbata, and *Besl. hort. aest. ord.* 6. *fol.* 3. /. 1, as suggested by Mr. Knowlton, Althaea cannabina. *Dcd.* 645, *repr. in Lob. obs.* 374, *Sf ic.* i. 655, *cop. in Dalech.* 593, # *repr. in* M. verbenaca. *Ger. by Johns.* 931, is probably M. moscbata.) ALCEA. *Dale* 191. *Geoffr.* iii. 50. *Mill. Jos.* 21. *Rutty* 12.

Alcea vulgaris minor. *Chom.* 705.
712. GOSSYPIUM. Calyx double; outer trifid. *Capsule* trilocular and quadrilocular. *Seeds* wrapped up in wool. *From L. S,-Swartz.* 1. GOSSYPIUM *herbaceum.* Leaves quinquelobate; lobes acute. Stem herbaceous. *Obs.* 8268. Specimen from M. Hertel.—*L. a Murr.* 628; *sp.* 975. *Hort. l-ew.* ii. 453. *Lour.* ii. 505. Segments of the outer calyx denlato-incise and entire at the margin.
G. foliis quinquelobis. *L. ups.* 203

G. sive Xylon. *Rait eur.* 135. Cultivated in Malta.—*Dalech.* 221. *Dod.* 66, *repr. in Lob. dbs.* 371; ic. i. 650, # *Ger.*

by Johns. 901, 6? cop, in
Gossipinm frutescens annuum.' Pari-, theatr. 1552, if
Xylon Gossypium, Stap. 425.
Xylon. *Fuchs.* 529. c. 208, *cop. in*
Xylon, sive Gossipium herbaceum. *Bauh. J. i, a.* 343. /. 1. /. 2. Лам *hist.* 1064. *Boerh.* i. 273.
Gossipium. *Cam. epit.* 203.
GOSSYPIUM. *Berg.* 590. *Herrn.* 361. *Linn.* 198. *Murr.* iii. 367. *Schoepf* 108. Bombas. *Akt.* ii. 331. Da/c 192. *Mill. Jos.* 88. ScArorf. 548. *0 perennis.* Stem perennial. From *Rumph.* (G. iiulicum. JL. a *Willd.* iii. 803, is marked as annual and biennial, the stem described as herbaceous, and the lobes of the leaves as obtuse.) GOSSIPIUM vulgare. *Rumph.* iv. 33. *t.* 12.
Lobes of the leaves acute. Corresponds with tho specific character of G. barbadense excepting that
Rumphius describes the wool as firmly adhering to
' the seeds.
i, $. GOSSYPIUM arborcum. Leaves palmate; lobe» lanceolate, mucronate. Stem fruticose. *L. sp.* 975; *mant.* 436. *Hort. kew.* ii. 453. *Lour.* ii. 506. Segments of the outer calyx incise.—*Park. theatr.* 1552. Leaves represented as incise. Gossipium arboreum, Gotncmsegiar. *Alp. aeg.fol.* 29. p. 1, *cop. in a Vesl.* ii. 38. r. *19 St abr. in* Xylon arborcum. *Bauh. J. i. a.* 346. Segments of the calyx entire.—*Raii hist.* 1064. G. herbaceum, sive Xylon maderaspatense, rubicundo flore, penlaphyllum. *Pluk. aim.* 172; *phyt. t.* 188. /. 3, is called herbaceous, and has an outer calyx with entire segments. CUD U-PAR1TI. *Rheede* i. 55. /. 31. Xylon malabaricum, Cudupuriti dictum. *Raii hist. 3.* GGSSYPIUM *Titifolinm.* Leaves trilobate and " qninquelobate, with 1 gland underneath; lobes semi» ovate, inucronate. Petioles and peduncles hirsute, minutely tuberculate. *Obs.* 8270. Specimen from Prof. Jos. F. Jacquin.—*L. a WilM.* Hi. 804. Сел
' G. lrutescens auunum, folio vitis ampliorc quinque fido. *Pluk. aim.* 172; *phyt.* t. 188. /. 2. No fructifications.
,:'; ÓOSSJPIUM latifolium. *Rumph.* iv. 37. *t.* IS.

''' Calyces lacmiate.
4. GOSSYPIUNf *barbadense.* Upper leaves tri loin te, lower quinquelobate; lobes divaricate. Branches petioles and peduncles nearly glabrous, dotted. Wool slightly adhering to the seeds. *Obs.* 8776.
Specimen gathered by Dr. Wright in Jamaica.
Account of the seeds and lower leaves from *Sarnrtz.* ' *'obs.* 266. *L. 3p.* 975; *a Willd.* iii. 806. *Hort, leew.* ii. 453. G. foliis trilobis integerrimis. *L. ups. 20i.* G. frntcscens annuum, folio trilobo, barbadense. *Pluk. aim.* 172; *phyl. t.* 188./. 1. la fruit.
G. brasiUanum, ñore flavo. *Sfoane cat.* 156.
Branches, dots black. *Leaves,* upper nearly glabrous above, tomentose underneath; margin entire. *Petioles* with black dots. *Peduncles* with black dots. *Calyx,* outer, segments incise. *Obs.* 877S. GOSSYPIUM fruticosura, foliis trilobis, seminibus rnajoribus. Browne 283.
713. HIBISCUS. *Calyx* double; outer monophyllous triphyltoib and polyph, lions. *Capsule* quinquclocular, quinquevalve; cells polyspermous and monospermous..' *Obs.* 6229. 8786. 8357. *L.* 1. *Cells polyspermous. Outer caly.T monophyUous,* 1. HIBISCUS *clatus.* Leaves cordate, subrotund; margin entire. Peduncles very short, uniflorous. Outer calyx seraiqninquefid. From *Swarlz. prodr,* 102, cS' *ind. occid.* 1218. *Dorm* 168. Malva arborea, folio rotundo, qortice in funes ductili, flore miniato maximo liliacco. *Sloane cat.* 95; *hist. i.* 215. *t.* 131. *f.* 2. 3. *HIBISCUS* arboreus, foliis angulato-cordatis, flore amplo croceo, ligno violacco. Browne 284.
2. HIBISCUS *titiaefolius.* Leaves cordate, acuminate, angular crenate and entire at the margin.
Stem arboreous. Outer calyx semidecerafid. *Obs.* 8357. Specimen gathered by Dr. Wright in Jamaica.—*Sal. R. hort.* 383. H. tiliaceus. *L. sp.* 977. *Hort. Lezc.* ii. 454. *Forst. G. esc.* 73. *Lour.* ii. 509. Althaea maritima arborescens diffusa, foliis orbiculato cordatis leniter crenatis subtus cinercis. *Brownt* 284. Malva arborea maritima, folio subrotundo mi-

nore acuminato subtus candido, coriicc in funes ductili, flore Jut o. *Sloane rat.* 95; *hist.* i. 215. *t.* 134.
/. 4. In fruit. Pariti, scu Tali-pariti. *Rheede* i. 53. *t.* 30. Alcea malabarica, abutili folio, flore minore ex albo flavescenteexteriussubaspero. *Raii hist.* 1070. NOVELLA. *Rumph.* ii. 218. i. 72.
2. *Cells polyspermous. Outer calyx triphyllous.* 3. HIBISCUS *populifolius.*—Leaves cordate; margin entire. Stem arboreous. *L.—Sal. R. hort.* 383.
H. populneus. *L. sp.* 976. *H. K,* ii. 454. Bupariti. *Rheede* i. 51. *t.* 29.
Alcea malabarica, abutili folio, flore majore ex albo flavescente. *Ra-i hist.* 1069.
NOVELLA litorea. *Rumph.* ii. 224. *t.* 74.
3. *Cells polyspermous. Outer calyx polyphyUous. Stem aculeate.*
'h; 4. HIBISCUS *vilifolius.* Stem herbaceous. Leaves quinquangular, acute, serrate. Flowers cernuous.
Capsula with 5 wings. From *L. sp.* 980; *mant.* 569, *Sf a Gmel.* ii. 1062.
Althaea indica, vitis folio, florc amplo flavo pendente.
Uerm. hort. 26. *t.* 28.
EATU BELOEREN. *Rheede* vi. 79. *f.* 46.
Raii hist. 1880.
5. HIBISCUS *appendiculatus.* Aculei recurvate. Leaves palmate and trilobate. Outer calyces with appendages. Stipulae semkordate. Flowers pedunculate. From
H. surattensis. *L. sp.* 979; *mant.* 436; *a Murr.* 630. *Hort. Item.* ii. 457. *Lour.* ii. 512.
JIERBA CRINALIUM domestica. *Rumph.* iv. 40. *t.* 16. .fj. HIBISCUS *cannabifolius.*—Leaves serrate, with I gland underneath, upper palmate and quinquepartite. Stem aculeate. Flowers sessile. *L.* Kctmia indica, foliis digitatis, flore magno sulphureo umbone atro-purpureo, petiolis spinosis. *Ehret t,* 6. /. 1. Alcea benghalensis spinosissima, acetosae sapore, flore luteo pallido umbone purpurascente. *Commet. J. hort.* i. 35.1.
18. Alcea americana. *Clus. hist.* ii. *96, repr. in* Sabdarifa. *Ger. by Johns.* 936, & *dbr. in* Sabdarifa, seu Alcea americana. *Park. par.* 363. f,
S67. /. 3. HIBISCUS cannabintis. *L. sp.* 979. *Bonn* 169. —*Roxb.* ii. 48. *t.* 190.

4. *Cells polyspermous. Outer calyx polyphyllous. Stem unarmed.* 7. HIBISCUS *rosiftorus.*—Leaves ovate, acuminate, serrate. Stem arboreous. *L.* H. Rosa sinensis. *L. sp.* 977. *H. K.* ii. 455. *Lour.* ii. 510. FLOS FESTALIS. *Rumph.* iv. 24. « *simplex.* Corolla single.—*H. K. a. Curt. mag. I.* 158. *β plenus.* Corolla double.—*H. K.*

Alcea javanica arborescens, flore pleno rubicundo» *Breyn. cent.* 121. /. 56. *Rati hist.* 1068.

Schem-pariti. *Rheede* ii. 25. *t.* 16.

Bonga raja rubra plena. *Rumph.* iv. 24. *t.* S.

8. HIBISCUS *petioliflorus.*—Leaves ovate, acuminate) serrate. Flowers on the petioles. Stem simple. *L.* Alcea rosca peregrina, forte Rosa moscheutos Plinii.

Corn. 144. *t.* 145, *abrt in Hist. ox. s.* 5. *t.* 19» *f.*6. HIBISCUS Moscheutos. *L sp.* 975,-Schoepf 9. HIBISCUS *mutabilis.* Leaves cordate, quinquangu" Iar, obsoletely serrate. Stem arboreous. *L. sp.* 977. //. *K.* ii. 455. *Lour.* ii. 511. Althaea arborea. Rosa sinensis. *Hist. ox. s.* 5. *t.* 18. rowS.*f.* 2. Hina pariti. *Rheede* vi. 66. *t.* 38 *to* 42. FLOS HORARIUS. *Rumpk.* iv. 27. *t.* 9.

10. HIBISCUS *Abelmoschus.* Leaves cordate, lobate and angidar; lobes and angles from 3 to 7; Iobe» acuminate, crenato-serrate. Stem hispid. *Obs.* 6229. In Sir H. Hunloke's garden *L. sp.* 980. *Hort. hew.* ii. 457. *Mill. Ph. diet. n.* 3.

H. foliis peltato-cordatis septemangularibus serratis hispidis. *L. ups.* 206. H. hispidus, foliis quinqiietobis, lobis acutis, semine muscato. *Browne* 285. Alcoa hirsuta,flavoflore, & semine mosenato. *Marcgr.* 45. *Sloane cat.* 98. Varies with sinuate and rounder leaves—which variety probably the same with ray specimen. Obs. 3485. Ketmia aegyptiaca, semine moschato. *Boerh.* i. 272. Alcea aegyptiaca villosa. *Raii hist.* 1066. Alcea acgyptia moschata, Abelmosch dicta. *ParL theatr.* 303. Granum moschatum. *Rumph.* iv. 38. *t.* 15. Ab el mosch, seu Mosch arabum. *Alp. a Vesl.* iu 207. Bammia rauschata. *Alp. a Vest.* ii. (. 66. Cattu-gasturi. *Rheede* ii. 71. *t*-38. » Stem shrubby; smaller branches herbaceous, with a brownish purple streak above the axillae; streaks decurrent on each side parallel to the decurrent margin of the petiole. *Leaves* hispid, quinquefido-septilobafe being cloven before and lobate behind, septilobate, angular with from 3 to 7 angles, and sometimes nearly hastate. *Petioles* hispid. *Stipulae* subulate, hispid. *Peduncles* axillary, solitary, about as long as the corolla, pubescent; hairs crowded, slightly deflex. *Calyx,* outer with from 6 to 11 subulutolinear phylla; inner from half as long again to thrice as long as the outer, sex fid and quinquefid, bursting to near the base on one side. *Petals* 6, oblongooobovate, pale yellow, with a brownish purple bloteh at the base; upper margin of the bloteh obliquely rounded. *Stamina* as long as the calyx. *Filaments* the loose ends shorter than the antherae. *Antherae* on the outside from near the base to the end of the united filaments, about 20, roundish. *Pistil* longer than the stamina. *Germen* pyramidal, pubescent, quinquelocular; cells polyspermous. *Styles* 5,*umled* below, purple at the end. *Stigmata* 5, oval, brownish purple. *Obs.* 6229.—*Stem* hispid. *Leaves* hispid, sexlobate and qainquelobate, crenate; lobes triangular, acuminate; sinuses concave. *Obs.* 3485. Specimen gathered by Broughton in Jamaica.—*Leaves* roundish, somewhat cuneiform at the base, quinquangular. *Seeds* vhen rubbed of the scent of musk. *Obs.* 3485. Specimen in fruit from the garden of Fothergill. ABELMOSCHUS. *Berg.* 591. *Lew. disp. by Rother.* 81, *Linn.* 168. *Mutt.* iii. 376. *Fog.* 173. Abelmosch. *Alst.* ii. 321. Bamia moschata. *Dale* 192. *Lew.* i. 200. *Mill. Jos.* 74.

Vol. *3.* M m 11. HIBISCUS *Sabdariffa.* Leaves serrate; lower undivided, ovate; upper trilobate and quinquelobate. Flowers nearly sessile. *Obs.* 8271. Specimen gathered by Dr. Wright in Jamaica, probably in a garden.—*L. sp.* 978; *rnant.* 436. *Swarlz. obs.* 269. *Hort. hew.* ii. 457.

H. gossypifolius. *Mill. Ph. diet. n.* 10.

H. rufescens acetosus, foliis trilobis. *Browne* 285.

Ketmia indica, gossypii folio, acetosae sapore. *Boerh»* i. 272.

Alcea acetosa indica mitis, foliis superioribus gossypii in modum tripartito-divisis. *Pluk. aim.* 15; *phyt. t.* 6. /. 2.

Alcoa acetosa, trifido folio, indiae occidentalis. *Sloane cat.* 99.

Althaea indica, gossipii folio, acetosae sapore. *Rait hist.* 1900. *Calyx* outer enneaphyllous; phylla subulate; inner monoph yllous, bursting on one side; mouth *seau* quinquefid. *Germen* ovate, longer than the outer calyx, novilocular. *Obs.* 8271.

RED SORREL. *Long.* iii. 805. 12. HIBISCUS *esciilentus.* Leaves quinquelobate. Outer calyx deciduous, decaphyllous; inner semiquinquend, bursting longitudinally. *Obs.* 8786. Specimen gathered by Dr. Wright in Jamaica, and from *L. a Willd.* iii. 827; *sp.* 980. *B. K.* ii. 458.

H. fcifolius. *Mill. Ph. diet. n.* 15.

II. ramosus hirsutus, foliis Iobatis irregulariter erenatis, fructu longiori. *Browne* 285.

Alcea americana annua, flore albo maximo, fructu pyramidali sulcato. *Commel. J. hort.* i, 37. *t.* 19. Alcea maxima, malvae roseae folio, fructu decagono recto crassiore breviore esculento. *Sloane cat.* 98; *hist.* i. 223. *t.* 133. /. 3.

Fruit. Alcea brasiliensis. *Rati hist.* 1068.

Quingombo. *Marcgr.* 31. Leaves quinquefido palmate. HIBISCUS esculentus. *Bry.* 373. *Clark, James in med. facts* vii. 307. *Lour.* ii. 512. *Schoepf* 109. *Sonniniu.* 4. *Wright in med.journ.* viii. 262. Ochra. *Edw. Bryan* i. 199. *Graing.* 19. 36. 714. MESUA, *Calyx* tetraphyllous. *Petals* 4. *Pistil* 1. JV« tetragonous, monospermous. *L.* 1. MESUA *ferrea. L. sp.* 734; *mant.* 402. Belutta Tsjampakam. *Rhcede* iii. 63. *t.* 53. Belutta Tsjampacam, sive Castanea rosea indica, *Raii hist.* 1680. NAGASSARIUM *Rumph.* vii. 3. «. 2, 715. CAMELLIA. *Calyx* imbricate; inner phylla larger, i, 1. CAMELLIA *acuminata.*—Leaves acutely serrate, acuminate. *Thunb.* Thea chinensis, pimentae jamaicensis folio, flare rpseo simplici. *Pet. gaz.* 52. *t.* 33. /. 4.

Sa. *Kaempf. am.* 850. *t.* 851.

Corolla quinquefido-partite, deciduous, vermilion coloured; segments obovate, incumbent. *Obs.* 2641. In a garden. CAMELLIA *japónica. L. sp.* 982. *Hort. kew.* ii. 460. *Curt. mag. t.* 42. *J acq.*

coll. i. 117; *ic.* iii. *t.* 553. *Thunb.jap.* 272;—*trav.* iy. 38. 2. CAMELLIcmarginala.—Leaves obtusely serrate, emarginate. *Thurtb.* C. Sasanqua. *Thunb. jap.* 273. *t.* 29. S AS AN QUA. *Kaempf. am.* 853, 3. CAMELLIA *drupifera.* Leaves ovato-oblong, sub» crenate. Flowers 2 and 3 together. Nuts qua» drilocular. *Lour.* ii. 499, 716. METEORUS. *Calyx* superior, quadrifid. *Corolla* hypocraterifoTiBj limb quadrifid. *Drupe* monosperraous, crowned,. *From Lour.*
I. METEORUS *coceineus. Lour,* ii. 499.
717. BARRINGTONIA. *Calyx* superior, dipbyllous. *Petals* 4. *Drupe.* Nut quadrilocular. *L. ßl. suppl.* 50. *Forst. J, and G.* 75. *t.* 38. 38 a. 38 *b.* 1. BARRINGTONIA *speciosa. Forst. J. and G.* 76; *G. austral, n.* 255. *L. ßU suppl.* 312.
Butonica speciosa. *Hort. kew.* ii. 439.
Mammea asiatica. *Osb.* ii. 62. *L. sp.* 781.
La Commersona. *Sonn. nouv. guin.* 14. *t.* 8. 9.
BUTONICA. *Rumph.* iii. 179.*t.*114.
718. GUSTAVIA.
Calyx superior, quadrifid and scxfid. *Petals* 4 and 6. *Berry* dry, quadrilocular and quinquelocular. *From L. a Willd.* # *L.JU. suppl.* 51. 1. GUSTAVIA *tetrapetala.* Petals 4. *From G.* augusta. *L. a Willd.* iii. 846; *a Murr.* 620. *L. fl. suppl.* 313. Pirigara tetrapetala. *AubU* 486. *t.* 192. (Pirigara hexapetala. *Aubl.* 490. *t.* 193, has a calyx with subulate segments.) *JANJPARANDJBA. Pis. bras.* 121, *repr in* Japarandiba. *Marcgr.* 109. In fruit.— *Raii hist.* 1646. 719. CORDYLA. *Calyx* inferior, quadrifid. *Corolla* none. *Berry* unilocular, stipitate. *From Lour,*
I. CORDYLA *africana. Lour.* ii. 300.

CPSIA information can be obtained at www.ICGtesting.com
Printed in the USA
BVOW03s1236120615

404417BV00018B/212/P